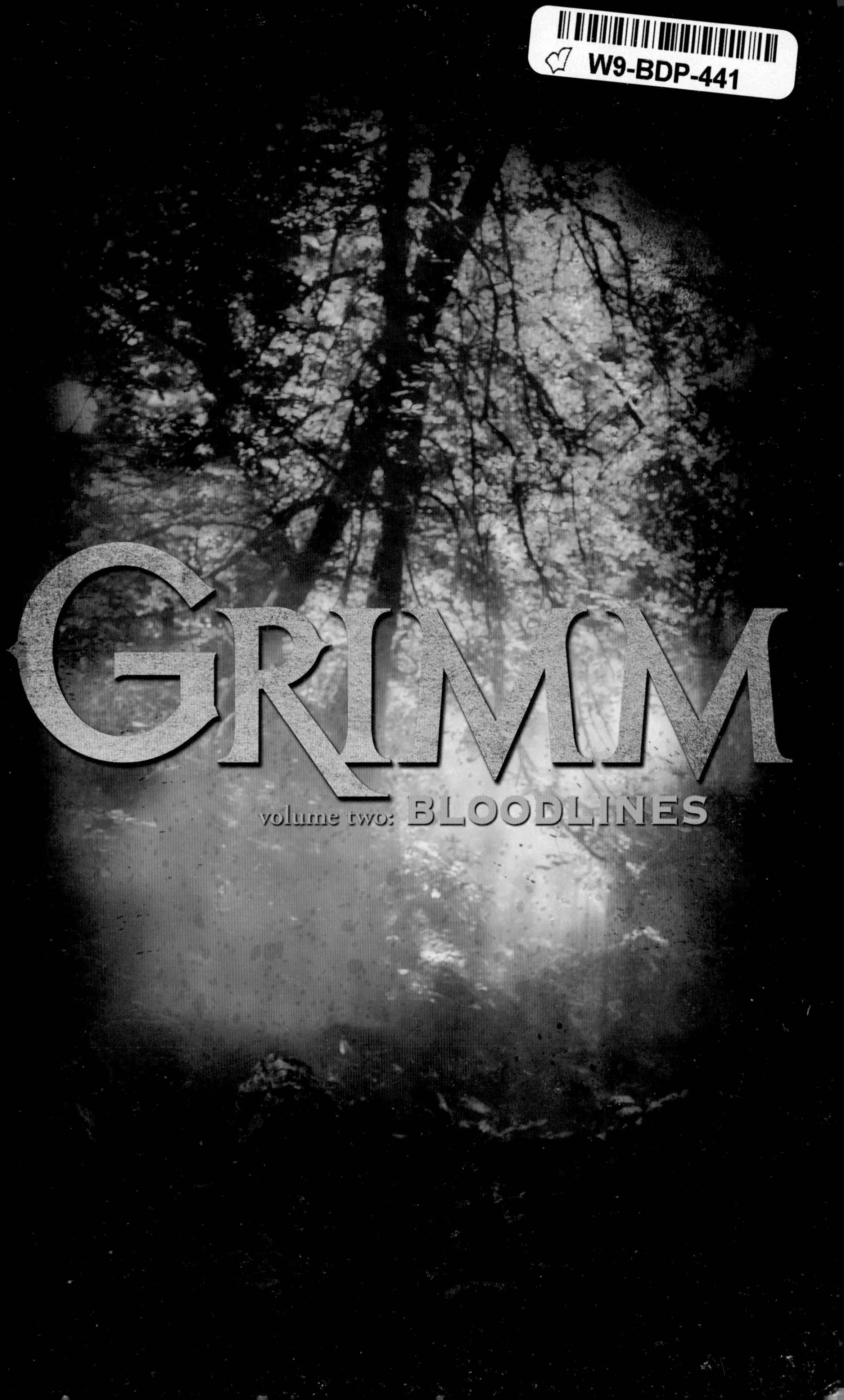

GRIMM

volume two: BLOODLINES

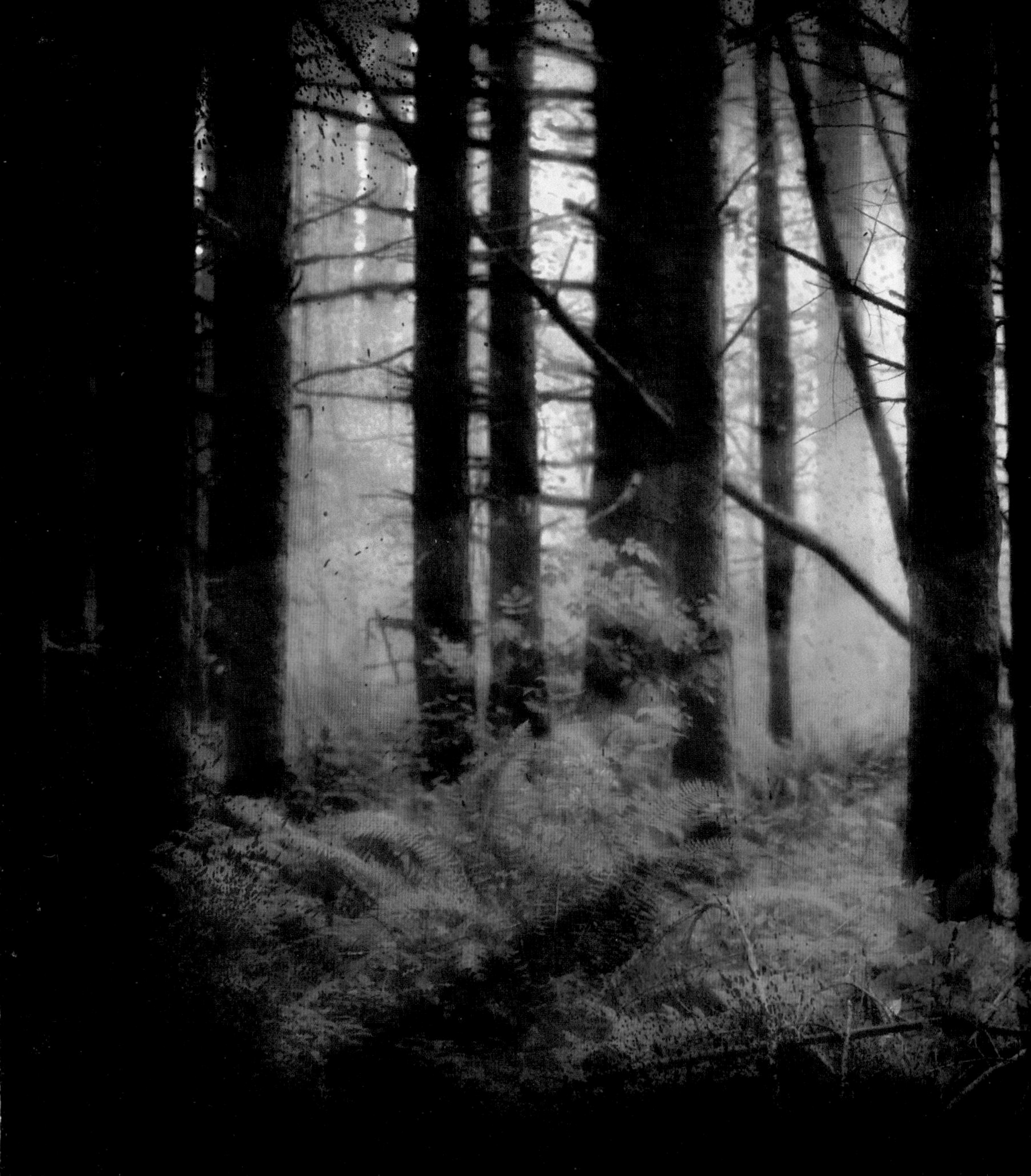

DYNAMITE®

Nick Barrucci, CEO / Publisher
Juan Collado, President / COO
Rich Young, Director Business Development
Keith Davidsen, Marketing Manager

Joe Rybandt, Senior Editor
Hannah Elder, Associate Editor
Josh Green, Traffic Coordinator
Molly Mahan, Assistant Editor

Josh Johnson, Art Director
Jason Ullmeyer, Senior Graphic Designer
Katie Hidalgo, Graphic Designer
Chris Caniano, Production Assistant

GRIMM

volume two: BLOODLINES

Plot by

JIM KOUF & DAVID GREENWALT

Script by

MARC GAFFEN & KYLE McVEY

Art by

ROD RODOLFO

Colors by

THIAGO DAL BELLO

Letters by

MARSHALL DILLON

Collection design by JOSH JOHNSON

Special thanks to

CHRIS LUCERO, LYNN KOUF, KIM NIEMI & ED PRINCE

Based on the NBC Television series "Grimm."

ISBN-10: 1-60690-518-X   ISBN-13: 978-1-60690-518-0
First Printing 10 9 8 7 6 5 4 3 2 1

Printed in China.

For information regarding press, media rights, foreign rights, licensing, promotions, and advertising e-mail: marketing@dynamite.com

NBC

Visit us online at **www.DYNAMITE.com**
Follow us on Twitter **@dynamitecomics**
Like us on Facebook **/Dynamitecomics**
Watch us on YouTube **/Dynamitecomics**

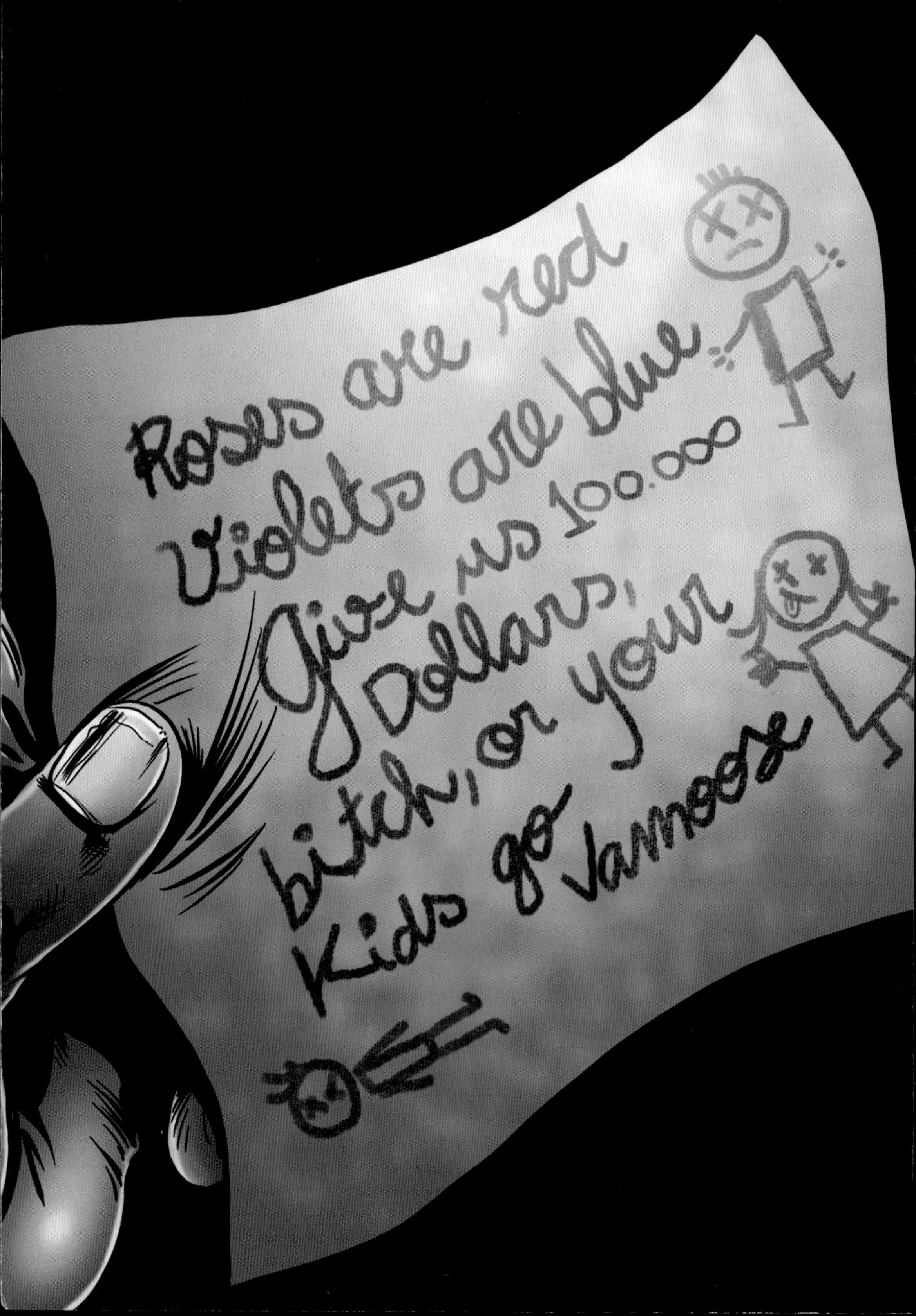
Roses are red
Violets are blue
Give us 100.000
Dollars,
bitch, or your
Kids go
Vamoose

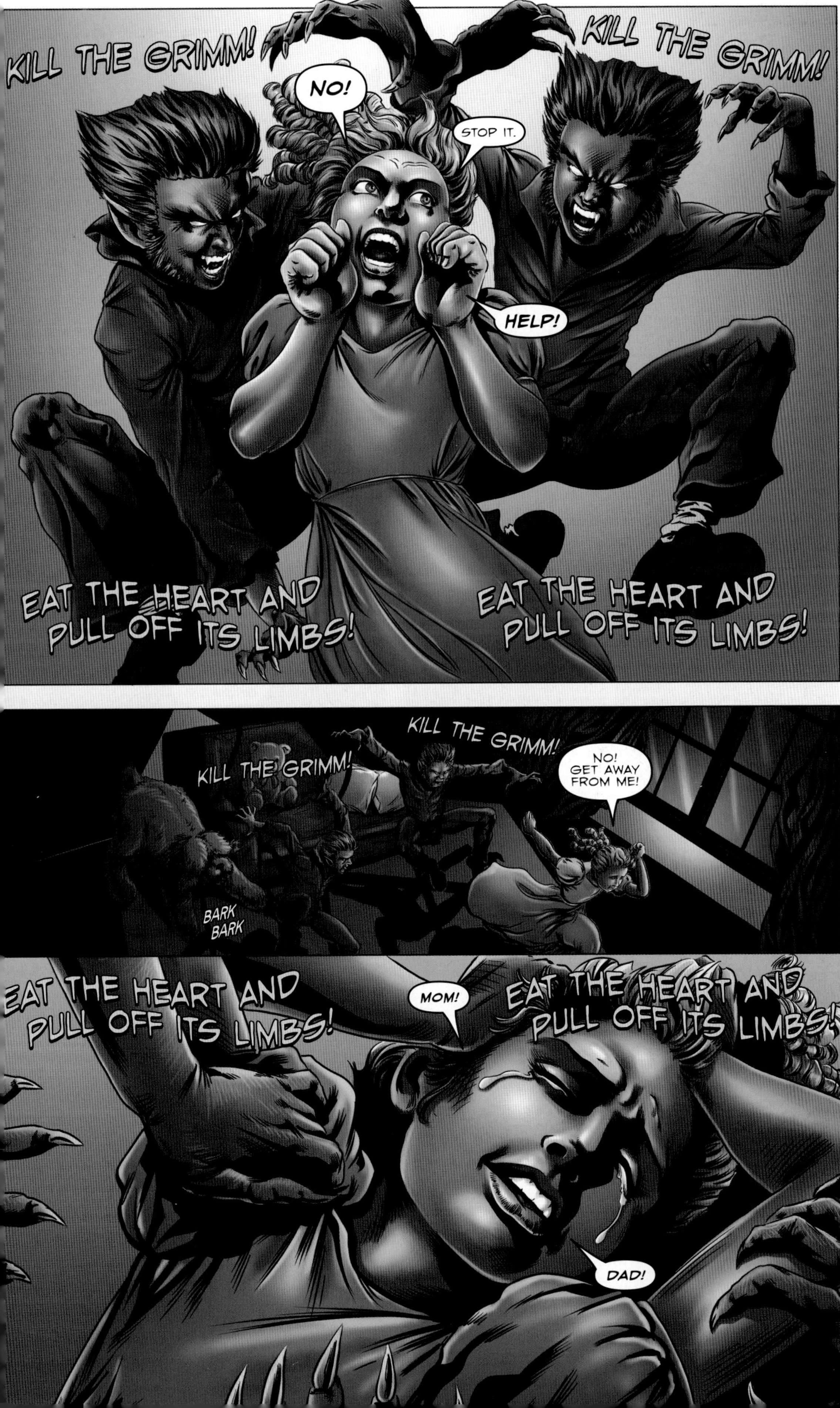
KILL THE GRIMM!
KILL THE GRIMM!
NO!
STOP IT.
HELP!
EAT THE HEART AND PULL OFF ITS LIMBS!
EAT THE HEART AND PULL OFF ITS LIMBS!
KILL THE GRIMM!
KILL THE GRIMM!
NO! GET AWAY FROM ME!
BARK BARK
EAT THE HEART AND PULL OFF ITS LIMBS!
MOM!
EAT THE HEART AND PULL OFF ITS LIMBS!
DAD!

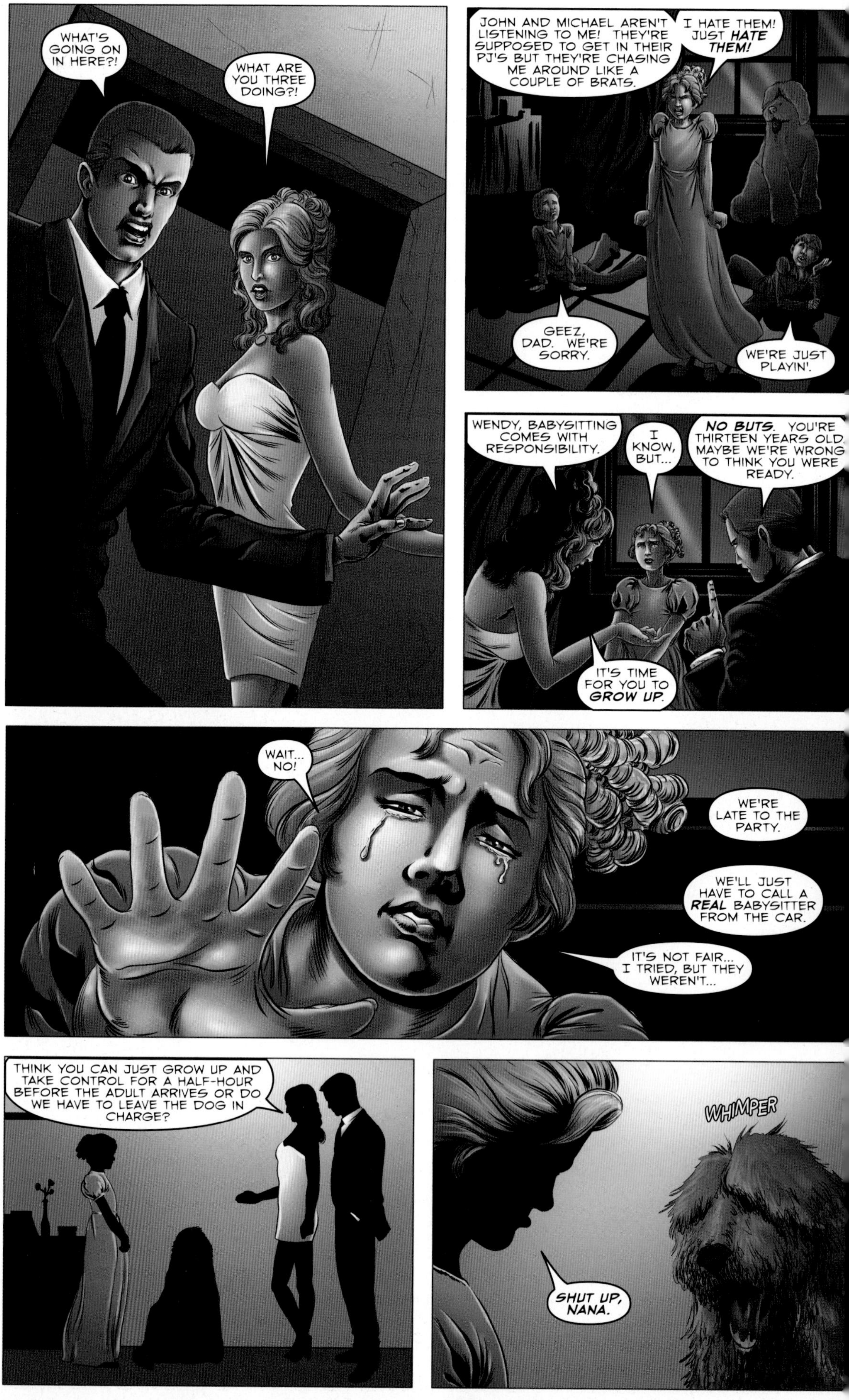
WHAT'S GOING ON IN HERE?!
WHAT ARE YOU THREE DOING?!
JOHN AND MICHAEL AREN'T LISTENING TO ME! THEY'RE SUPPOSED TO GET IN THEIR PJ'S BUT THEY'RE CHASING ME AROUND LIKE A COUPLE OF BRATS.
I HATE THEM! JUST HATE THEM!
GEEZ, DAD. WE'RE SORRY.
WE'RE JUST PLAYIN'.
WENDY, BABYSITTING COMES WITH RESPONSIBILITY.
I KNOW, BUT...
NO BUTS. YOU'RE THIRTEEN YEARS OLD. MAYBE WE'RE WRONG TO THINK YOU WERE READY.
IT'S TIME FOR YOU TO GROW UP.
WAIT... NO!
WE'RE LATE TO THE PARTY.
WE'LL JUST HAVE TO CALL A REAL BABYSITTER FROM THE CAR.
IT'S NOT FAIR... I TRIED, BUT THEY WEREN'T...
THINK YOU CAN JUST GROW UP AND TAKE CONTROL FOR A HALF-HOUR BEFORE THE ADULT ARRIVES OR DO WE HAVE TO LEAVE THE DOG IN CHARGE?
WHIMPER
SHUT UP, NANA.

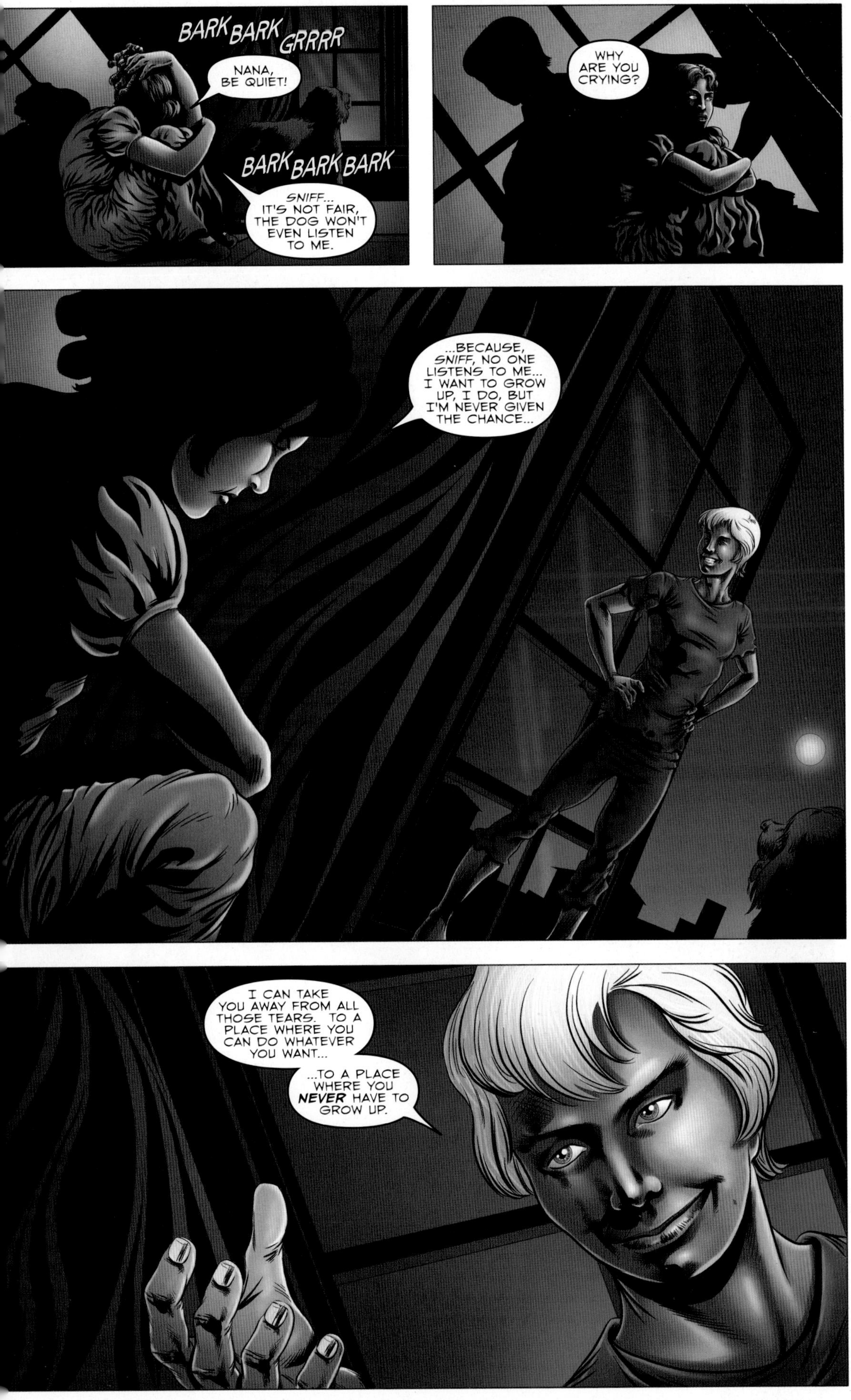

BARK BARK GRRRR
NANA, BE QUIET!
BARK BARK BARK
SNIFF... IT'S NOT FAIR, THE DOG WON'T EVEN LISTEN TO ME.
WHY ARE YOU CRYING?
...BECAUSE, SNIFF, NO ONE LISTENS TO ME... I WANT TO GROW UP, I DO, BUT I'M NEVER GIVEN THE CHANCE...
I CAN TAKE YOU AWAY FROM ALL THOSE TEARS. TO A PLACE WHERE YOU CAN DO WHATEVER YOU WANT...
...TO A PLACE WHERE YOU NEVER HAVE TO GROW UP.

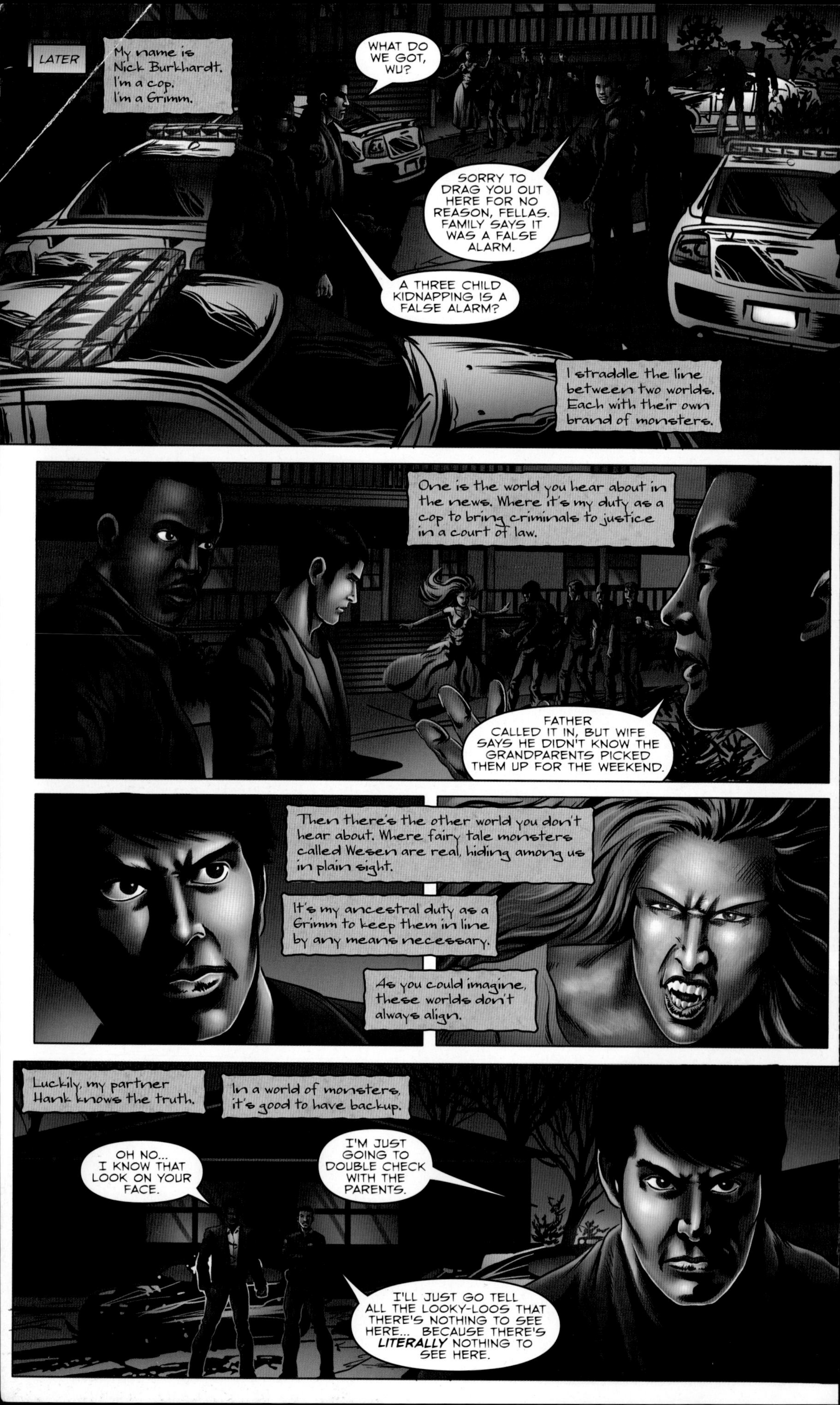
LATER
My name is Nick Burkhardt. I'm a cop. I'm a Grimm.
WHAT DO WE GOT, WU?
SORRY TO DRAG YOU OUT HERE FOR NO REASON, FELLAS. FAMILY SAYS IT WAS A FALSE ALARM.
A THREE CHILD KIDNAPPING IS A FALSE ALARM?
I straddle the line between two worlds. Each with their own brand of monsters.
One is the world you hear about in the news. Where it's my duty as a cop to bring criminals to justice in a court of law.
FATHER CALLED IT IN, BUT WIFE SAYS HE DIDN'T KNOW THE GRANDPARENTS PICKED THEM UP FOR THE WEEKEND.
Then there's the other world you don't hear about. Where fairy tale monsters called Wesen are real, hiding among us in plain sight.
It's my ancestral duty as a Grimm to keep them in line by any means necessary.
As you could imagine, these worlds don't always align.
Luckily, my partner Hank knows the truth.
In a world of monsters, it's good to have backup.
OH NO... I KNOW THAT LOOK ON YOUR FACE.
I'M JUST GOING TO DOUBLE CHECK WITH THE PARENTS.
I'LL JUST GO TELL ALL THE LOOKY-LOOS THAT THERE'S NOTHING TO SEE HERE... BECAUSE THERE'S *LITERALLY* NOTHING TO SEE HERE.

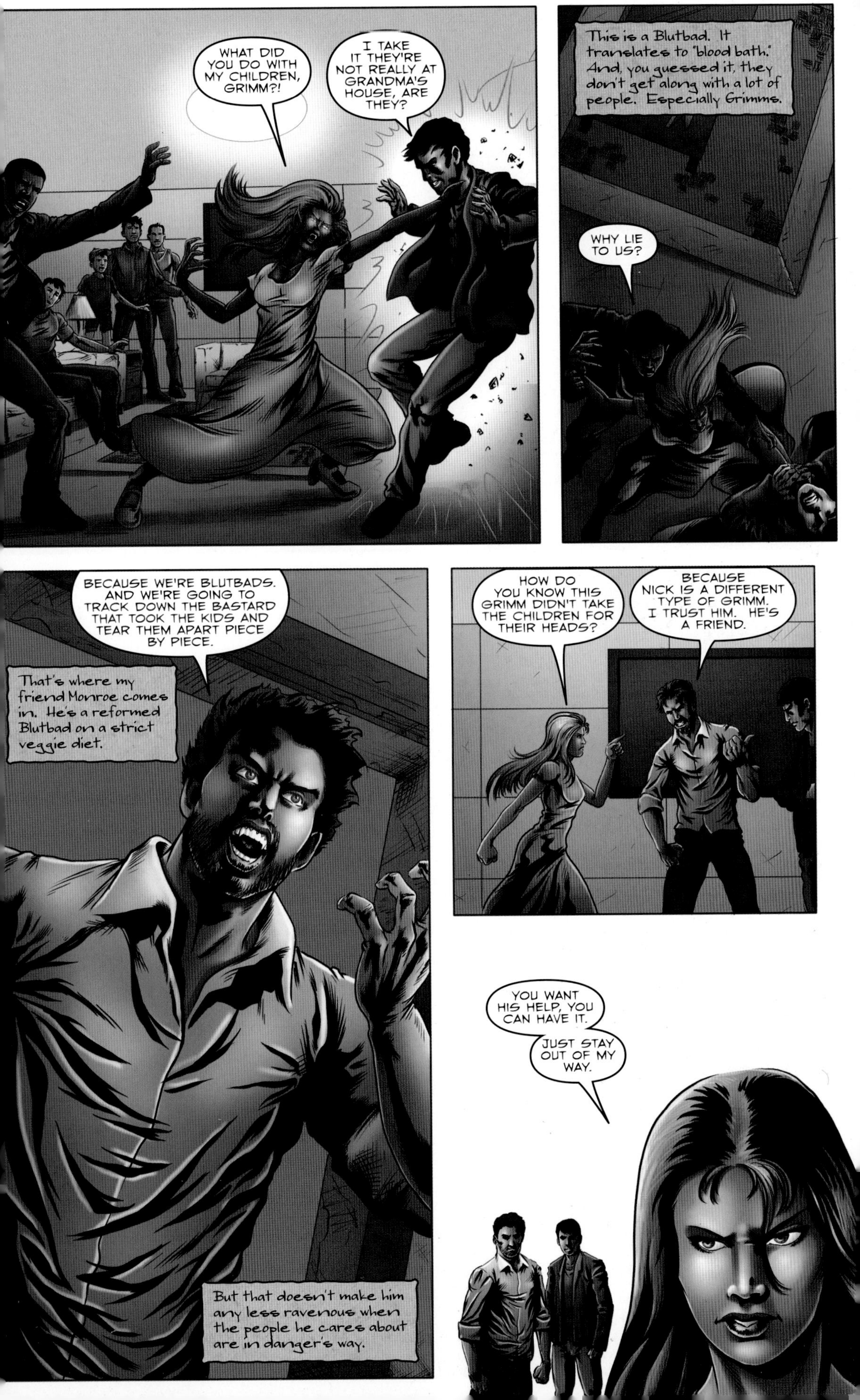
WHAT DID YOU DO WITH MY CHILDREN, GRIMM?!
I TAKE IT THEY'RE NOT REALLY AT GRANDMA'S HOUSE, ARE THEY?
This is a Blutbad. It translates to "blood bath." And, you guessed it, they don't get along with a lot of people. Especially Grimms.
WHY LIE TO US?
BECAUSE WE'RE BLUTBADS. AND WE'RE GOING TO TRACK DOWN THE BASTARD THAT TOOK THE KIDS AND TEAR THEM APART PIECE BY PIECE.
That's where my friend Monroe comes in. He's a reformed Blutbad on a strict veggie diet.
But that doesn't make him any less ravenous when the people he cares about are in danger's way.
HOW DO YOU KNOW THIS GRIMM DIDN'T TAKE THE CHILDREN FOR THEIR HEADS?
BECAUSE NICK IS A DIFFERENT TYPE OF GRIMM. I TRUST HIM. HE'S A FRIEND.
YOU WANT HIS HELP, YOU CAN HAVE IT.
JUST STAY OUT OF MY WAY.

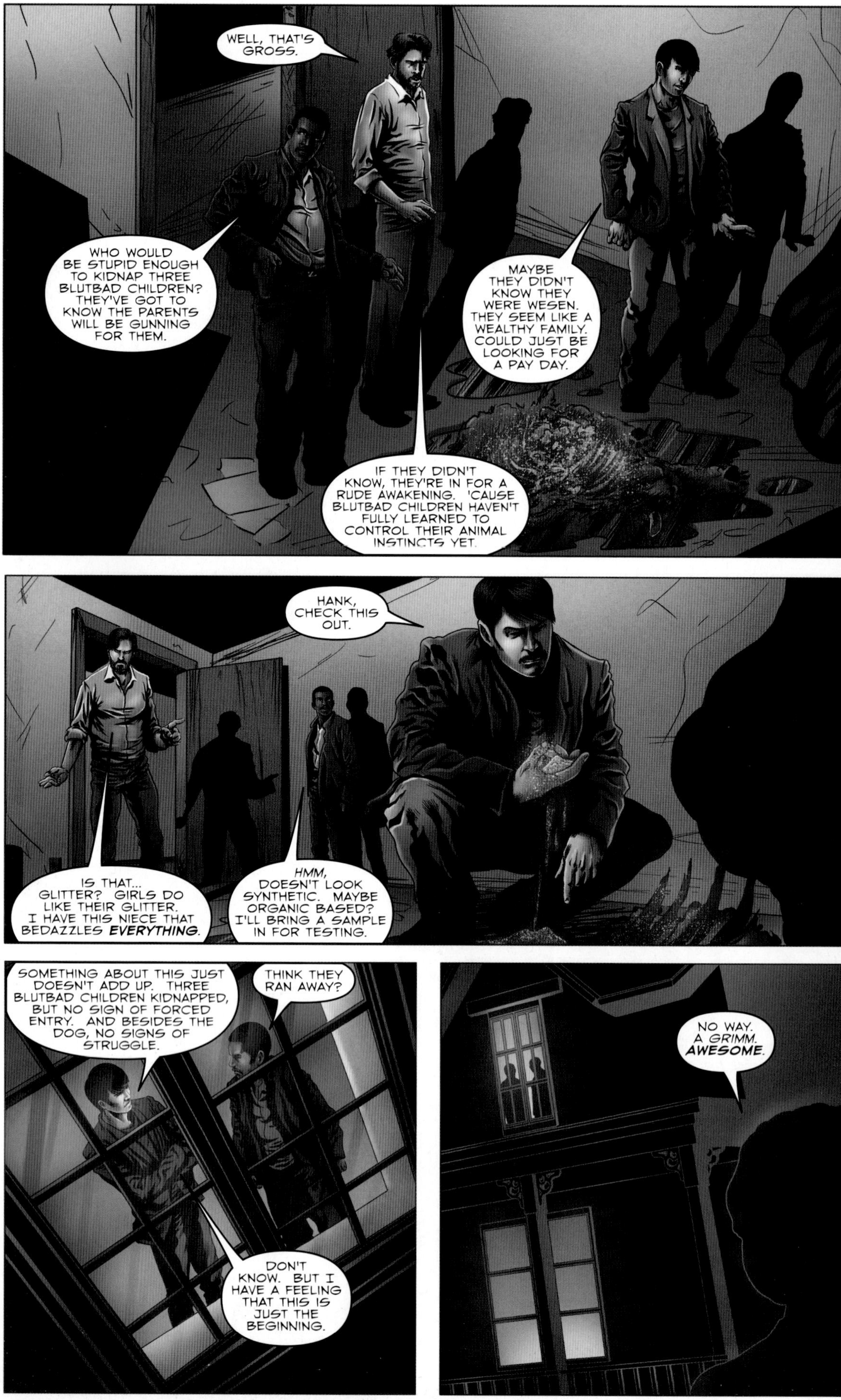

WELL, THAT'S GROSS.
WHO WOULD BE STUPID ENOUGH TO KIDNAP THREE BLUTBAD CHILDREN? THEY'VE GOT TO KNOW THE PARENTS WILL BE GUNNING FOR THEM.
MAYBE THEY DIDN'T KNOW THEY WERE WESEN. THEY SEEM LIKE A WEALTHY FAMILY. COULD JUST BE LOOKING FOR A PAY DAY.
IF THEY DIDN'T KNOW, THEY'RE IN FOR A RUDE AWAKENING. 'CAUSE BLUTBAD CHILDREN HAVEN'T FULLY LEARNED TO CONTROL THEIR ANIMAL INSTINCTS YET.
HANK, CHECK THIS OUT.
IS THAT... GLITTER? GIRLS DO LIKE THEIR GLITTER. I HAVE THIS NIECE THAT BEDAZZLES ***EVERYTHING***.
HMM, DOESN'T LOOK SYNTHETIC. MAYBE ORGANIC BASED? I'LL BRING A SAMPLE IN FOR TESTING.
SOMETHING ABOUT THIS JUST DOESN'T ADD UP. THREE BLUTBAD CHILDREN KIDNAPPED, BUT NO SIGN OF FORCED ENTRY. AND BESIDES THE DOG, NO SIGNS OF STRUGGLE.
THINK THEY RAN AWAY?
DON'T KNOW. BUT I HAVE A FEELING THAT THIS IS JUST THE BEGINNING.
NO WAY. A GRIMM. ***AWESOME***.

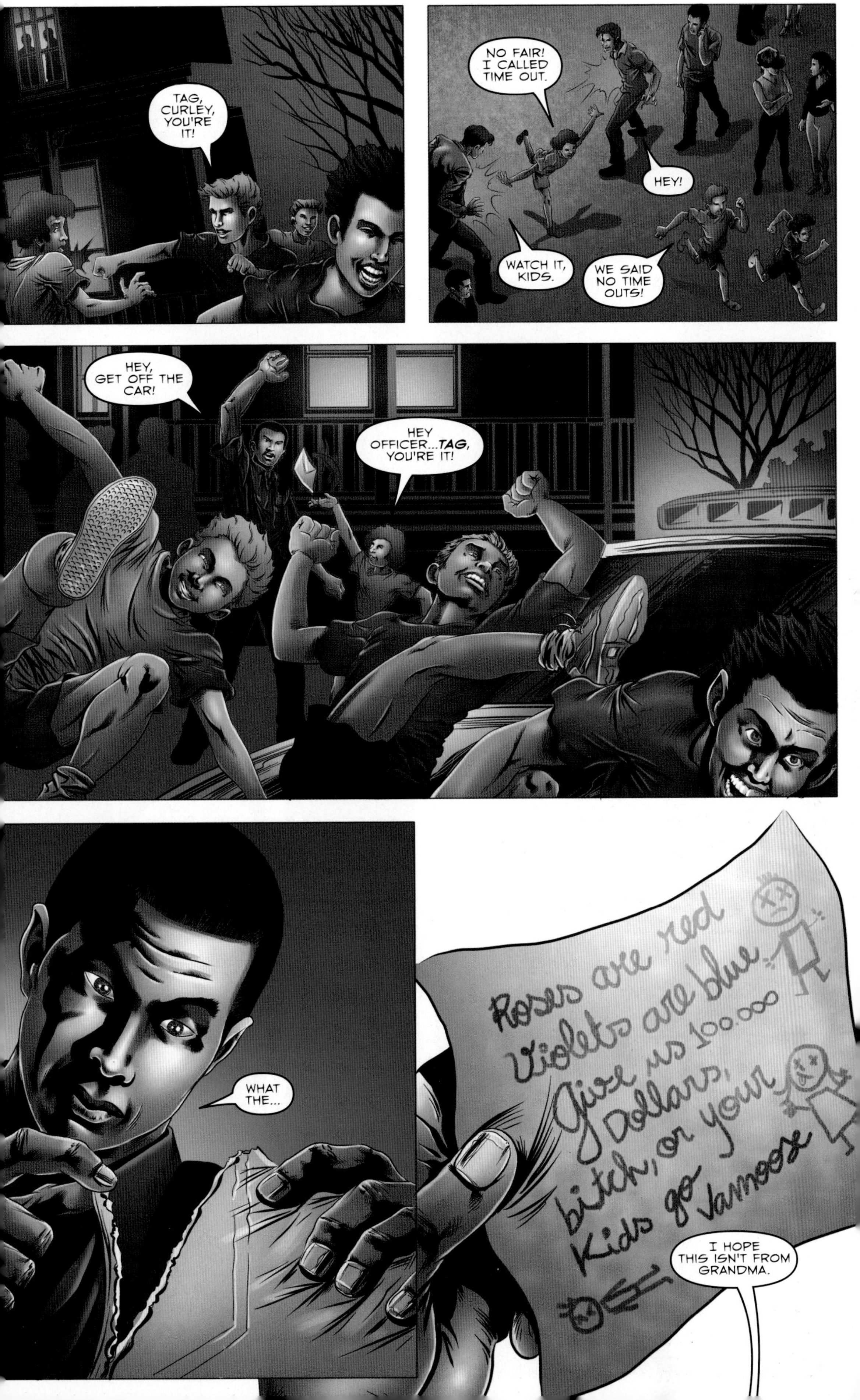
TAG, CURLEY, YOU'RE IT!
NO FAIR! I CALLED TIME OUT.
HEY!
WATCH IT, KIDS.
WE SAID NO TIME OUTS!
HEY, GET OFF THE CAR!
HEY OFFICER...TAG, YOU'RE IT!
WHAT THE...
Roses are red
Violets are blue
Give us 100.000
Dollars,
bitch, or your
Kids go Vamoose
I HOPE THIS ISN'T FROM GRANDMA.

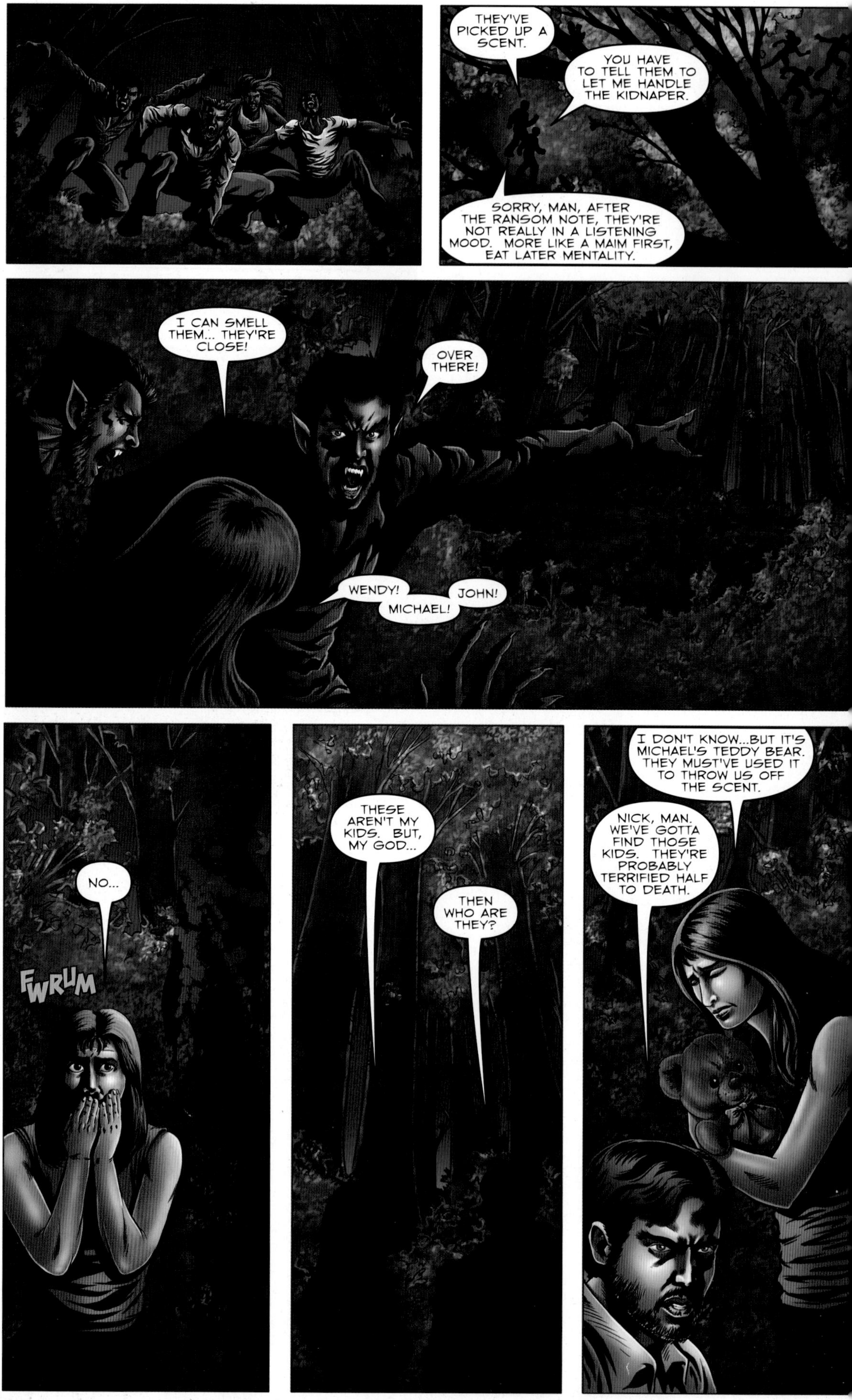

THEY'VE PICKED UP A SCENT.
YOU HAVE TO TELL THEM TO LET ME HANDLE THE KIDNAPER.
SORRY, MAN, AFTER THE RANSOM NOTE, THEY'RE NOT REALLY IN A LISTENING MOOD. MORE LIKE A MAIM FIRST, EAT LATER MENTALITY.
I CAN SMELL THEM... THEY'RE CLOSE!
OVER THERE!
WENDY!
MICHAEL!
JOHN!
NO...
FWRUM
THESE AREN'T MY KIDS. BUT, MY GOD...
THEN WHO ARE THEY?
I DON'T KNOW...BUT IT'S MICHAEL'S TEDDY BEAR. THEY MUST'VE USED IT TO THROW US OFF THE SCENT.
NICK, MAN. WE'VE GOTTA FIND THOSE KIDS. THEY'RE PROBABLY TERRIFIED HALF TO DEATH.

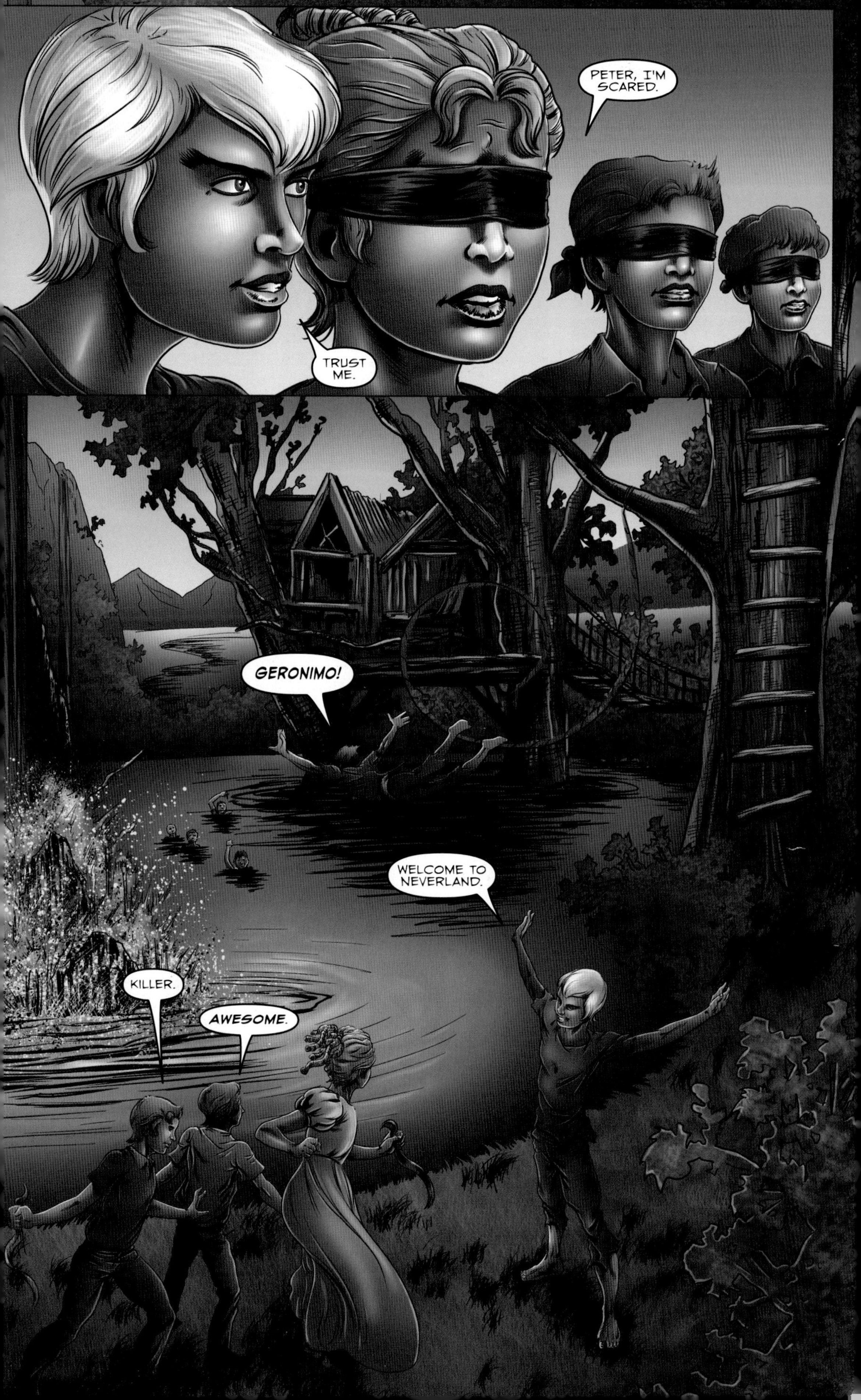
PETER, I'M SCARED.
TRUST ME.
GERONIMO!
WELCOME TO NEVERLAND.
KILLER.
AWESOME.

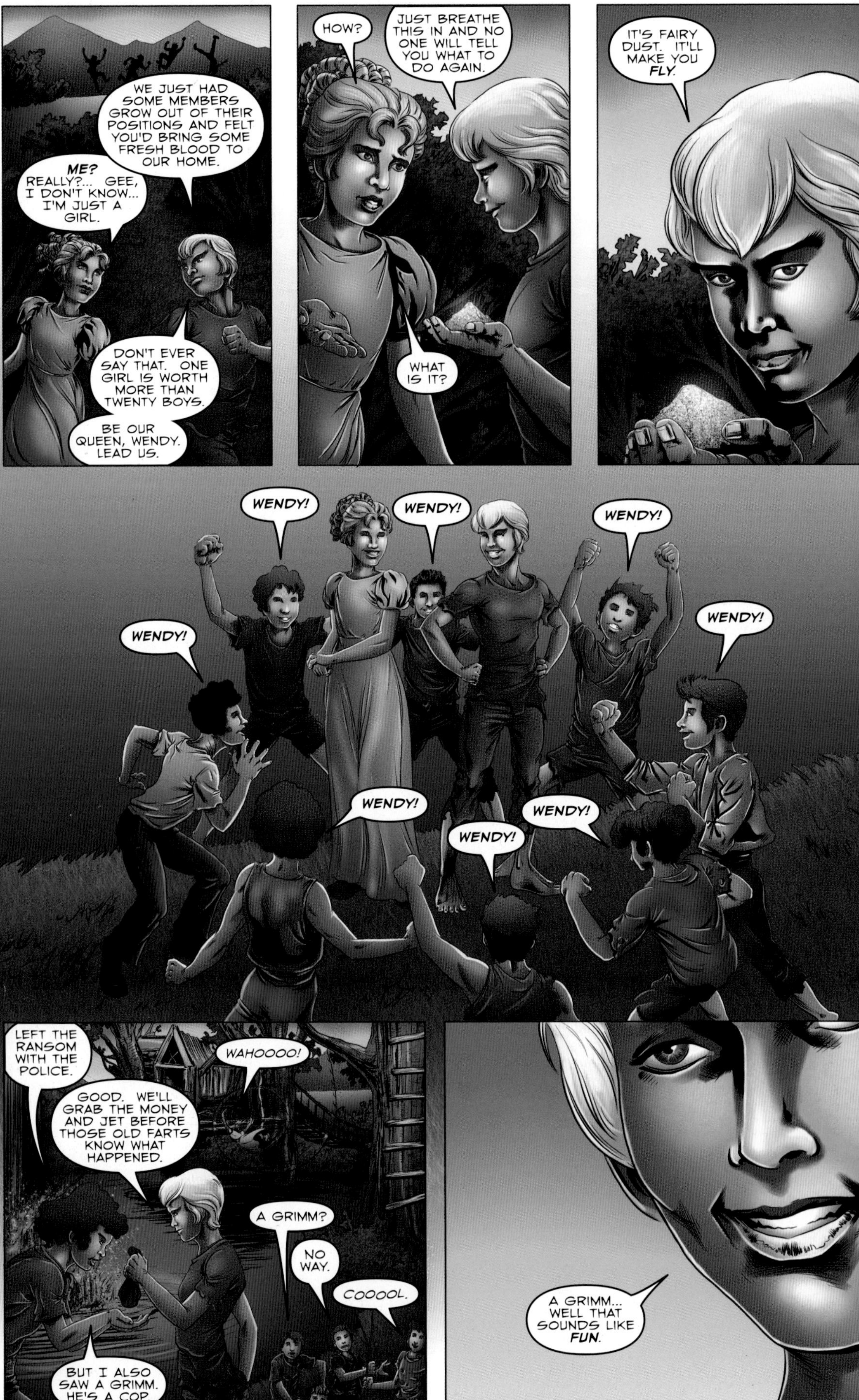
WE JUST HAD SOME MEMBERS GROW OUT OF THEIR POSITIONS AND FELT YOU'D BRING SOME FRESH BLOOD TO OUR HOME.
ME? REALLY?... GEE, I DON'T KNOW... I'M JUST A GIRL.
DON'T EVER SAY THAT. ONE GIRL IS WORTH MORE THAN TWENTY BOYS.
BE OUR QUEEN, WENDY. LEAD US.
HOW?
JUST BREATHE THIS IN AND NO ONE WILL TELL YOU WHAT TO DO AGAIN.
WHAT IS IT?
IT'S FAIRY DUST. IT'LL MAKE YOU FLY.
WENDY!
WENDY!
WENDY!
WENDY!
WENDY!
WENDY!
WENDY!
WENDY!
LEFT THE RANSOM WITH THE POLICE.
WAHOOOO!
GOOD. WE'LL GRAB THE MONEY AND JET BEFORE THOSE OLD FARTS KNOW WHAT HAPPENED.
BUT I ALSO SAW A GRIMM. HE'S A COP.
A GRIMM?
NO WAY.
COOOOL.
A GRIMM... WELL THAT SOUNDS LIKE FUN.

SO WHAT DID YOU FIND OUT?

THREE BODIES CAME BACK AS THE JAMES CHILDREN. KIDNAPPED FROM SPOKANE SIX YEARS AGO.

STORY IS EERILY SIMILAR TO THE DAVIES' KIDS DOWN TO THE NOTE WRITTEN IN CRAYON. PARENTS PAID, BUT THE KIDS WERE NEVER RETURNED.

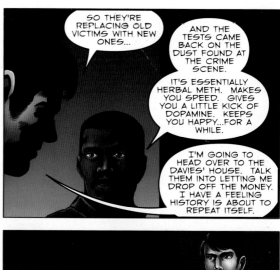

SO THEY'RE REPLACING OLD VICTIMS WITH NEW ONES...

AND THE TESTS CAME BACK ON THE DUST FOUND AT THE CRIME SCENE.

IT'S ESSENTIALLY HERBAL METH. MAKES YOU SPEED. GIVES YOU A LITTLE KICK OF DOPAMINE. KEEPS YOU HAPPY...FOR A WHILE.

I'M GOING TO HEAD OVER TO THE DAVIES' HOUSE. TALK THEM INTO LETTING ME DROP OFF THE MONEY. I HAVE A FEELING HISTORY IS ABOUT TO REPEAT ITSELF.

EAT THE HEART AND PULL OFF ITS LIMBS...

KID, WHAT'RE YOU DOING? YOU OKAY?

HEY, MISTER, WANT TO PLAY?

YOU LOST? WHERE ARE YOUR...

TAG! YOU'RE IT.

GRIMMS AREN'T ALL THAT SPECIAL. YOU'RE LAZY, FAT, AND SLOW JUST LIKE ALL GROWN UPS.

I WANT THE MONEY OR THE KIDS WILL NEVER BE SEEN AGAIN.

WHO ARE YOU?

"I'M YOUTH, I'M JOY, I'M A LITTLE BIRD THAT HAS BROKEN OUT OF THE EGG."

FWRUM

SMACK

NO MORE GAMES. YOU'RE GOING TO TAKE ME TO THE KIDS. *NOW.*

BUT WE'RE HAVING SO MUCH FUN...

HOW 'BOUT WE PLAY HIDE AND SEEK? TRY TO HIDE, SEE IF I CAN'T FIND YOU.

HELP! STRANGER!

HELP! HE'S HURTING ME!

FWRUM

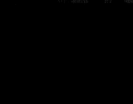

WHAT'S GOING ON HERE?!

NICK, HAVE YOU LOST YOUR MIND?

LET ME GO, IT'S A TRICK...!

WHAT ARE YOU DOING TO THAT KID?!

WE NEED TO FIND THOSE KIDS. BEFORE IT'S TOO LATE.

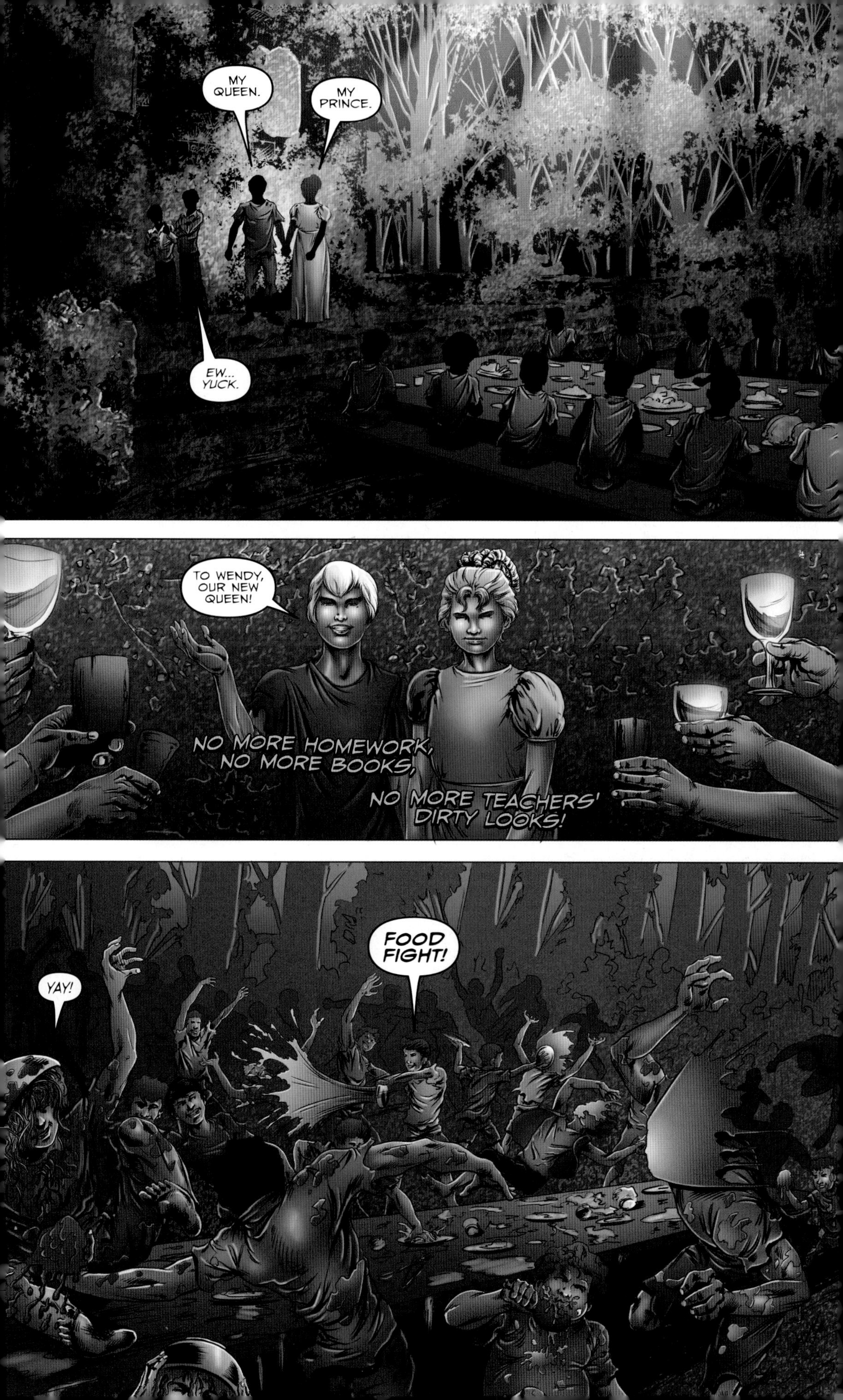
MY QUEEN.
MY PRINCE.
EW... YUCK.
TO WENDY, OUR NEW QUEEN!
NO MORE HOMEWORK, NO MORE BOOKS,
NO MORE TEACHERS' DIRTY LOOKS!
YAY!
FOOD FIGHT!

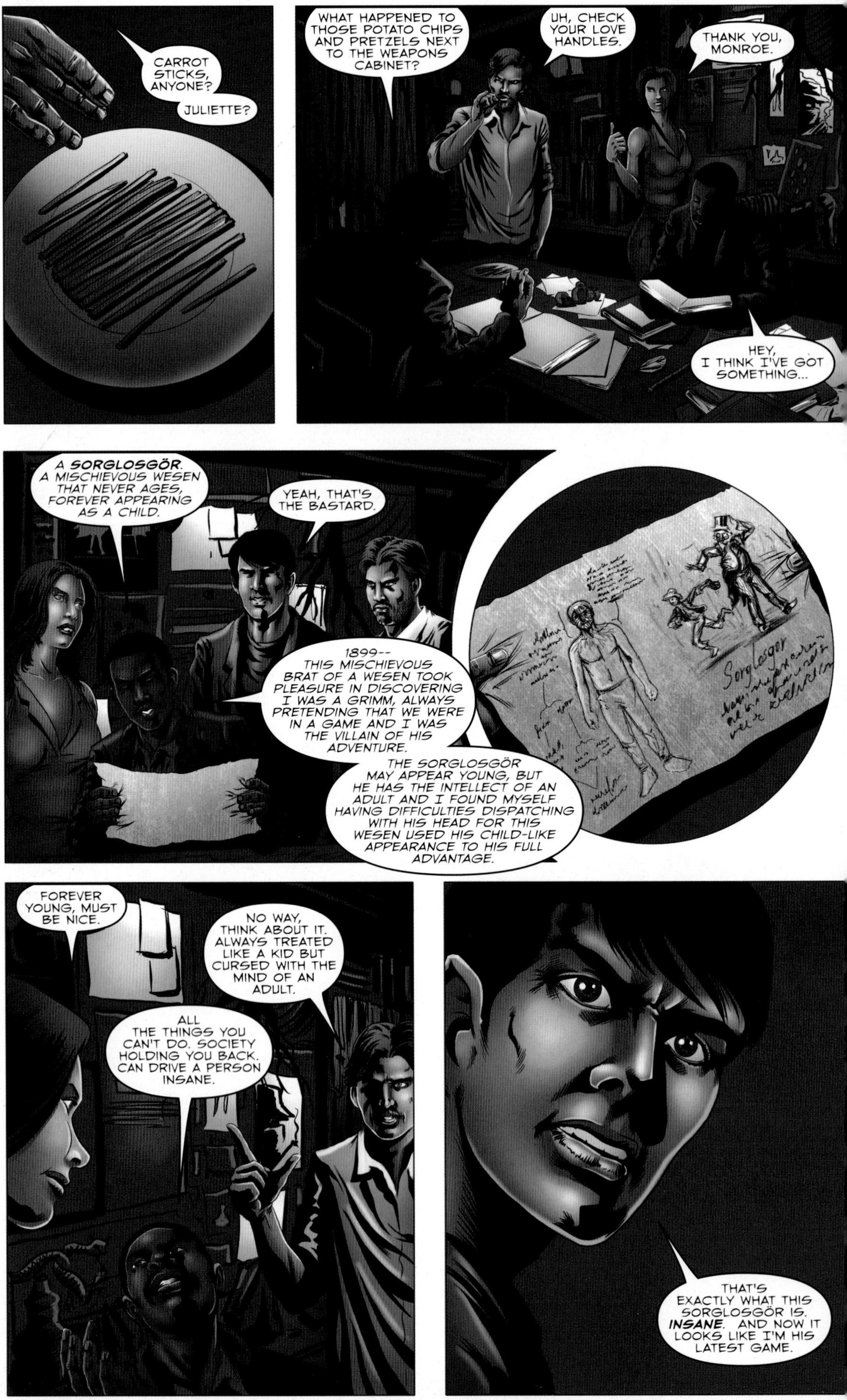
CARROT STICKS, ANYONE?
JULIETTE?
WHAT HAPPENED TO THOSE POTATO CHIPS AND PRETZELS NEXT TO THE WEAPONS CABINET?
UH, CHECK YOUR LOVE HANDLES.
THANK YOU, MONROE.
HEY, I THINK I'VE GOT SOMETHING...
A SORGLOSGÖR. A MISCHIEVOUS WESEN THAT NEVER AGES, FOREVER APPEARING AS A CHILD.
YEAH, THAT'S THE BASTARD.
1899-- THIS MISCHIEVOUS BRAT OF A WESEN TOOK PLEASURE IN DISCOVERING I WAS A GRIMM, ALWAYS PRETENDING THAT WE WERE IN A GAME AND I WAS THE VILLAIN OF HIS ADVENTURE.
THE SORGLOSGÖR MAY APPEAR YOUNG, BUT HE HAS THE INTELLECT OF AN ADULT AND I FOUND MYSELF HAVING DIFFICULTIES DISPATCHING WITH HIS HEAD FOR THIS WESEN USED HIS CHILD-LIKE APPEARANCE TO HIS FULL ADVANTAGE.
Sorglosgor
FOREVER YOUNG, MUST BE NICE.
NO WAY, THINK ABOUT IT. ALWAYS TREATED LIKE A KID BUT CURSED WITH THE MIND OF AN ADULT.
ALL THE THINGS YOU CAN'T DO. SOCIETY HOLDING YOU BACK. CAN DRIVE A PERSON INSANE.
THAT'S EXACTLY WHAT THIS SORGLOSGÖR IS. INSANE. AND NOW IT LOOKS LIKE I'M HIS LATEST GAME.

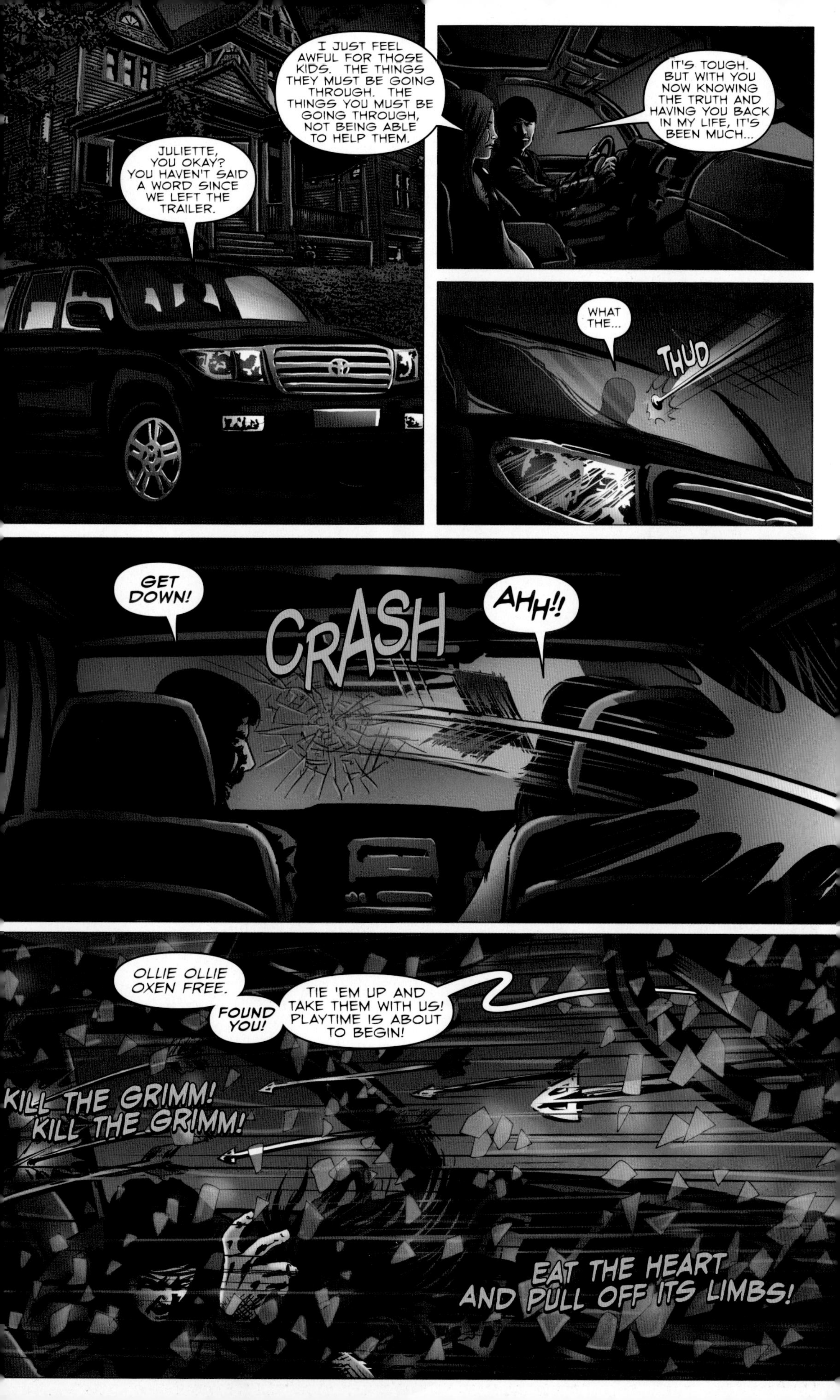
JULIETTE, YOU OKAY? YOU HAVEN'T SAID A WORD SINCE WE LEFT THE TRAILER.
I JUST FEEL AWFUL FOR THOSE KIDS. THE THINGS THEY MUST BE GOING THROUGH. THE THINGS YOU MUST BE GOING THROUGH, NOT BEING ABLE TO HELP THEM.
IT'S TOUGH. BUT WITH YOU NOW KNOWING THE TRUTH AND HAVING YOU BACK IN MY LIFE, IT'S BEEN MUCH...
WHAT THE...
THUD
GET DOWN!
CRASH
AHH!!
OLLIE OLLIE OXEN FREE.
FOUND YOU!
TIE 'EM UP AND TAKE THEM WITH US! PLAYTIME IS ABOUT TO BEGIN!
KILL THE GRIMM! KILL THE GRIMM!
EAT THE HEART AND PULL OFF ITS LIMBS!

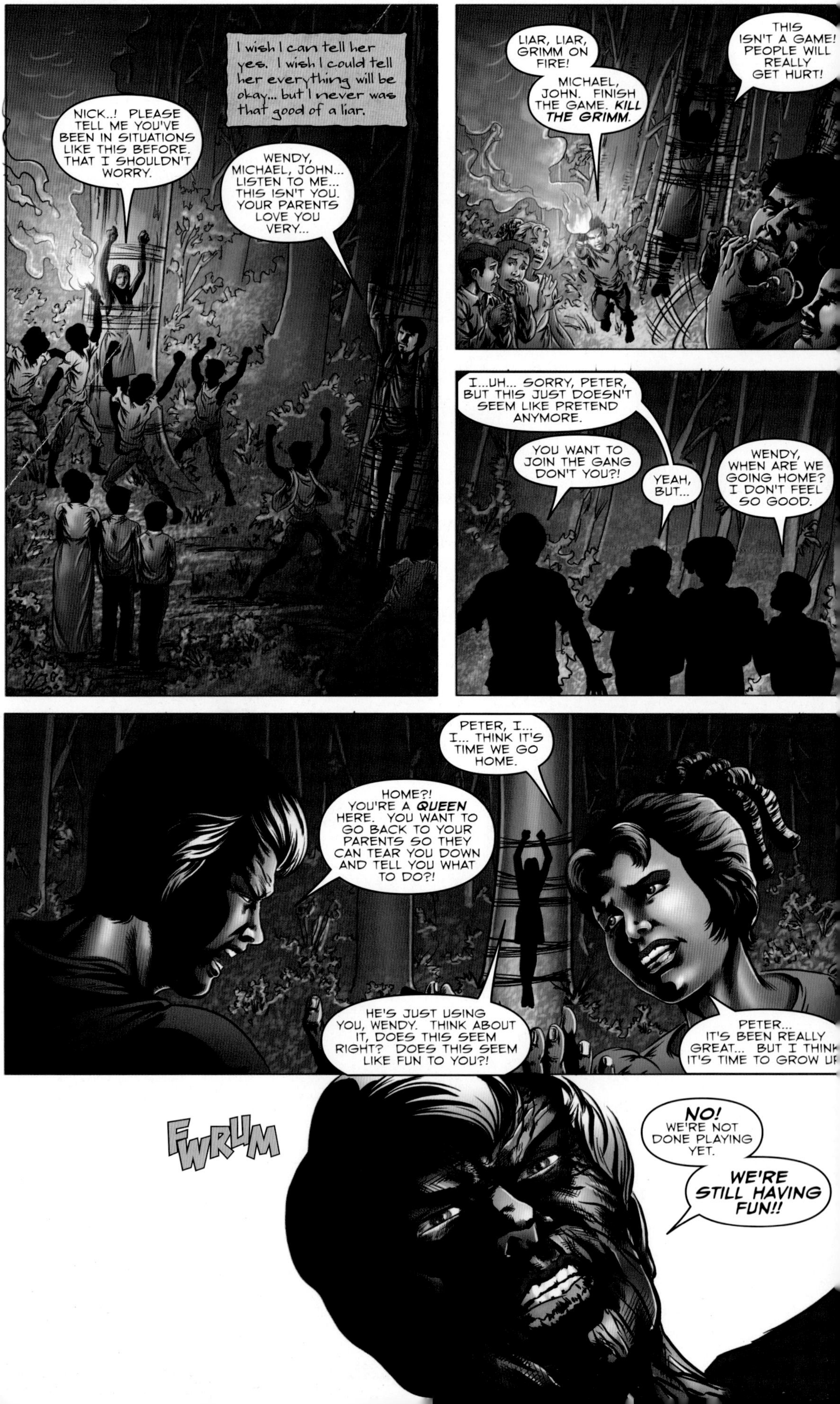

I wish I can tell her yes. I wish I could tell her everything will be okay... but I never was that good of a liar.
NICK..! PLEASE TELL ME YOU'VE BEEN IN SITUATIONS LIKE THIS BEFORE. THAT I SHOULDN'T WORRY.
WENDY, MICHAEL, JOHN... LISTEN TO ME... THIS ISN'T YOU. YOUR PARENTS LOVE YOU VERY...
LIAR, LIAR, GRIMM ON FIRE!
MICHAEL, JOHN. FINISH THE GAME. KILL THE GRIMM.
THIS ISN'T A GAME! PEOPLE WILL REALLY GET HURT!
I...UH... SORRY, PETER, BUT THIS JUST DOESN'T SEEM LIKE PRETEND ANYMORE.
YOU WANT TO JOIN THE GANG DON'T YOU?!
YEAH, BUT...
WENDY, WHEN ARE WE GOING HOME? I DON'T FEEL SO GOOD.
PETER, I... I... THINK IT'S TIME WE GO HOME.
HOME?! YOU'RE A QUEEN HERE. YOU WANT TO GO BACK TO YOUR PARENTS SO THEY CAN TEAR YOU DOWN AND TELL YOU WHAT TO DO?!
HE'S JUST USING YOU, WENDY. THINK ABOUT IT, DOES THIS SEEM RIGHT? DOES THIS SEEM LIKE FUN TO YOU?!
PETER... IT'S BEEN REALLY GREAT... BUT I THINK IT'S TIME TO GROW UP
FWRUM
NO! WE'RE NOT DONE PLAYING YET.
WE'RE STILL HAVING FUN!!

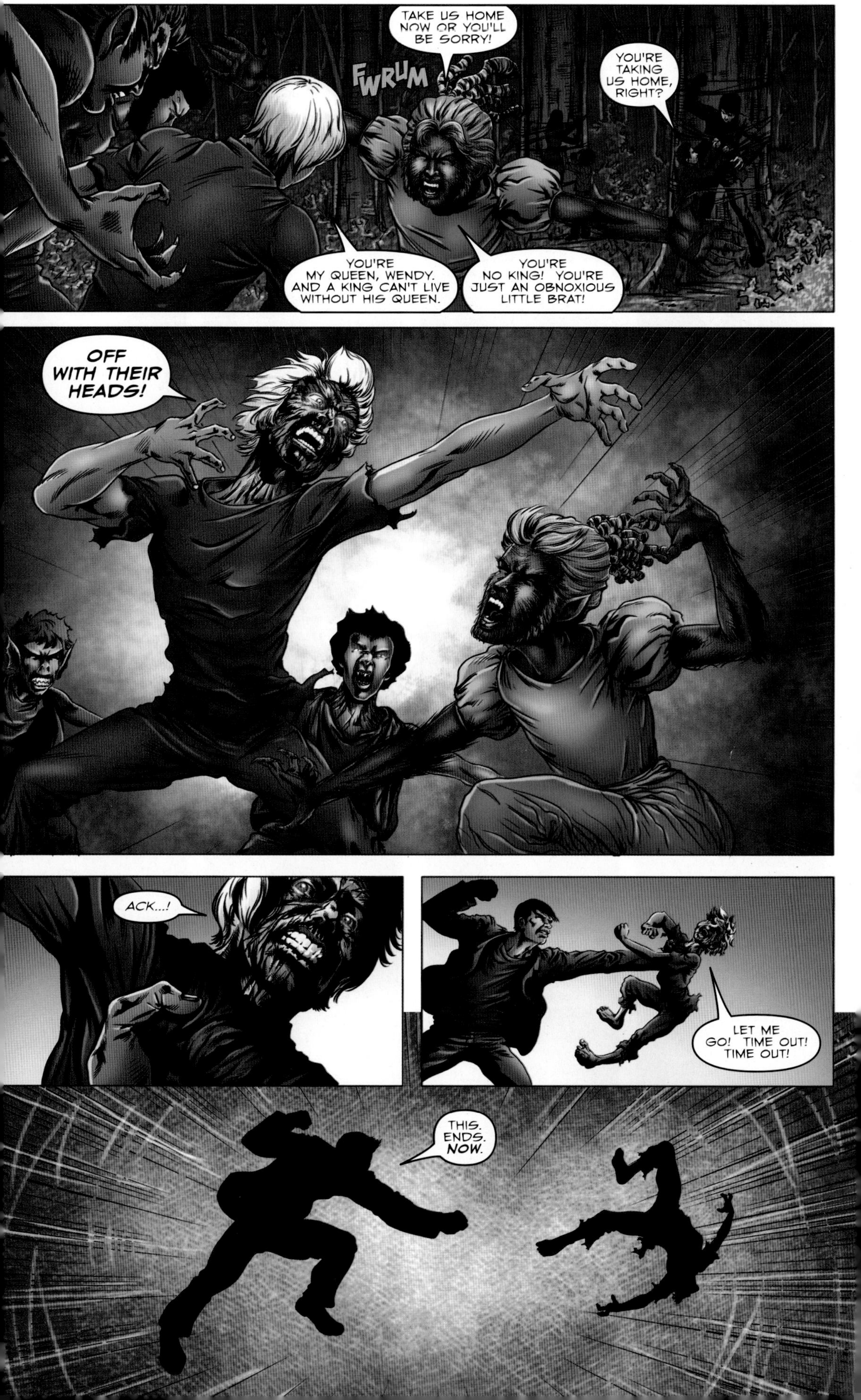
TAKE US HOME NOW OR YOU'LL BE SORRY!
FWRUM
YOU'RE TAKING US HOME, RIGHT?
YOU'RE MY QUEEN, WENDY. AND A KING CAN'T LIVE WITHOUT HIS QUEEN.
YOU'RE NO KING! YOU'RE JUST AN OBNOXIOUS LITTLE BRAT!
OFF WITH THEIR HEADS!
ACK...!
LET ME GO! TIME OUT! TIME OUT!
THIS. ENDS. NOW.

YOU CAN'T TELL ME WHAT TO DO! NO ONE CAN!

I don't hate this Sorglosgör. I pity him.

♪THE ITSY BITSY SPIDER CRAWLED UP THE WATER SPOUT...♪

Having to create this fantasy to hide who he really is inside.

All that pent up frustration would drive anyone crazy.

I know, because having to live a secret life as a Grimm nearly killed me. And nearly lost me Juliette.

♪DOWN CAME THE RAIN, AND WASHED THE SPIDER OUT.♪

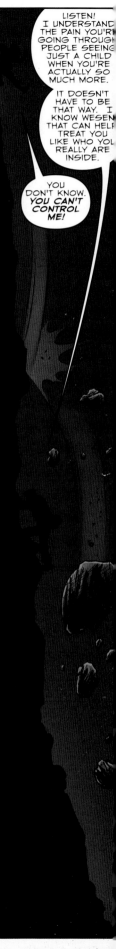

LISTEN! I UNDERSTAND THE PAIN YOU'R'E GOING THROUGH, PEOPLE SEEING JUST A CHILD WHEN YOU'RE ACTUALLY SO MUCH MORE.

IT DOESN'T HAVE TO BE THAT WAY. I KNOW WESEN THAT CAN HELP TREAT YOU LIKE WHO YOU REALLY ARE INSIDE.

YOU DON'T KNOW. YOU CAN'T CONTROL ME!

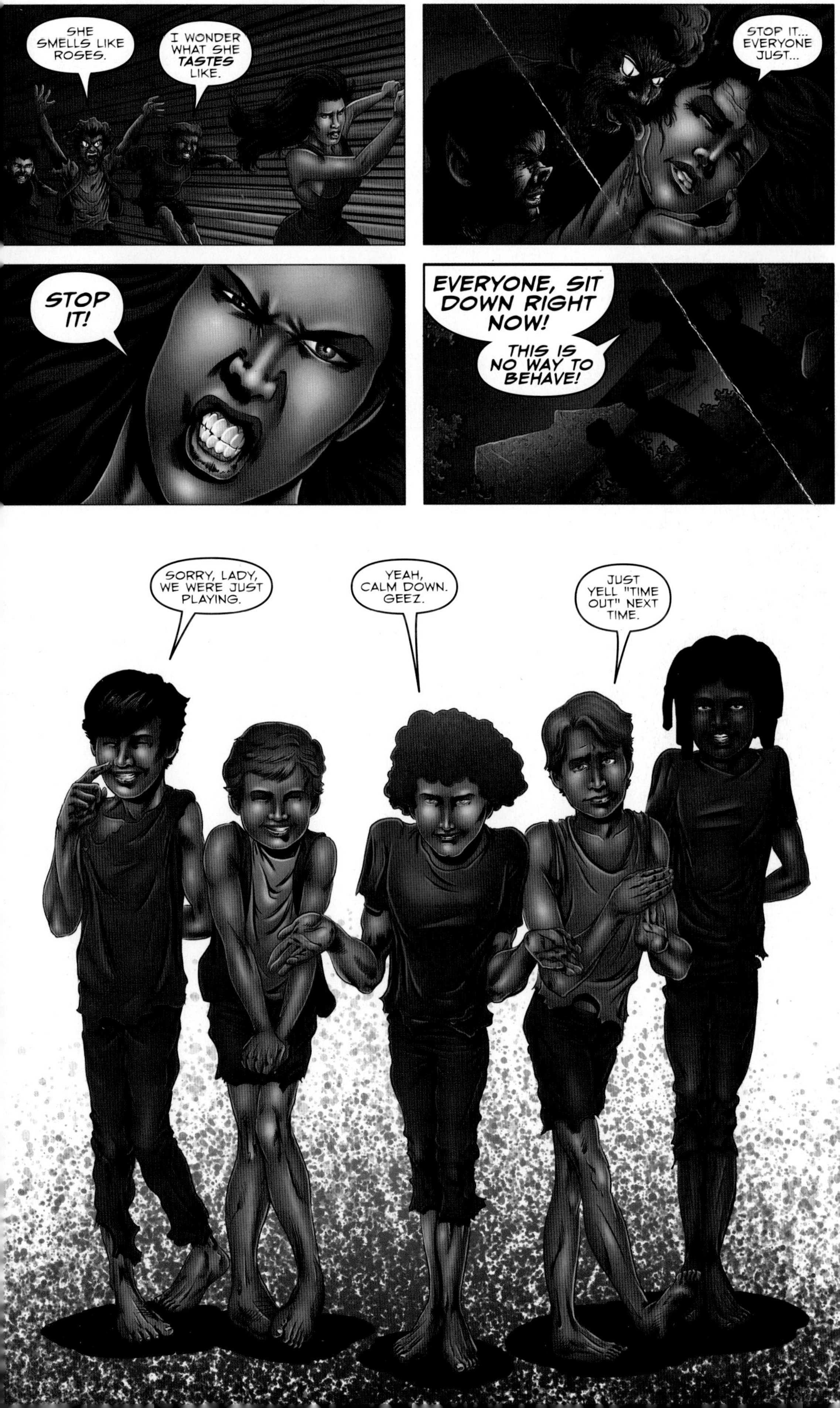
SHE SMELLS LIKE ROSES.
I WONDER WHAT SHE *TASTES* LIKE.
STOP IT... EVERYONE JUST...
STOP IT!
EVERYONE, SIT DOWN RIGHT NOW!
THIS IS NO WAY TO BEHAVE!
SORRY, LADY, WE WERE JUST PLAYING.
YEAH, CALM DOWN. GEEZ.
JUST YELL "TIME OUT" NEXT TIME.

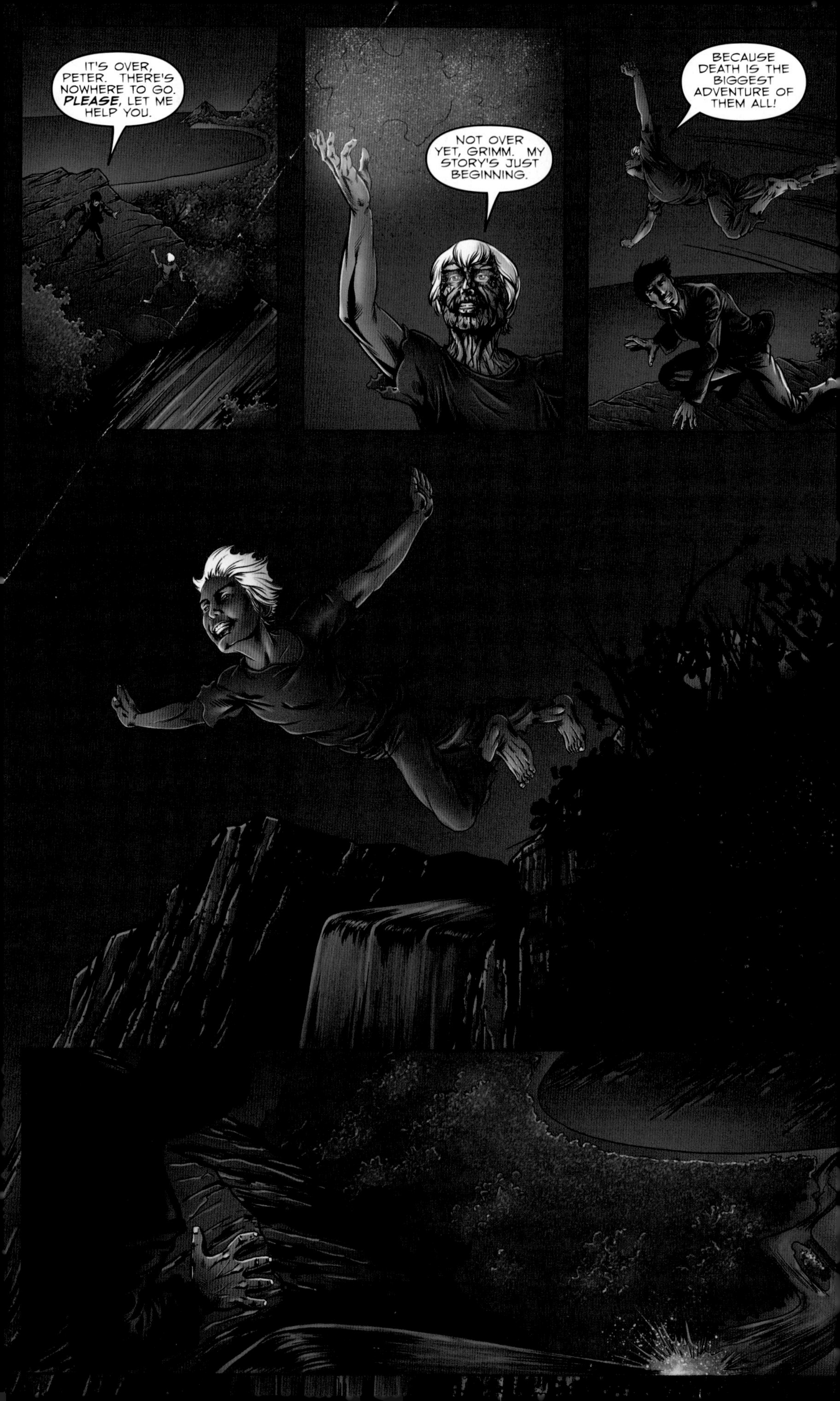
IT'S OVER, PETER. THERE'S NOWHERE TO GO. ***PLEASE***, LET ME HELP YOU.
NOT OVER YET, GRIMM. MY STORY'S JUST BEGINNING.
BECAUSE DEATH IS THE BIGGEST ADVENTURE OF THEM ALL!

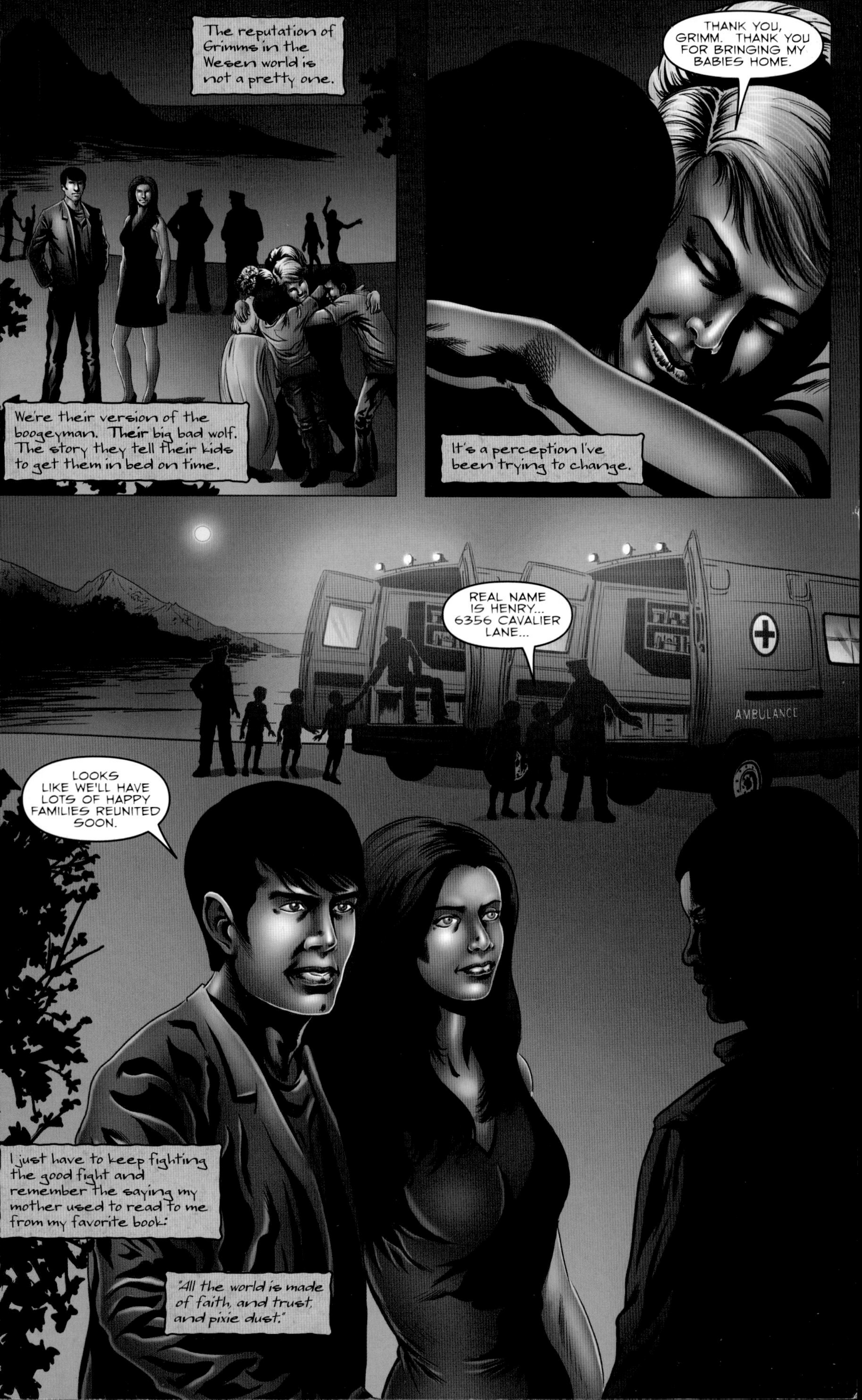
The reputation of Grimms in the Wesen world is not a pretty one.
We're their version of the boogeyman. Their big bad wolf. The story they tell their kids to get them in bed on time.
THANK YOU, GRIMM. THANK YOU FOR BRINGING MY BABIES HOME.
It's a perception I've been trying to change.
REAL NAME IS HENRY... 6356 CAVALIER LANE...
AMBULANCE
LOOKS LIKE WE'LL HAVE LOTS OF HAPPY FAMILIES REUNITED SOON.
I just have to keep fighting the good fight and remember the saying my mother used to read to me from my favorite book:
"All the world is made of faith, and trust, and pixie dust."

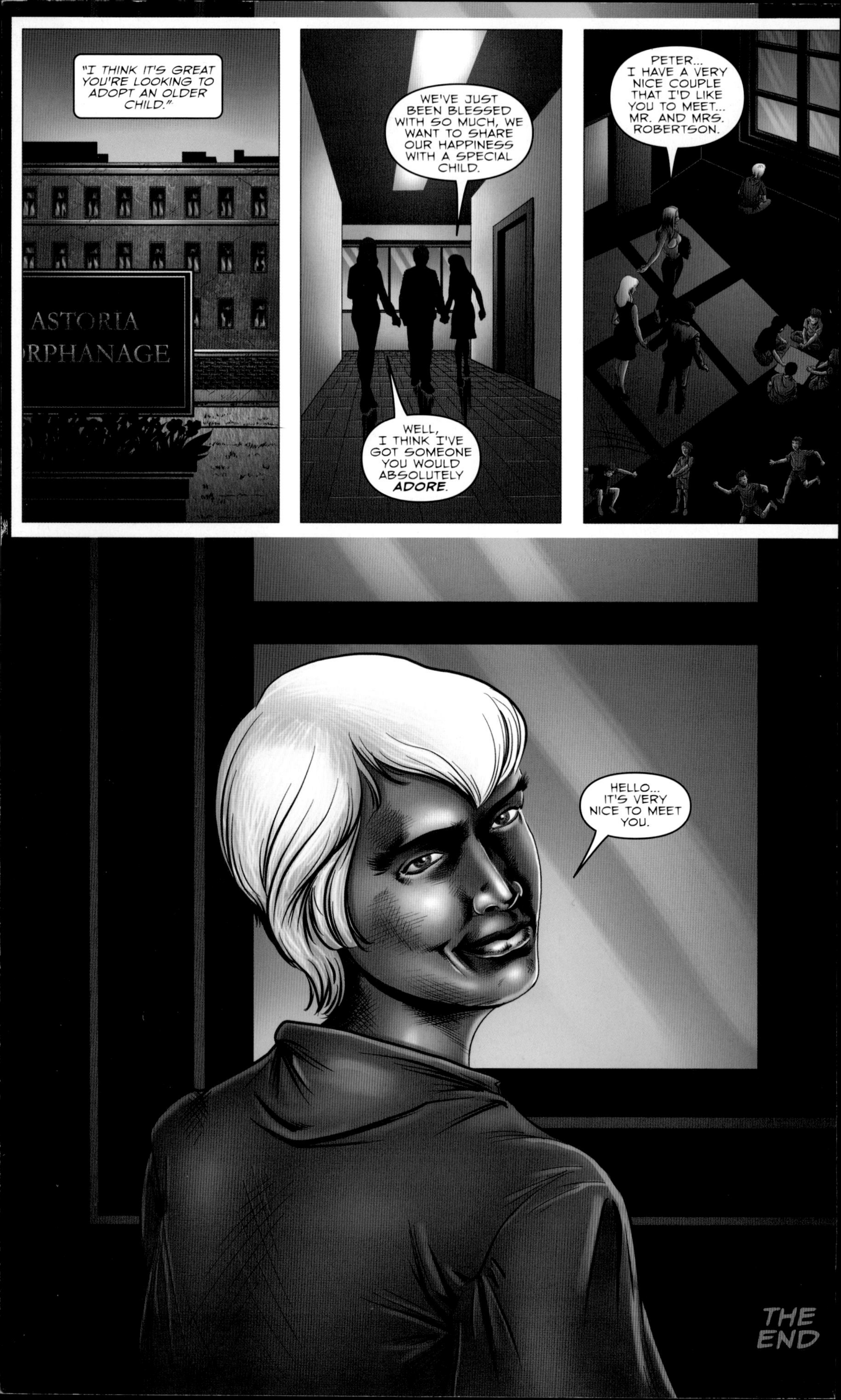
"I THINK IT'S GREAT YOU'RE LOOKING TO ADOPT AN OLDER CHILD."
ASTORIA ORPHANAGE
WE'VE JUST BEEN BLESSED WITH SO MUCH, WE WANT TO SHARE OUR HAPPINESS WITH A SPECIAL CHILD.
WELL, I THINK I'VE GOT SOMEONE YOU WOULD ABSOLUTELY *ADORE*.
PETER... I HAVE A VERY NICE COUPLE THAT I'D LIKE YOU TO MEET... MR. AND MRS. ROBERTSON.
HELLO... IT'S VERY NICE TO MEET YOU.
THE END

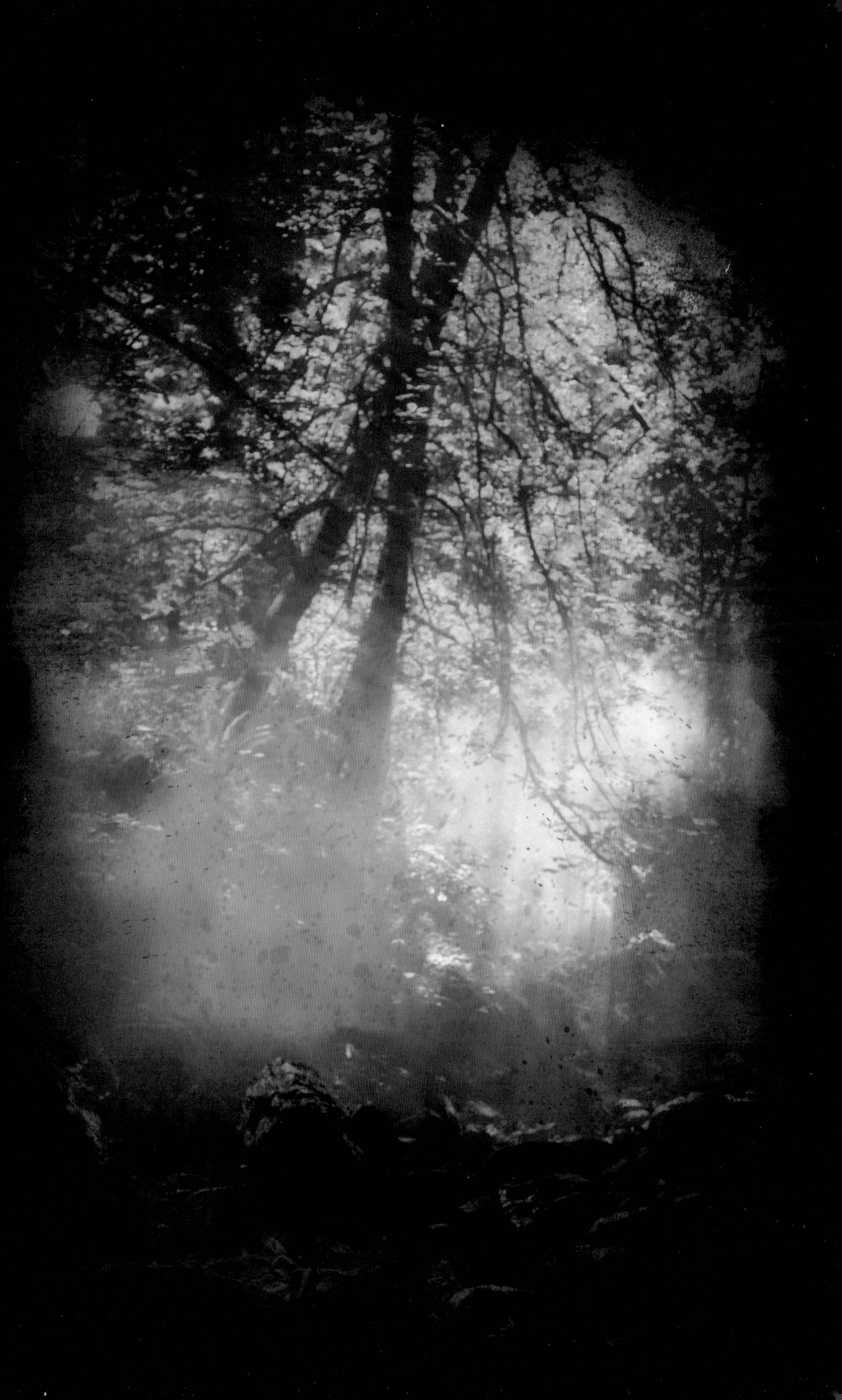

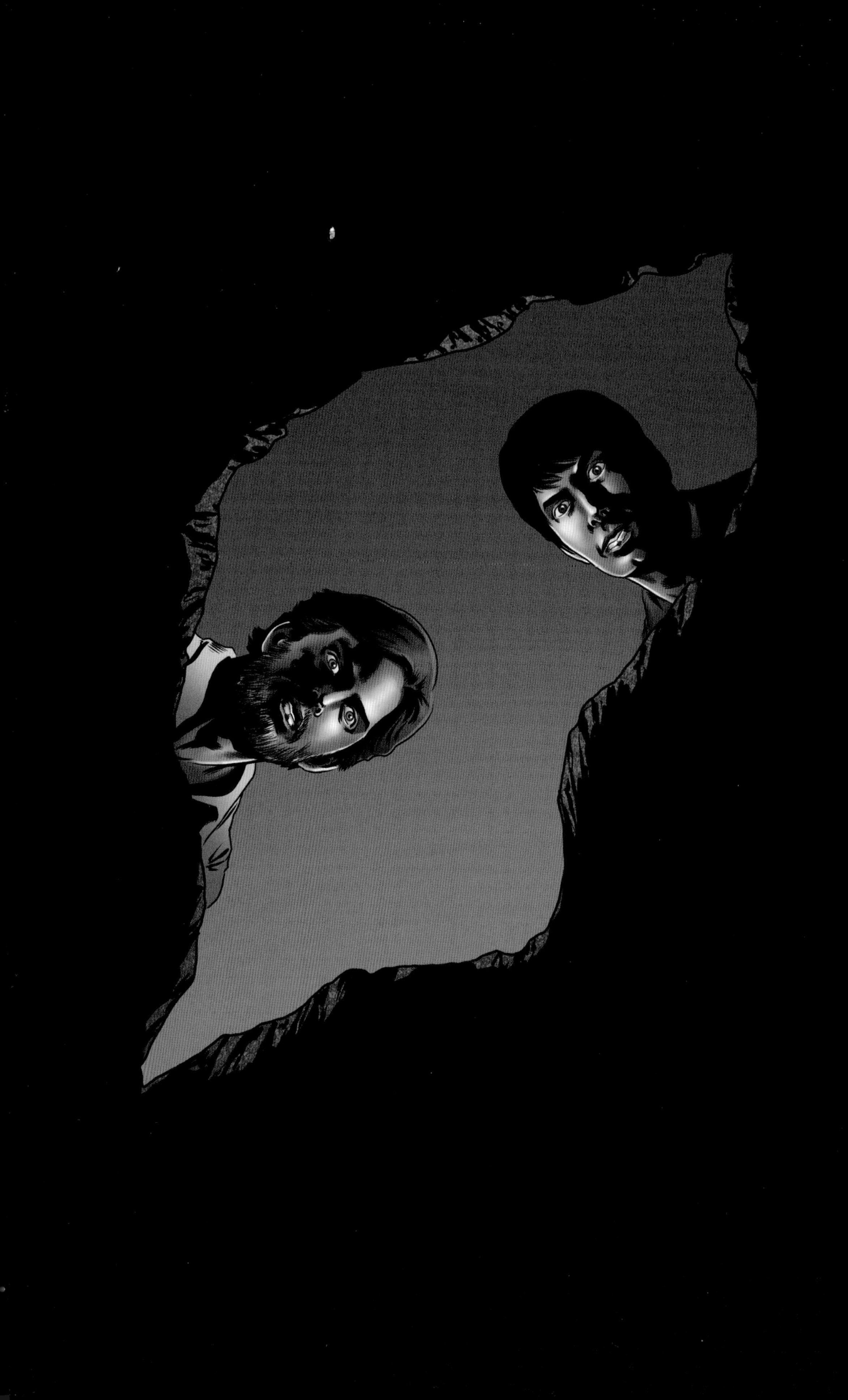

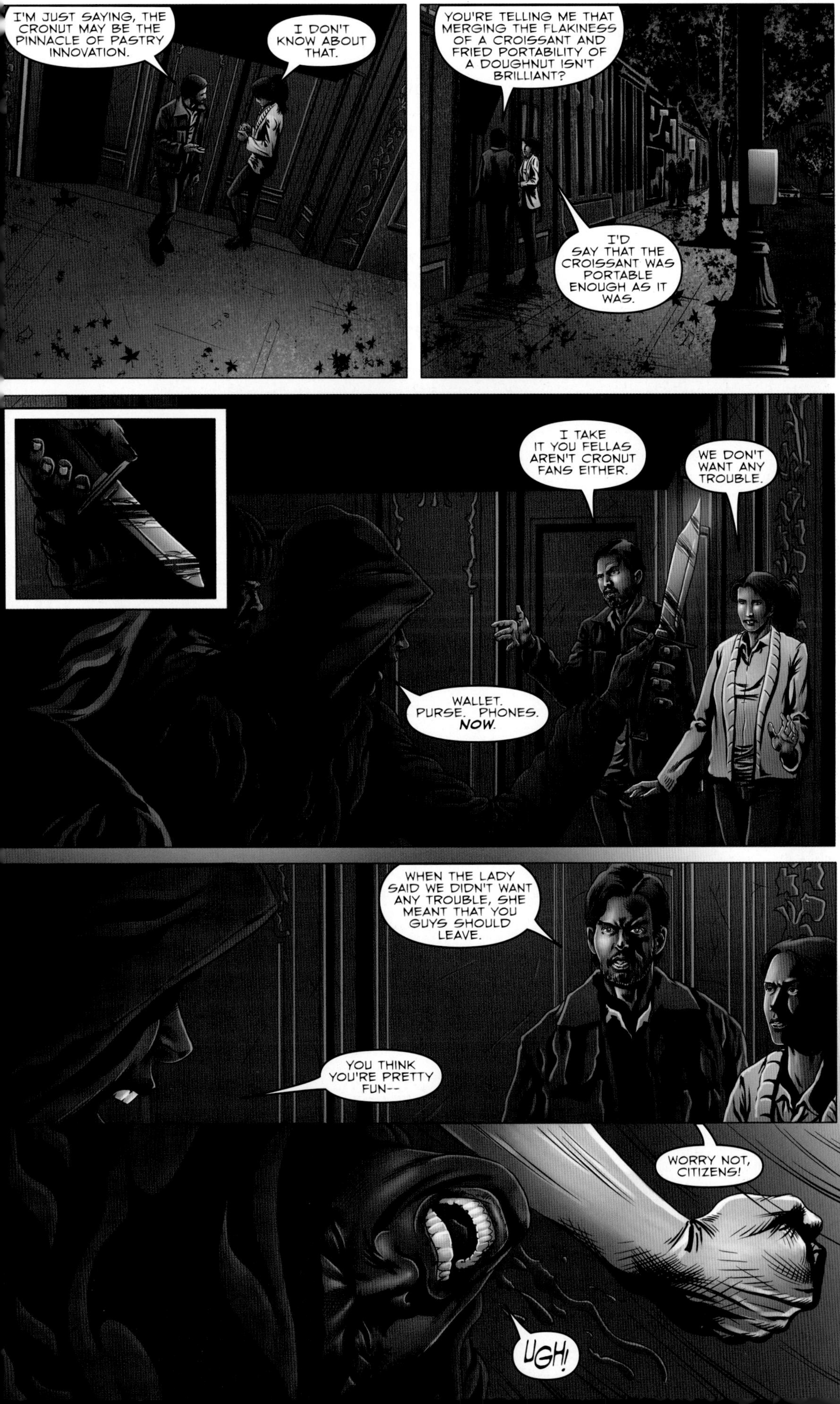

I'M JUST SAYING, THE CRONUT MAY BE THE PINNACLE OF PASTRY INNOVATION.
I DON'T KNOW ABOUT THAT.
YOU'RE TELLING ME THAT MERGING THE FLAKINESS OF A CROISSANT AND FRIED PORTABILITY OF A DOUGHNUT ISN'T BRILLIANT?
I'D SAY THAT THE CROISSANT WAS PORTABLE ENOUGH AS IT WAS.
I TAKE IT YOU FELLAS AREN'T CRONUT FANS EITHER.
WE DON'T WANT ANY TROUBLE.
WALLET. PURSE. PHONES. *NOW*.
WHEN THE LADY SAID WE DIDN'T WANT ANY TROUBLE, SHE MEANT THAT YOU GUYS SHOULD LEAVE.
YOU THINK YOU'RE PRETTY FUN--
WORRY NOT, CITIZENS!
UGH!

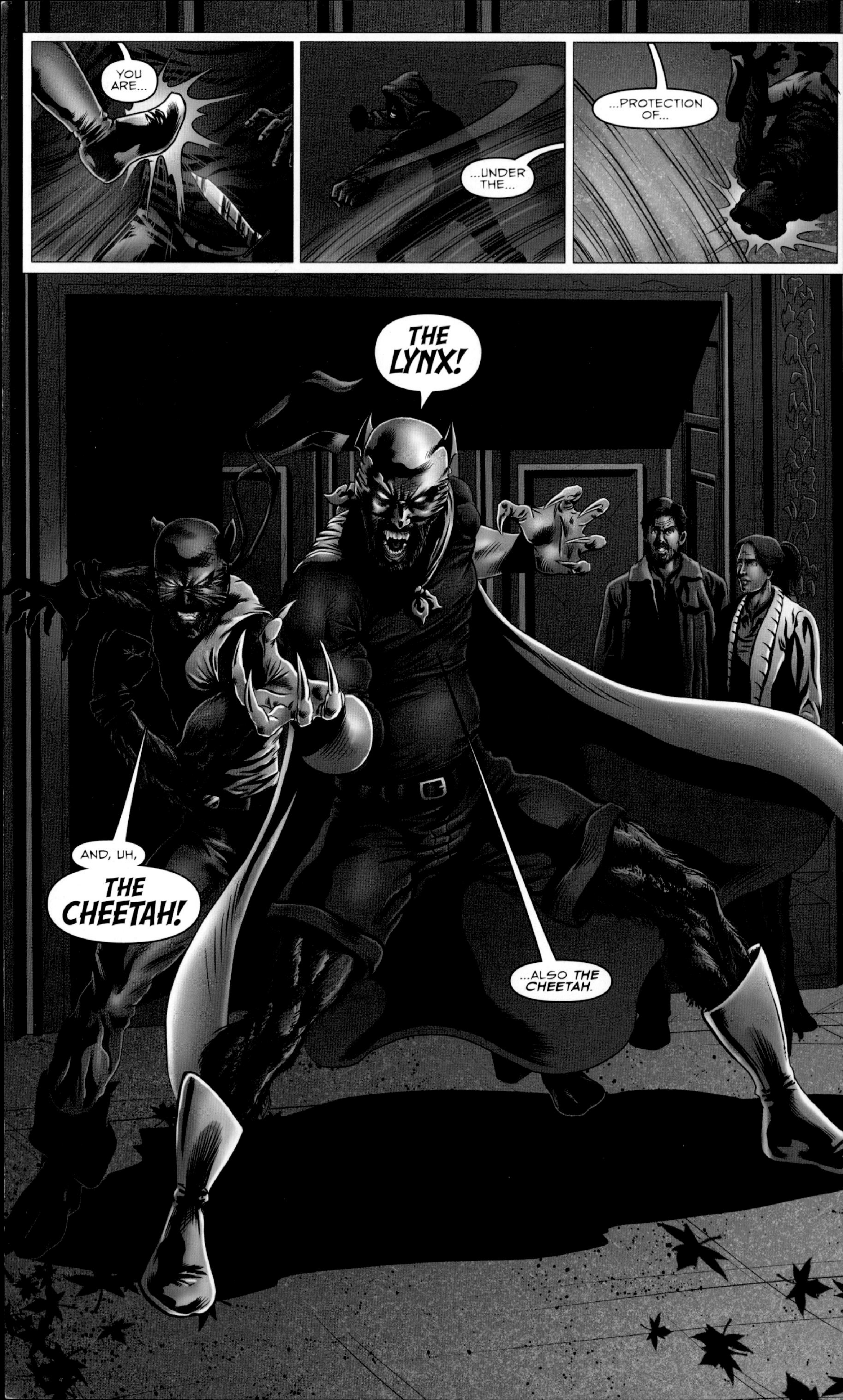
YOU ARE...
...UNDER THE...
...PROTECTION OF...
THE LYNX!
AND, UH,
THE CHEETAH!
...ALSO THE CHEETAH.

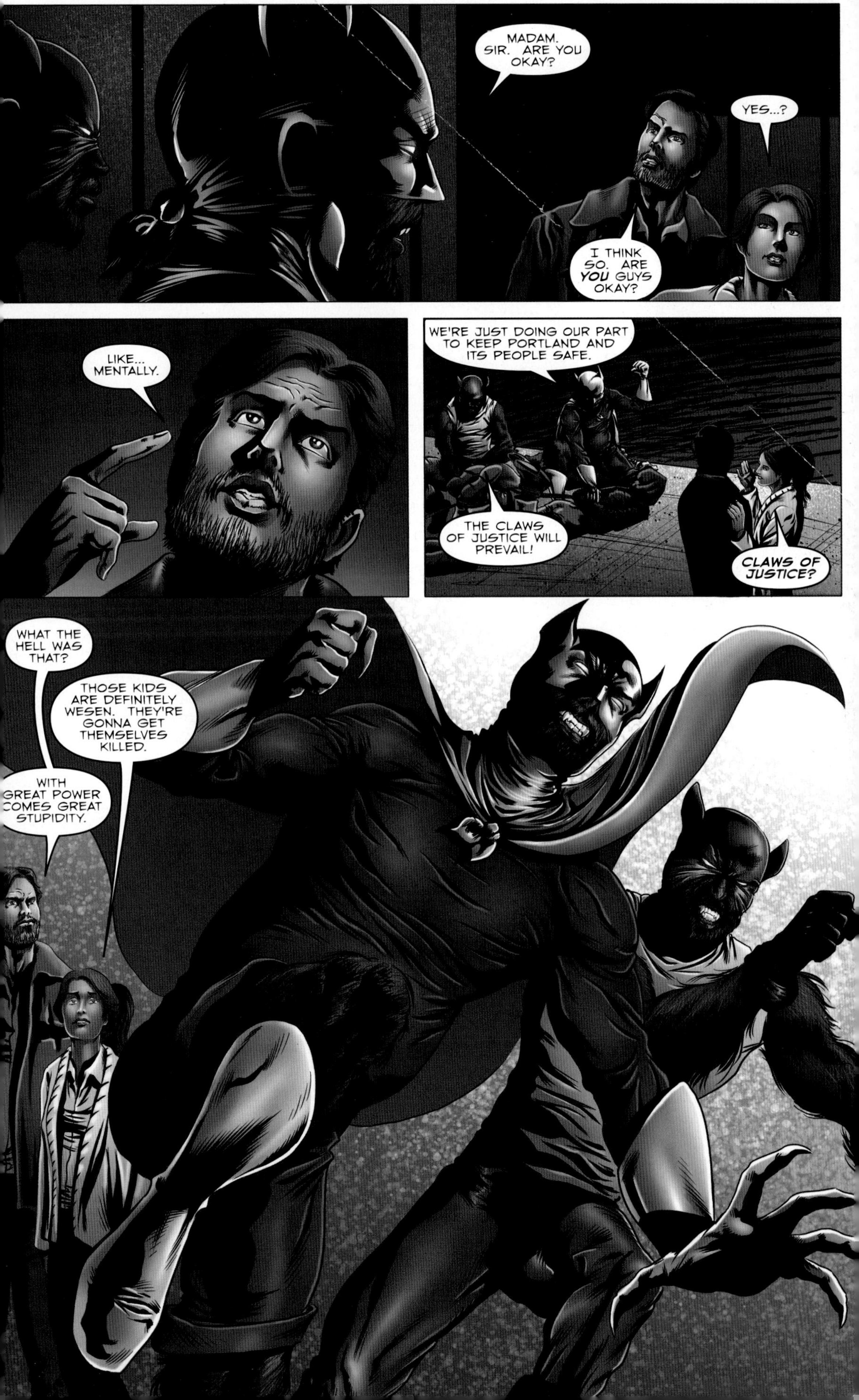
MADAM. SIR. ARE YOU OKAY?
YES...?
I THINK SO. ARE YOU GUYS OKAY?
LIKE... MENTALLY.
WE'RE JUST DOING OUR PART TO KEEP PORTLAND AND ITS PEOPLE SAFE.
THE CLAWS OF JUSTICE WILL PREVAIL!
CLAWS OF JUSTICE?
WHAT THE HELL WAS THAT?
THOSE KIDS ARE DEFINITELY WESEN. THEY'RE GONNA GET THEMSELVES KILLED.
WITH GREAT POWER COMES GREAT STUPIDITY.

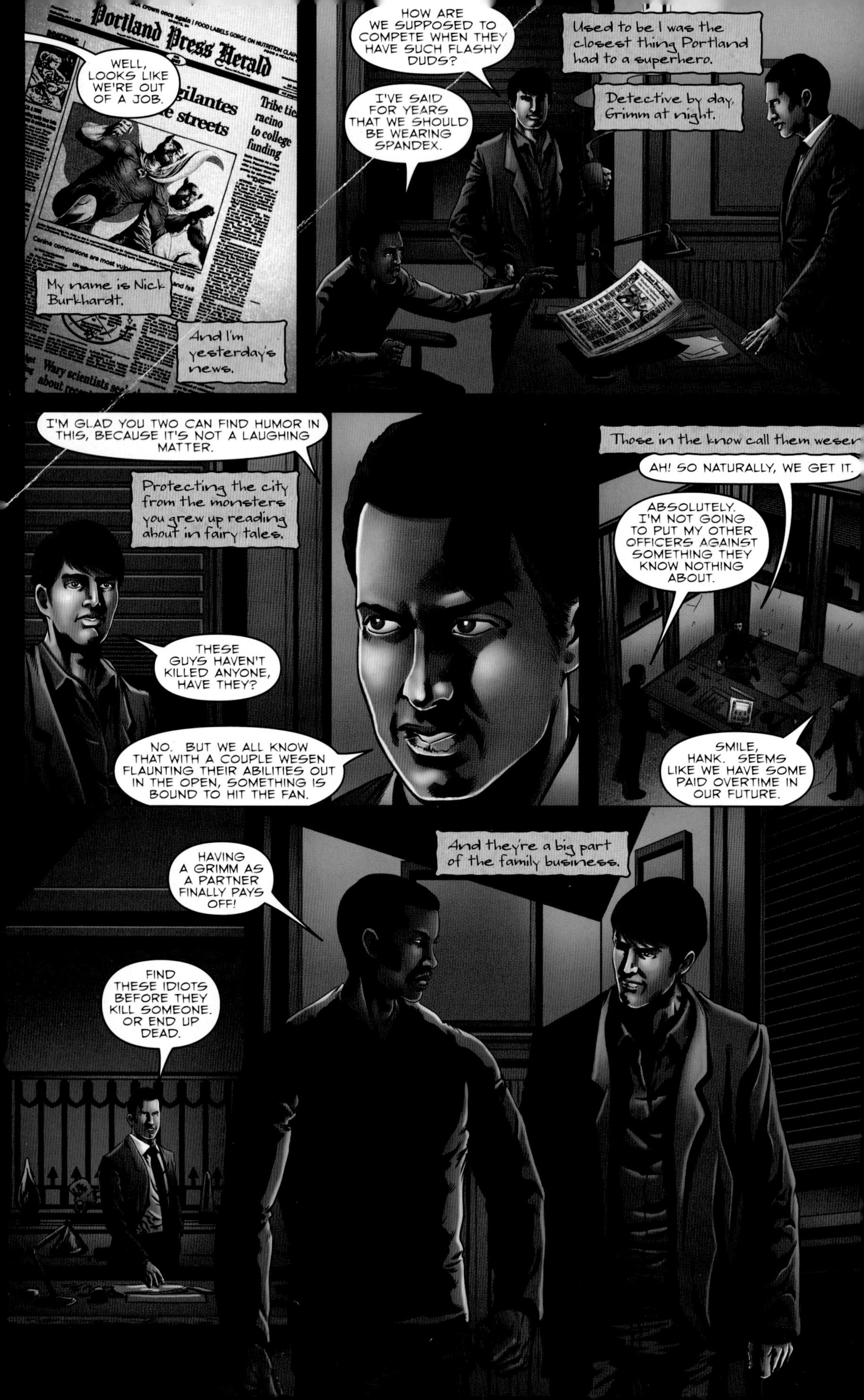

Portland Press Herald
WELL, LOOKS LIKE WE'RE OUT OF A JOB.
My name is Nick Burkhardt.
And I'm yesterday's news.
HOW ARE WE SUPPOSED TO COMPETE WHEN THEY HAVE SUCH FLASHY DUDS?
I'VE SAID FOR YEARS THAT WE SHOULD BE WEARING SPANDEX.
Used to be I was the closest thing Portland had to a superhero.
Detective by day, Grimm at night.
I'M GLAD YOU TWO CAN FIND HUMOR IN THIS, BECAUSE IT'S NOT A LAUGHING MATTER.
Protecting the city from the monsters you grew up reading about in fairy tales.
THESE GUYS HAVEN'T KILLED ANYONE, HAVE THEY?
NO. BUT WE ALL KNOW THAT WITH A COUPLE WESEN FLAUNTING THEIR ABILITIES OUT IN THE OPEN, SOMETHING IS BOUND TO HIT THE FAN.
Those in the know call them weser
AH! SO NATURALLY, WE GET IT.
ABSOLUTELY. I'M NOT GOING TO PUT MY OTHER OFFICERS AGAINST SOMETHING THEY KNOW NOTHING ABOUT.
SMILE, HANK. SEEMS LIKE WE HAVE SOME PAID OVERTIME IN OUR FUTURE.
HAVING A GRIMM AS A PARTNER FINALLY PAYS OFF!
And they're a big part of the family business.
FIND THESE IDIOTS BEFORE THEY KILL SOMEONE. OR END UP DEAD.

LOOK AT ALL THESE PEOPLE.

CLUELESS.

COMPLETELY UNAWARE THAT THEY'RE IN THE PRESENCE OF A GENUINE SUPERHERO...

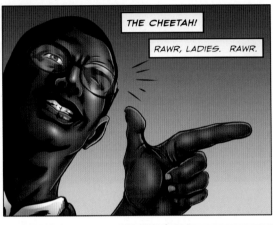

THE CHEETAH!

RAWR, LADIES. RAWR.

AAAHHH!

WHAM

REAL GRACEFUL THERE, SUPES.

THAT WAS A HELL OF A DIVE, BEN.

YEA WELL. I DON'T WANT PEOPLE TO THINK THAT I'M TOO COORDINATED.

PEOPLE FEAR PERFECTION, PENNY.

HAHAHA, SURE. THEN YOU'RE A HERO. LEADING THE CHARGE FOR DEFECTIVE PEOPLE EVERYWHERE.

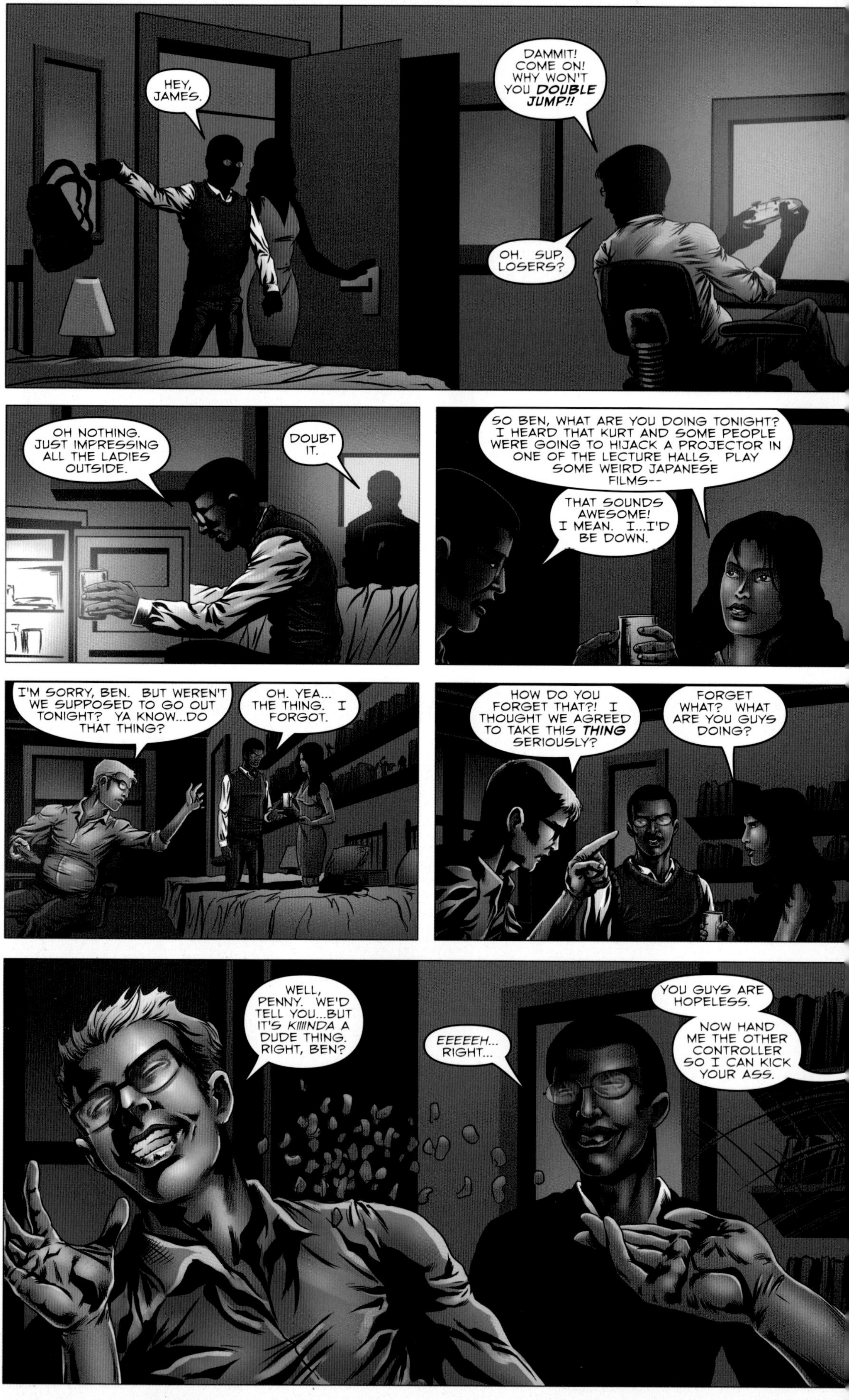
HEY, JAMES.
DAMMIT! COME ON! WHY WON'T YOU DOUBLE JUMP!!
OH. SUP, LOSERS?
OH NOTHING. JUST IMPRESSING ALL THE LADIES OUTSIDE.
DOUBT IT.
SO BEN, WHAT ARE YOU DOING TONIGHT? I HEARD THAT KURT AND SOME PEOPLE WERE GOING TO HIJACK A PROJECTOR IN ONE OF THE LECTURE HALLS. PLAY SOME WEIRD JAPANESE FILMS--
THAT SOUNDS AWESOME! I MEAN. I...I'D BE DOWN.
I'M SORRY, BEN. BUT WEREN'T WE SUPPOSED TO GO OUT TONIGHT? YA KNOW...DO THAT THING?
OH. YEA... THE THING. I FORGOT.
HOW DO YOU FORGET THAT?! I THOUGHT WE AGREED TO TAKE THIS THING SERIOUSLY?
FORGET WHAT? WHAT ARE YOU GUYS DOING?
WELL, PENNY. WE'D TELL YOU...BUT IT'S KIIIINDA A DUDE THING. RIGHT, BEN?
EEEEEH... RIGHT...
YOU GUYS ARE HOPELESS.
NOW HAND ME THE OTHER CONTROLLER SO I CAN KICK YOUR ASS.

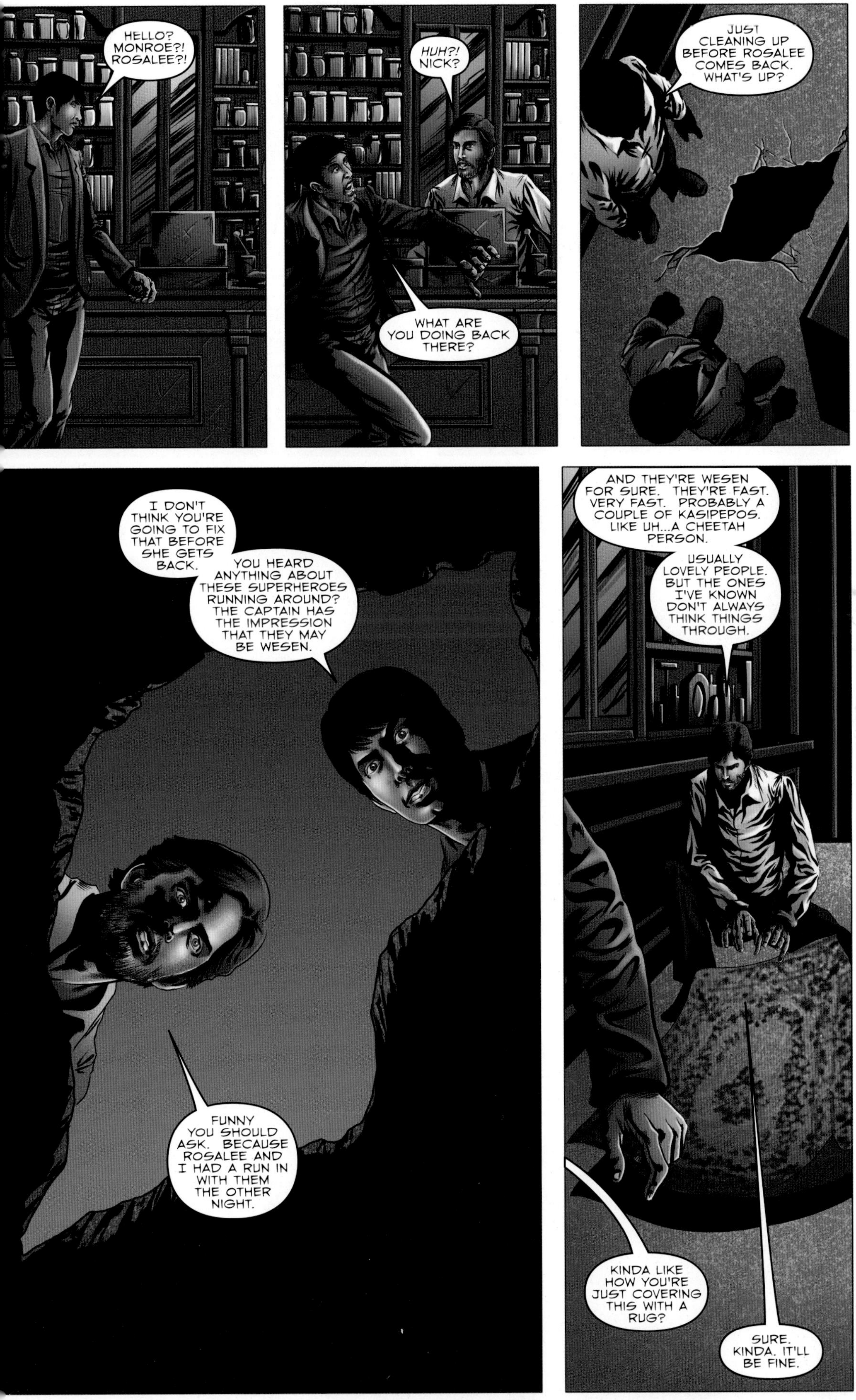
HELLO? MONROE?! ROSALEE?!
HUH?! NICK?
WHAT ARE YOU DOING BACK THERE?
JUST CLEANING UP BEFORE ROSALEE COMES BACK. WHAT'S UP?
I DON'T THINK YOU'RE GOING TO FIX THAT BEFORE SHE GETS BACK.
YOU HEARD ANYTHING ABOUT THESE SUPERHEROES RUNNING AROUND? THE CAPTAIN HAS THE IMPRESSION THAT THEY MAY BE WESEN.
FUNNY YOU SHOULD ASK. BECAUSE ROSALEE AND I HAD A RUN IN WITH THEM THE OTHER NIGHT.
AND THEY'RE WESEN FOR SURE. THEY'RE FAST. VERY FAST. PROBABLY A COUPLE OF KASIPEPOS. LIKE UH...A CHEETAH PERSON.
USUALLY LOVELY PEOPLE. BUT THE ONES I'VE KNOWN DON'T ALWAYS THINK THINGS THROUGH.
KINDA LIKE HOW YOU'RE JUST COVERING THIS WITH A RUG?
SURE. KINDA. IT'LL BE FINE.

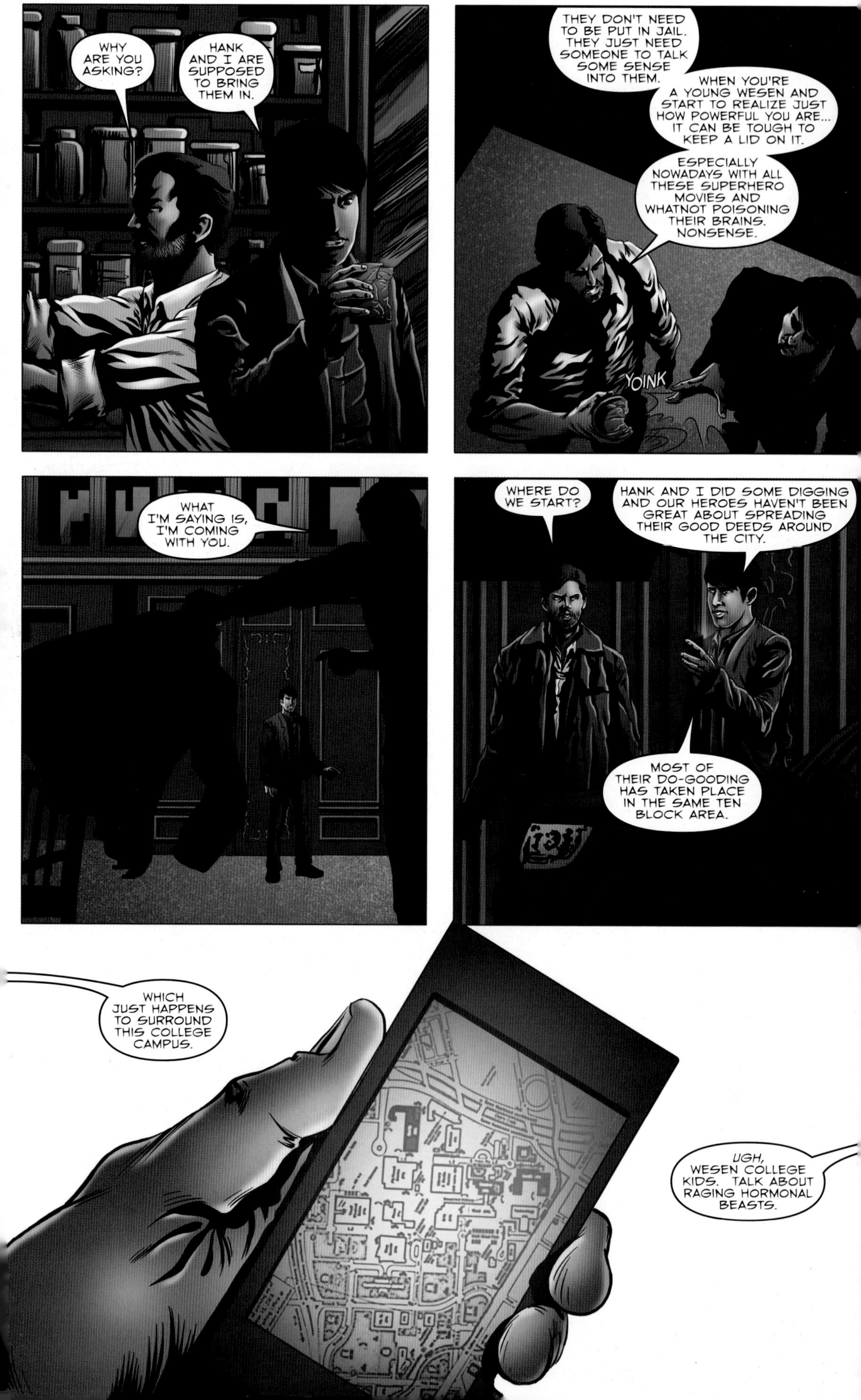
WHY ARE YOU ASKING?
HANK AND I ARE SUPPOSED TO BRING THEM IN.
THEY DON'T NEED TO BE PUT IN JAIL. THEY JUST NEED SOMEONE TO TALK SOME SENSE INTO THEM.
WHEN YOU'RE A YOUNG WESEN AND START TO REALIZE JUST HOW POWERFUL YOU ARE... IT CAN BE TOUGH TO KEEP A LID ON IT.
ESPECIALLY NOWADAYS WITH ALL THESE SUPERHERO MOVIES AND WHATNOT POISONING THEIR BRAINS. NONSENSE.
YOINK
WHAT I'M SAYING IS, I'M COMING WITH YOU.
WHERE DO WE START?
HANK AND I DID SOME DIGGING AND OUR HEROES HAVEN'T BEEN GREAT ABOUT SPREADING THEIR GOOD DEEDS AROUND THE CITY.
MOST OF THEIR DO-GOODING HAS TAKEN PLACE IN THE SAME TEN BLOCK AREA.
WHICH JUST HAPPENS TO SURROUND THIS COLLEGE CAMPUS.
UGH, WESEN COLLEGE KIDS. TALK ABOUT RAGING HORMONAL BEASTS.

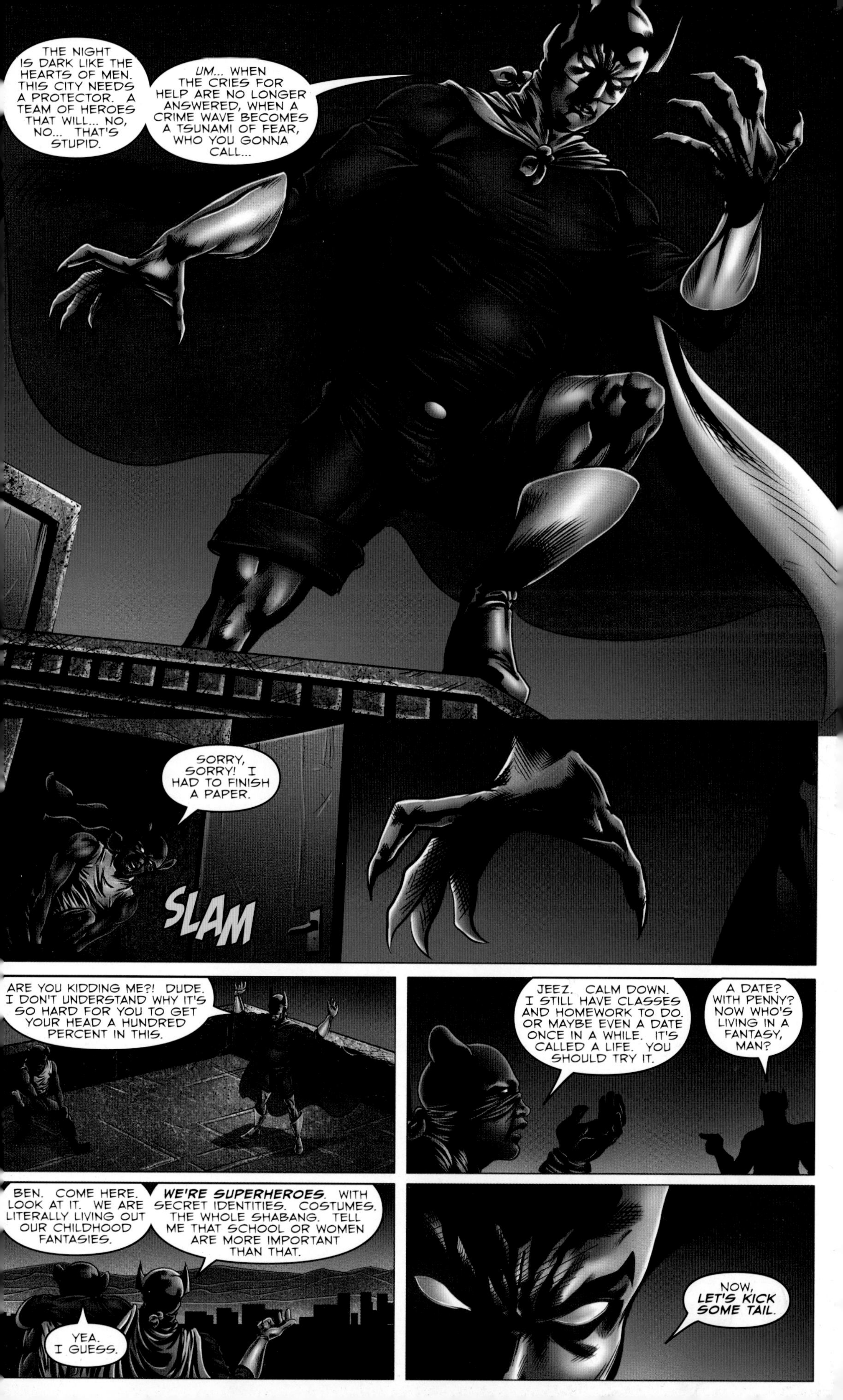
THE NIGHT IS DARK LIKE THE HEARTS OF MEN. THIS CITY NEEDS A PROTECTOR. A TEAM OF HEROES THAT WILL... NO, NO... THAT'S STUPID.
UM... WHEN THE CRIES FOR HELP ARE NO LONGER ANSWERED, WHEN A CRIME WAVE BECOMES A TSUNAMI OF FEAR, WHO YOU GONNA CALL...
SORRY, SORRY! I HAD TO FINISH A PAPER.
SLAM
ARE YOU KIDDING ME?! DUDE. I DON'T UNDERSTAND WHY IT'S SO HARD FOR YOU TO GET YOUR HEAD A HUNDRED PERCENT IN THIS.
JEEZ. CALM DOWN. I STILL HAVE CLASSES AND HOMEWORK TO DO. OR MAYBE EVEN A DATE ONCE IN A WHILE. IT'S CALLED A LIFE. YOU SHOULD TRY IT.
A DATE? WITH PENNY? NOW WHO'S LIVING IN A FANTASY, MAN?
BEN. COME HERE. LOOK AT IT. WE ARE LITERALLY LIVING OUT OUR CHILDHOOD FANTASIES.
WE'RE SUPERHEROES. WITH SECRET IDENTITIES. COSTUMES. THE WHOLE SHABANG. TELL ME THAT SCHOOL OR WOMEN ARE MORE IMPORTANT THAN THAT.
YEA. I GUESS.
NOW, LET'S KICK SOME TAIL.

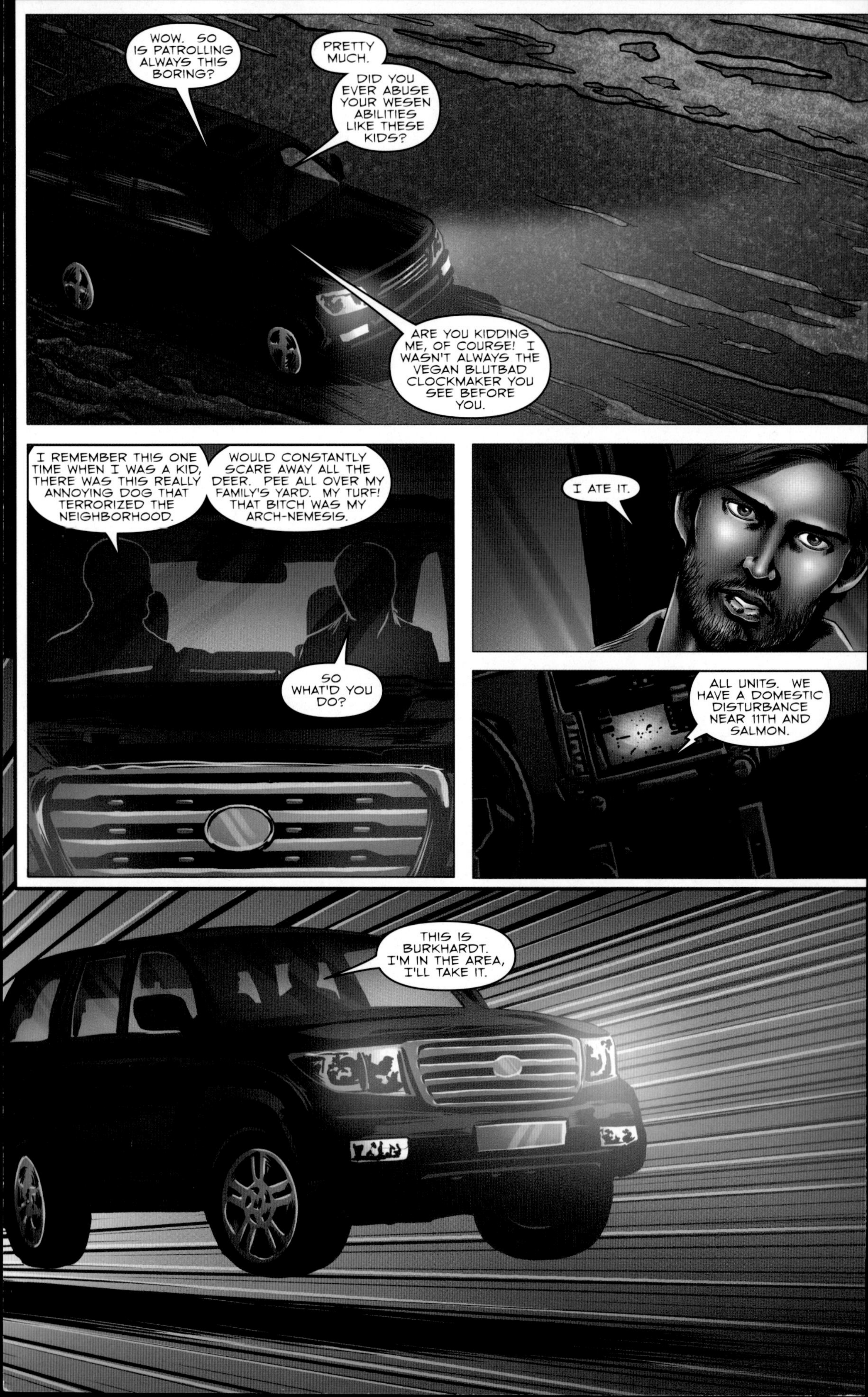
WOW. SO IS PATROLLING ALWAYS THIS BORING?
PRETTY MUCH.
DID YOU EVER ABUSE YOUR WESEN ABILITIES LIKE THESE KIDS?
ARE YOU KIDDING ME, OF COURSE! I WASN'T ALWAYS THE VEGAN BLUTBAD CLOCKMAKER YOU SEE BEFORE YOU.
I REMEMBER THIS ONE TIME WHEN I WAS A KID, THERE WAS THIS REALLY ANNOYING DOG THAT TERRORIZED THE NEIGHBORHOOD.
WOULD CONSTANTLY SCARE AWAY ALL THE DEER. PEE ALL OVER MY FAMILY'S YARD. MY TURF! THAT BITCH WAS MY ARCH-NEMESIS.
SO WHAT'D YOU DO?
I ATE IT.
ALL UNITS. WE HAVE A DOMESTIC DISTURBANCE NEAR 11TH AND SALMON.
THIS IS BURKHARDT. I'M IN THE AREA, I'LL TAKE IT.

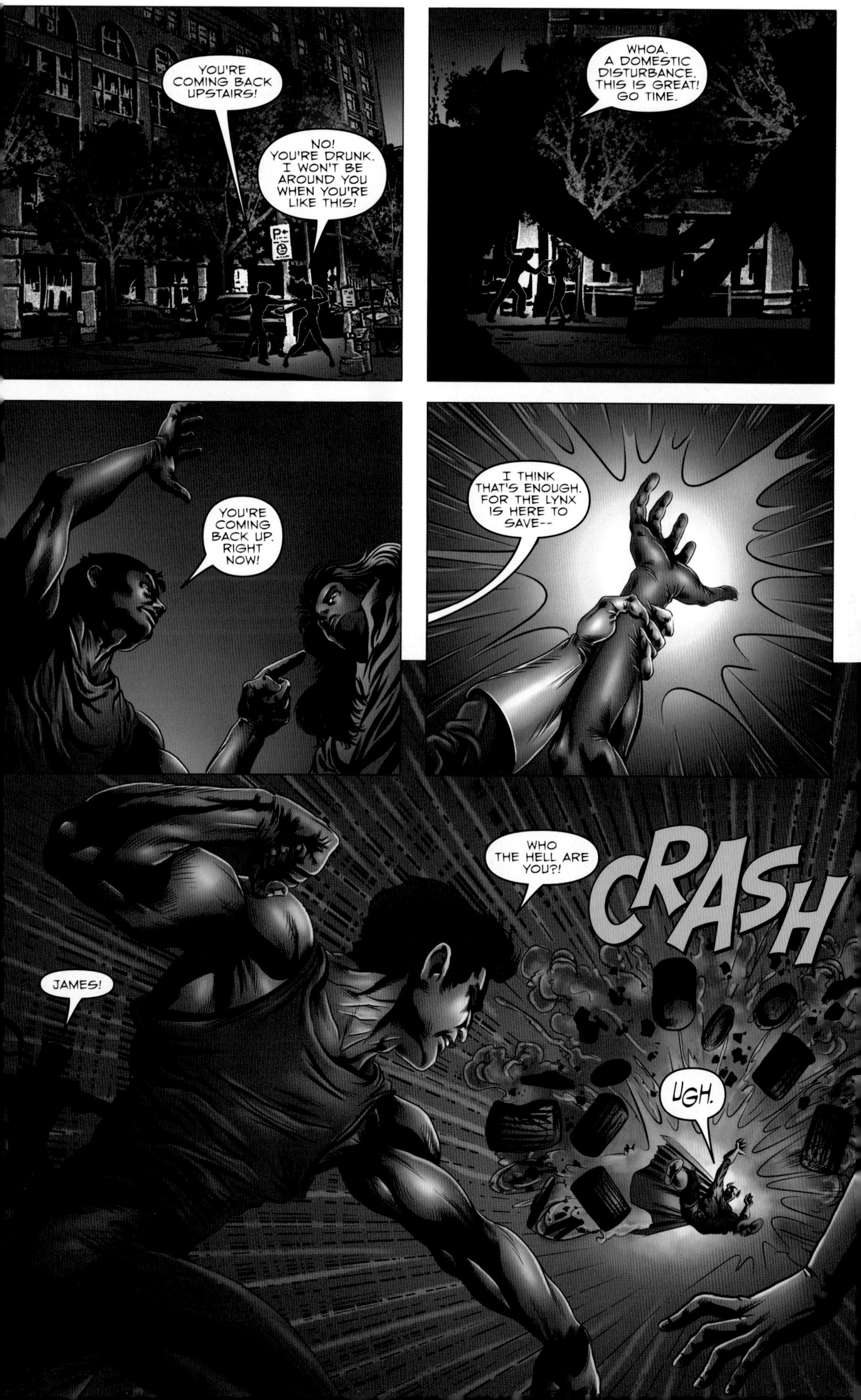
YOU'RE COMING BACK UPSTAIRS!
NO! YOU'RE DRUNK. I WON'T BE AROUND YOU WHEN YOU'RE LIKE THIS!
WHOA. A DOMESTIC DISTURBANCE. THIS IS GREAT! GO TIME.
YOU'RE COMING BACK UP. RIGHT NOW!
I THINK THAT'S ENOUGH. FOR THE LYNX IS HERE TO SAVE--
WHO THE HELL ARE YOU?!
CRASH
JAMES!
UGH.

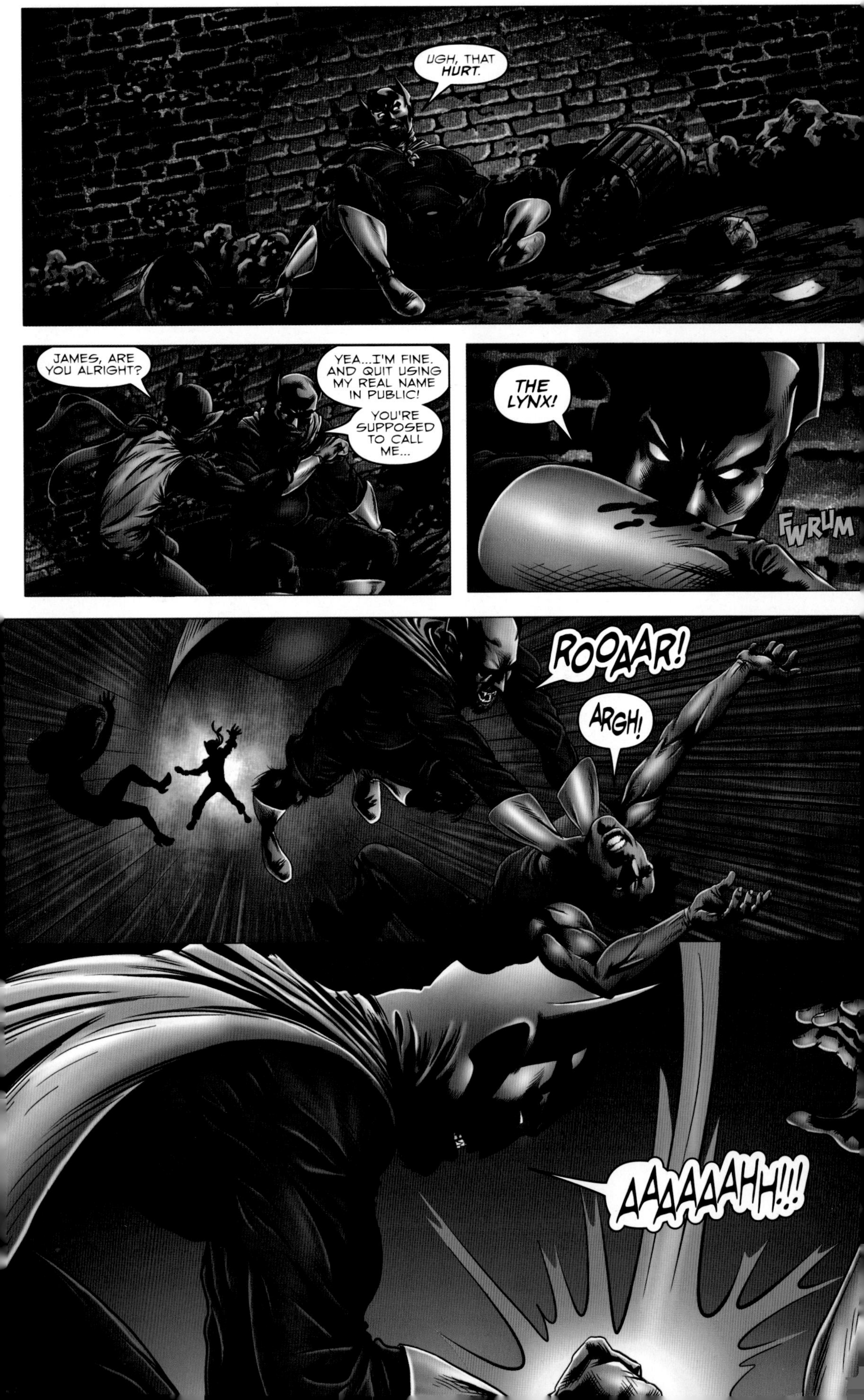
UGH, THAT HURT.
JAMES, ARE YOU ALRIGHT?
YEA...I'M FINE. AND QUIT USING MY REAL NAME IN PUBLIC!
YOU'RE SUPPOSED TO CALL ME...
THE LYNX!
FWRUM
ROOAAR!
ARGH!
AAAAAHH!!!

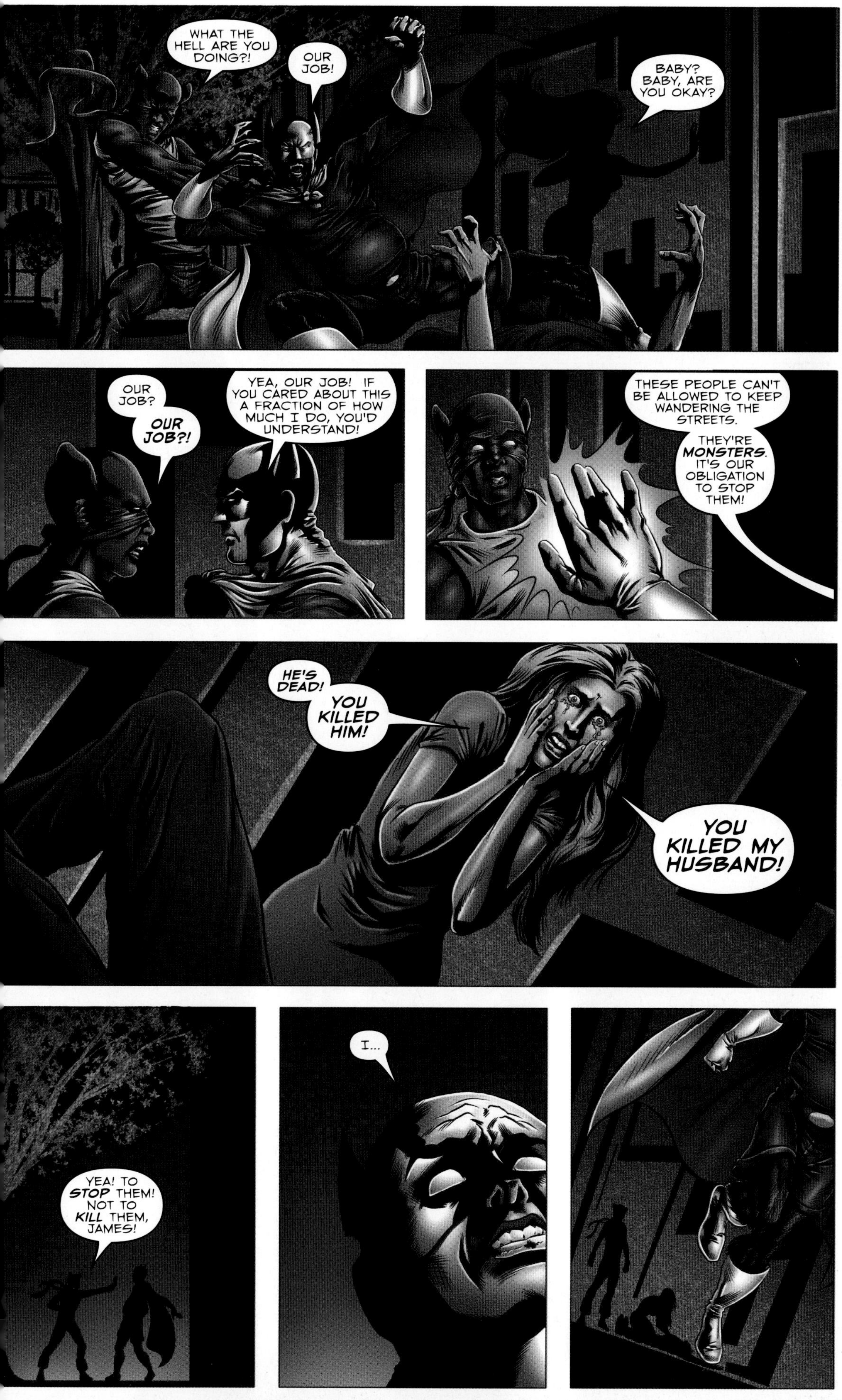

WHAT THE HELL ARE YOU DOING?!
OUR JOB!
BABY? BABY, ARE YOU OKAY?
OUR JOB? OUR JOB?!
YEA, OUR JOB! IF YOU CARED ABOUT THIS A FRACTION OF HOW MUCH I DO, YOU'D UNDERSTAND!
THESE PEOPLE CAN'T BE ALLOWED TO KEEP WANDERING THE STREETS.
THEY'RE MONSTERS. IT'S OUR OBLIGATION TO STOP THEM!
HE'S DEAD!
YOU KILLED HIM!
YOU KILLED MY HUSBAND!
YEA! TO STOP THEM! NOT TO KILL THEM, JAMES!
I...

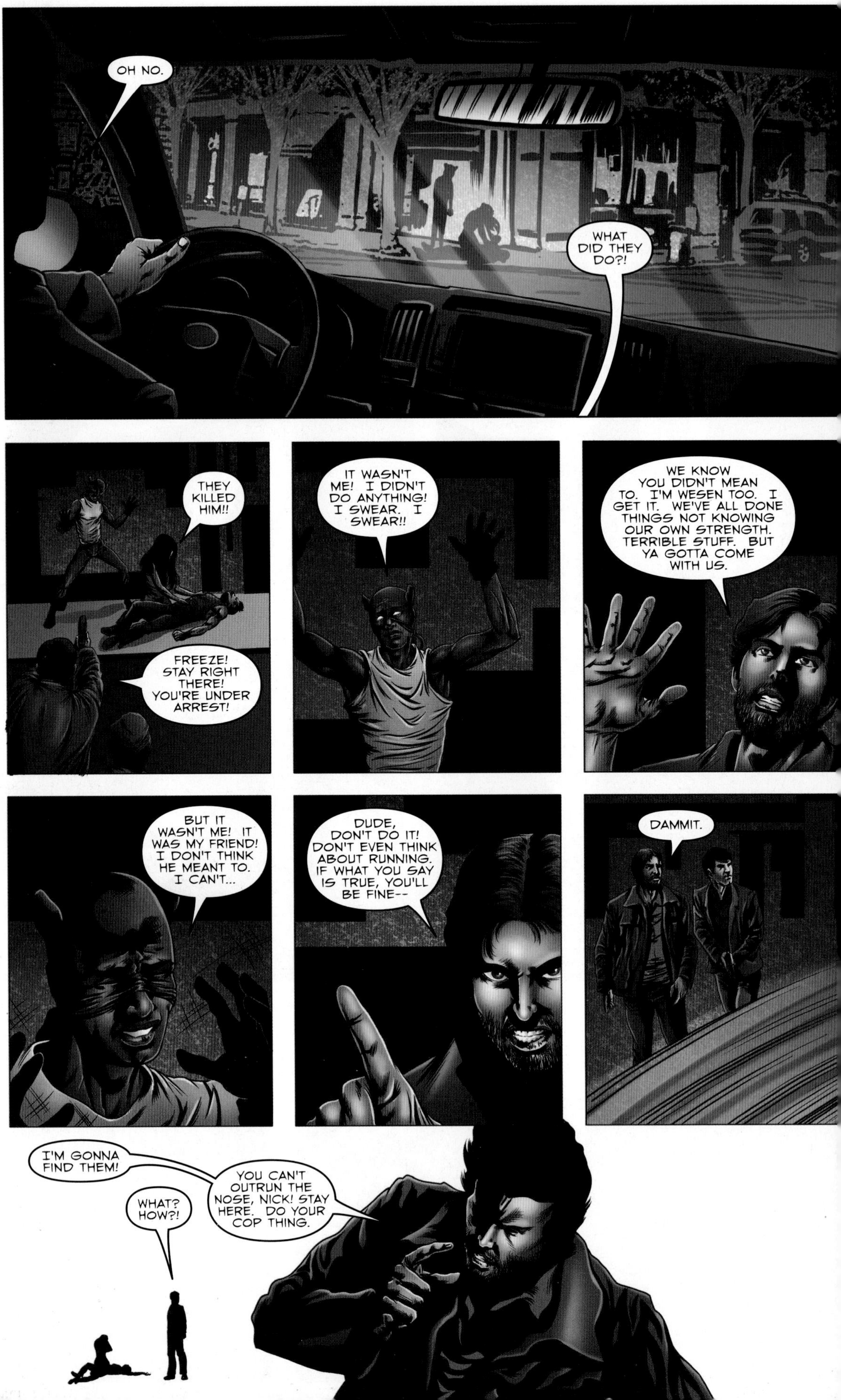
OH NO.
WHAT DID THEY DO?!
THEY KILLED HIM!!
FREEZE! STAY RIGHT THERE! YOU'RE UNDER ARREST!
IT WASN'T ME! I DIDN'T DO ANYTHING! I SWEAR. I SWEAR!!
WE KNOW YOU DIDN'T MEAN TO. I'M WESEN TOO. I GET IT. WE'VE ALL DONE THINGS NOT KNOWING OUR OWN STRENGTH. TERRIBLE STUFF. BUT YA GOTTA COME WITH US.
BUT IT WASN'T ME! IT WAS MY FRIEND! I DON'T THINK HE MEANT TO. I CAN'T...
DUDE, DON'T DO IT! DON'T EVEN THINK ABOUT RUNNING. IF WHAT YOU SAY IS TRUE, YOU'LL BE FINE--
DAMMIT.
I'M GONNA FIND THEM!
YOU CAN'T OUTRUN THE NOSE, NICK! STAY HERE. DO YOUR COP THING.
WHAT? HOW?!

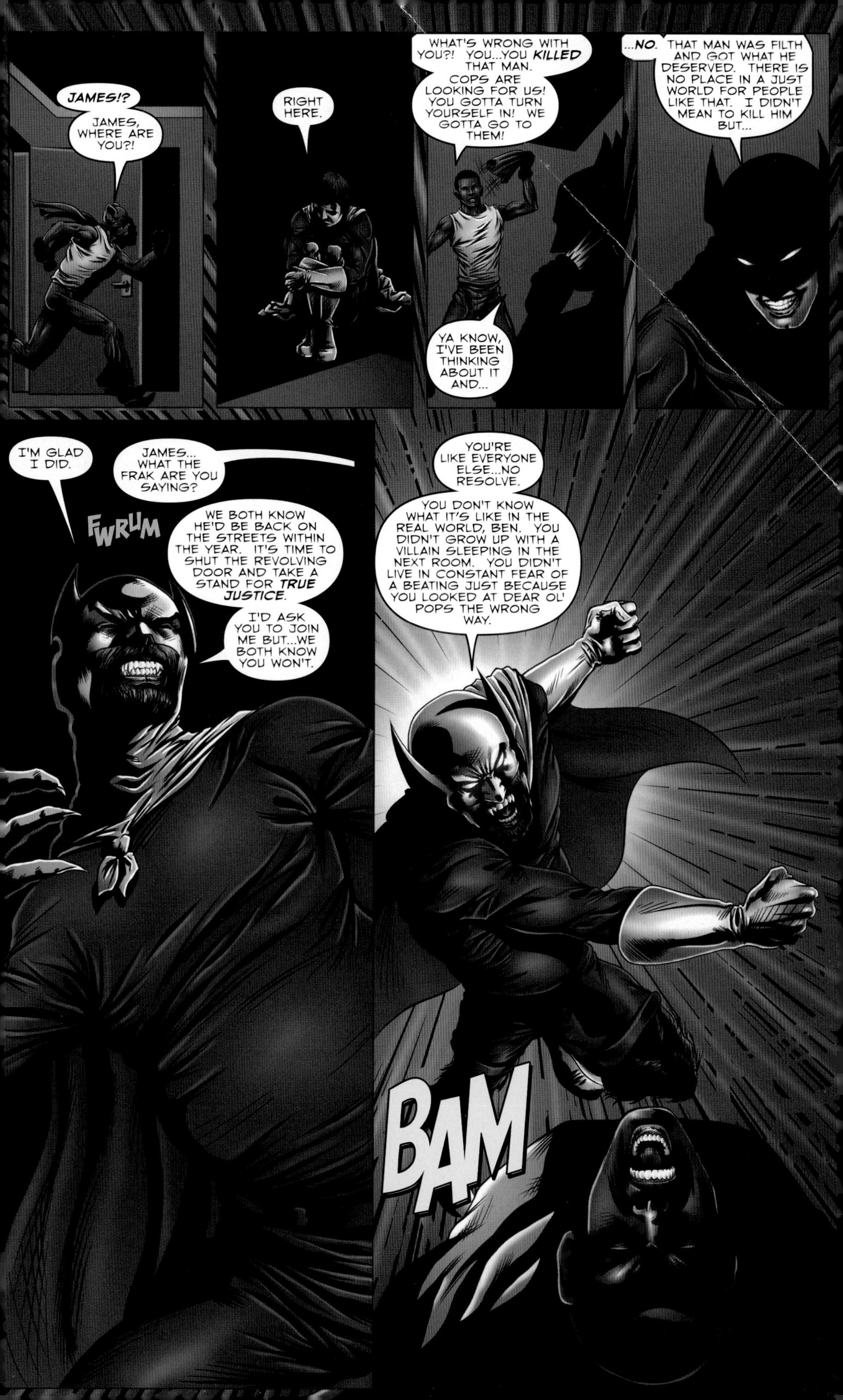
JAMES!?
JAMES, WHERE ARE YOU?!
RIGHT HERE.
WHAT'S WRONG WITH YOU?! YOU...YOU KILLED THAT MAN. COPS ARE LOOKING FOR US! YOU GOTTA TURN YOURSELF IN! WE GOTTA GO TO THEM!
YA KNOW, I'VE BEEN THINKING ABOUT IT AND...
...NO. THAT MAN WAS FILTH AND GOT WHAT HE DESERVED. THERE IS NO PLACE IN A JUST WORLD FOR PEOPLE LIKE THAT. I DIDN'T MEAN TO KILL HIM BUT...
I'M GLAD I DID.
JAMES... WHAT THE FRAK ARE YOU SAYING?
FWRUM
WE BOTH KNOW HE'D BE BACK ON THE STREETS WITHIN THE YEAR. IT'S TIME TO SHUT THE REVOLVING DOOR AND TAKE A STAND FOR TRUE JUSTICE.
I'D ASK YOU TO JOIN ME BUT...WE BOTH KNOW YOU WON'T.
YOU'RE LIKE EVERYONE ELSE...NO RESOLVE.
YOU DON'T KNOW WHAT IT'S LIKE IN THE REAL WORLD, BEN. YOU DIDN'T GROW UP WITH A VILLAIN SLEEPING IN THE NEXT ROOM. YOU DIDN'T LIVE IN CONSTANT FEAR OF A BEATING JUST BECAUSE YOU LOOKED AT DEAR OL' POPS THE WRONG WAY.
BAM

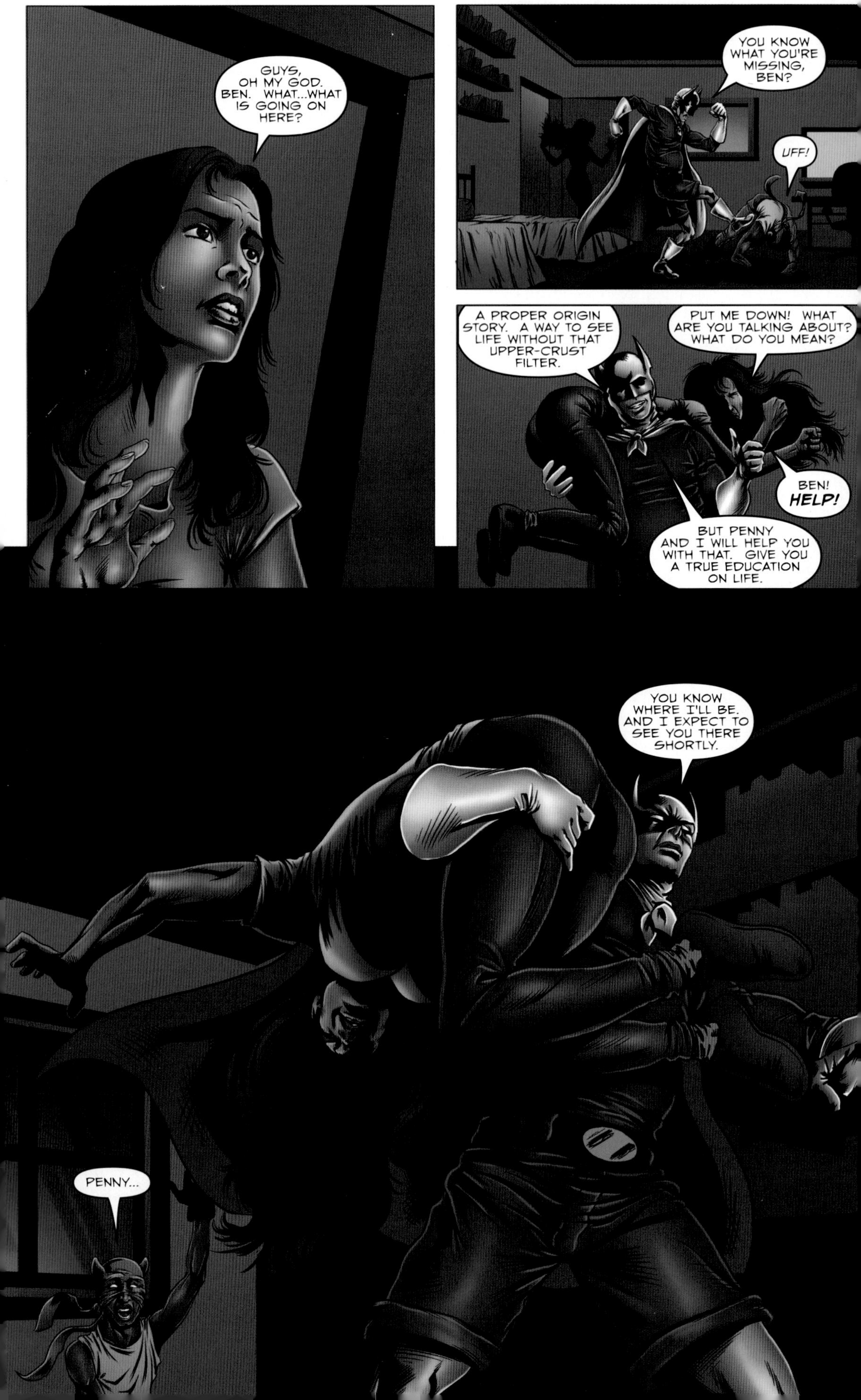

GUYS, OH MY GOD. BEN. WHAT...WHAT IS GOING ON HERE?
YOU KNOW WHAT YOU'RE MISSING, BEN?
UFF!
A PROPER ORIGIN STORY. A WAY TO SEE LIFE WITHOUT THAT UPPER-CRUST FILTER.
PUT ME DOWN! WHAT ARE YOU TALKING ABOUT? WHAT DO YOU MEAN?
BEN! HELP!
BUT PENNY AND I WILL HELP YOU WITH THAT. GIVE YOU A TRUE EDUCATION ON LIFE.
YOU KNOW WHERE I'LL BE. AND I EXPECT TO SEE YOU THERE SHORTLY.
PENNY...

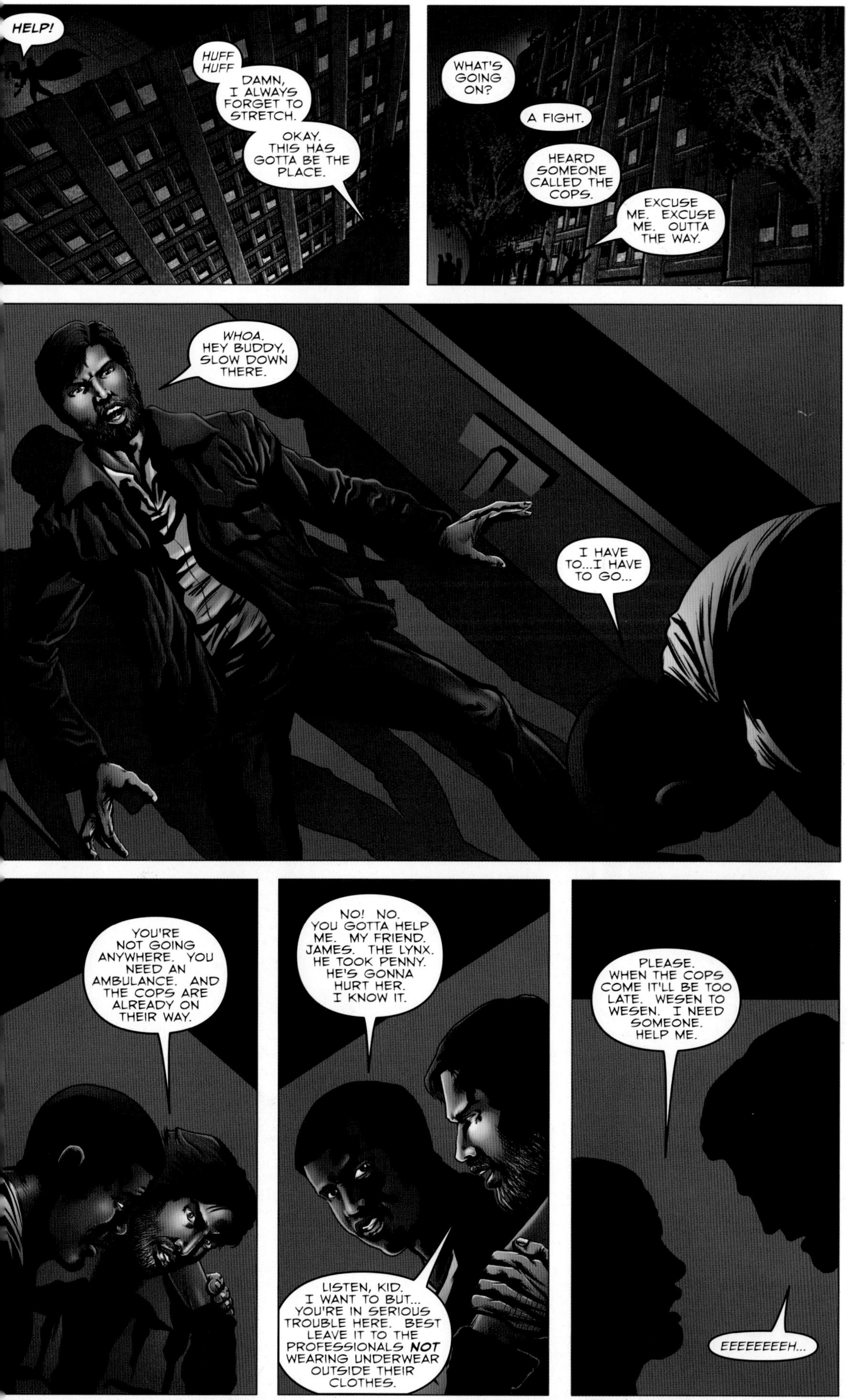
HELP!
HUFF HUFF
DAMN, I ALWAYS FORGET TO STRETCH.
OKAY. THIS HAS GOTTA BE THE PLACE.
WHAT'S GOING ON?
A FIGHT.
HEARD SOMEONE CALLED THE COPS.
EXCUSE ME. EXCUSE ME. OUTTA THE WAY.
WHOA. HEY BUDDY, SLOW DOWN THERE.
I HAVE TO...I HAVE TO GO...
YOU'RE NOT GOING ANYWHERE. YOU NEED AN AMBULANCE. AND THE COPS ARE ALREADY ON THEIR WAY.
NO! NO. YOU GOTTA HELP ME. MY FRIEND. JAMES. THE LYNX. HE TOOK PENNY. HE'S GONNA HURT HER. I KNOW IT.
LISTEN, KID. I WANT TO BUT... YOU'RE IN SERIOUS TROUBLE HERE. BEST LEAVE IT TO THE PROFESSIONALS NOT WEARING UNDERWEAR OUTSIDE THEIR CLOTHES.
PLEASE. WHEN THE COPS COME IT'LL BE TOO LATE. WESEN TO WESEN. I NEED SOMEONE. HELP ME.
EEEEEEEEH...

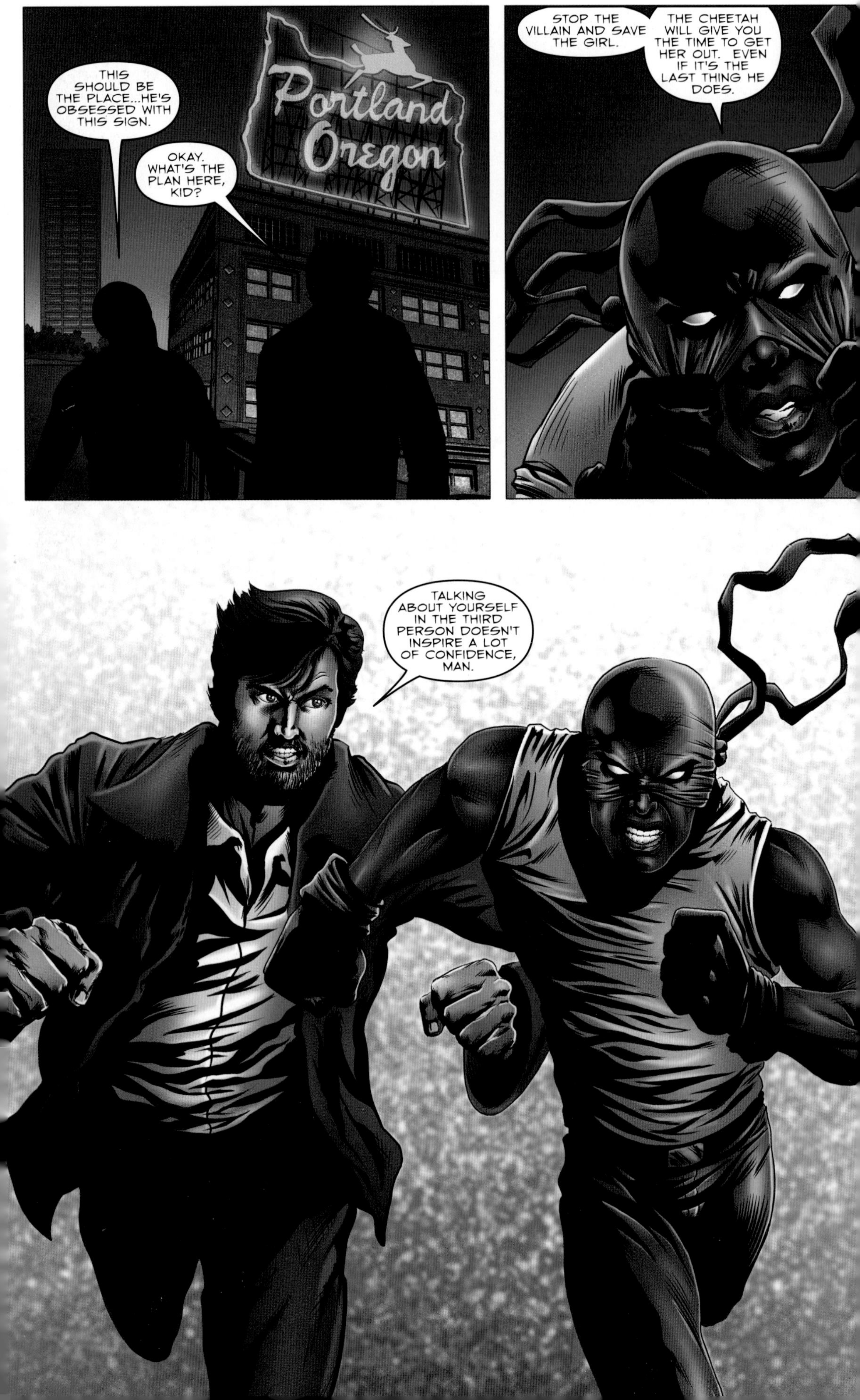
Portland Oregon
THIS SHOULD BE THE PLACE...HE'S OBSESSED WITH THIS SIGN.
OKAY. WHAT'S THE PLAN HERE, KID?
STOP THE VILLAIN AND SAVE THE GIRL.
THE CHEETAH WILL GIVE YOU THE TIME TO GET HER OUT. EVEN IF IT'S THE LAST THING HE DOES.
TALKING ABOUT YOURSELF IN THE THIRD PERSON DOESN'T INSPIRE A LOT OF CONFIDENCE, MAN.

PHEW. THAT IS QUITE A DROP. IF I DO SAY SO MYSELF.

JAMES HAVE YOU GONE *INSANE!?* WHY ARE DOING THIS?

TO HELP MY BEST FRIEND! HE NEEDS TO SEE THAT ALL WE'VE BEEN DOING IS FOR THE GREATER GOOD. ALL HE NEEDS IS A NUDGE.

EVERY SUPERHERO NEEDS THEIR ORIGIN STORY, PENNY. A TRAGEDY THAT WILL PROPEL THEM TO GREATNESS. YOU'RE GOING TO BE BEN'S.

IT ACTUALLY SOUNDS EVEN COOLER WHEN I SAY IT OUT LOUD.

JAMES!!

STEP AWAY FROM HER! THIS IS BETWEEN YOU AND ME!

AND YOUR FRIEND THERE?

HI, I'M MONROE. A BLUTBAD. IT'S NICE TO MEET YOU.

WHATEVER. BEN. IN THE END, YOU'LL THANK ME FOR DOING THIS. I PROMISE.

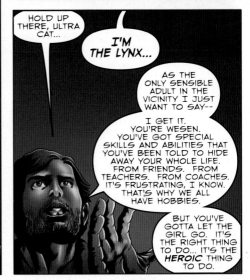

HOLD UP THERE, ULTRA CAT...

I'M THE LYNX...

AS THE ONLY SENSIBLE ADULT IN THE VICINITY I JUST WANT TO SAY--

I GET IT. YOU'RE WESEN. YOU'VE GOT SPECIAL SKILLS AND ABILITIES THAT YOU'VE BEEN TOLD TO HIDE AWAY YOUR WHOLE LIFE. FROM FRIENDS. FROM TEACHERS. FROM COACHES. IT'S FRUSTRATING, I KNOW. THAT'S WHY WE ALL HAVE HOBBIES.

BUT YOU'VE GOTTA LET THE GIRL GO. IT'S THE RIGHT THING TO DO... IT'S THE *HEROIC* THING TO DO.

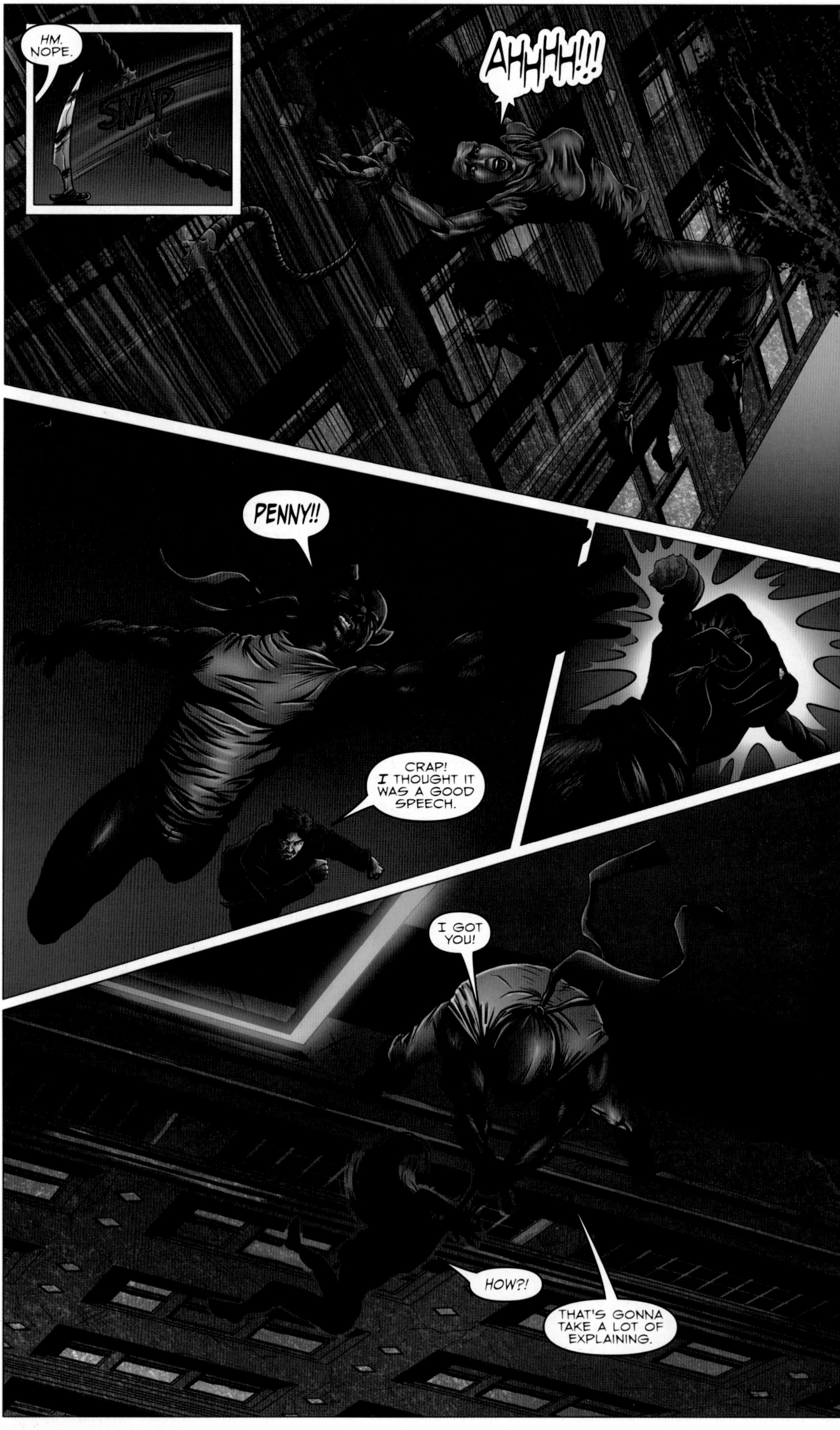
HM. NOPE.
SNAP
AHHHH!!!
PENNY!!
CRAP! I THOUGHT IT WAS A GOOD SPEECH.
I GOT YOU!
HOW?!
THAT'S GONNA TAKE A LOT OF EXPLAINING.

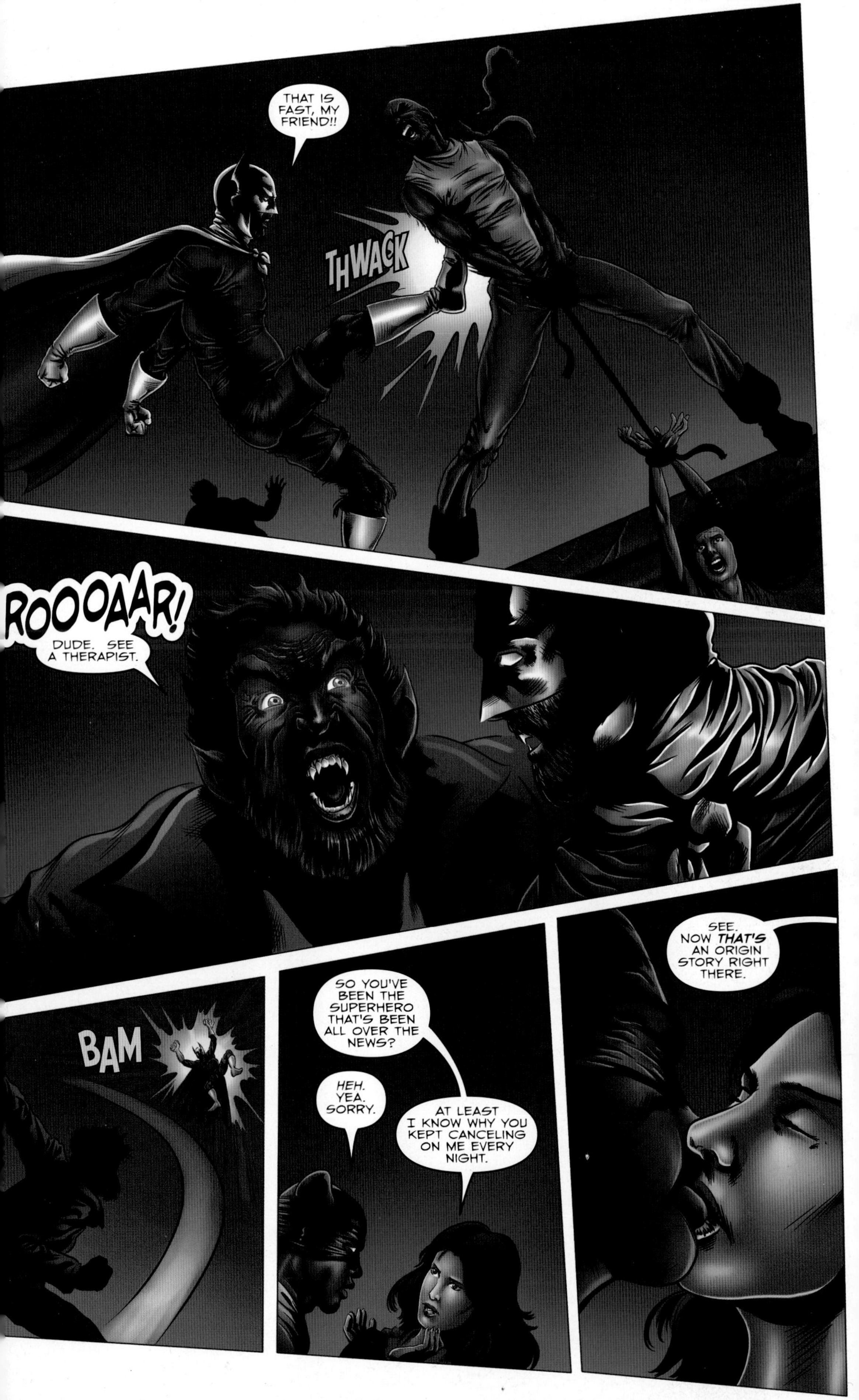

THAT IS FAST, MY FRIEND!!
THWACK
ROOOAAR!
DUDE. SEE A THERAPIST.
BAM
SO YOU'VE BEEN THE SUPERHERO THAT'S BEEN ALL OVER THE NEWS?
HEH. YEA. SORRY.
AT LEAST I KNOW WHY YOU KEPT CANCELING ON ME EVERY NIGHT.
SEE. NOW *THAT'S* AN ORIGIN STORY RIGHT THERE.

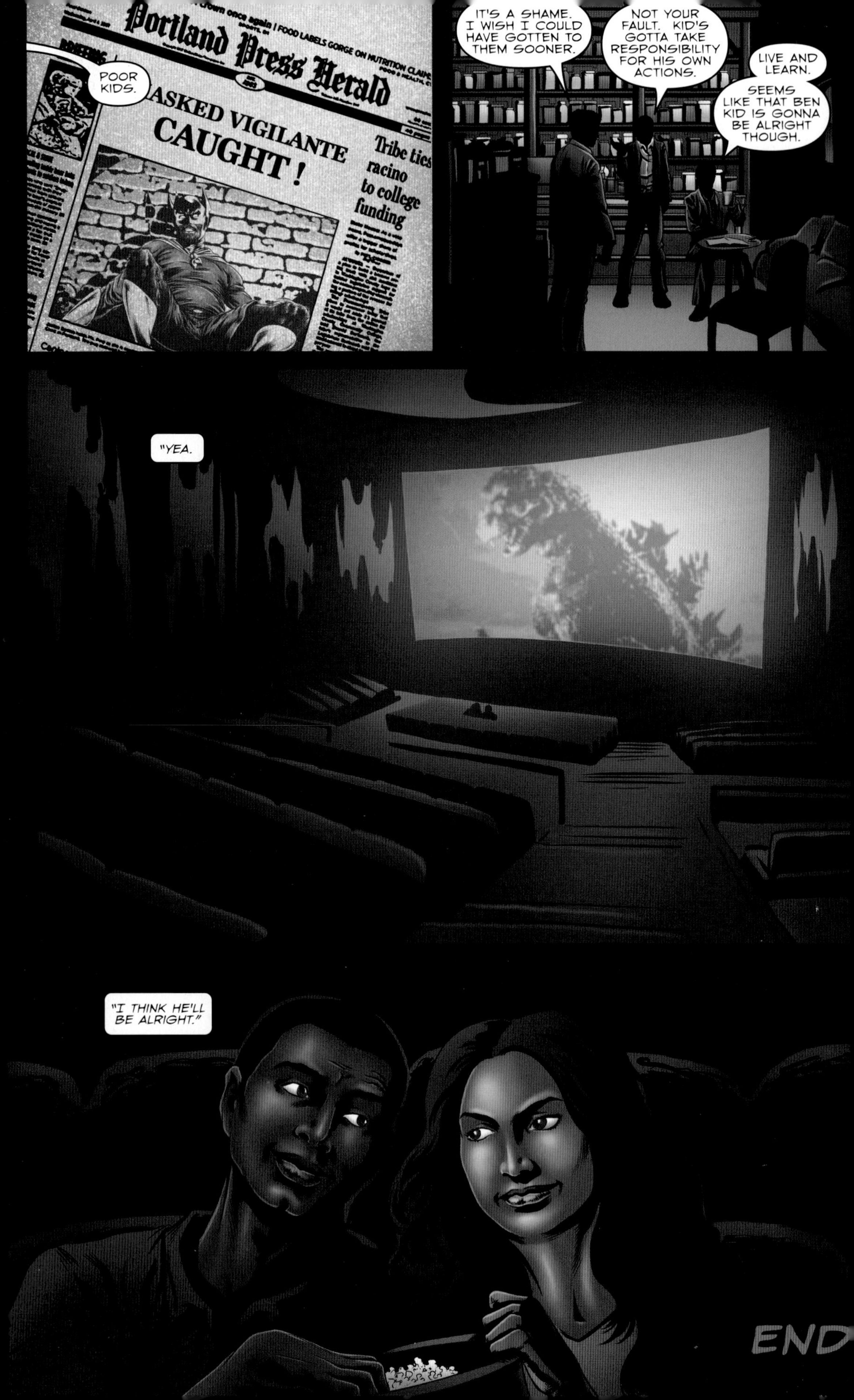
Portland Press Herald
ASKED VIGILANTE CAUGHT!
Tribe ties racino to college funding
POOR KIDS.
IT'S A SHAME. I WISH I COULD HAVE GOTTEN TO THEM SOONER.
NOT YOUR FAULT. KID'S GOTTA TAKE RESPONSIBILITY FOR HIS OWN ACTIONS.
LIVE AND LEARN.
SEEMS LIKE THAT BEN KID IS GONNA BE ALRIGHT THOUGH.
"YEA.
"I THINK HE'LL BE ALRIGHT."
END

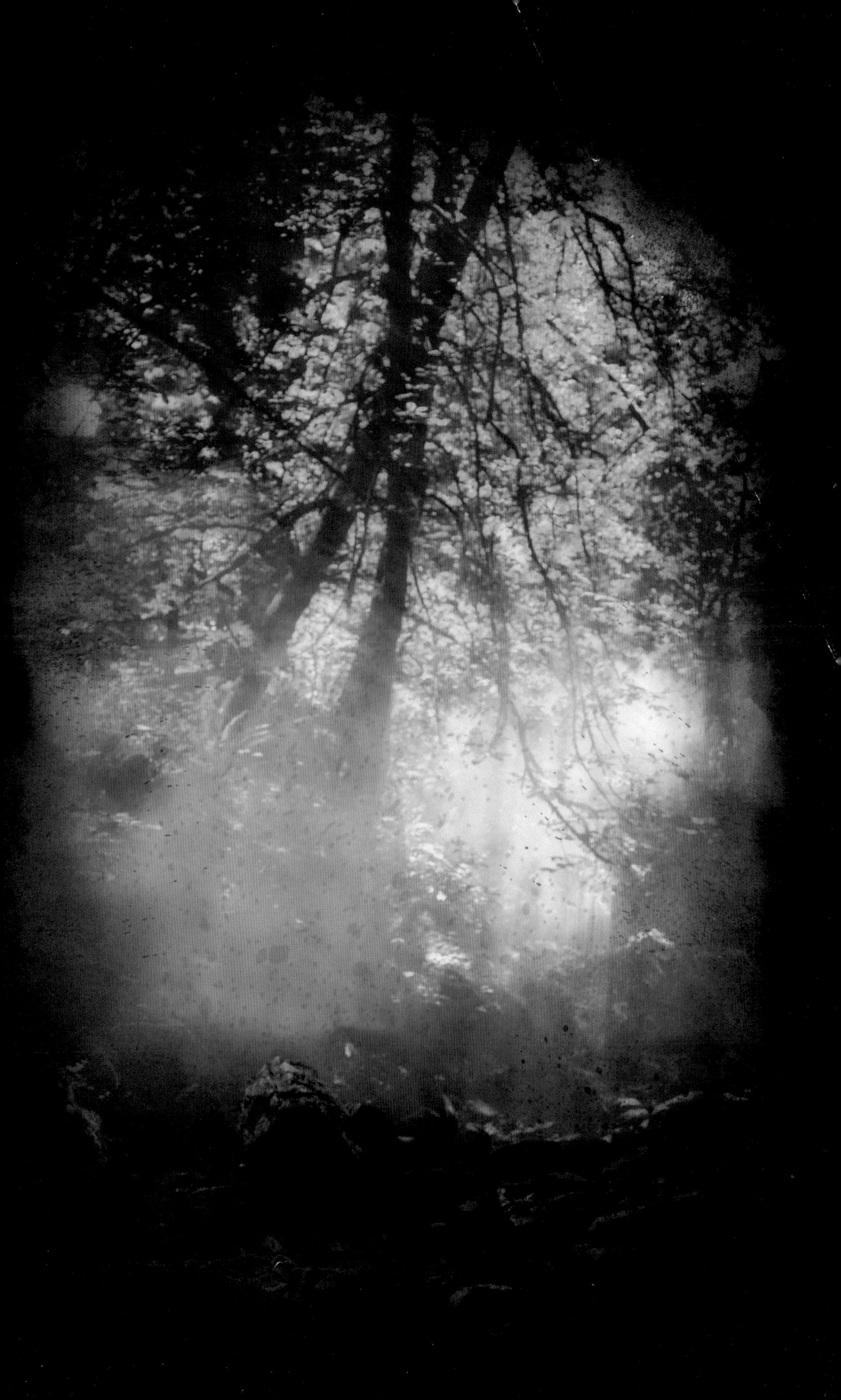

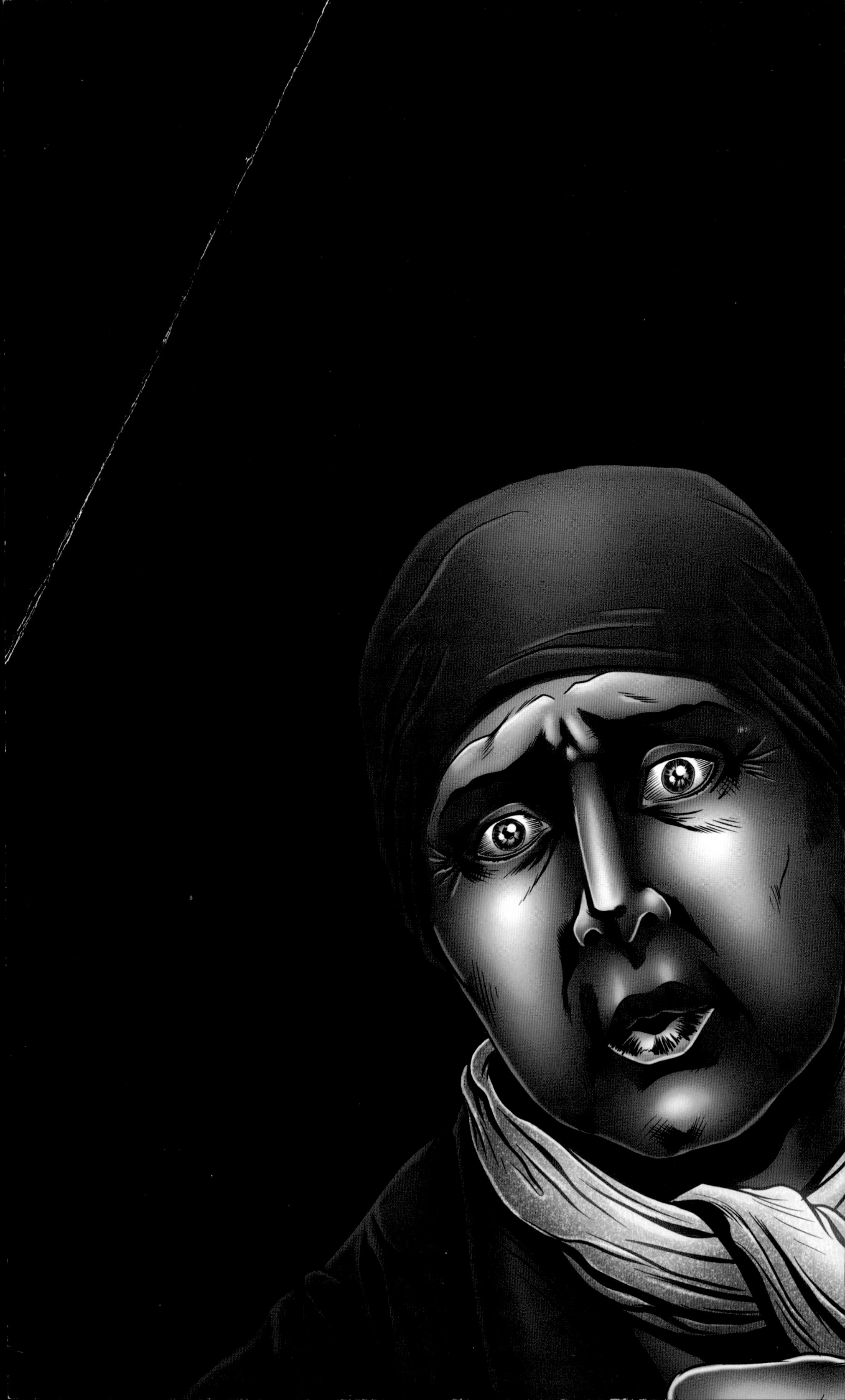

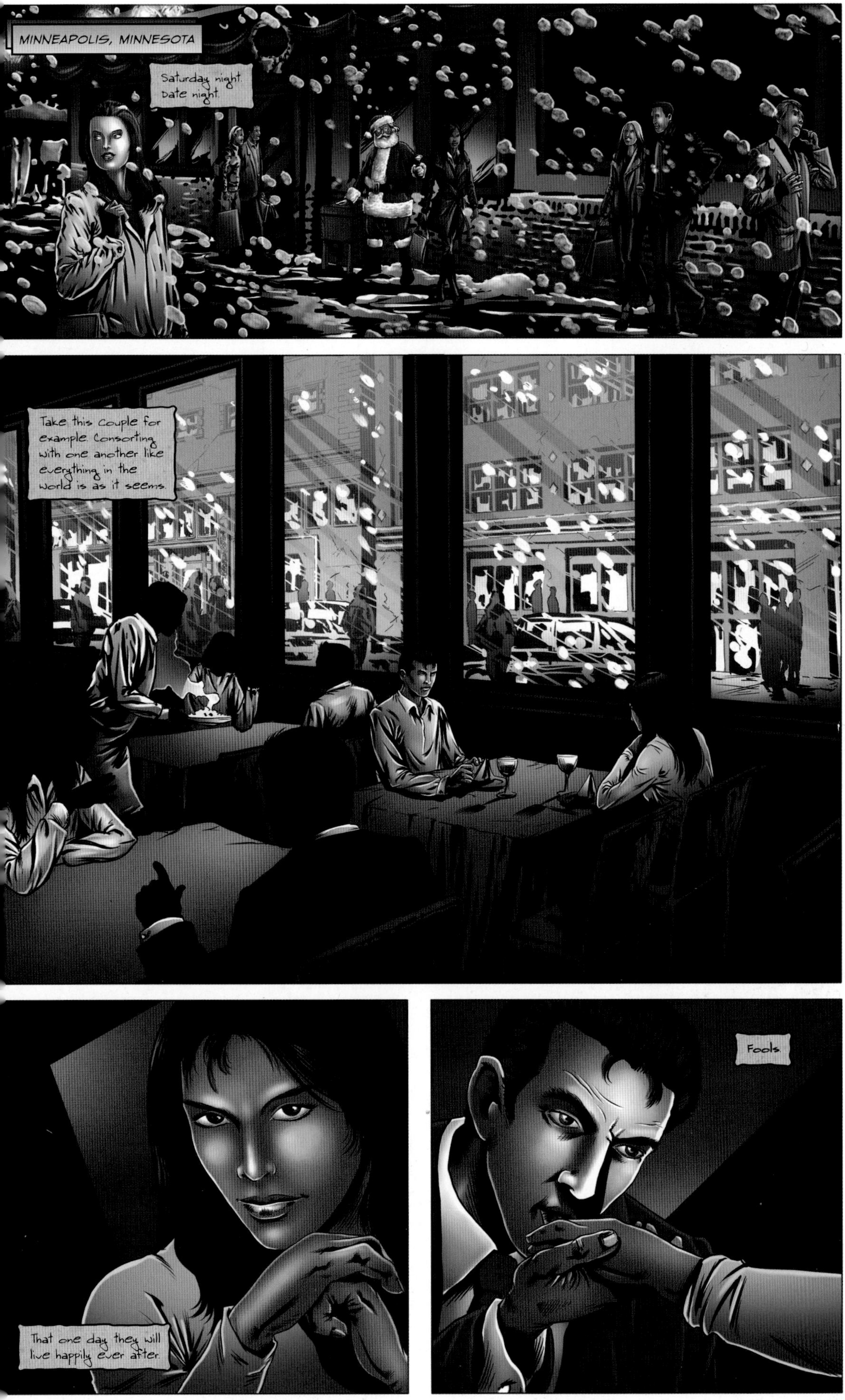
MINNEAPOLIS, MINNESOTA
Saturday night. Date night.
Take this couple for example. Consorting with one another like everything in the world is as it seems.
That one day they will live happily ever after.
Fools.

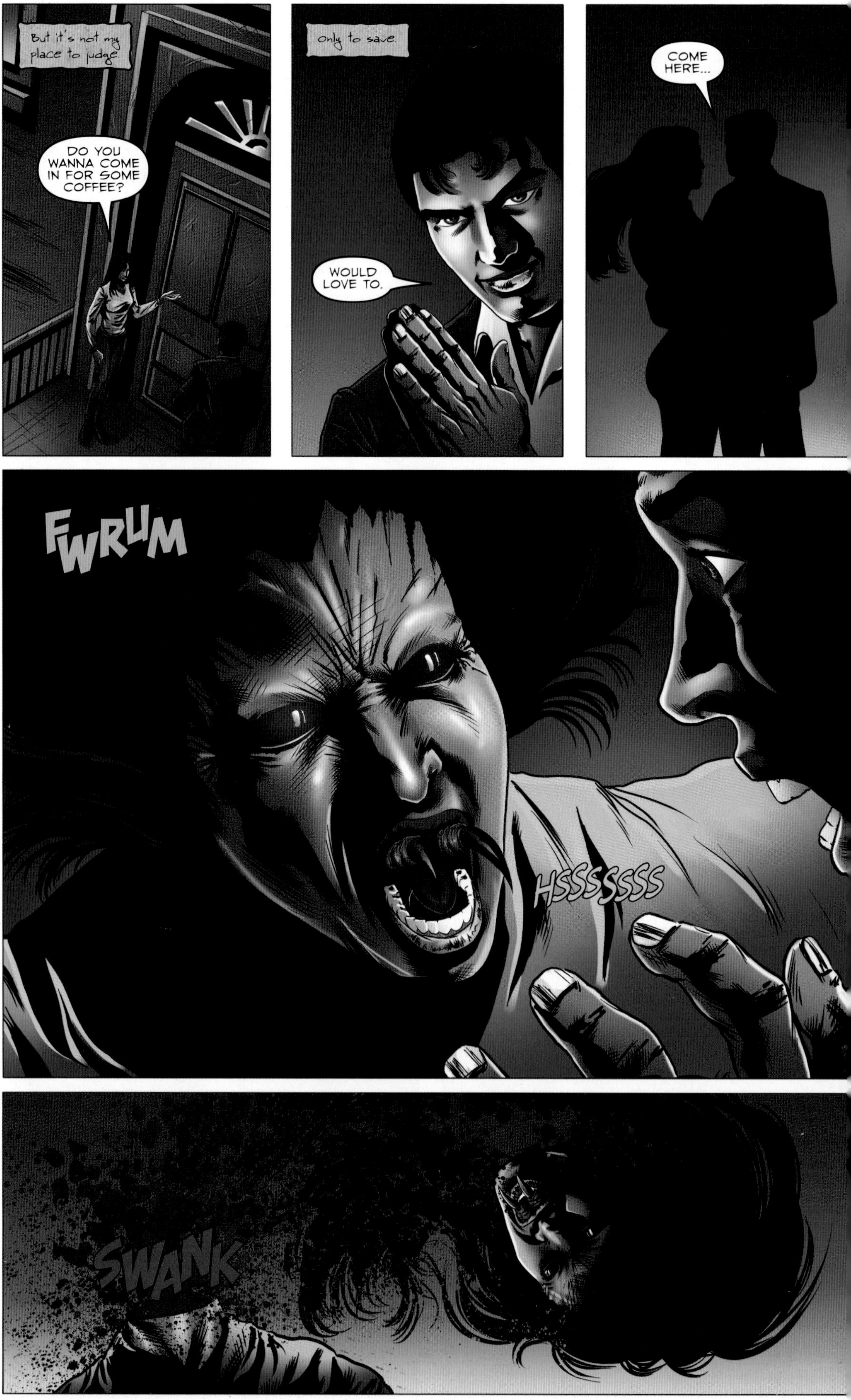
But it's not my place to judge.
DO YOU WANNA COME IN FOR SOME COFFEE?
only to save.
WOULD LOVE TO.
COME HERE...
FWRUM
HSSSSSSS
SWANK

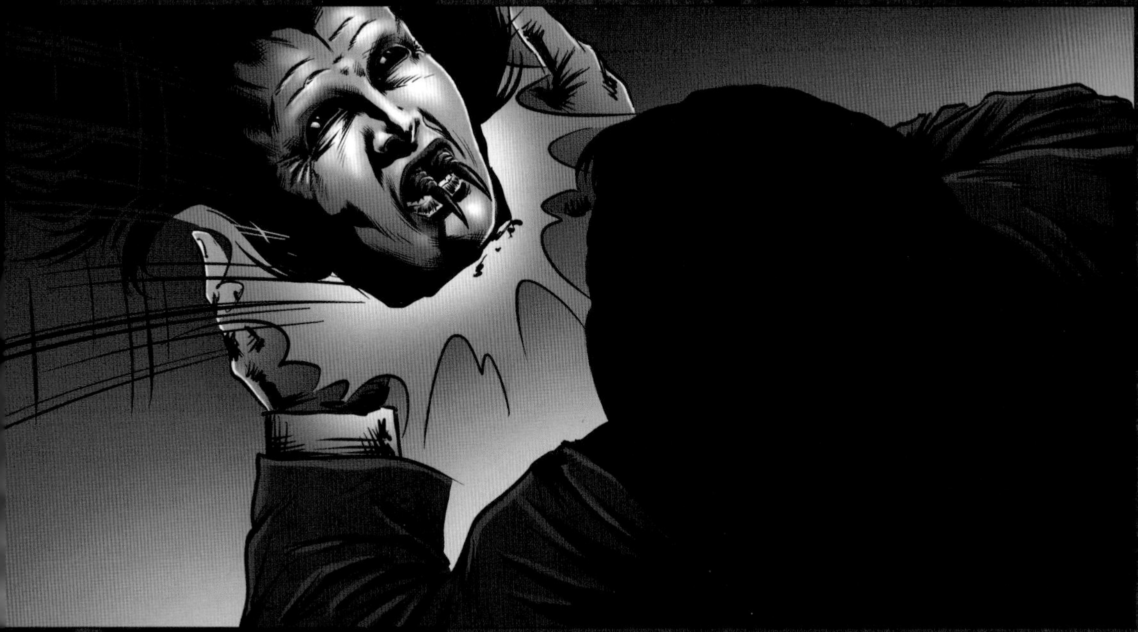

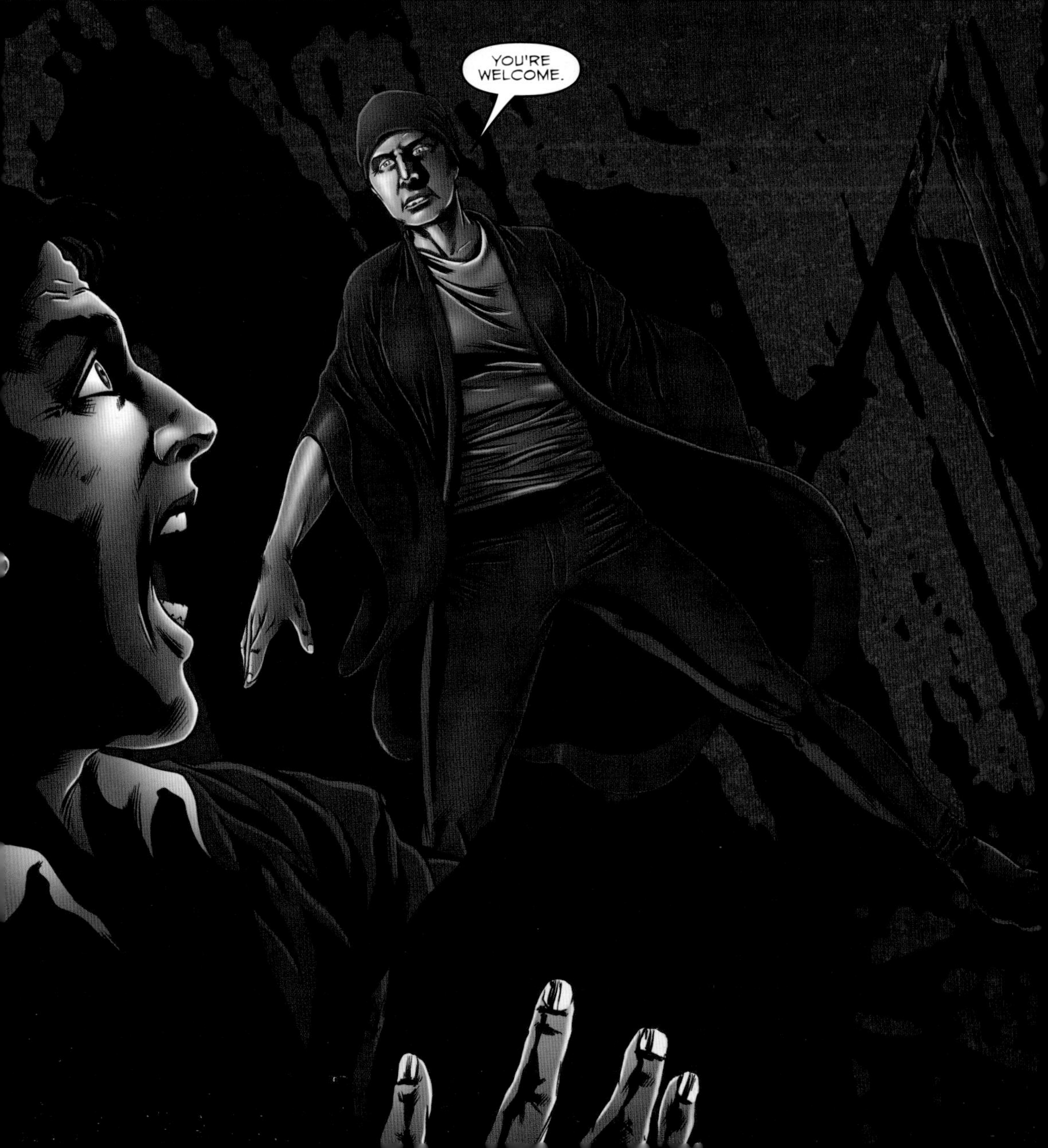
YOU'RE WELCOME.

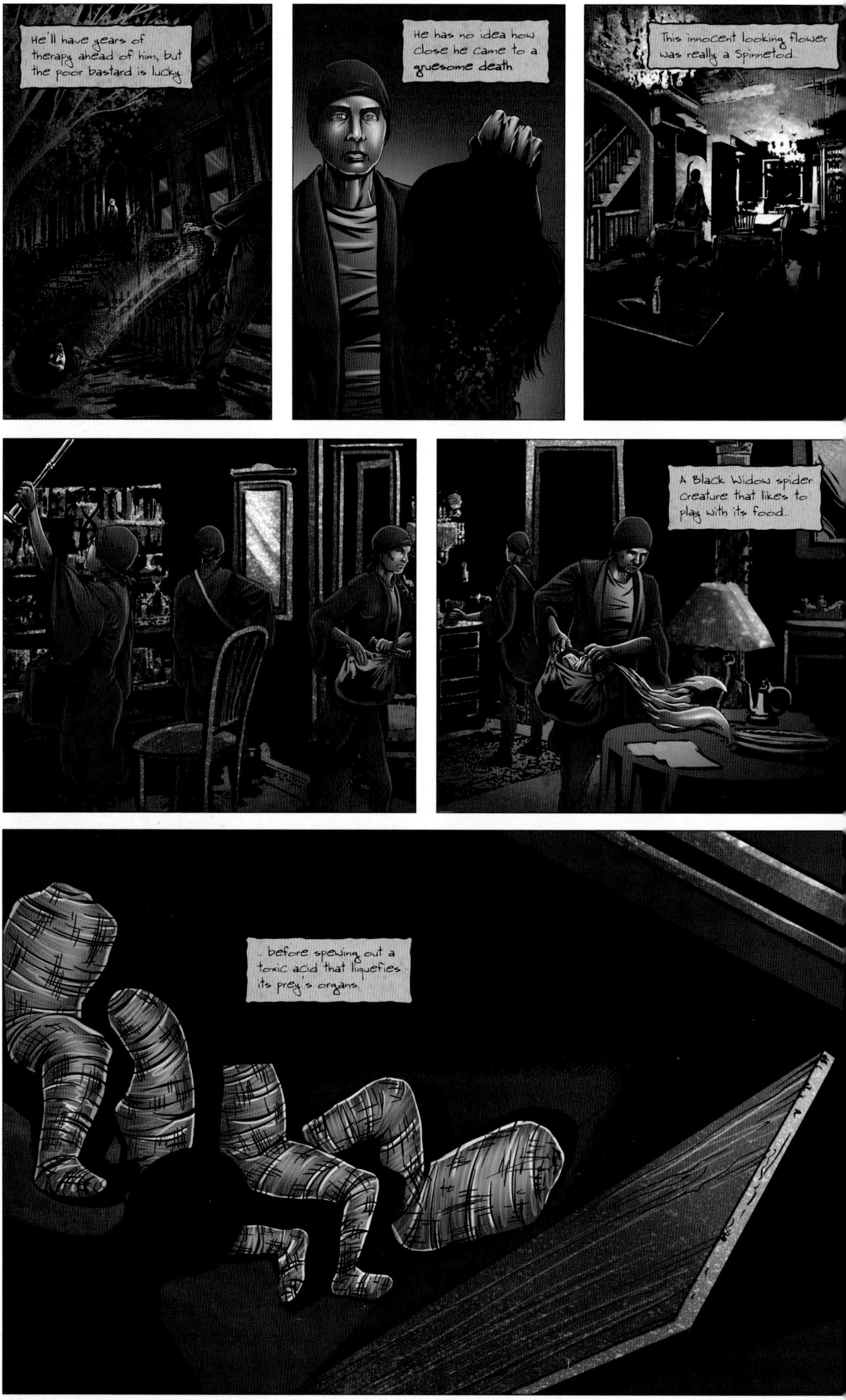
He'll have years of therapy ahead of him, but the poor bastard is lucky.
He has no idea how close he came to a gruesome death.
This innocent looking flower was really a Spinnetod...
A Black Widow spider creature that likes to play with its food...
...before spewing out a toxic acid that liquefies its prey's organs.

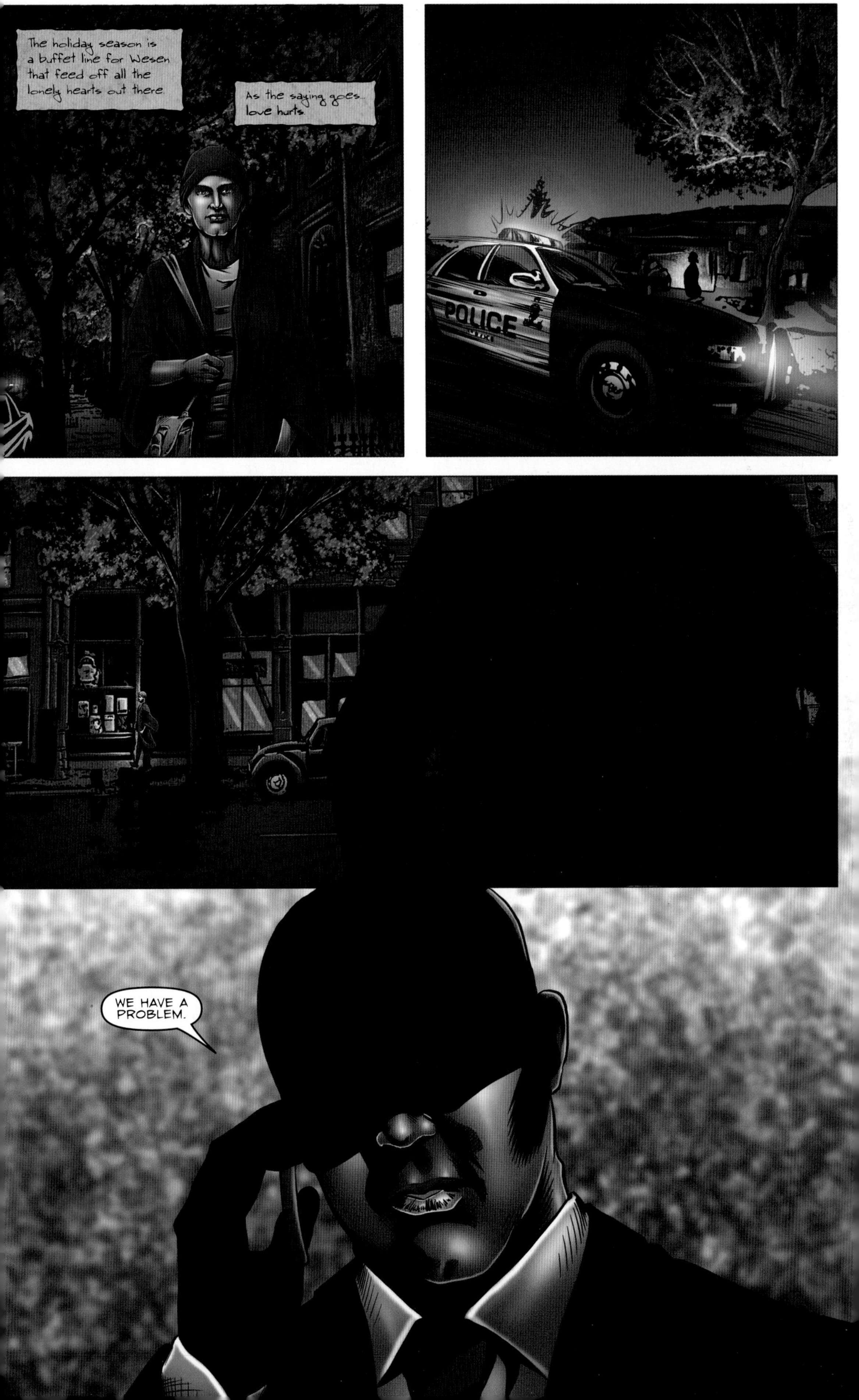

The holiday season is a buffet line for Wesen that feed off all the lonely hearts out there.
As the saying goes... love hurts.
POLICE
WE HAVE A PROBLEM.

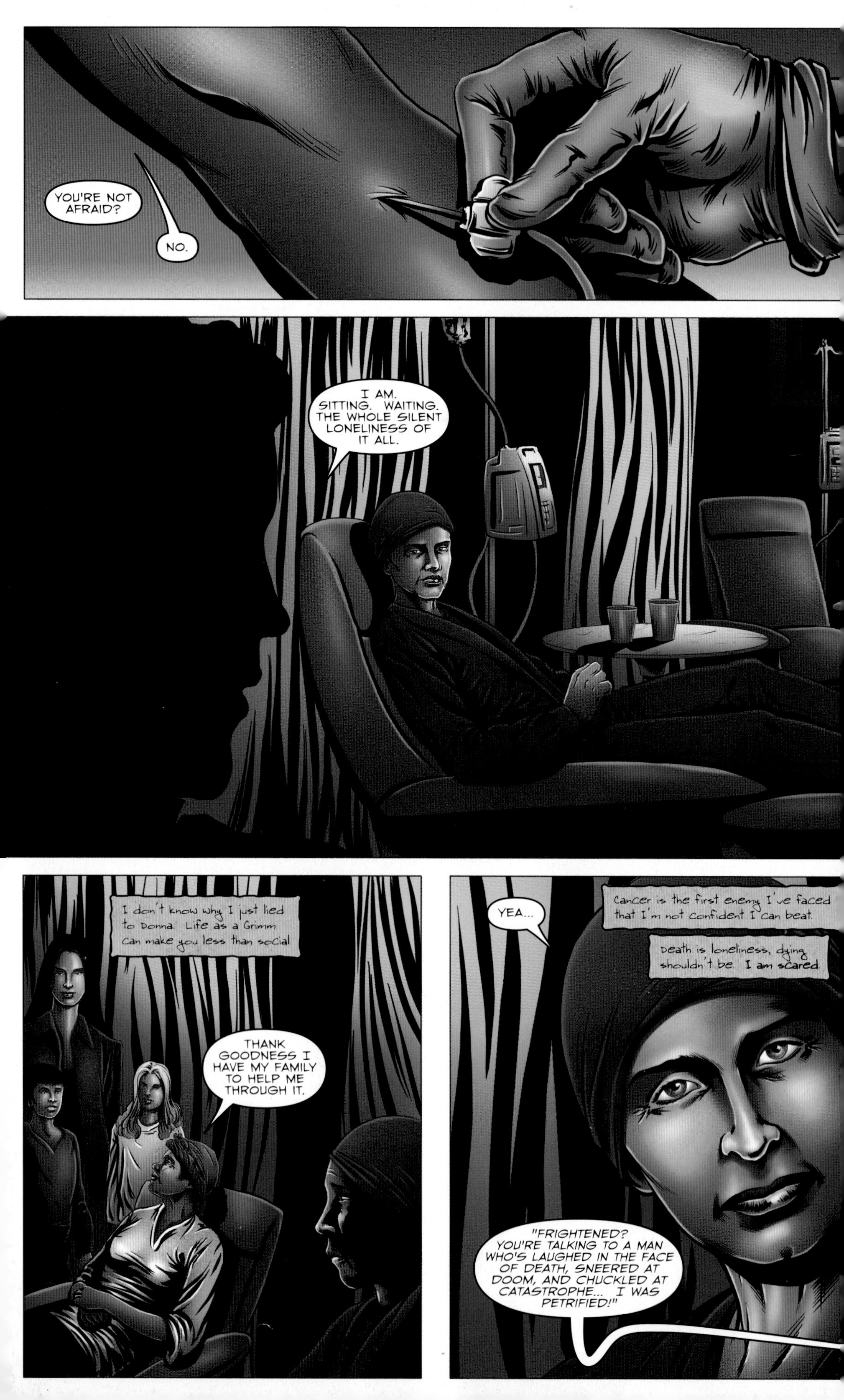
YOU'RE NOT AFRAID?
NO.
I AM. SITTING. WAITING. THE WHOLE SILENT LONELINESS OF IT ALL.
I don't know why I just lied to Donna. Life as a Grimm can make you less than social.
THANK GOODNESS I HAVE MY FAMILY TO HELP ME THROUGH IT.
YEA...
Cancer is the first enemy I've faced that I'm not confident I can beat.
Death is loneliness, dying shouldn't be. I am scared.
"FRIGHTENED? YOU'RE TALKING TO A MAN WHO'S LAUGHED IN THE FACE OF DEATH, SNEERED AT DOOM, AND CHUCKLED AT CATASTROPHE... I WAS PETRIFIED!"

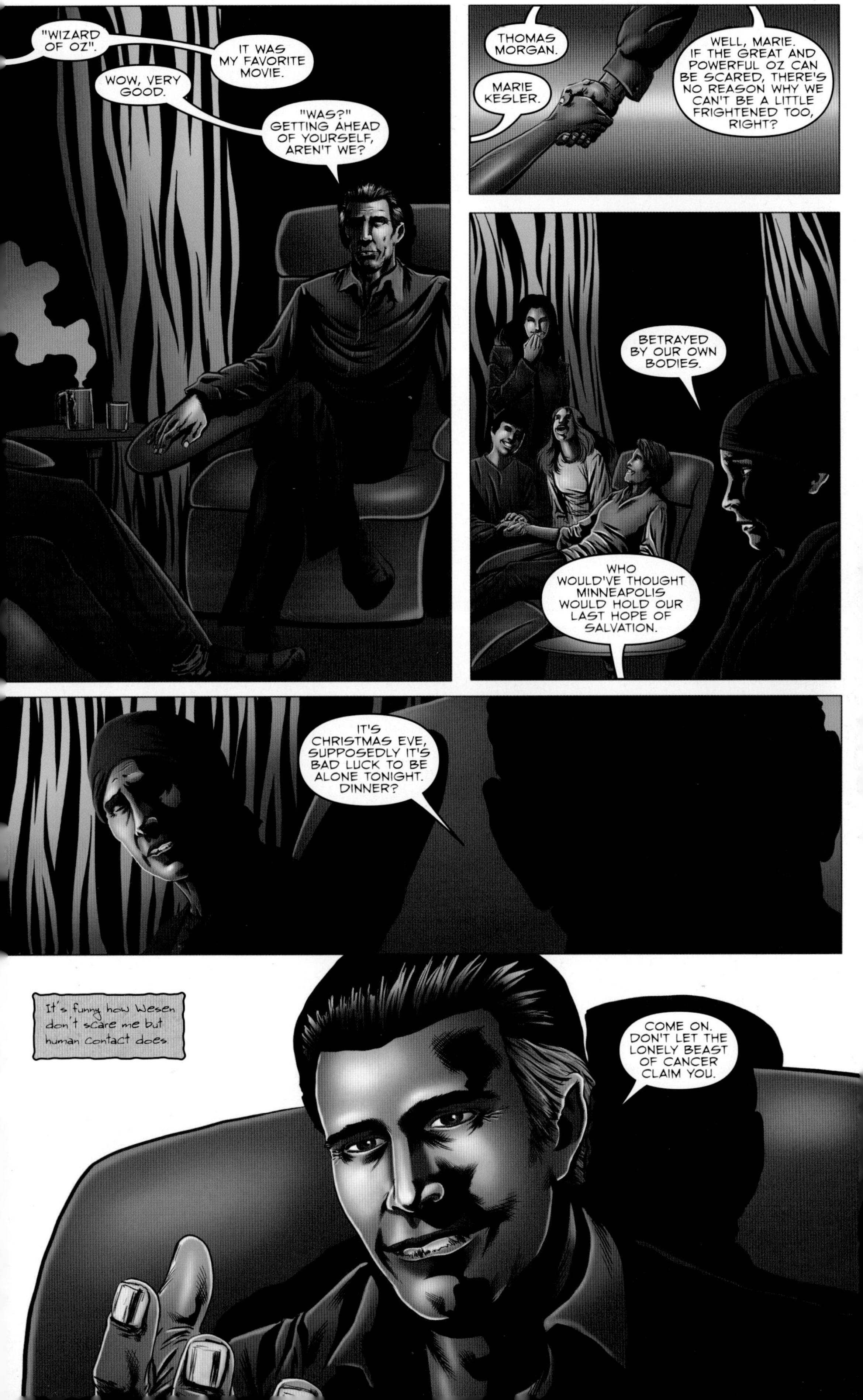
"WIZARD OF OZ".
IT WAS MY FAVORITE MOVIE.
WOW, VERY GOOD.
"WAS?" GETTING AHEAD OF YOURSELF, AREN'T WE?
THOMAS MORGAN.
MARIE KESLER.
WELL, MARIE. IF THE GREAT AND POWERFUL OZ CAN BE SCARED, THERE'S NO REASON WHY WE CAN'T BE A LITTLE FRIGHTENED TOO, RIGHT?
BETRAYED BY OUR OWN BODIES.
WHO WOULD'VE THOUGHT MINNEAPOLIS WOULD HOLD OUR LAST HOPE OF SALVATION.
IT'S CHRISTMAS EVE, SUPPOSEDLY IT'S BAD LUCK TO BE ALONE TONIGHT. DINNER?
It's funny how Wesen don't scare me but human contact does.
COME ON. DON'T LET THE LONELY BEAST OF CANCER CLAIM YOU.

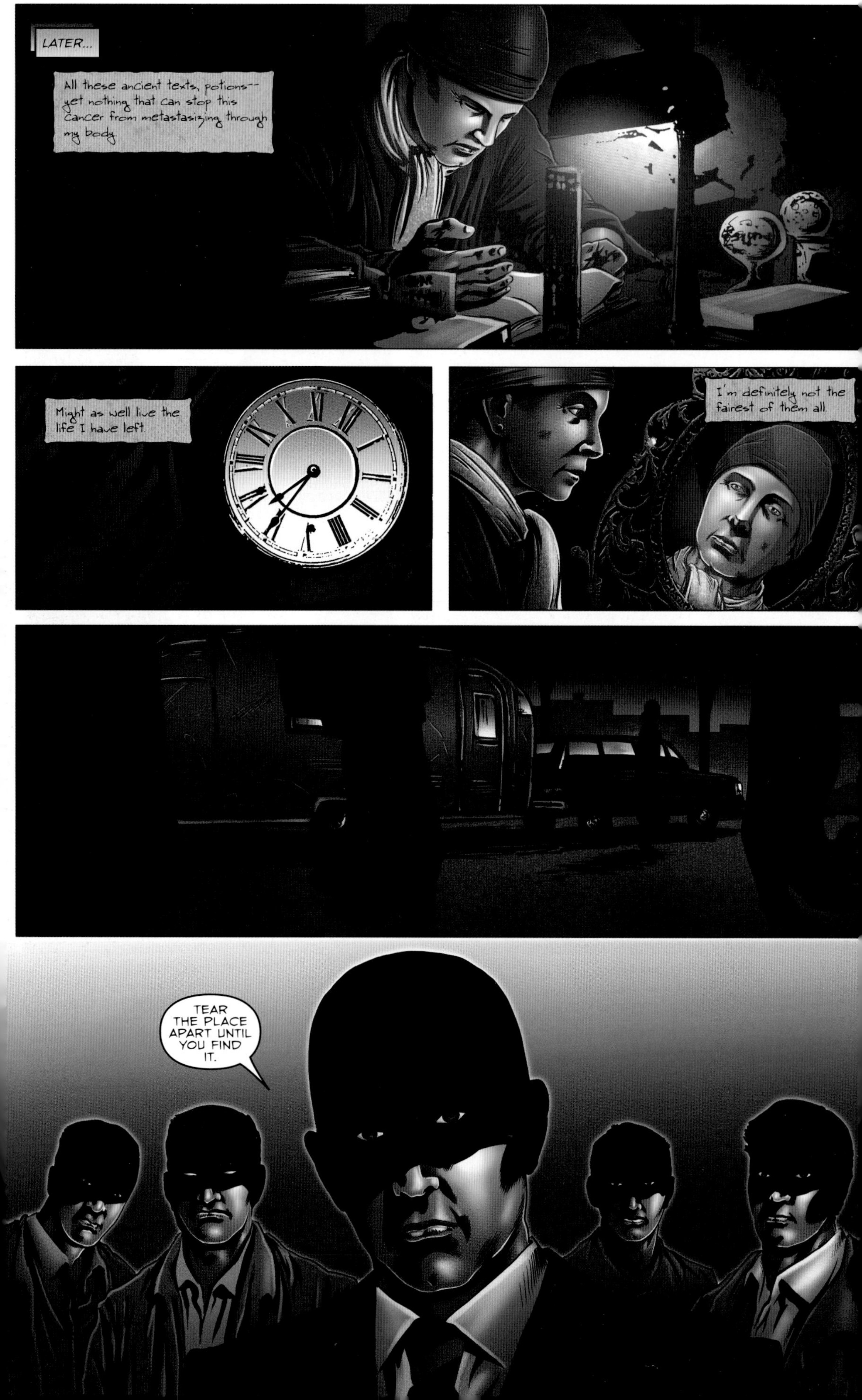
LATER...
All these ancient texts, potions--yet nothing that can stop this cancer from metastasizing through my body.
Might as well live the life I have left.
I'm definitely not the fairest of them all.
TEAR THE PLACE APART UNTIL YOU FIND IT.

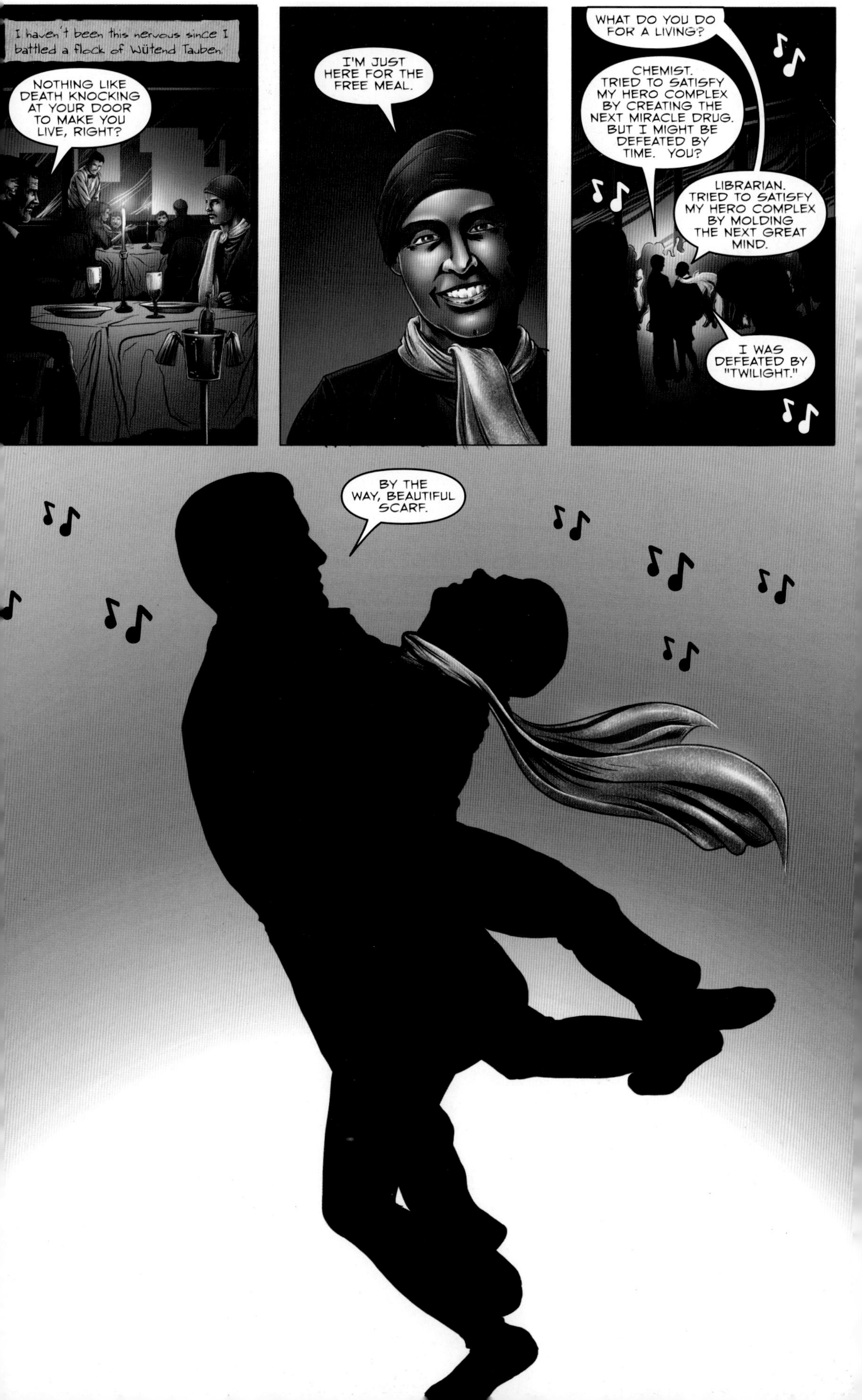

I haven't been this nervous since I battled a flock of Wütend Tauben.
NOTHING LIKE DEATH KNOCKING AT YOUR DOOR TO MAKE YOU LIVE, RIGHT?
I'M JUST HERE FOR THE FREE MEAL.
WHAT DO YOU DO FOR A LIVING?
CHEMIST. TRIED TO SATISFY MY HERO COMPLEX BY CREATING THE NEXT MIRACLE DRUG. BUT I MIGHT BE DEFEATED BY TIME. YOU?
LIBRARIAN. TRIED TO SATISFY MY HERO COMPLEX BY MOLDING THE NEXT GREAT MIND.
I WAS DEFEATED BY "TWILIGHT."
BY THE WAY, BEAUTIFUL SCARF.

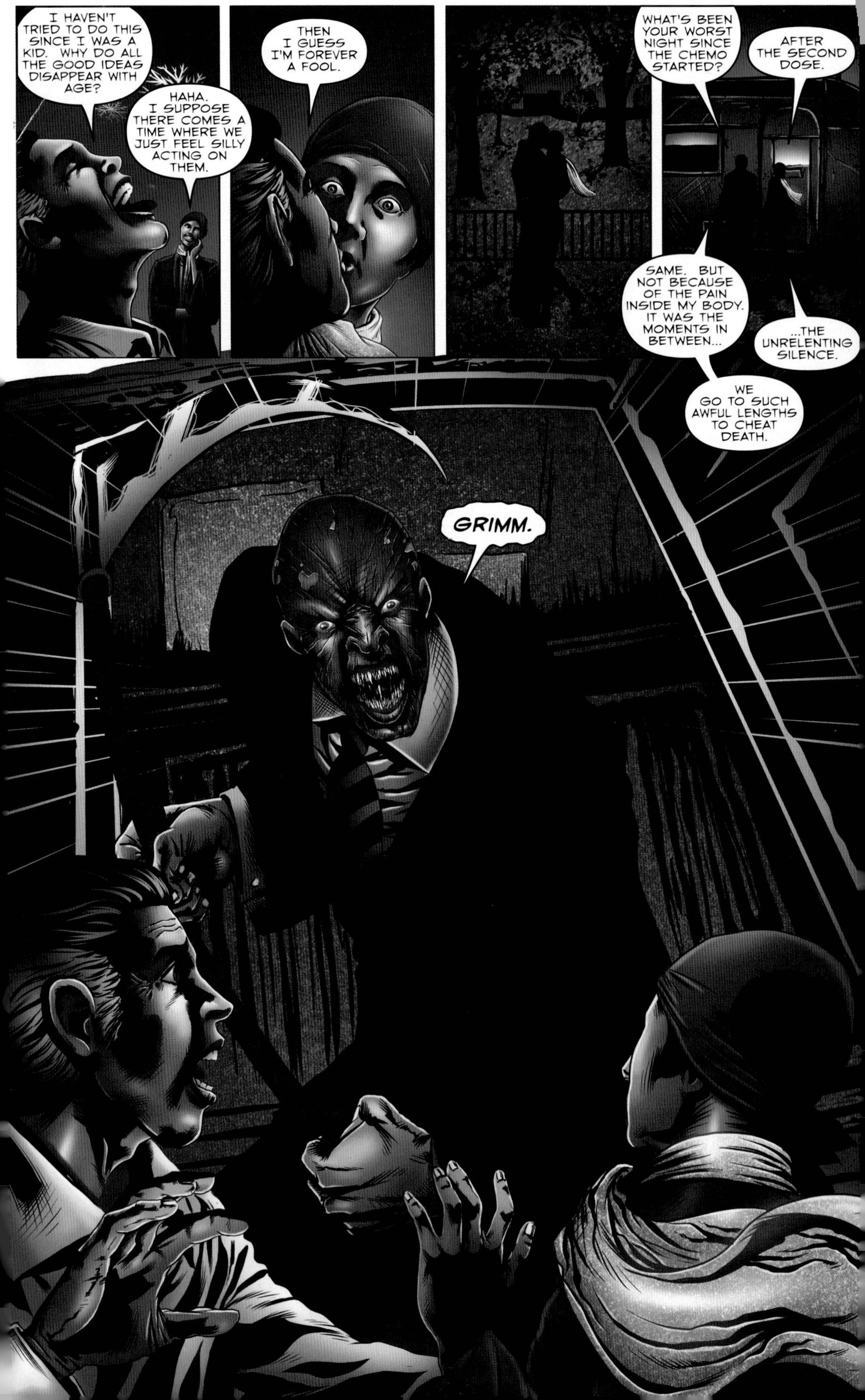
I HAVEN'T TRIED TO DO THIS SINCE I WAS A KID. WHY DO ALL THE GOOD IDEAS DISAPPEAR WITH AGE?
HAHA. I SUPPOSE THERE COMES A TIME WHERE WE JUST FEEL SILLY ACTING ON THEM.
THEN I GUESS I'M FOREVER A FOOL.
WHAT'S BEEN YOUR WORST NIGHT SINCE THE CHEMO STARTED?
AFTER THE SECOND DOSE.
SAME. BUT NOT BECAUSE OF THE PAIN INSIDE MY BODY. IT WAS THE MOMENTS IN BETWEEN...
...THE UNRELENTING SILENCE.
WE GO TO SUCH AWFUL LENGTHS TO CHEAT DEATH.
GRIMM.

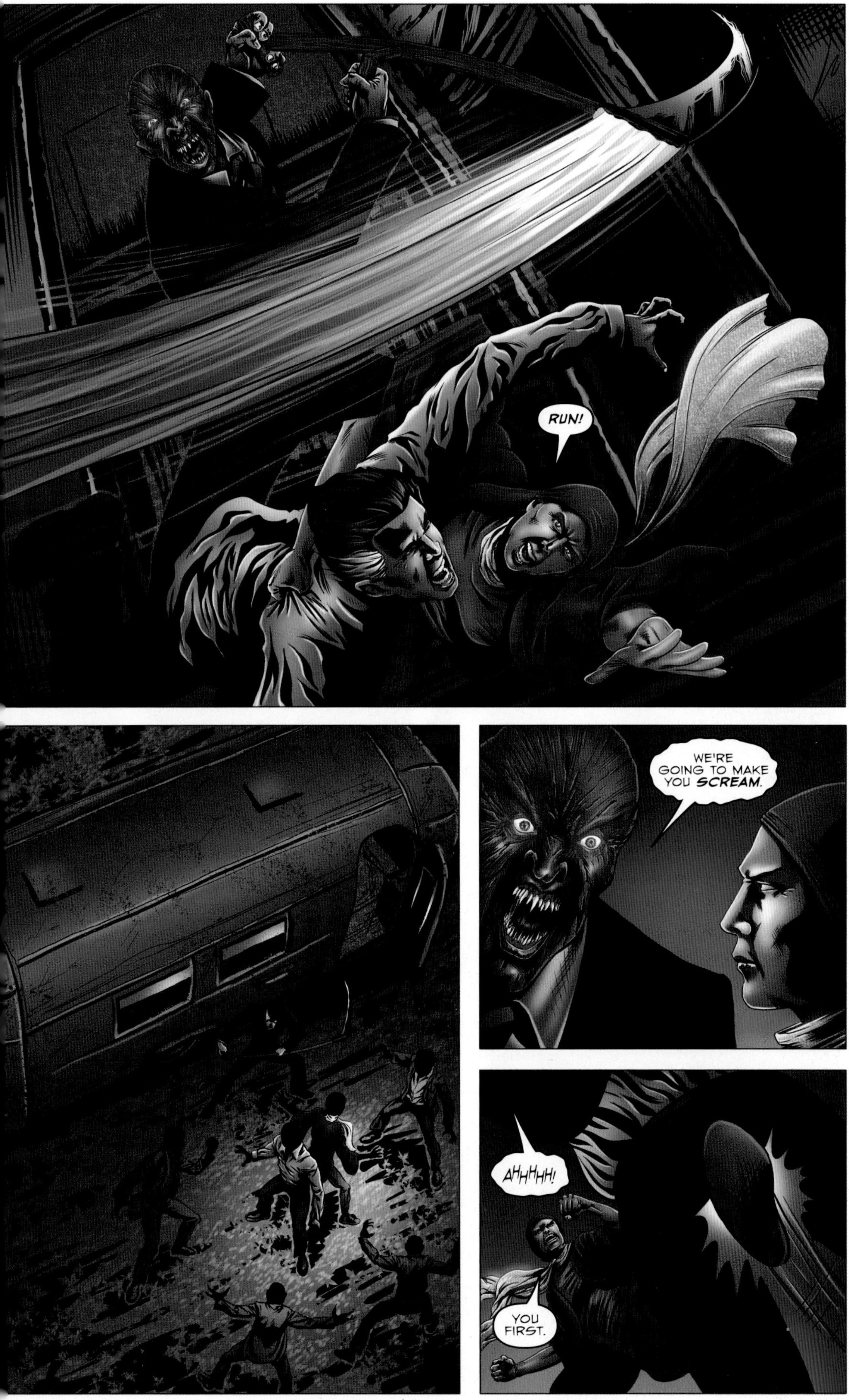
RUN!
WE'RE GOING TO MAKE YOU SCREAM.
AHHHHH!
YOU FIRST.

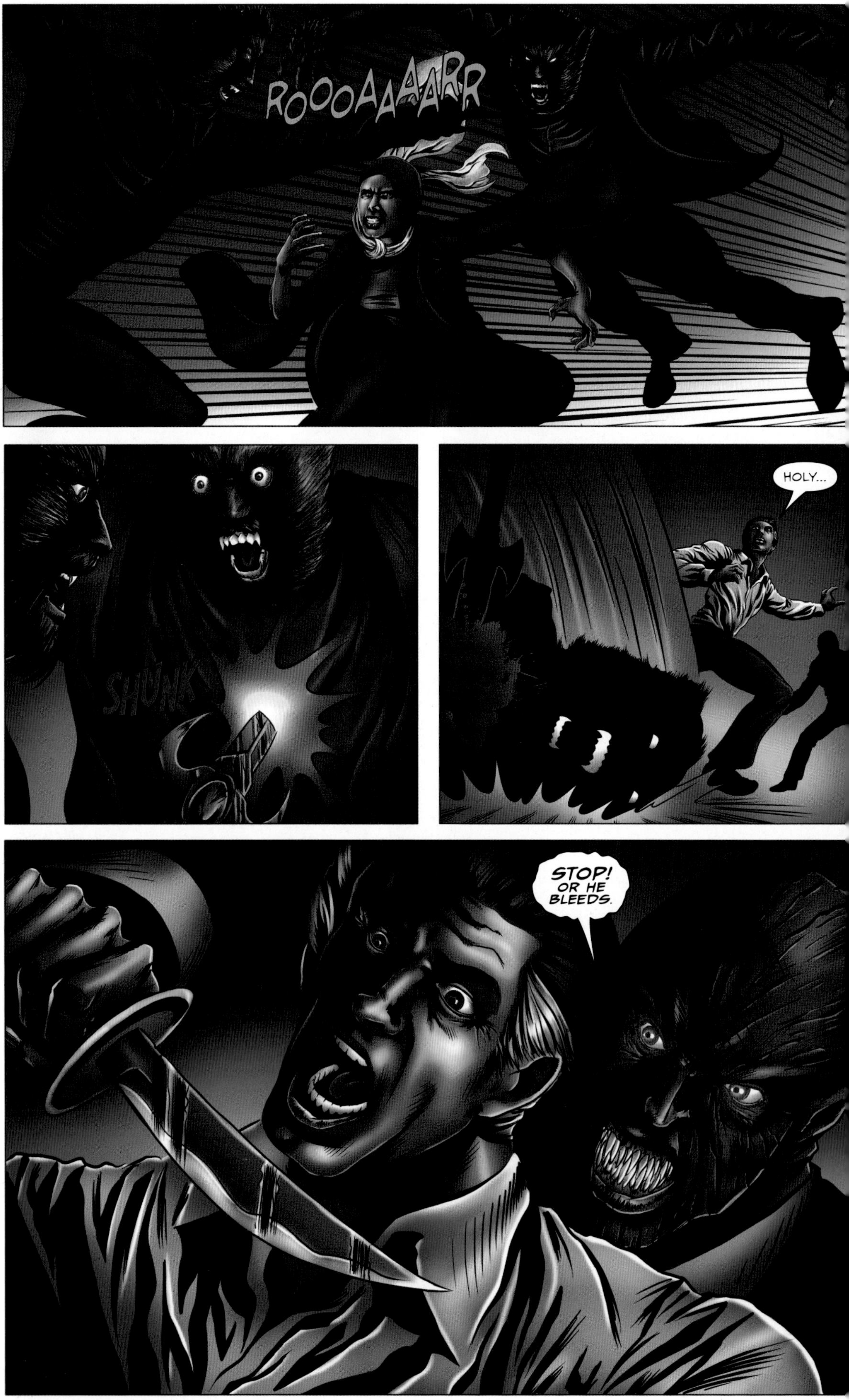
ROOOAAAARR
SHUNK
HOLY...
STOP! OR HE BLEEDS.

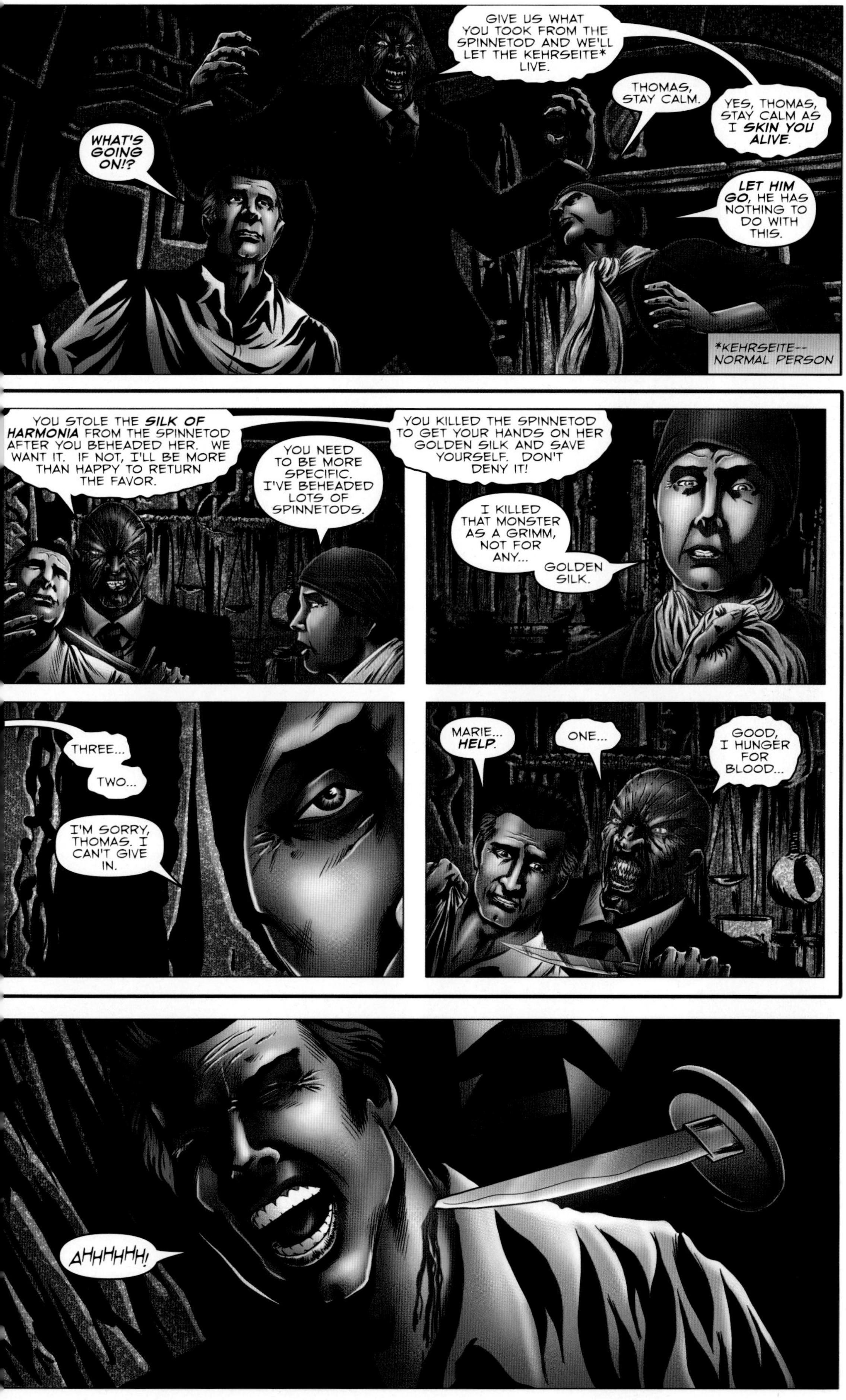
GIVE US WHAT YOU TOOK FROM THE SPINNETOD AND WE'LL LET THE KEHRSEITE* LIVE.
WHAT'S GOING ON!?
THOMAS, STAY CALM.
YES, THOMAS, STAY CALM AS I SKIN YOU ALIVE.
LET HIM GO, HE HAS NOTHING TO DO WITH THIS.
*KEHRSEITE-- NORMAL PERSON
YOU STOLE THE SILK OF HARMONIA FROM THE SPINNETOD AFTER YOU BEHEADED HER. WE WANT IT. IF NOT, I'LL BE MORE THAN HAPPY TO RETURN THE FAVOR.
YOU NEED TO BE MORE SPECIFIC. I'VE BEHEADED LOTS OF SPINNETODS.
YOU KILLED THE SPINNETOD TO GET YOUR HANDS ON HER GOLDEN SILK AND SAVE YOURSELF. DON'T DENY IT!
I KILLED THAT MONSTER AS A GRIMM, NOT FOR ANY...
GOLDEN SILK.
THREE...
TWO...
I'M SORRY, THOMAS. I CAN'T GIVE IN.
MARIE... HELP.
ONE...
GOOD, I HUNGER FOR BLOOD...
AHHHHHH!

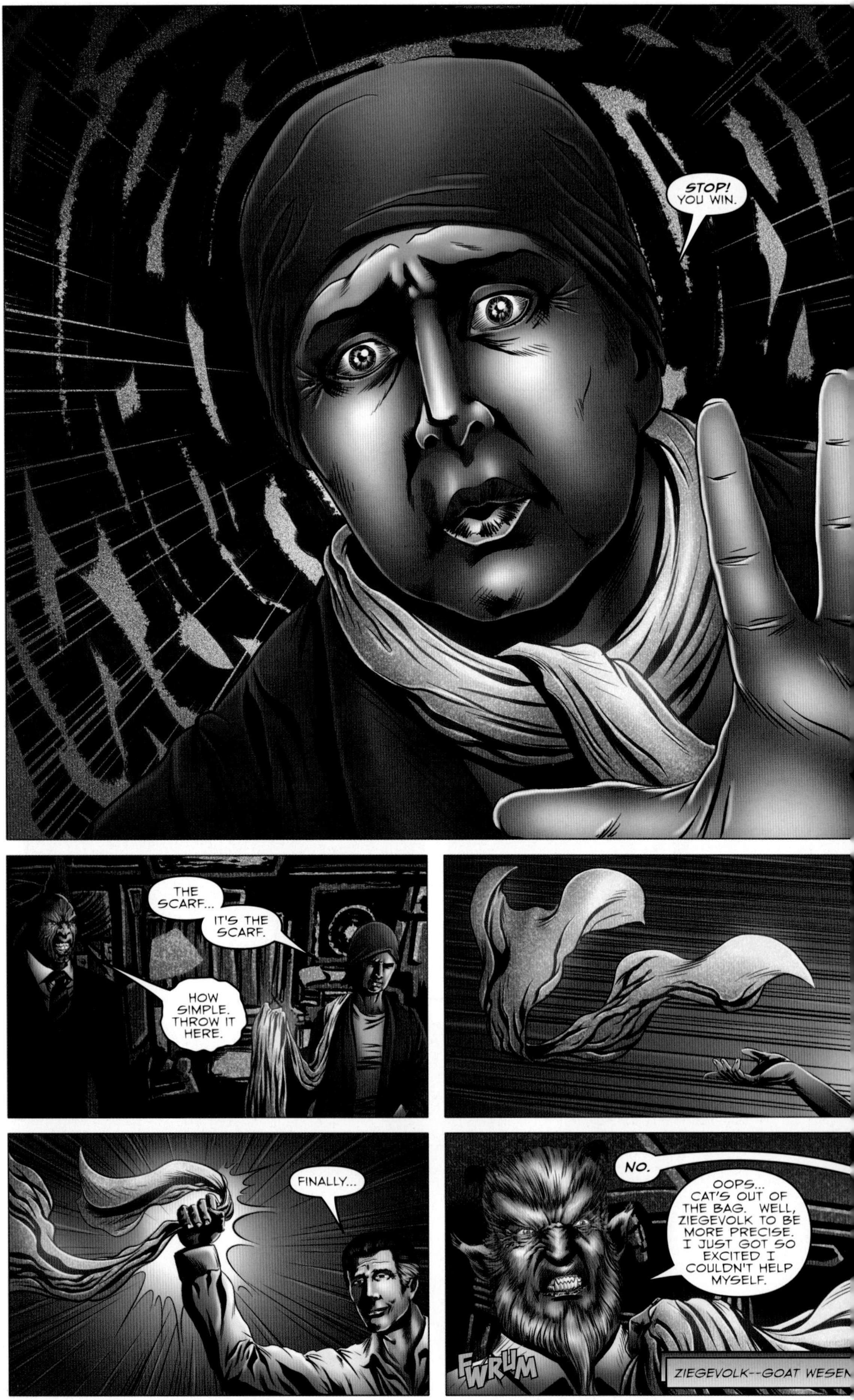
STOP! YOU WIN.
THE SCARF...
IT'S THE SCARF.
HOW SIMPLE. THROW IT HERE.
FINALLY...
NO.
OOPS... CAT'S OUT OF THE BAG. WELL, ZIEGEVOLK TO BE MORE PRECISE. I JUST GOT SO EXCITED I COULDN'T HELP MYSELF.
FWRUM
ZIEGEVOLK--GOAT WESEN

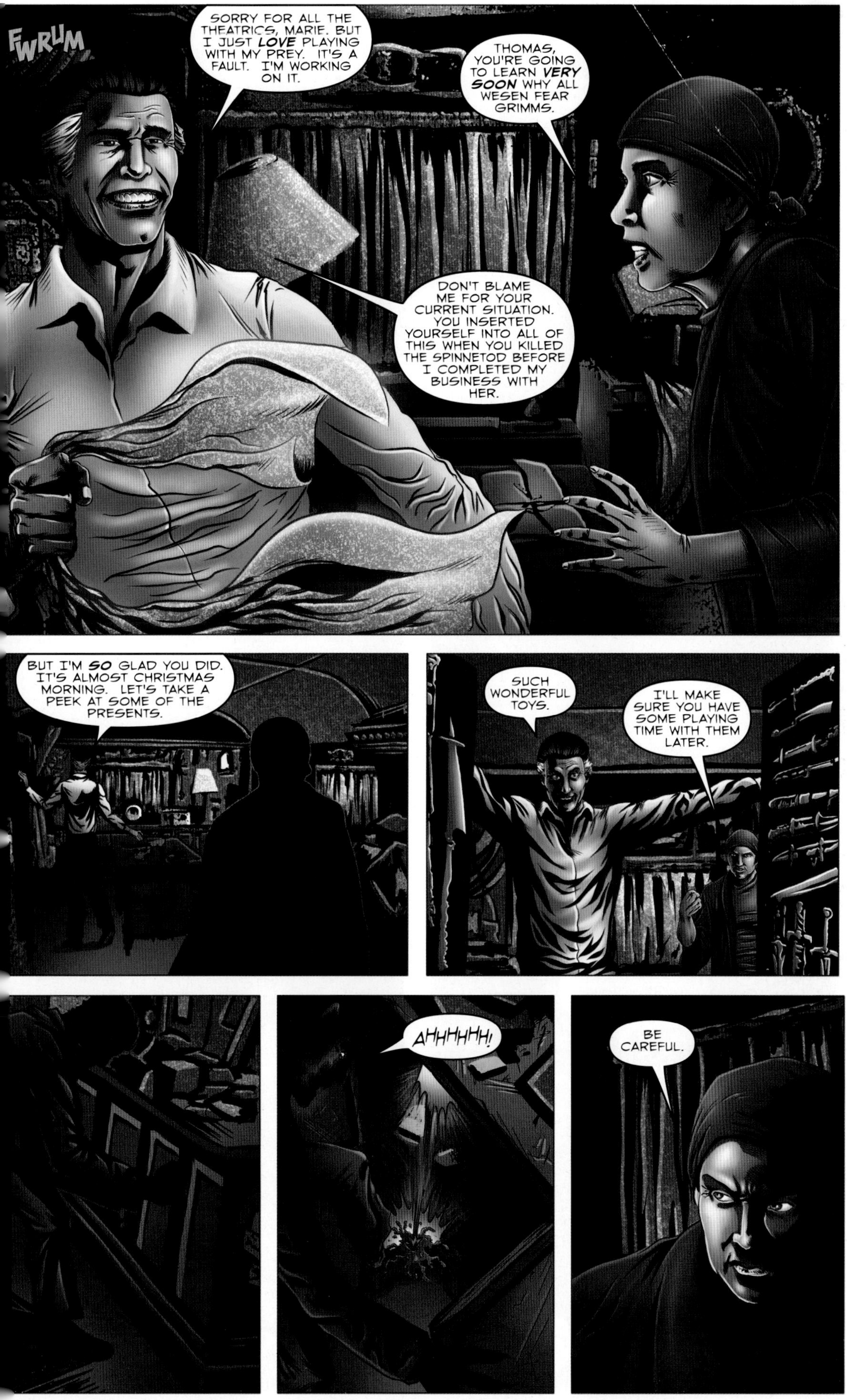
FWRUM
SORRY FOR ALL THE THEATRICS, MARIE. BUT I JUST LOVE PLAYING WITH MY PREY. IT'S A FAULT. I'M WORKING ON IT.
THOMAS, YOU'RE GOING TO LEARN VERY SOON WHY ALL WESEN FEAR GRIMMS.
DON'T BLAME ME FOR YOUR CURRENT SITUATION. YOU INSERTED YOURSELF INTO ALL OF THIS WHEN YOU KILLED THE SPINNETOD BEFORE I COMPLETED MY BUSINESS WITH HER.
BUT I'M SO GLAD YOU DID. IT'S ALMOST CHRISTMAS MORNING. LET'S TAKE A PEEK AT SOME OF THE PRESENTS.
SUCH WONDERFUL TOYS.
I'LL MAKE SURE YOU HAVE SOME PLAYING TIME WITH THEM LATER.
AHHHHHH!
BE CAREFUL.

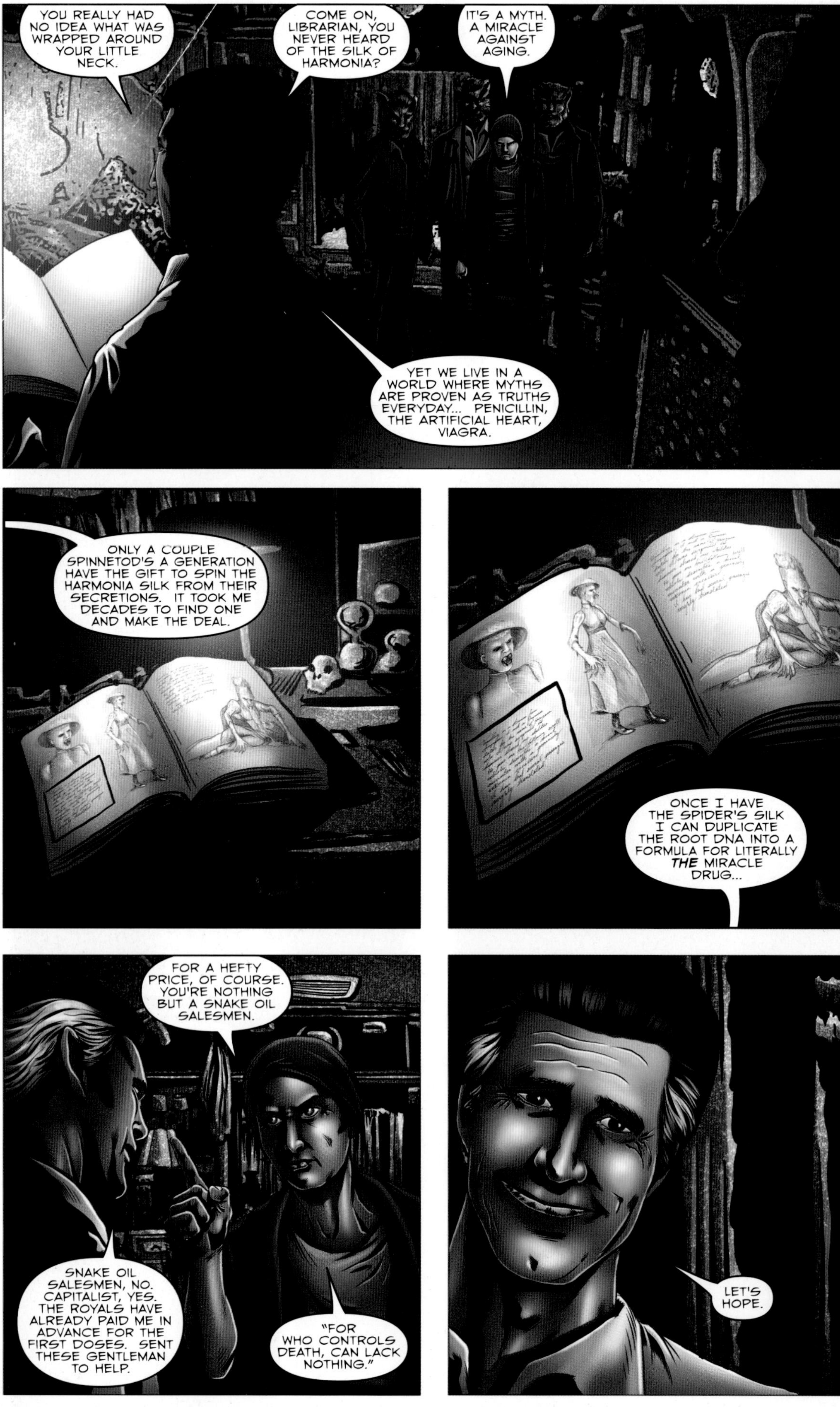
YOU REALLY HAD NO IDEA WHAT WAS WRAPPED AROUND YOUR LITTLE NECK.
COME ON, LIBRARIAN, YOU NEVER HEARD OF THE SILK OF HARMONIA?
IT'S A MYTH. A MIRACLE AGAINST AGING.
YET WE LIVE IN A WORLD WHERE MYTHS ARE PROVEN AS TRUTHS EVERYDAY... PENICILLIN, THE ARTIFICIAL HEART, VIAGRA.
ONLY A COUPLE SPINNETOD'S A GENERATION HAVE THE GIFT TO SPIN THE HARMONIA SILK FROM THEIR SECRETIONS. IT TOOK ME DECADES TO FIND ONE AND MAKE THE DEAL.
ONCE I HAVE THE SPIDER'S SILK I CAN DUPLICATE THE ROOT DNA INTO A FORMULA FOR LITERALLY *THE* MIRACLE DRUG...
FOR A HEFTY PRICE, OF COURSE. YOU'RE NOTHING BUT A SNAKE OIL SALESMEN.
SNAKE OIL SALESMEN, NO. CAPITALIST, YES. THE ROYALS HAVE ALREADY PAID ME IN ADVANCE FOR THE FIRST DOSES. SENT THESE GENTLEMAN TO HELP.
"FOR WHO CONTROLS DEATH, CAN LACK NOTHING."
LET'S HOPE.

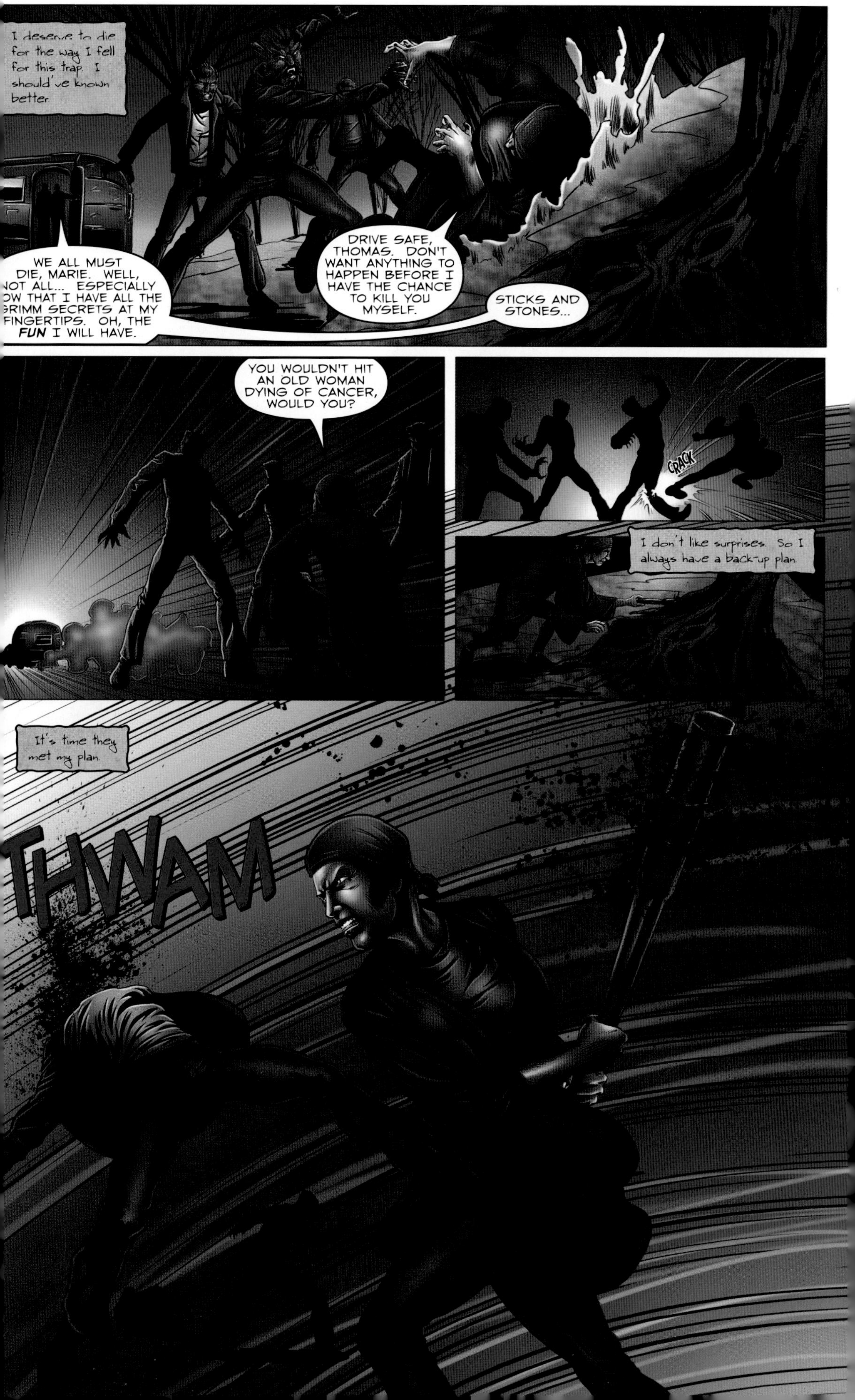

I deserve to die for the way I fell for this trap. I should've known better.
WE ALL MUST DIE, MARIE. WELL, NOT ALL... ESPECIALLY NOW THAT I HAVE ALL THE GRIMM SECRETS AT MY FINGERTIPS. OH, THE FUN I WILL HAVE.
DRIVE SAFE, THOMAS. DON'T WANT ANYTHING TO HAPPEN BEFORE I HAVE THE CHANCE TO KILL YOU MYSELF.
STICKS AND STONES...
YOU WOULDN'T HIT AN OLD WOMAN DYING OF CANCER, WOULD YOU?
CRACK
I don't like surprises. So I always have a back-up plan.
It's time they met my plan.
THWAM

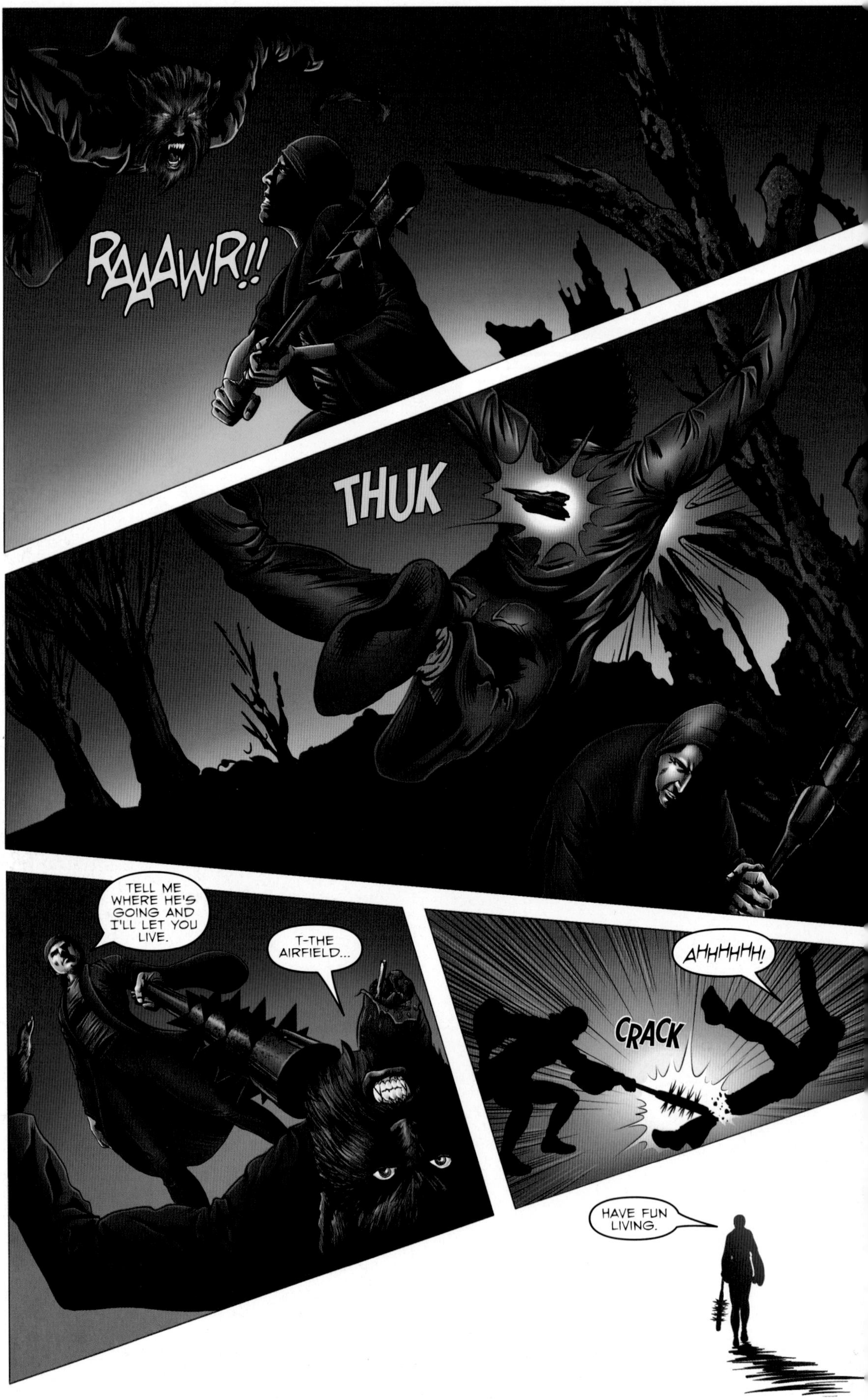
RAAAWR!!
THUK
TELL ME WHERE HE'S GOING AND I'LL LET YOU LIVE.
T-THE AIRFIELD...
AHHHHHH!
CRACK
HAVE FUN LIVING.

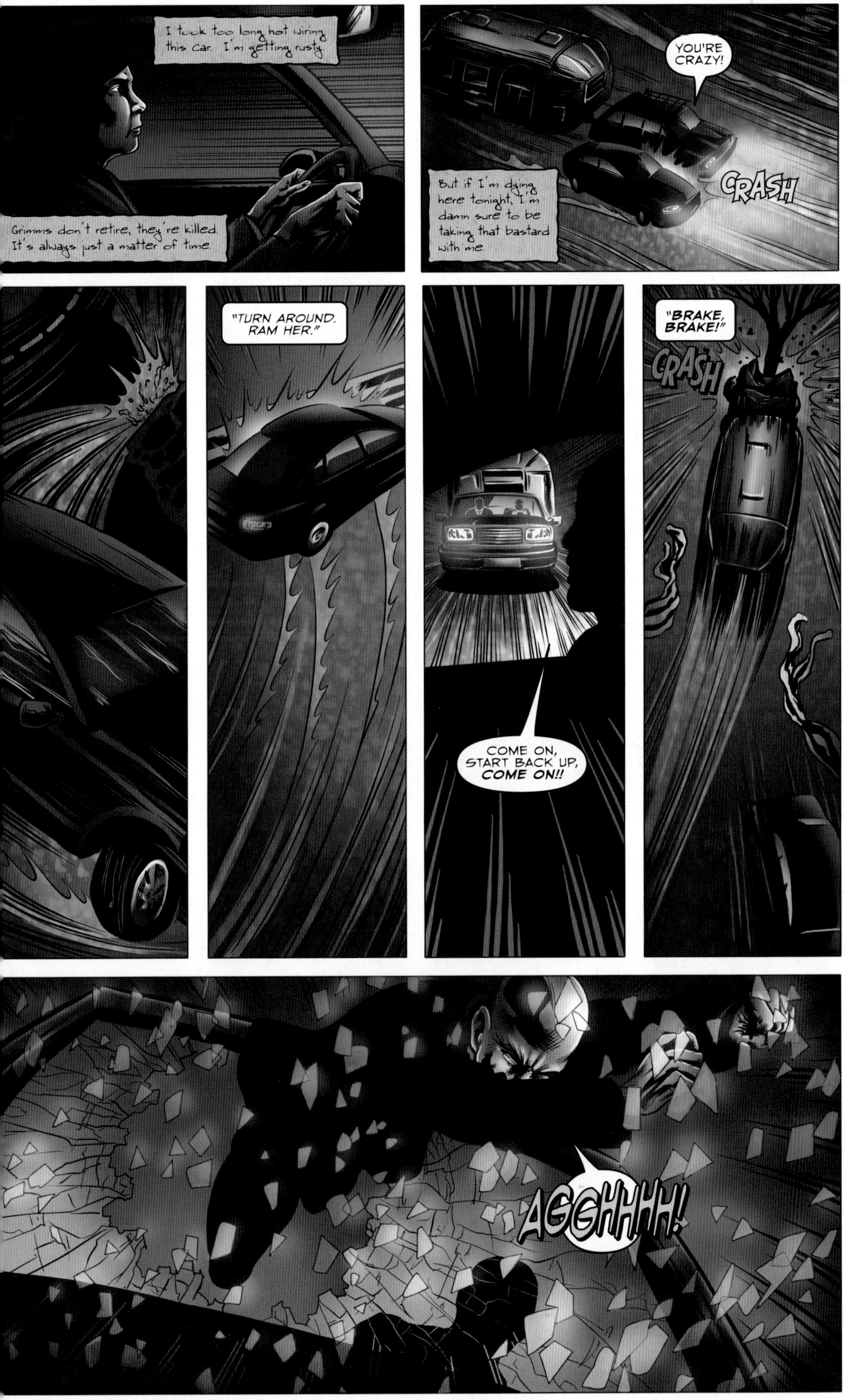

I took too long hot wiring this car. I'm getting rusty.
Grimms don't retire, they're killed. It's always just a matter of time.
YOU'RE CRAZY!
But if I'm dying here tonight, I'm damn sure to be taking that bastard with me.
CRASH
"TURN AROUND. RAM HER."
COME ON, START BACK UP, COME ON!!
"BRAKE, BRAKE!"
CRASH
AGGHHHH!

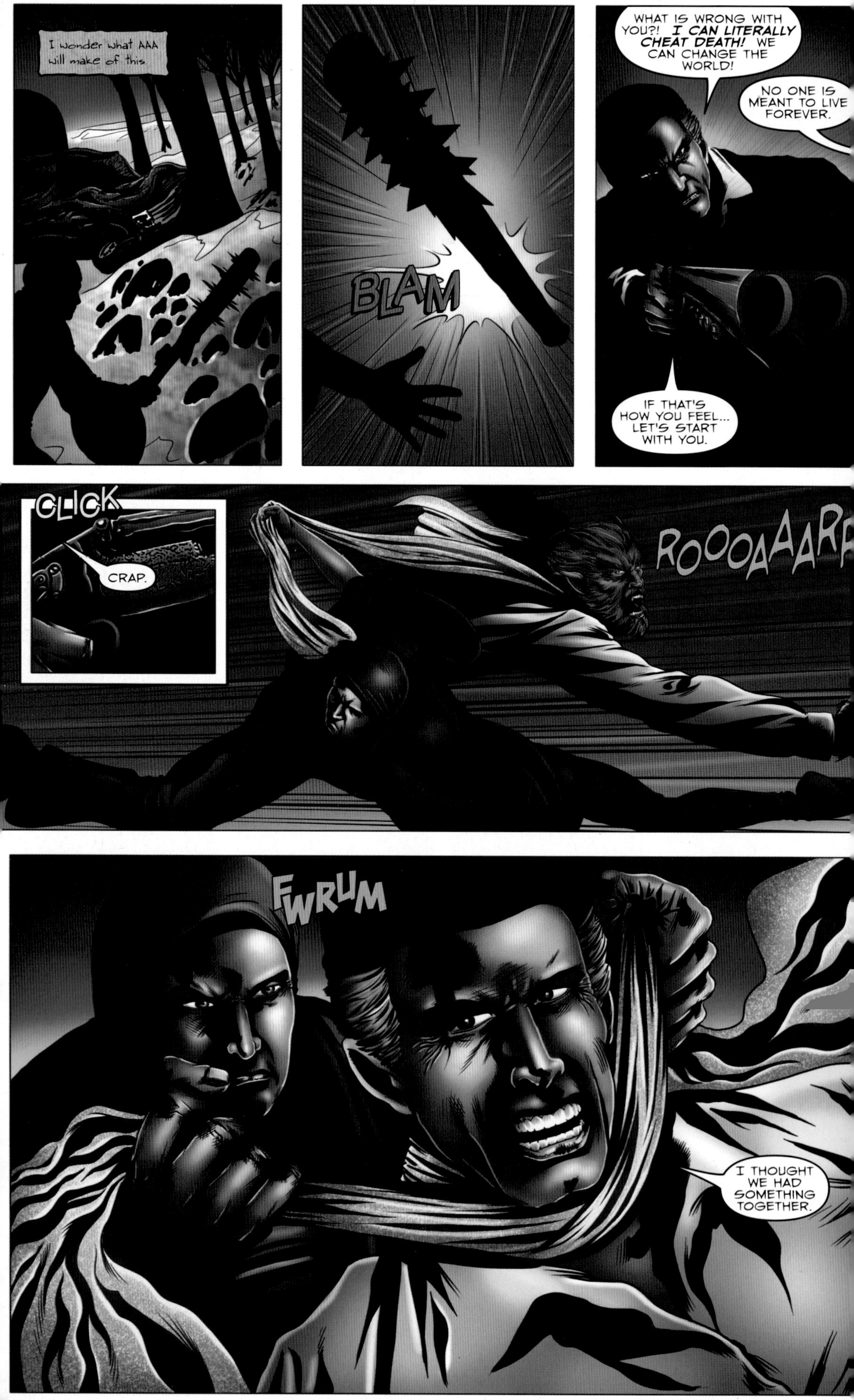
I wonder what AAA will make of this.
BLAM
WHAT IS WRONG WITH YOU?! I CAN LITERALLY CHEAT DEATH! WE CAN CHANGE THE WORLD!
NO ONE IS MEANT TO LIVE FOREVER.
IF THAT'S HOW YOU FEEL... LET'S START WITH YOU.
CLICK
CRAP.
ROOOAAARR
FWRUM
I THOUGHT WE HAD SOMETHING TOGETHER.

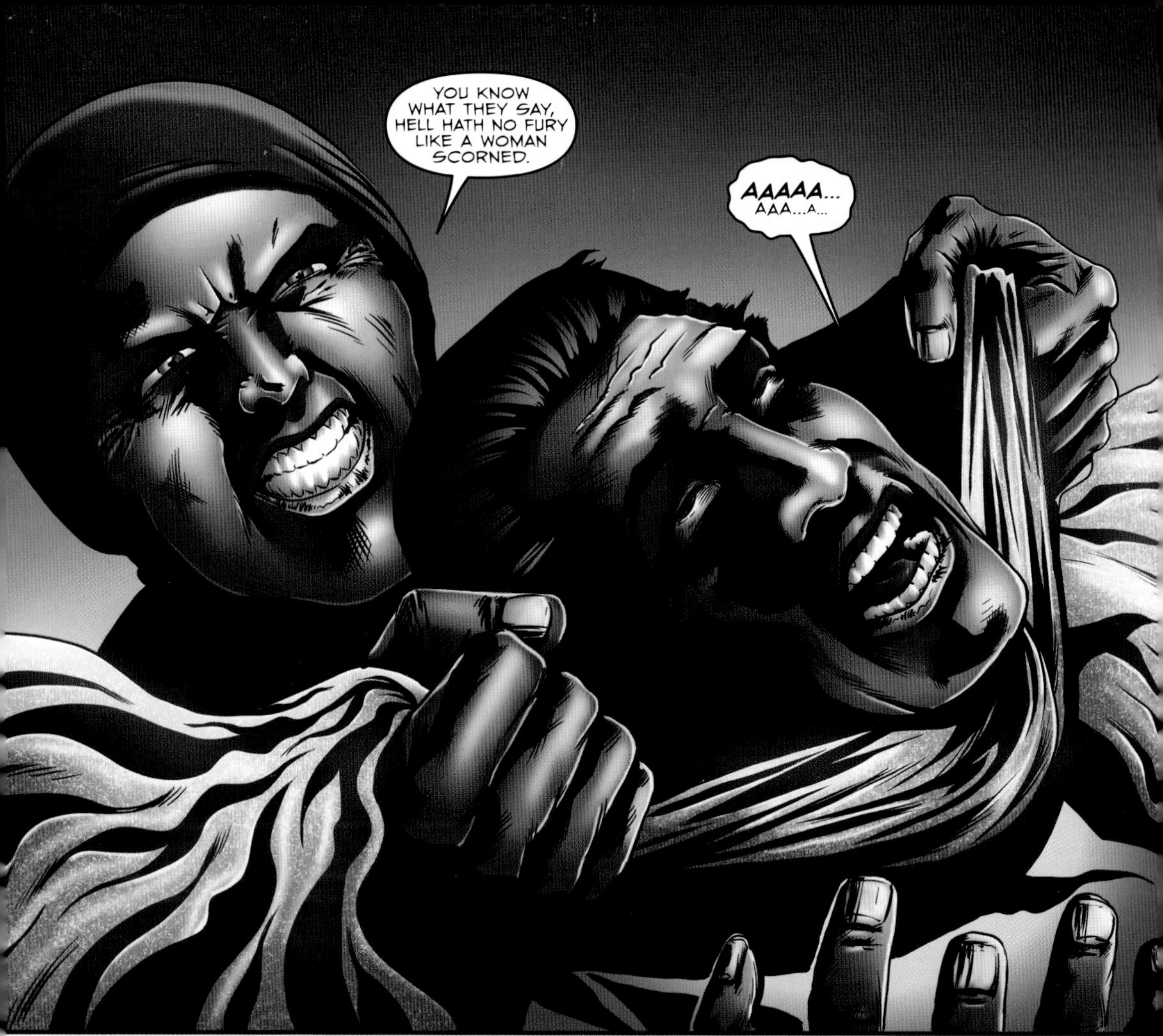
YOU KNOW WHAT THEY SAY, HELL HATH NO FURY LIKE A WOMAN SCORNED.
AAAAA... AAA...A...
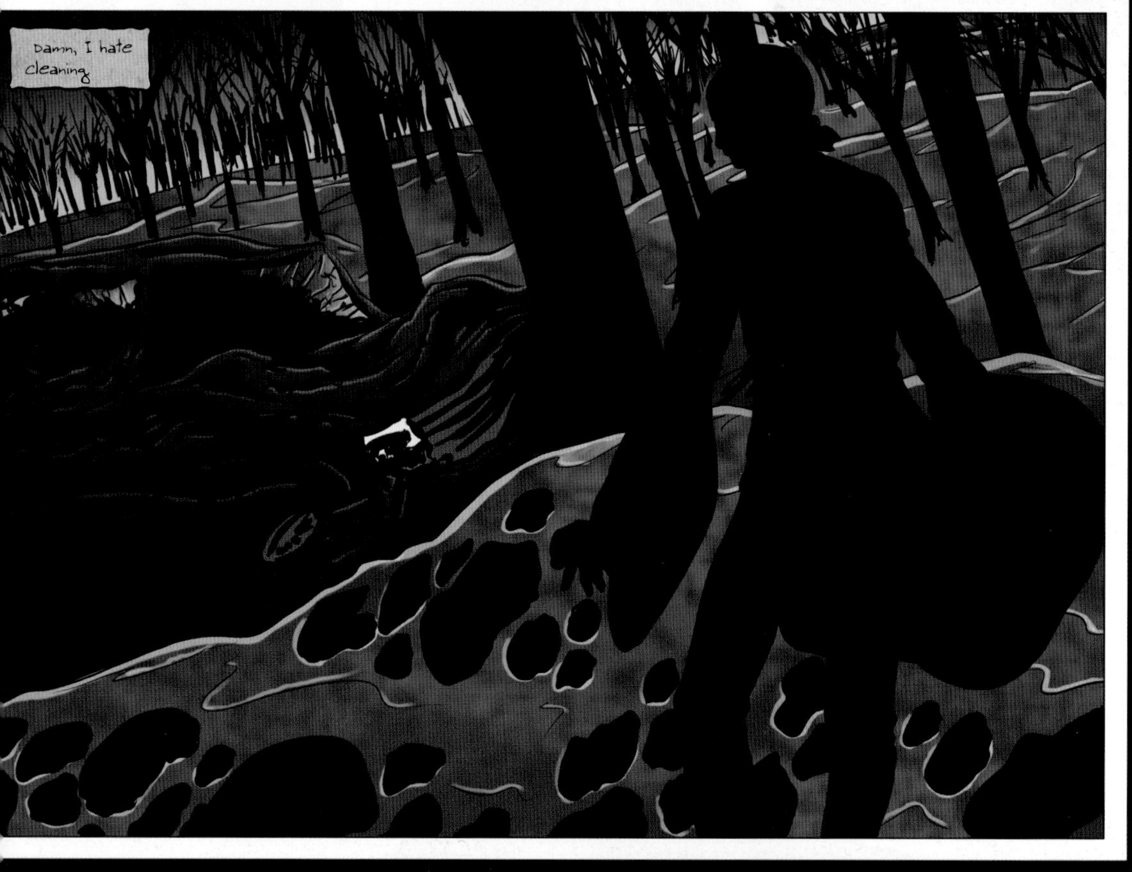
Damn, I hate cleaning.

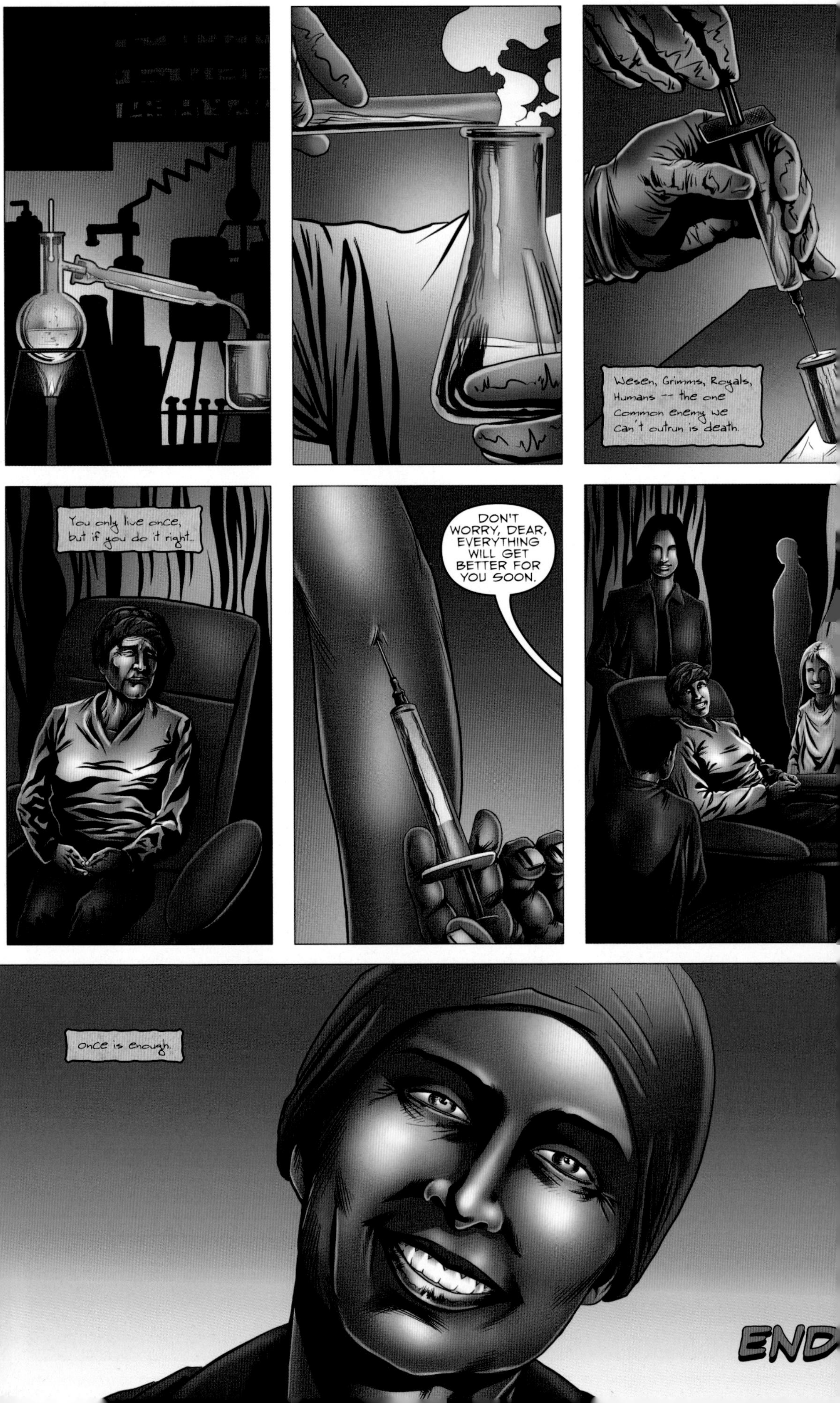
Wesen, Grimms, Royals, Humans -- the one common enemy we can't outrun is death.
You only live once, but if you do it right...
DON'T WORRY, DEAR, EVERYTHING WILL GET BETTER FOR YOU SOON.
once is enough.
END

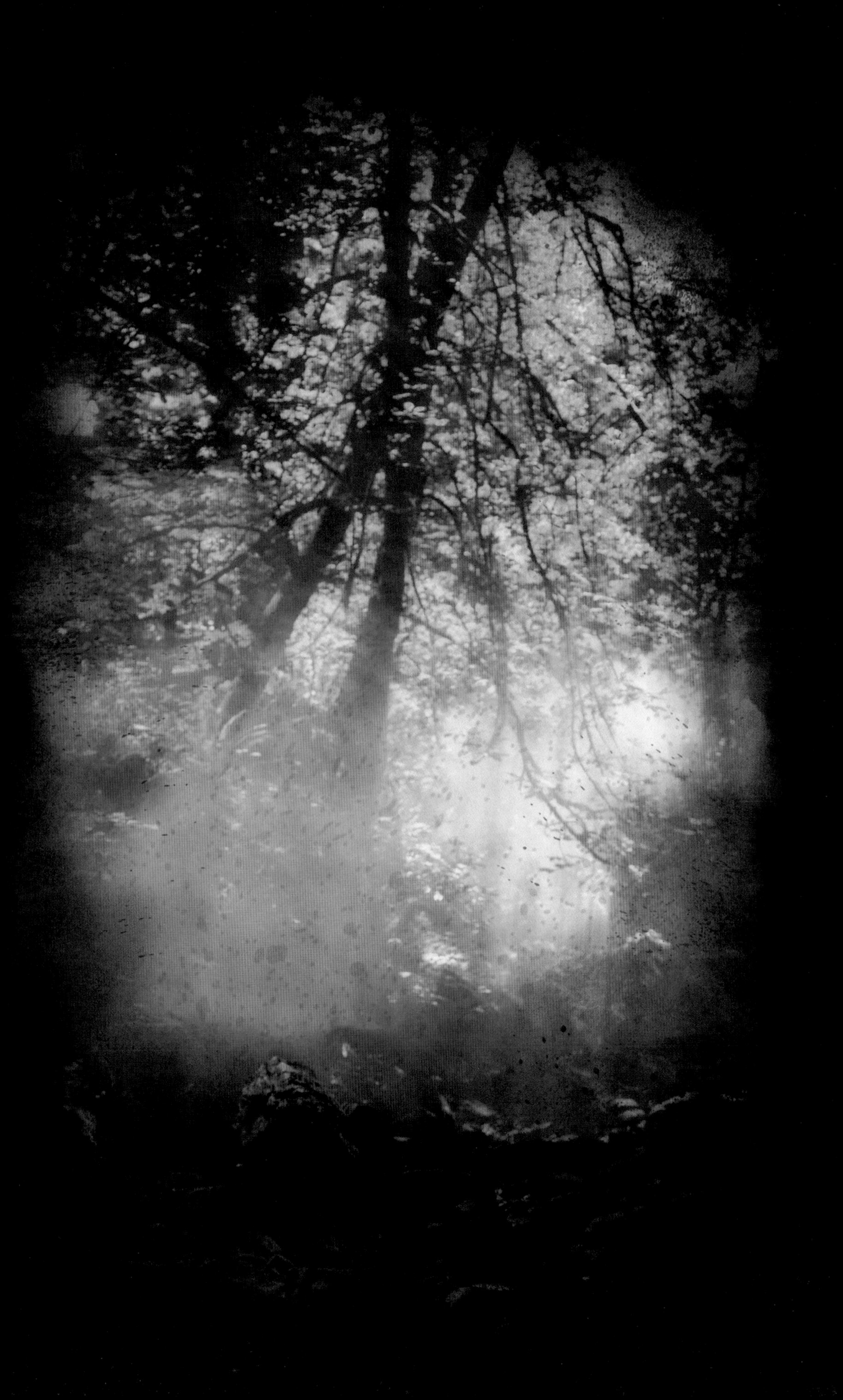

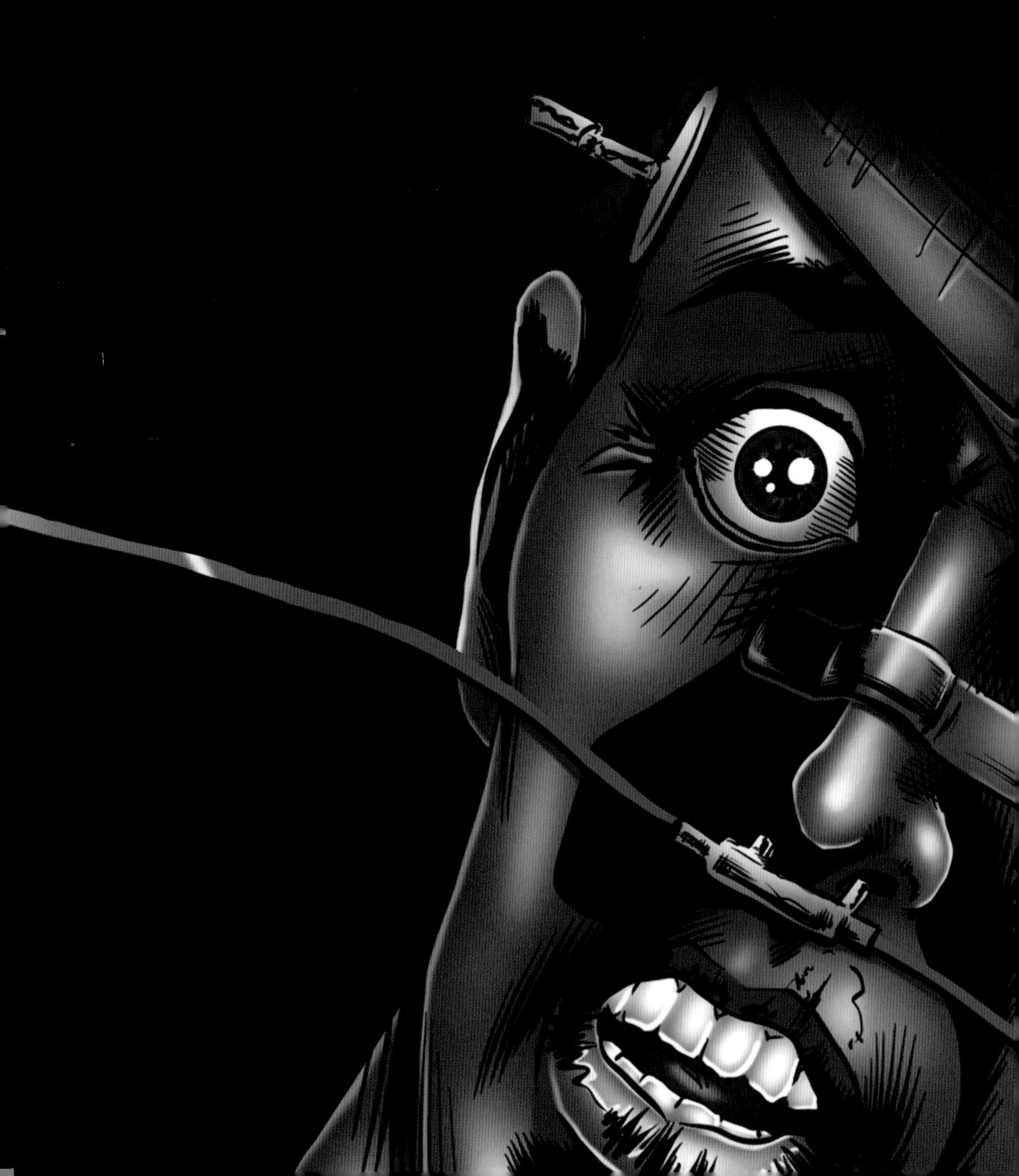

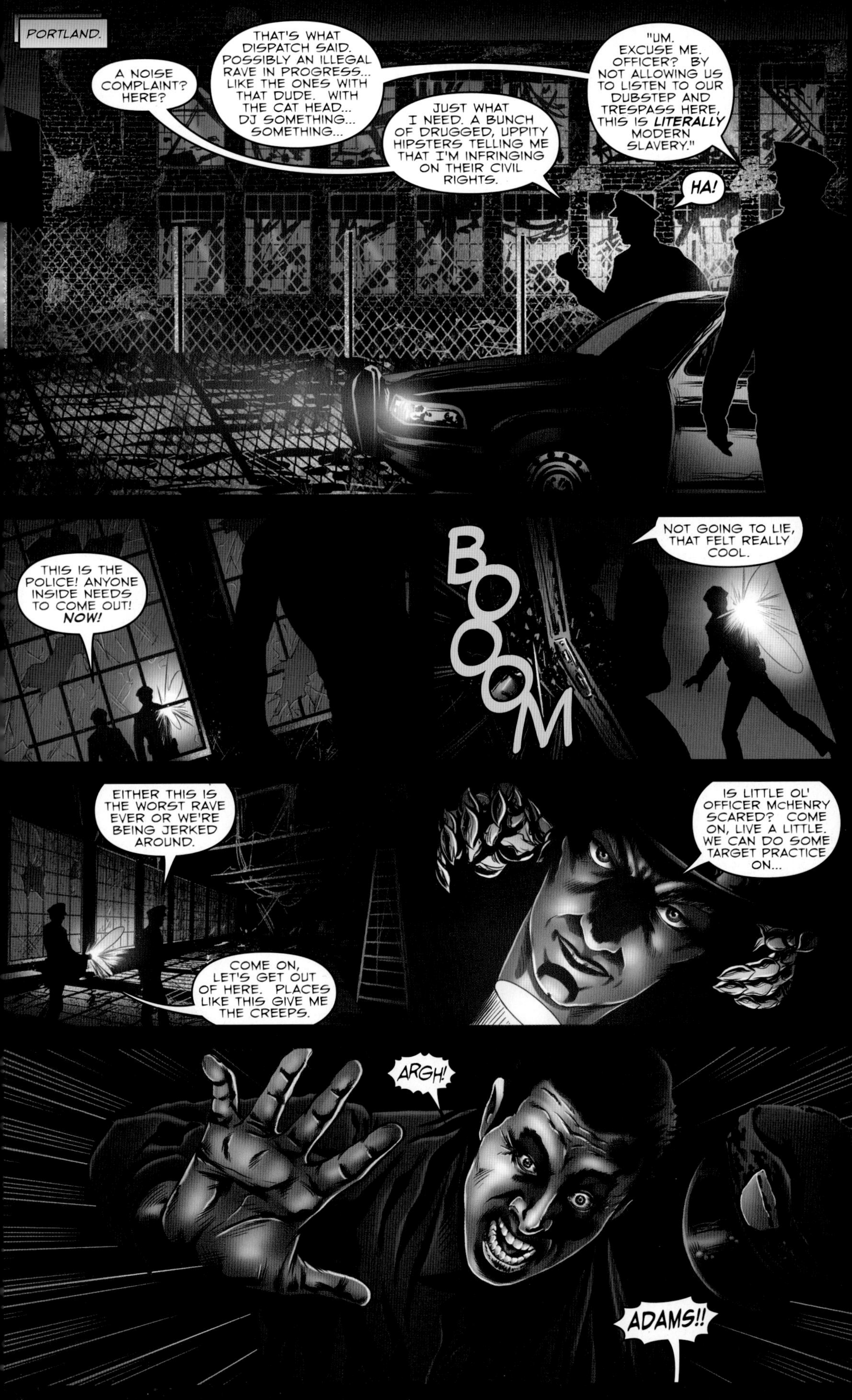
PORTLAND.
A NOISE COMPLAINT? HERE?
THAT'S WHAT DISPATCH SAID. POSSIBLY AN ILLEGAL RAVE IN PROGRESS... LIKE THE ONES WITH THAT DUDE. WITH THE CAT HEAD... DJ SOMETHING... SOMETHING...
JUST WHAT I NEED. A BUNCH OF DRUGGED, UPPITY HIPSTERS TELLING ME THAT I'M INFRINGING ON THEIR CIVIL RIGHTS.
"UM. EXCUSE ME. OFFICER? BY NOT ALLOWING US TO LISTEN TO OUR DUBSTEP AND TRESPASS HERE, THIS IS *LITERALLY* MODERN SLAVERY."
HA!
THIS IS THE POLICE! ANYONE INSIDE NEEDS TO COME OUT! *NOW!*
BOOOOM
NOT GOING TO LIE, THAT FELT REALLY COOL.
EITHER THIS IS THE WORST RAVE EVER OR WE'RE BEING JERKED AROUND.
COME ON, LET'S GET OUT OF HERE. PLACES LIKE THIS GIVE ME THE CREEPS.
IS LITTLE OL' OFFICER MCHENRY SCARED? COME ON, LIVE A LITTLE. WE CAN DO SOME TARGET PRACTICE ON...
ARGH!
ADAMS!!

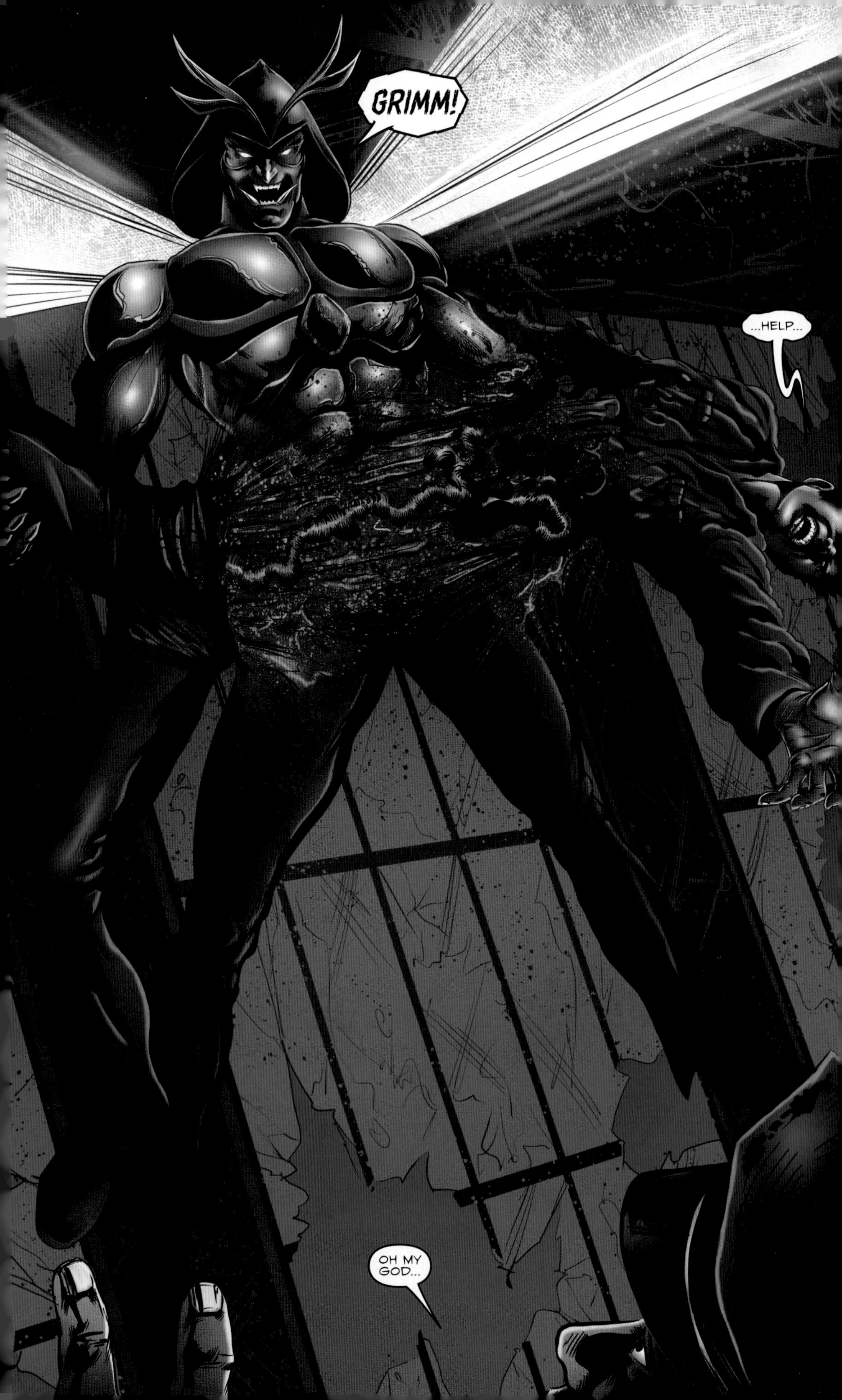
GRIMM!
...HELP...
OH MY GOD...

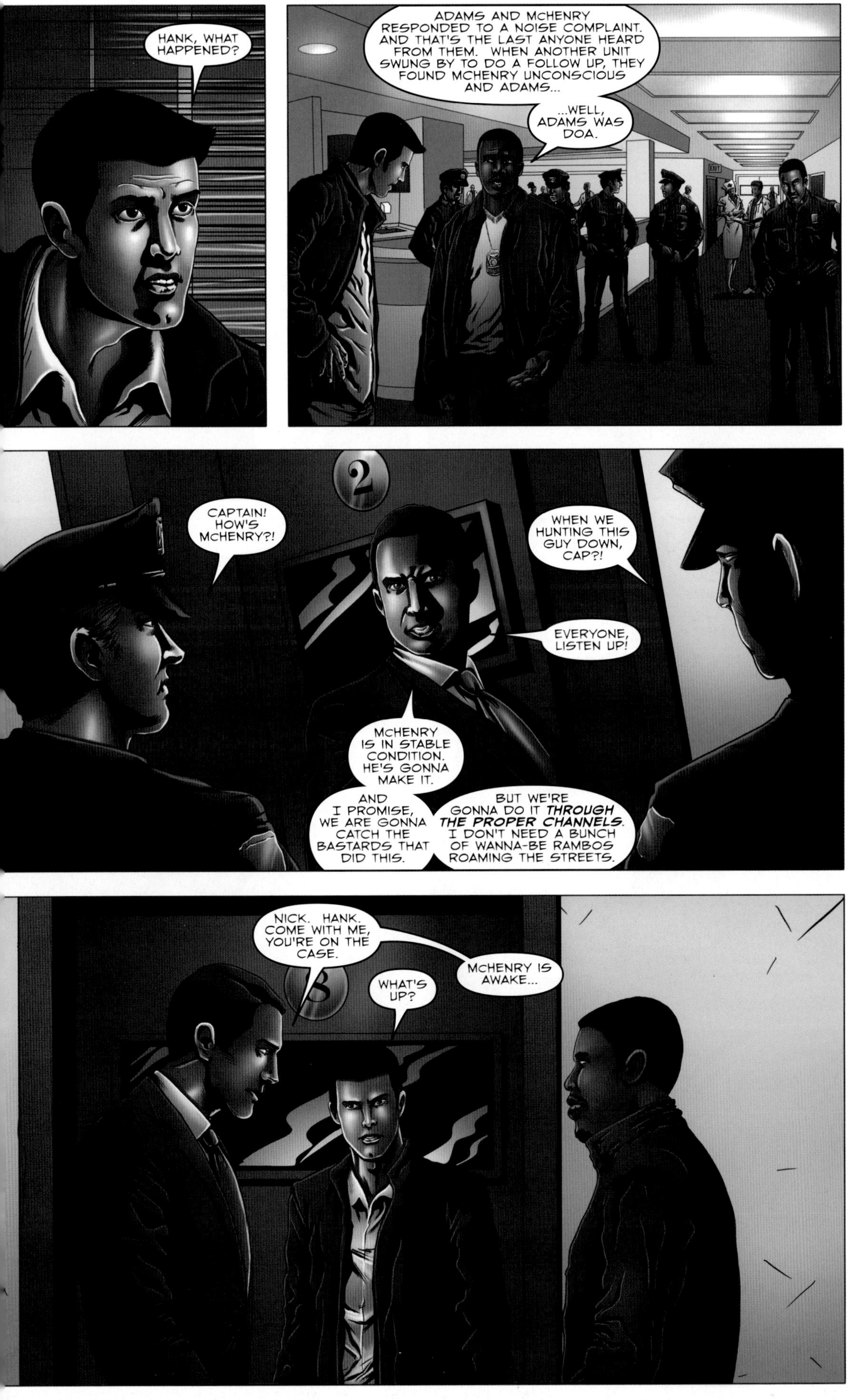
HANK, WHAT HAPPENED?
ADAMS AND MCHENRY RESPONDED TO A NOISE COMPLAINT. AND THAT'S THE LAST ANYONE HEARD FROM THEM. WHEN ANOTHER UNIT SWUNG BY TO DO A FOLLOW UP, THEY FOUND MCHENRY UNCONSCIOUS AND ADAMS...
...WELL, ADAMS WAS DOA.
EXIT
2
CAPTAIN! HOW'S McHENRY?!
WHEN WE HUNTING THIS GUY DOWN, CAP?!
EVERYONE, LISTEN UP!
McHENRY IS IN STABLE CONDITION. HE'S GONNA MAKE IT.
AND I PROMISE, WE ARE GONNA CATCH THE BASTARDS THAT DID THIS.
BUT WE'RE GONNA DO IT ***THROUGH THE PROPER CHANNELS***. I DON'T NEED A BUNCH OF WANNA-BE RAMBOS ROAMING THE STREETS.
NICK. HANK. COME WITH ME, YOU'RE ON THE CASE.
WHAT'S UP?
McHENRY IS AWAKE...

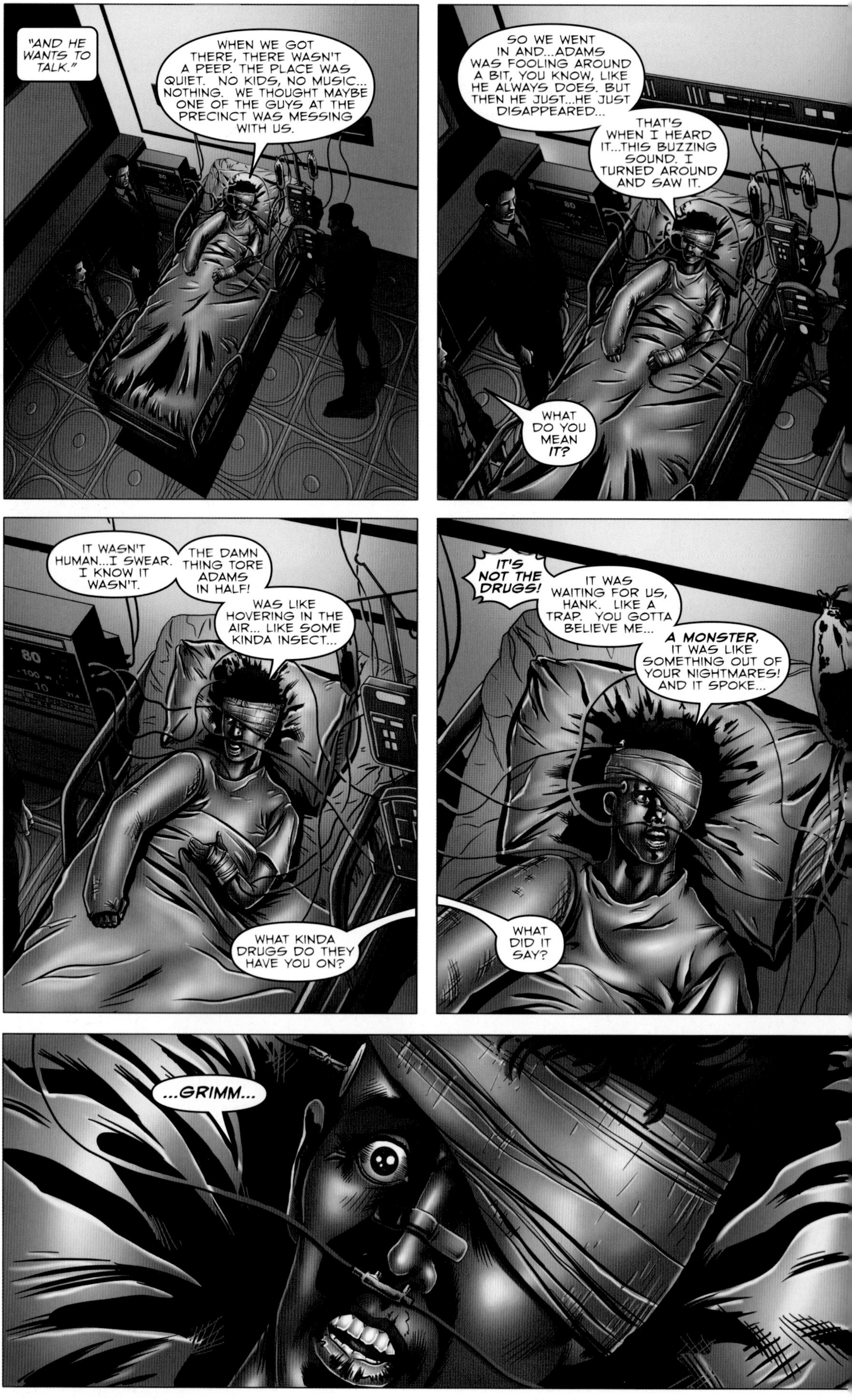
"AND HE WANTS TO TALK."
WHEN WE GOT THERE, THERE WASN'T A PEEP. THE PLACE WAS QUIET. NO KIDS, NO MUSIC... NOTHING. WE THOUGHT MAYBE ONE OF THE GUYS AT THE PRECINCT WAS MESSING WITH US.
SO WE WENT IN AND...ADAMS WAS FOOLING AROUND A BIT, YOU KNOW, LIKE HE ALWAYS DOES. BUT THEN HE JUST...HE JUST DISAPPEARED...
THAT'S WHEN I HEARD IT...THIS BUZZING SOUND. I TURNED AROUND AND SAW IT.
WHAT DO YOU MEAN IT?
IT WASN'T HUMAN...I SWEAR. I KNOW IT WASN'T.
THE DAMN THING TORE ADAMS IN HALF!
WAS LIKE HOVERING IN THE AIR... LIKE SOME KINDA INSECT...
WHAT KINDA DRUGS DO THEY HAVE YOU ON?
IT'S NOT THE DRUGS!
IT WAS WAITING FOR US, HANK. LIKE A TRAP. YOU GOTTA BELIEVE ME...
A MONSTER, IT WAS LIKE SOMETHING OUT OF YOUR NIGHTMARES! AND IT SPOKE...
WHAT DID IT SAY?
...GRIMM...

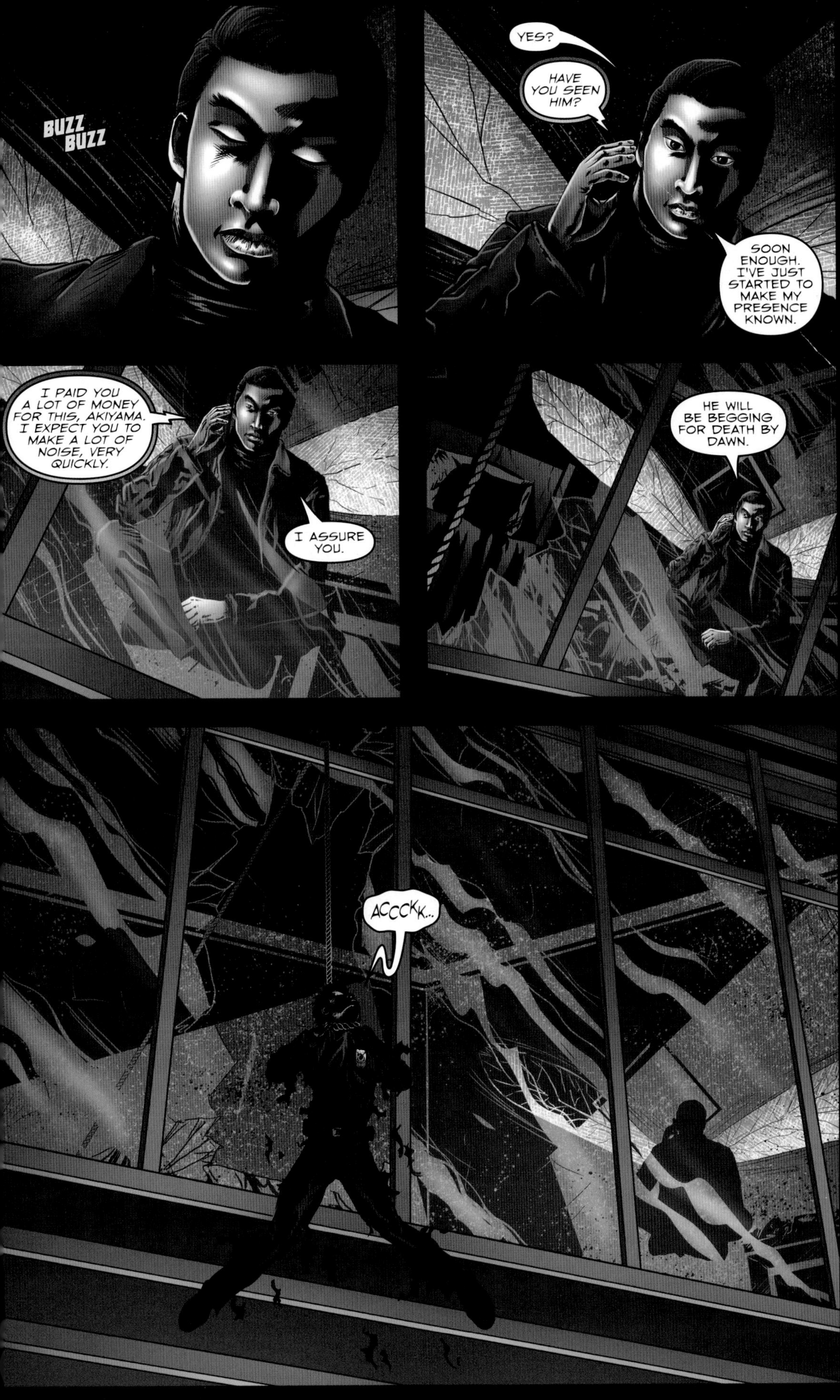
BUZZ BUZZ
YES?
HAVE YOU SEEN HIM?
SOON ENOUGH. I'VE JUST STARTED TO MAKE MY PRESENCE KNOWN.
I PAID YOU A LOT OF MONEY FOR THIS, AKIYAMA. I EXPECT YOU TO MAKE A LOT OF NOISE, VERY QUICKLY.
I ASSURE YOU.
HE WILL BE BEGGING FOR DEATH BY DAWN.
ACCCKK...

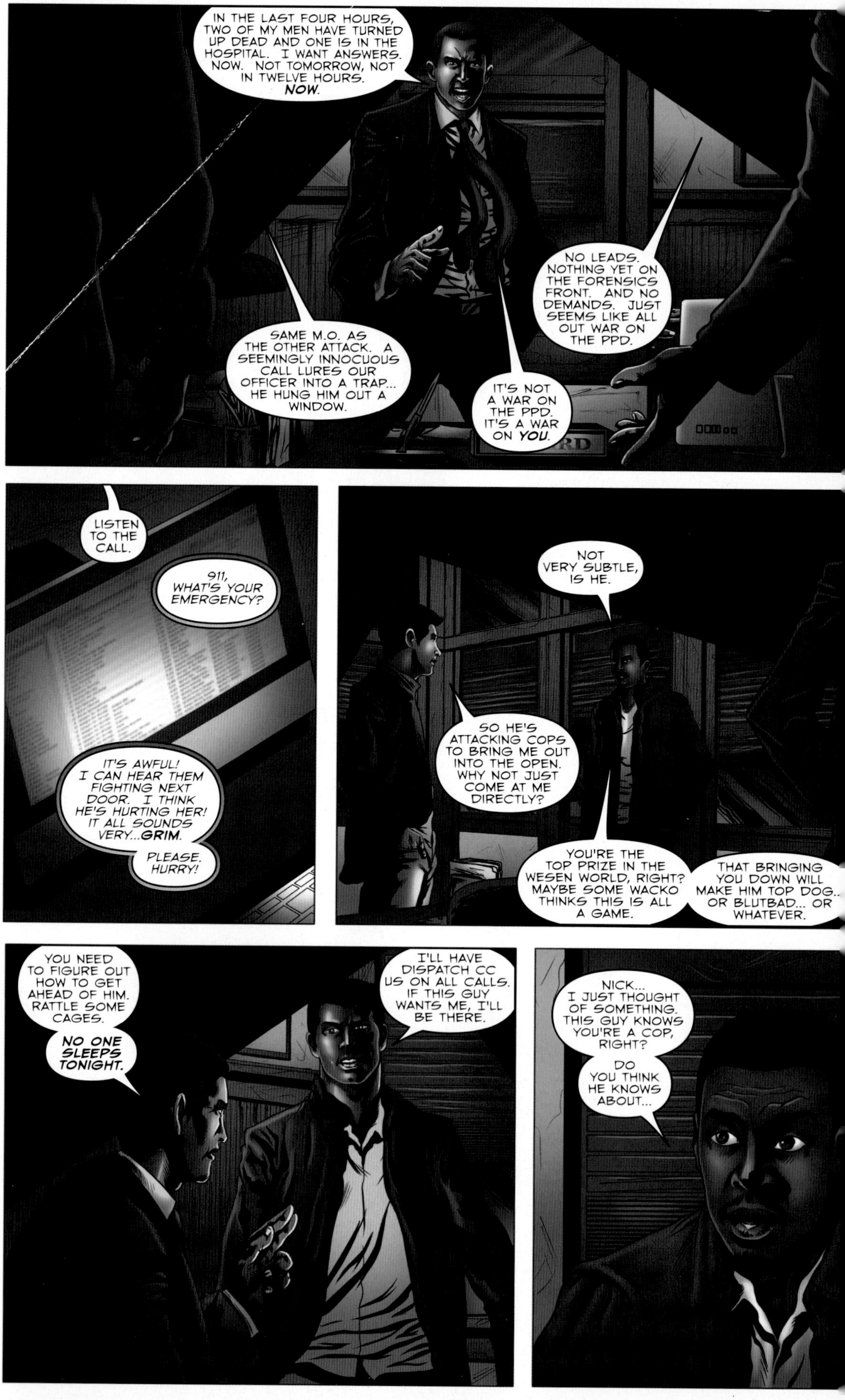
IN THE LAST FOUR HOURS, TWO OF MY MEN HAVE TURNED UP DEAD AND ONE IS IN THE HOSPITAL. I WANT ANSWERS. NOW. NOT TOMORROW, NOT IN TWELVE HOURS. NOW.
SAME M.O. AS THE OTHER ATTACK. A SEEMINGLY INNOCUOUS CALL LURES OUR OFFICER INTO A TRAP... HE HUNG HIM OUT A WINDOW.
NO LEADS. NOTHING YET ON THE FORENSICS FRONT. AND NO DEMANDS. JUST SEEMS LIKE ALL OUT WAR ON THE PPD.
IT'S NOT A WAR ON THE PPD. IT'S A WAR ON YOU.
LISTEN TO THE CALL.
911, WHAT'S YOUR EMERGENCY?
IT'S AWFUL! I CAN HEAR THEM FIGHTING NEXT DOOR. I THINK HE'S HURTING HER! IT ALL SOUNDS VERY...GRIM.
PLEASE. HURRY!
NOT VERY SUBTLE, IS HE.
SO HE'S ATTACKING COPS TO BRING ME OUT INTO THE OPEN. WHY NOT JUST COME AT ME DIRECTLY?
YOU'RE THE TOP PRIZE IN THE WESEN WORLD, RIGHT? MAYBE SOME WACKO THINKS THIS IS ALL A GAME.
THAT BRINGING YOU DOWN WILL MAKE HIM TOP DOG... OR BLUTBAD... OR WHATEVER.
YOU NEED TO FIGURE OUT HOW TO GET AHEAD OF HIM. RATTLE SOME CAGES.
NO ONE SLEEPS TONIGHT.
I'LL HAVE DISPATCH CC US ON ALL CALLS. IF THIS GUY WANTS ME, I'LL BE THERE.
NICK... I JUST THOUGHT OF SOMETHING. THIS GUY KNOWS YOU'RE A COP, RIGHT?
DO YOU THINK HE KNOWS ABOUT...

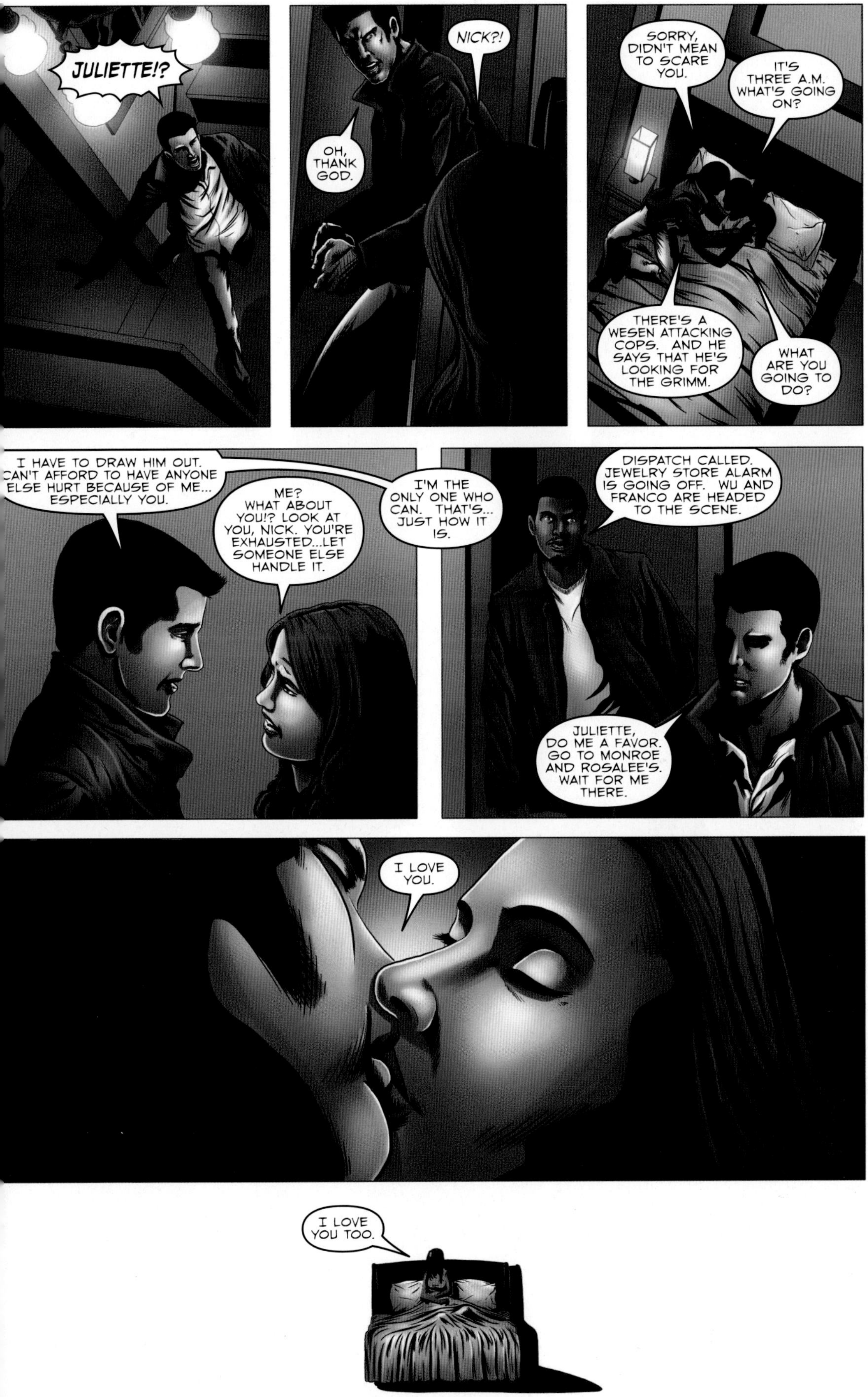
JULIETTE!?
NICK?!
OH, THANK GOD.
SORRY, DIDN'T MEAN TO SCARE YOU.
IT'S THREE A.M. WHAT'S GOING ON?
THERE'S A WESEN ATTACKING COPS. AND HE SAYS THAT HE'S LOOKING FOR THE GRIMM.
WHAT ARE YOU GOING TO DO?
I HAVE TO DRAW HIM OUT. CAN'T AFFORD TO HAVE ANYONE ELSE HURT BECAUSE OF ME... ESPECIALLY YOU.
ME? WHAT ABOUT YOU!? LOOK AT YOU, NICK. YOU'RE EXHAUSTED...LET SOMEONE ELSE HANDLE IT.
I'M THE ONLY ONE WHO CAN. THAT'S... JUST HOW IT IS.
DISPATCH CALLED. JEWELRY STORE ALARM IS GOING OFF. WU AND FRANCO ARE HEADED TO THE SCENE.
JULIETTE, DO ME A FAVOR. GO TO MONROE AND ROSALEE'S. WAIT FOR ME THERE.
I LOVE YOU.
I LOVE YOU TOO.

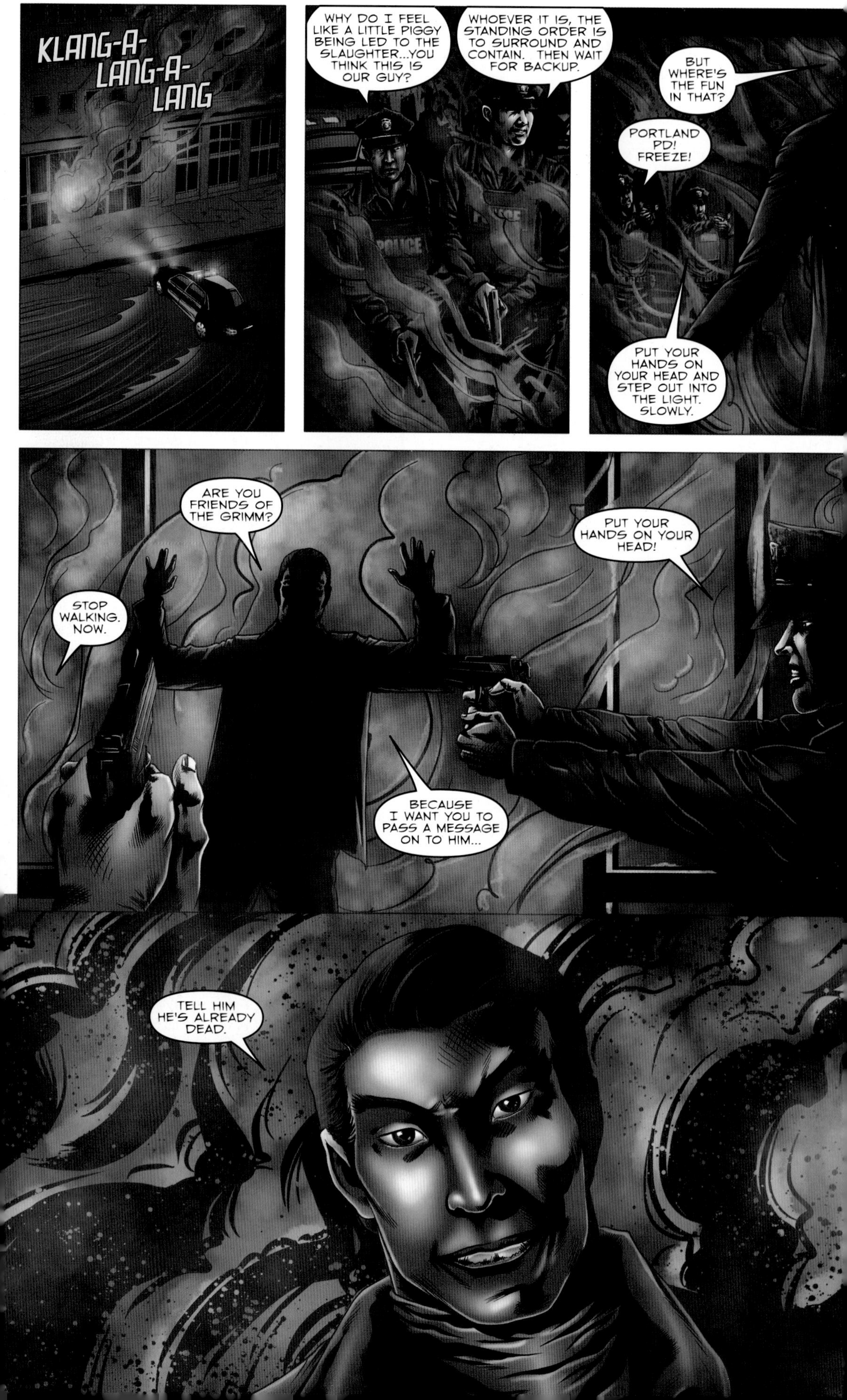
KLANG-A-LANG-A-LANG
WHY DO I FEEL LIKE A LITTLE PIGGY BEING LED TO THE SLAUGHTER...YOU THINK THIS IS OUR GUY?
WHOEVER IT IS, THE STANDING ORDER IS TO SURROUND AND CONTAIN. THEN WAIT FOR BACKUP.
BUT WHERE'S THE FUN IN THAT?
PORTLAND PD! FREEZE!
PUT YOUR HANDS ON YOUR HEAD AND STEP OUT INTO THE LIGHT. SLOWLY.
ARE YOU FRIENDS OF THE GRIMM?
PUT YOUR HANDS ON YOUR HEAD!
STOP WALKING. NOW.
BECAUSE I WANT YOU TO PASS A MESSAGE ON TO HIM...
TELL HIM HE'S ALREADY DEAD.

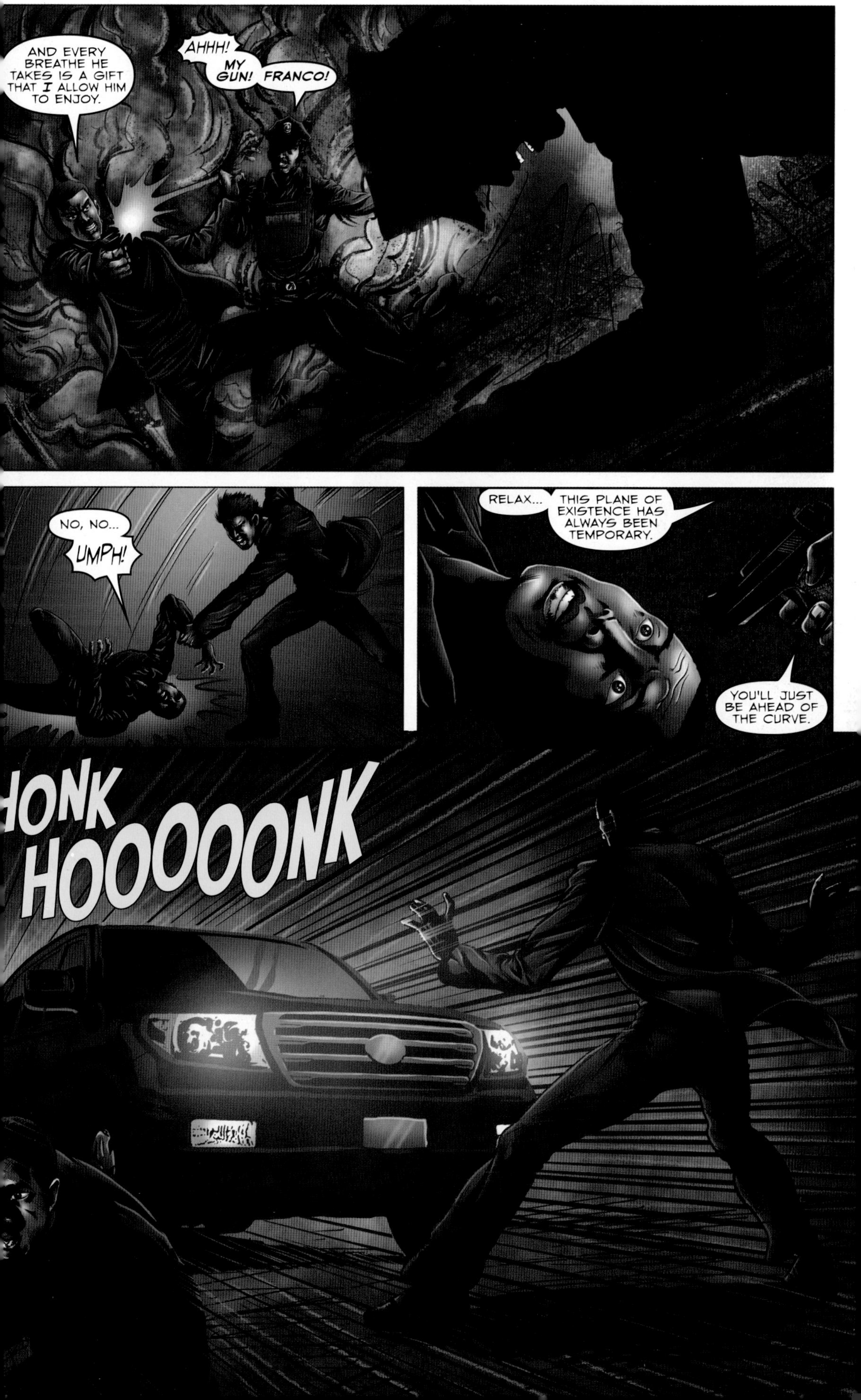

AND EVERY BREATHE HE TAKES IS A GIFT THAT I ALLOW HIM TO ENJOY.
AHHH! MY GUN!
FRANCO!
NO, NO...
UMPH!
RELAX...
THIS PLANE OF EXISTENCE HAS ALWAYS BEEN TEMPORARY.
YOU'LL JUST BE AHEAD OF THE CURVE.
HONK
HOOOOONK

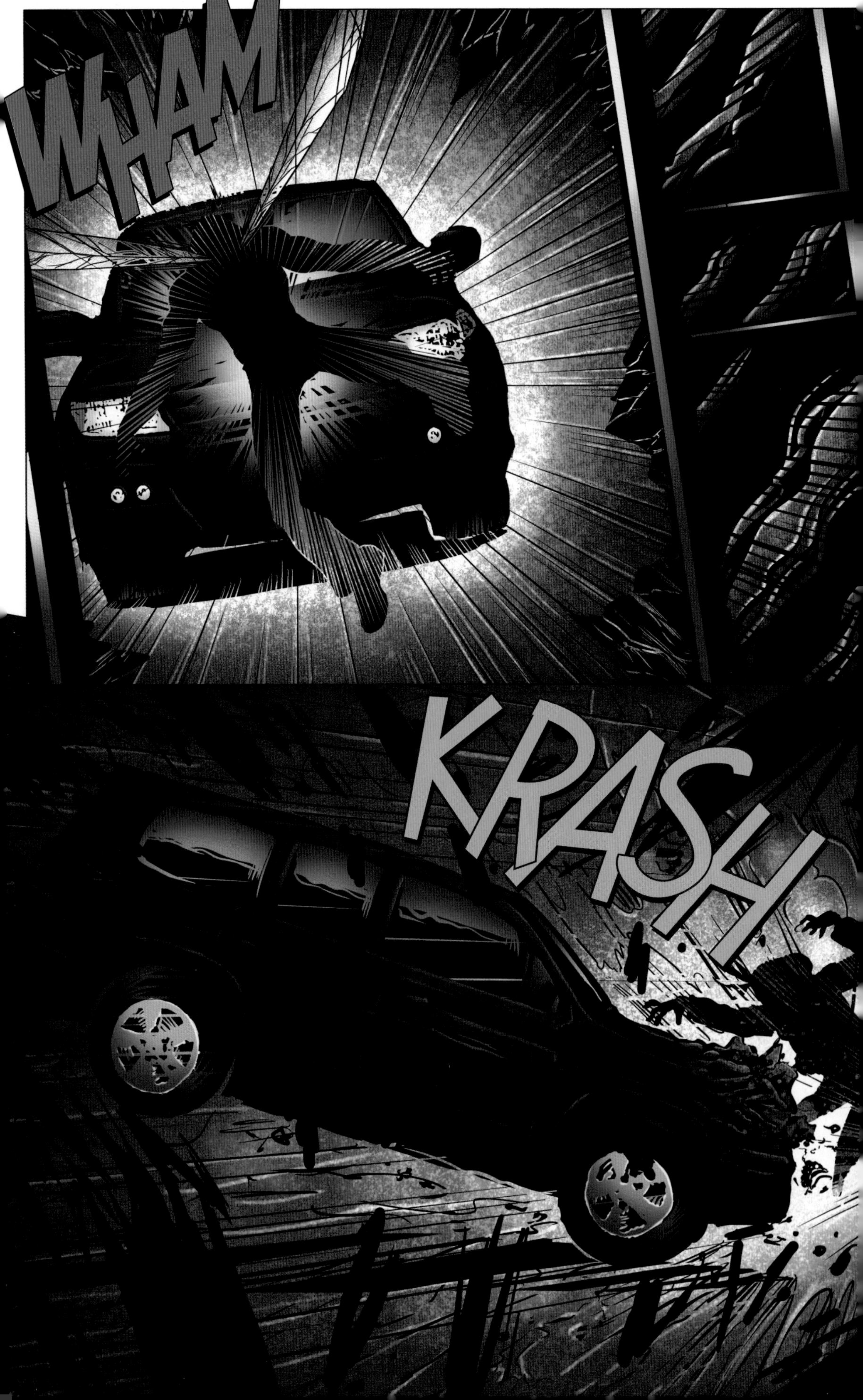
WHAM
KRASH

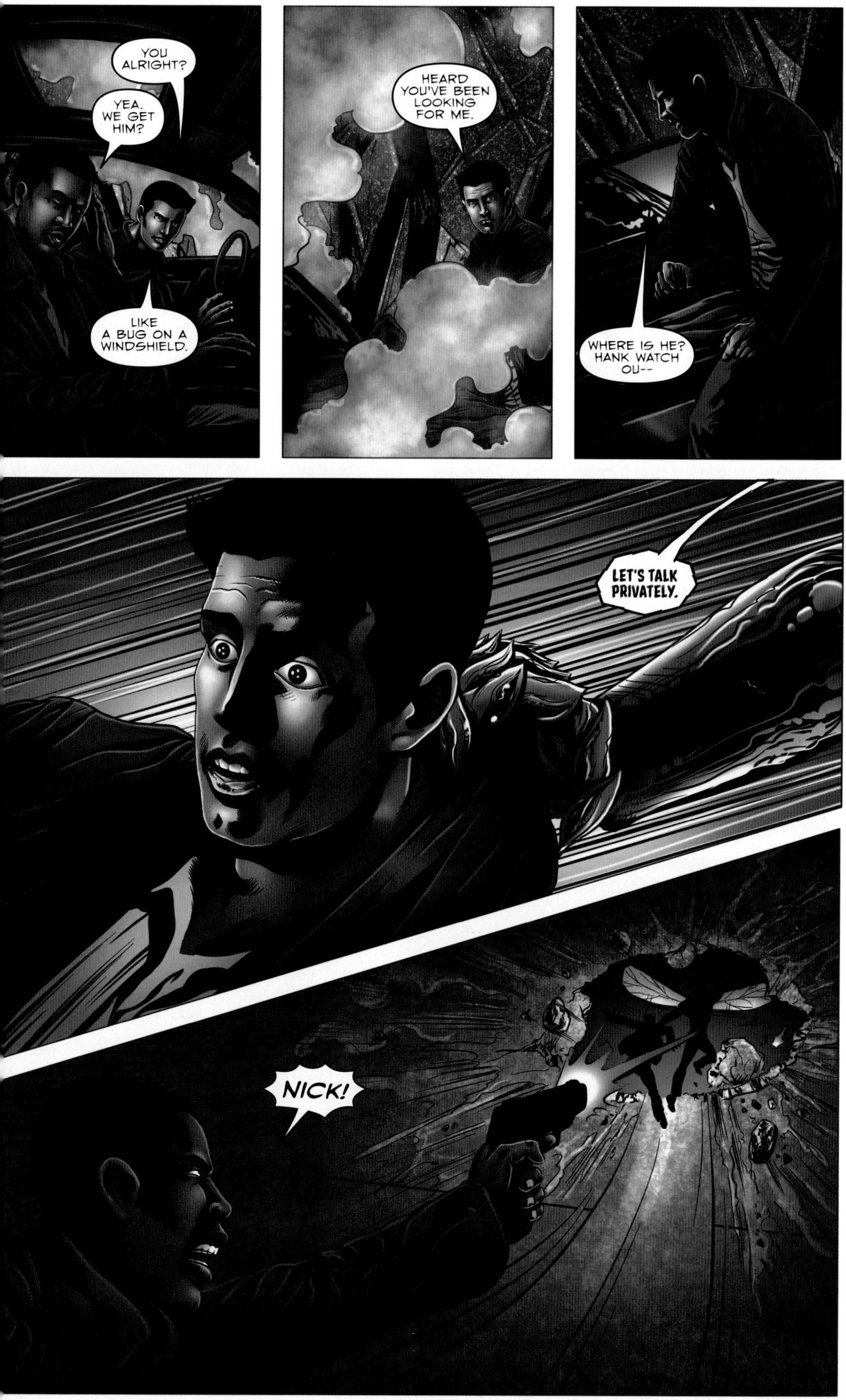
YOU ALRIGHT?
YEA. WE GET HIM?
LIKE A BUG ON A WINDSHIELD.
HEARD YOU'VE BEEN LOOKING FOR ME.
WHERE IS HE? HANK WATCH OU--
LET'S TALK PRIVATELY.
NICK!

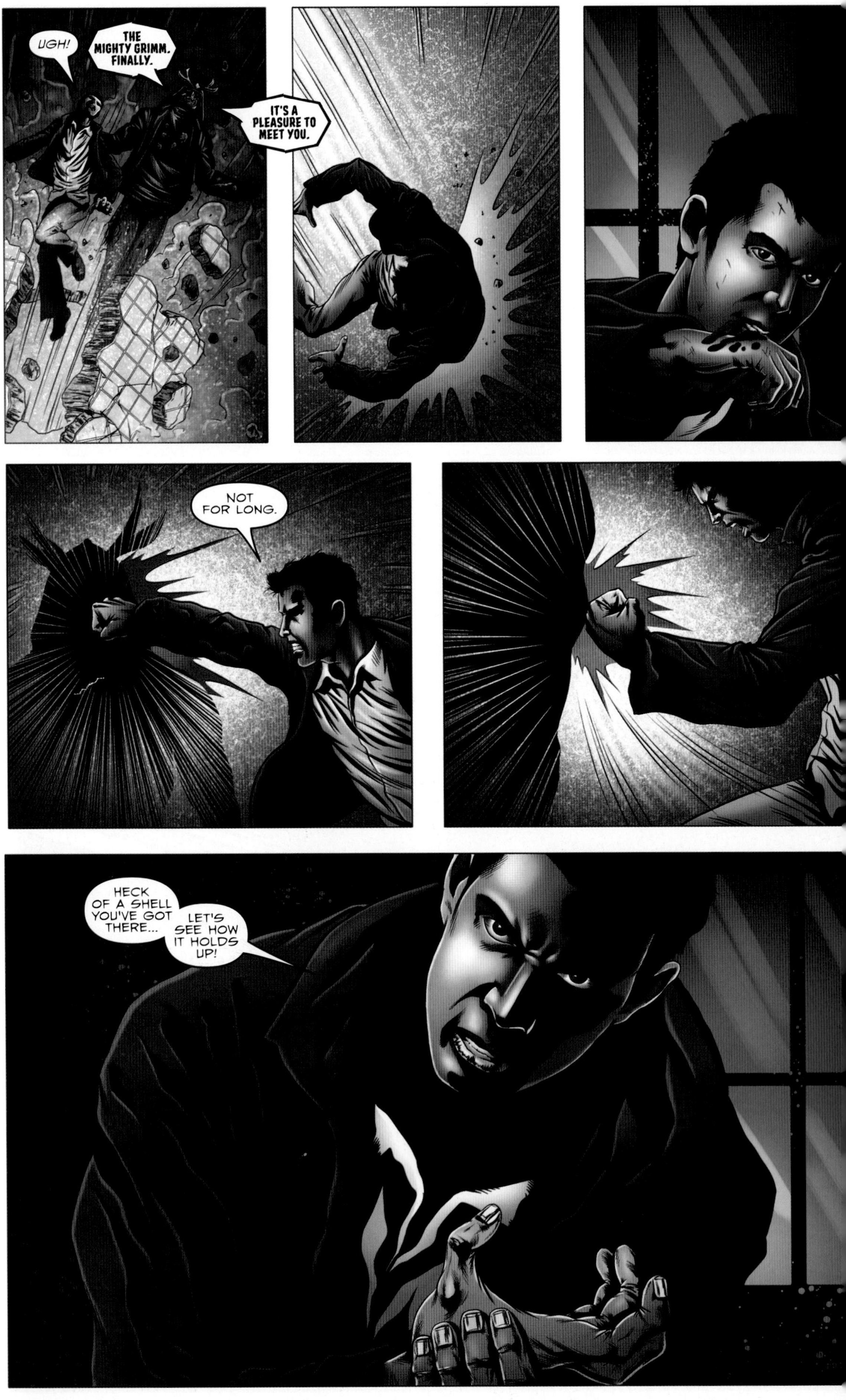
UGH!
THE MIGHTY GRIMM. FINALLY.
IT'S A PLEASURE TO MEET YOU.
NOT FOR LONG.
HECK OF A SHELL YOU'VE GOT THERE...
LET'S SEE HOW IT HOLDS UP!

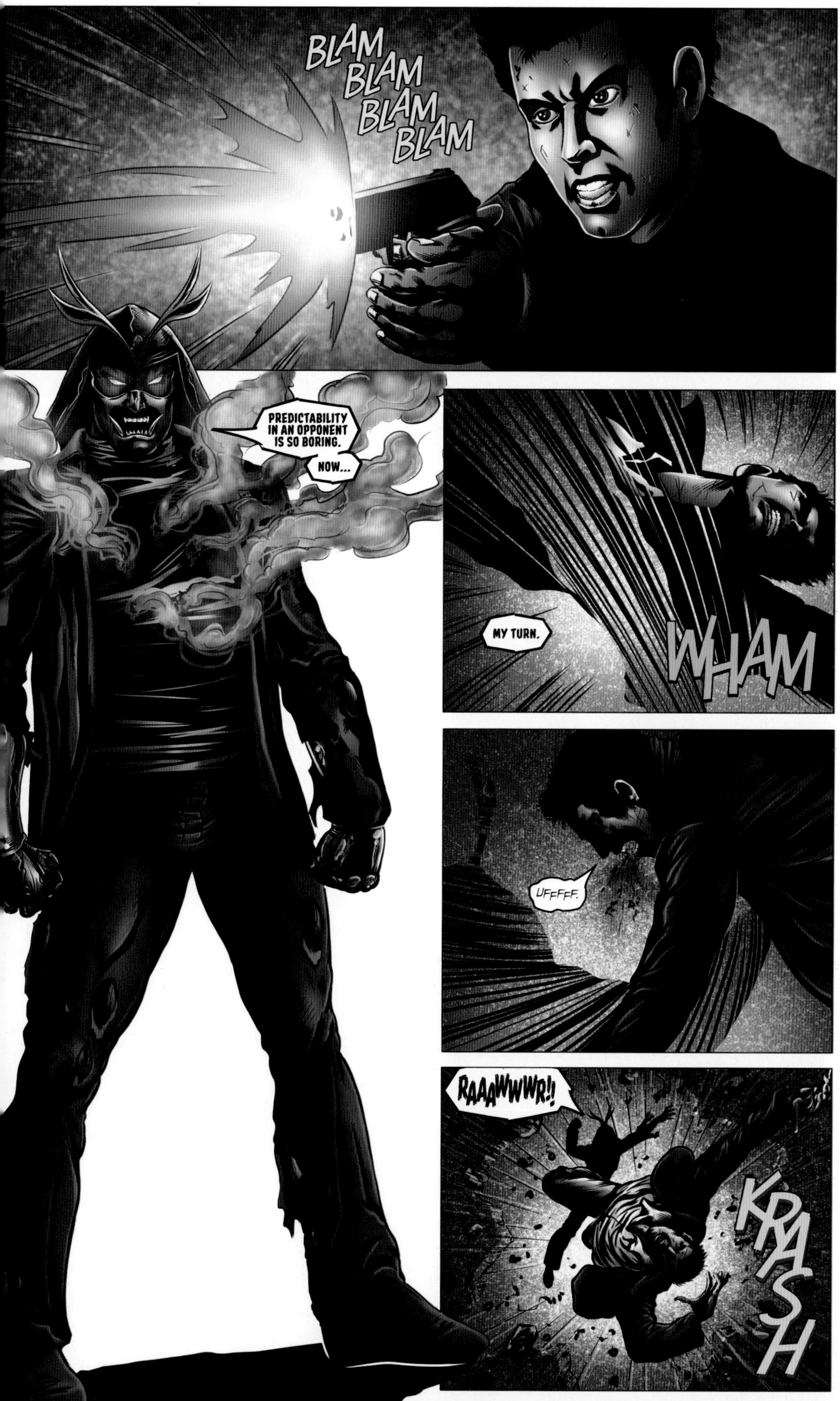
BLAM
BLAM
BLAM
BLAM
PREDICTABILITY IN AN OPPONENT IS SO BORING.
NOW...
MY TURN.
WHAM
UFFFFF.
RAAAWWWR!!
KRASH

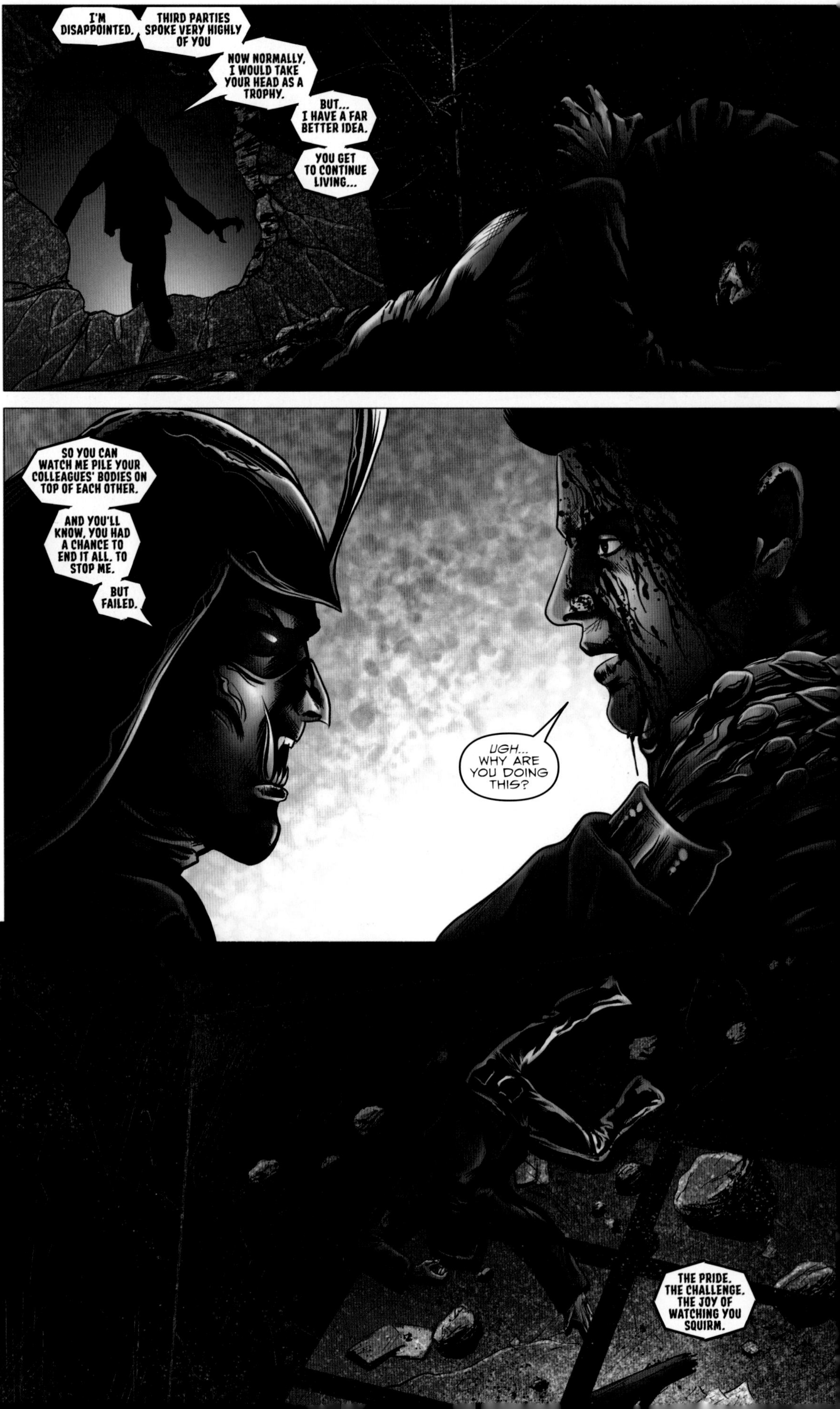
I'M DISAPPOINTED.
THIRD PARTIES SPOKE VERY HIGHLY OF YOU
NOW NORMALLY, I WOULD TAKE YOUR HEAD AS A TROPHY.
BUT... I HAVE A FAR BETTER IDEA.
YOU GET TO CONTINUE LIVING...
SO YOU CAN WATCH ME PILE YOUR COLLEAGUES' BODIES ON TOP OF EACH OTHER.
AND YOU'LL KNOW, YOU HAD A CHANCE TO END IT ALL. TO STOP ME.
BUT FAILED.
UGH... WHY ARE YOU DOING THIS?
THE PRIDE. THE CHALLENGE. THE JOY OF WATCHING YOU SQUIRM.

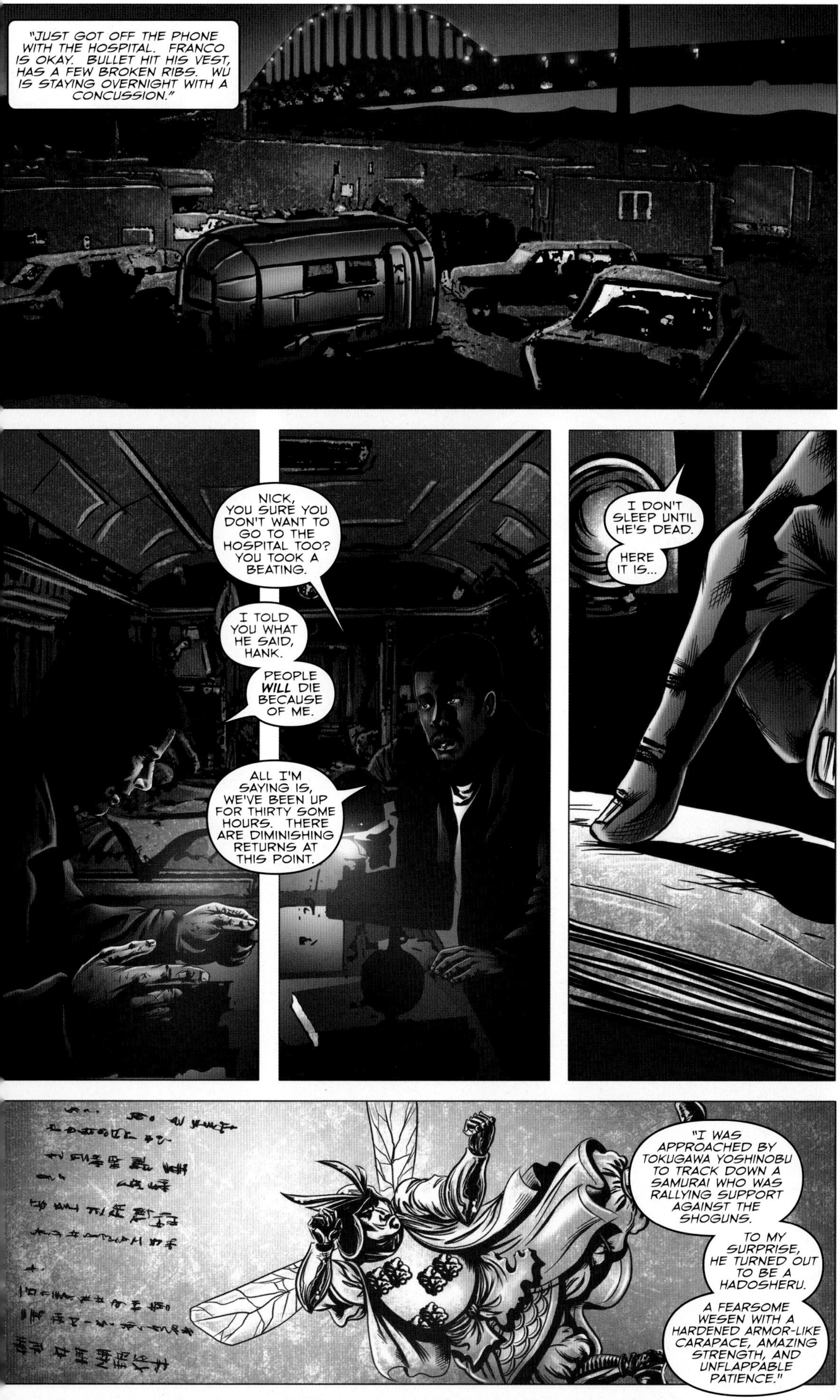
"JUST GOT OFF THE PHONE WITH THE HOSPITAL. FRANCO IS OKAY. BULLET HIT HIS VEST, HAS A FEW BROKEN RIBS. WU IS STAYING OVERNIGHT WITH A CONCUSSION."
NICK, YOU SURE YOU DON'T WANT TO GO TO THE HOSPITAL TOO? YOU TOOK A BEATING.
I TOLD YOU WHAT HE SAID, HANK.
PEOPLE **WILL** DIE BECAUSE OF ME.
ALL I'M SAYING IS, WE'VE BEEN UP FOR THIRTY SOME HOURS. THERE ARE DIMINISHING RETURNS AT THIS POINT.
I DON'T SLEEP UNTIL HE'S DEAD.
HERE IT IS...
"I WAS APPROACHED BY TOKUGAWA YOSHINOBU TO TRACK DOWN A SAMURAI WHO WAS RALLYING SUPPORT AGAINST THE SHOGUNS.
TO MY SURPRISE, HE TURNED OUT TO BE A HADOSHERU.
A FEARSOME WESEN WITH A HARDENED ARMOR-LIKE CARAPACE, AMAZING STRENGTH, AND UNFLAPPABLE PATIENCE."

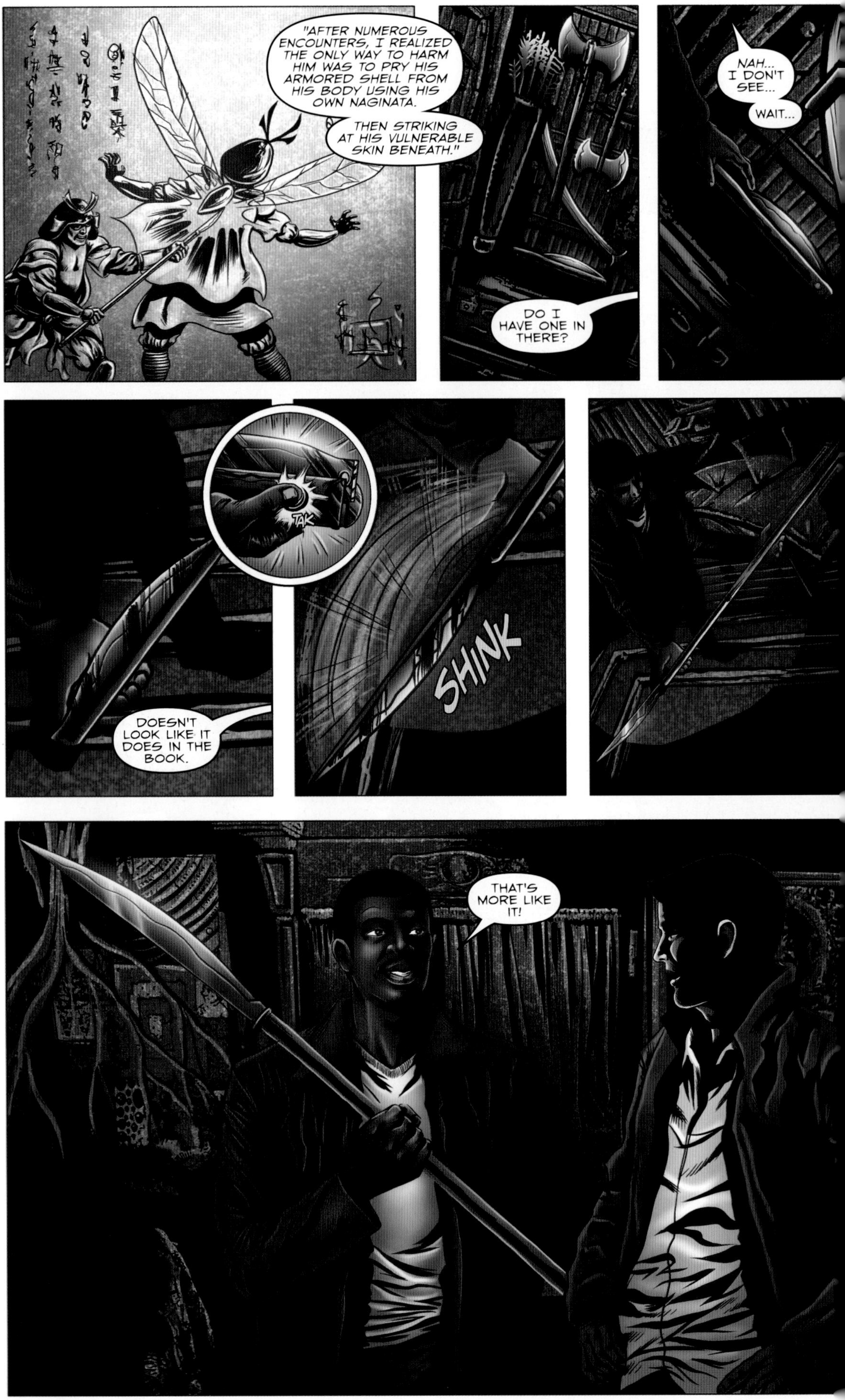
"AFTER NUMEROUS ENCOUNTERS, I REALIZED THE ONLY WAY TO HARM HIM WAS TO PRY HIS ARMORED SHELL FROM HIS BODY USING HIS OWN NAGINATA.
THEN STRIKING AT HIS VULNERABLE SKIN BENEATH."
DO I HAVE ONE IN THERE?
NAH... I DON'T SEE...
WAIT...
TAK
DOESN'T LOOK LIKE IT DOES IN THE BOOK.
SHINK
THAT'S MORE LIKE IT!

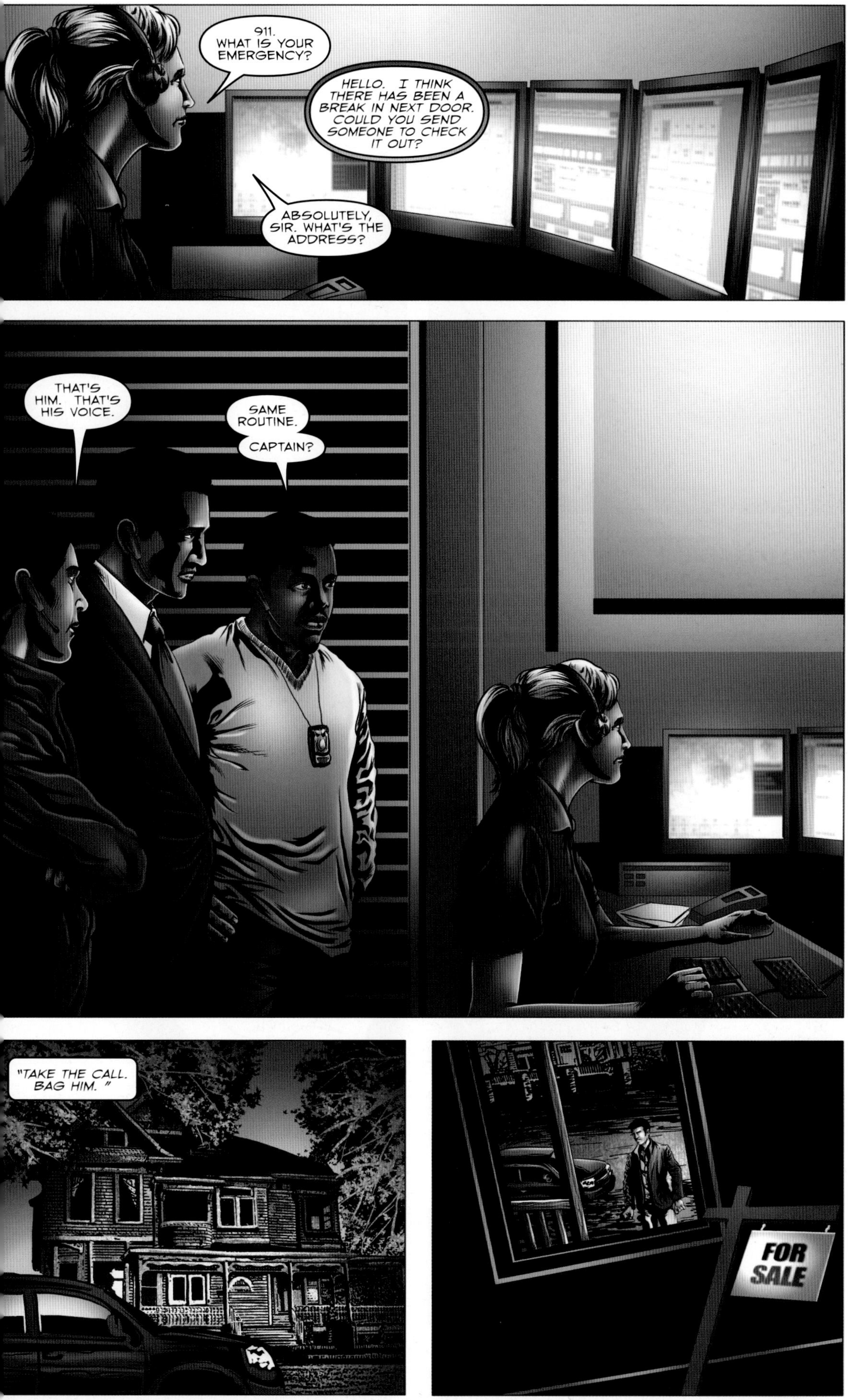
911. WHAT IS YOUR EMERGENCY?
HELLO. I THINK THERE HAS BEEN A BREAK IN NEXT DOOR. COULD YOU SEND SOMEONE TO CHECK IT OUT?
ABSOLUTELY, SIR. WHAT'S THE ADDRESS?
THAT'S HIM. THAT'S HIS VOICE.
SAME ROUTINE.
CAPTAIN?
"TAKE THE CALL. BAG HIM."
FOR SALE

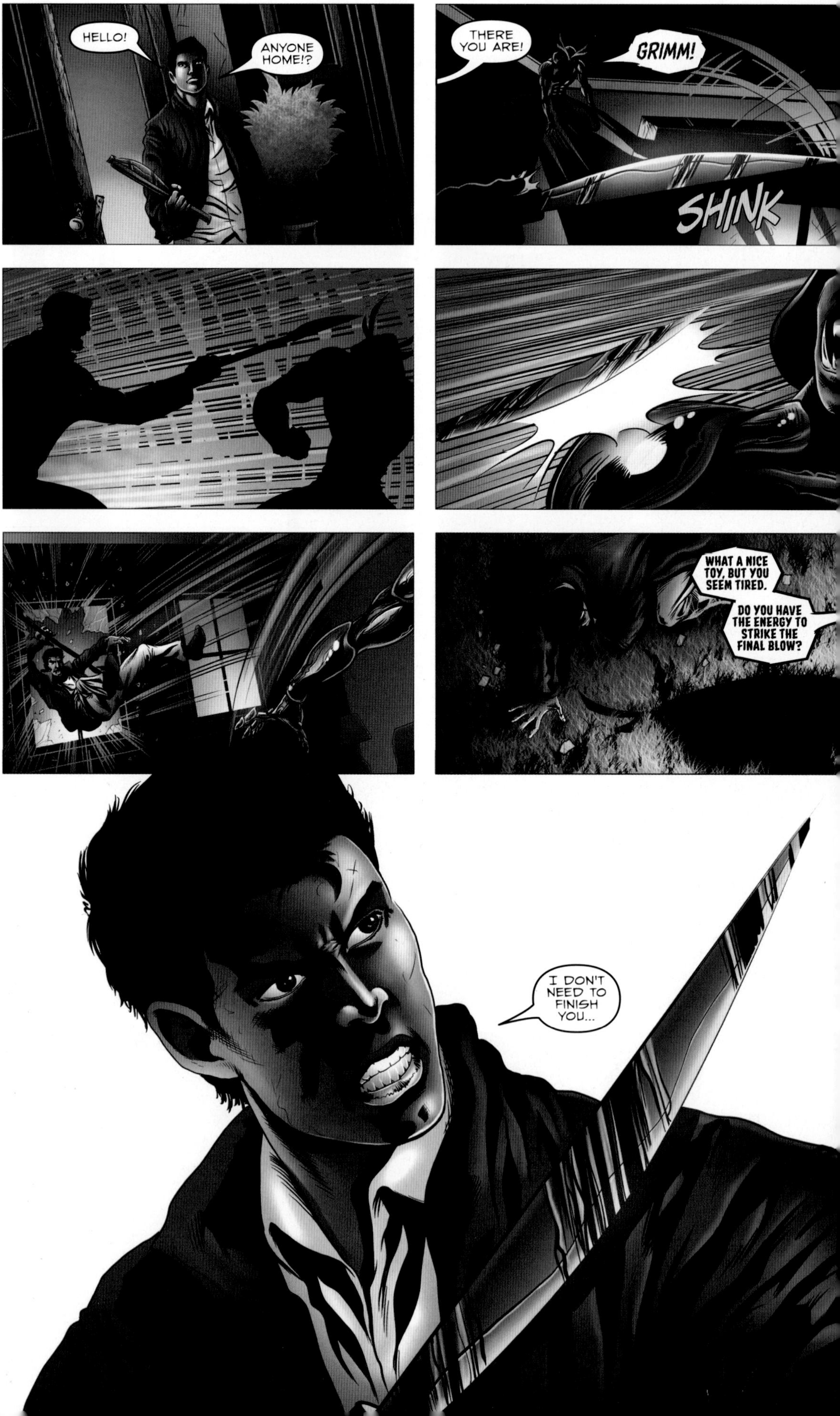
HELLO!
ANYONE HOME!?
THERE YOU ARE!
GRIMM!
SHINK
WHAT A NICE TOY, BUT YOU SEEM TIRED.
DO YOU HAVE THE ENERGY TO STRIKE THE FINAL BLOW?
I DON'T NEED TO FINISH YOU...

I JUST HAVE TO DO THE PREP WORK!

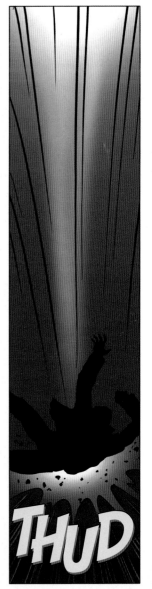

THUD

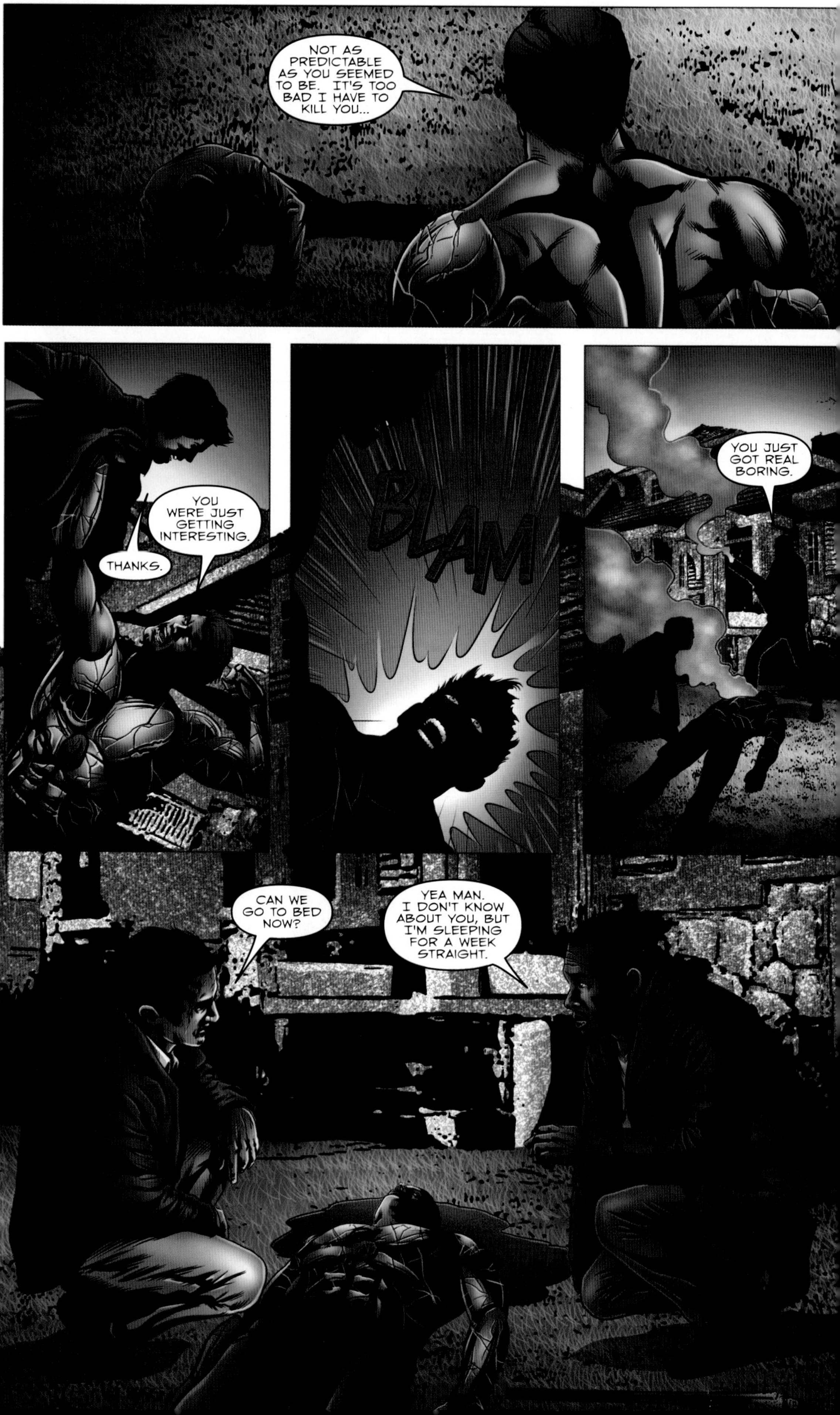
NOT AS PREDICTABLE AS YOU SEEMED TO BE. IT'S TOO BAD I HAVE TO KILL YOU...
YOU WERE JUST GETTING INTERESTING.
THANKS.
BLAM
YOU JUST GOT REAL BORING.
CAN WE GO TO BED NOW?
YEA MAN. I DON'T KNOW ABOUT YOU, BUT I'M SLEEPING FOR A WEEK STRAIGHT.

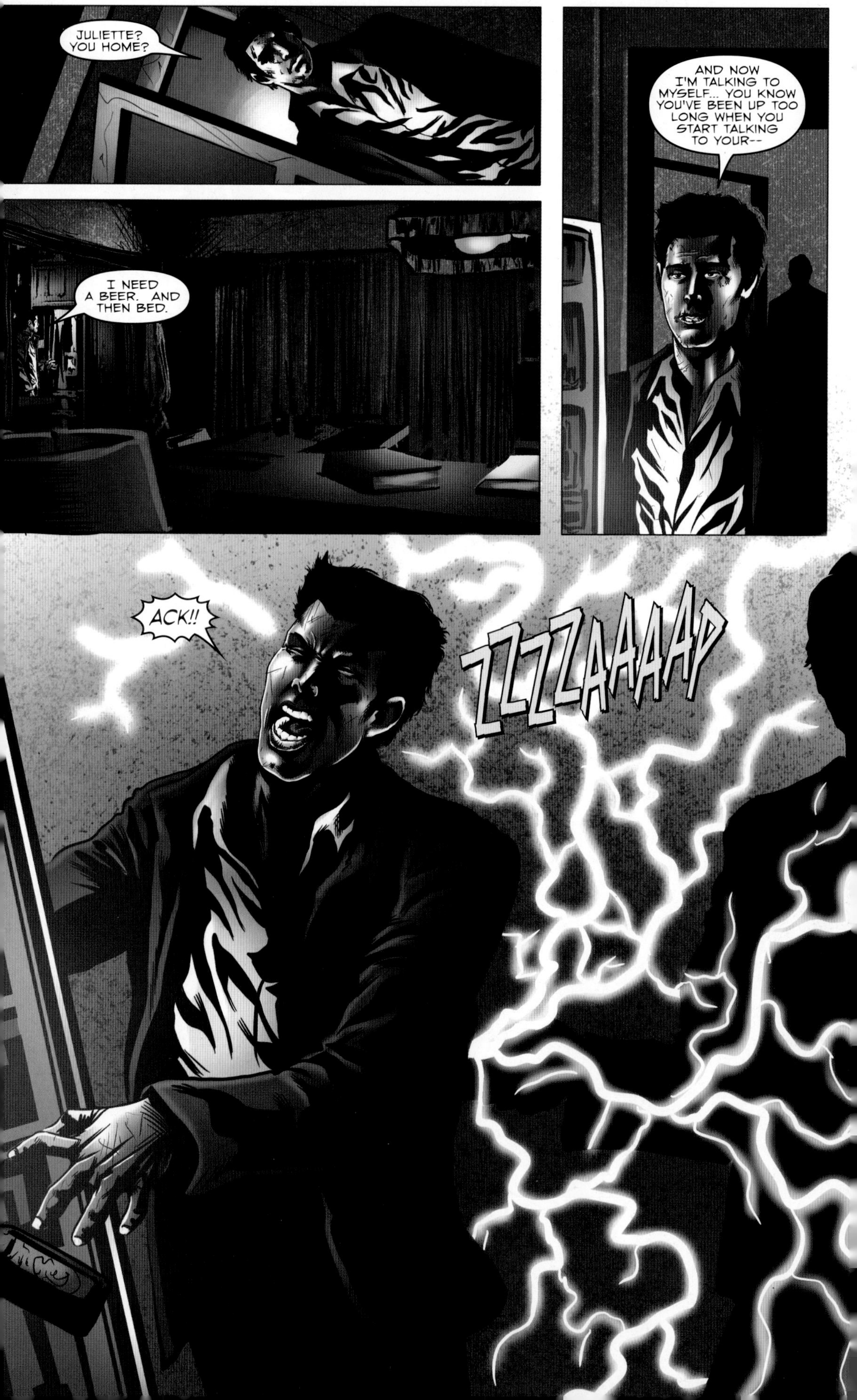

JULIETTE? YOU HOME?
I NEED A BEER. AND THEN BED.
AND NOW I'M TALKING TO MYSELF... YOU KNOW YOU'VE BEEN UP TOO LONG WHEN YOU START TALKING TO YOUR--
ACK!!
ZZZZAAAAP

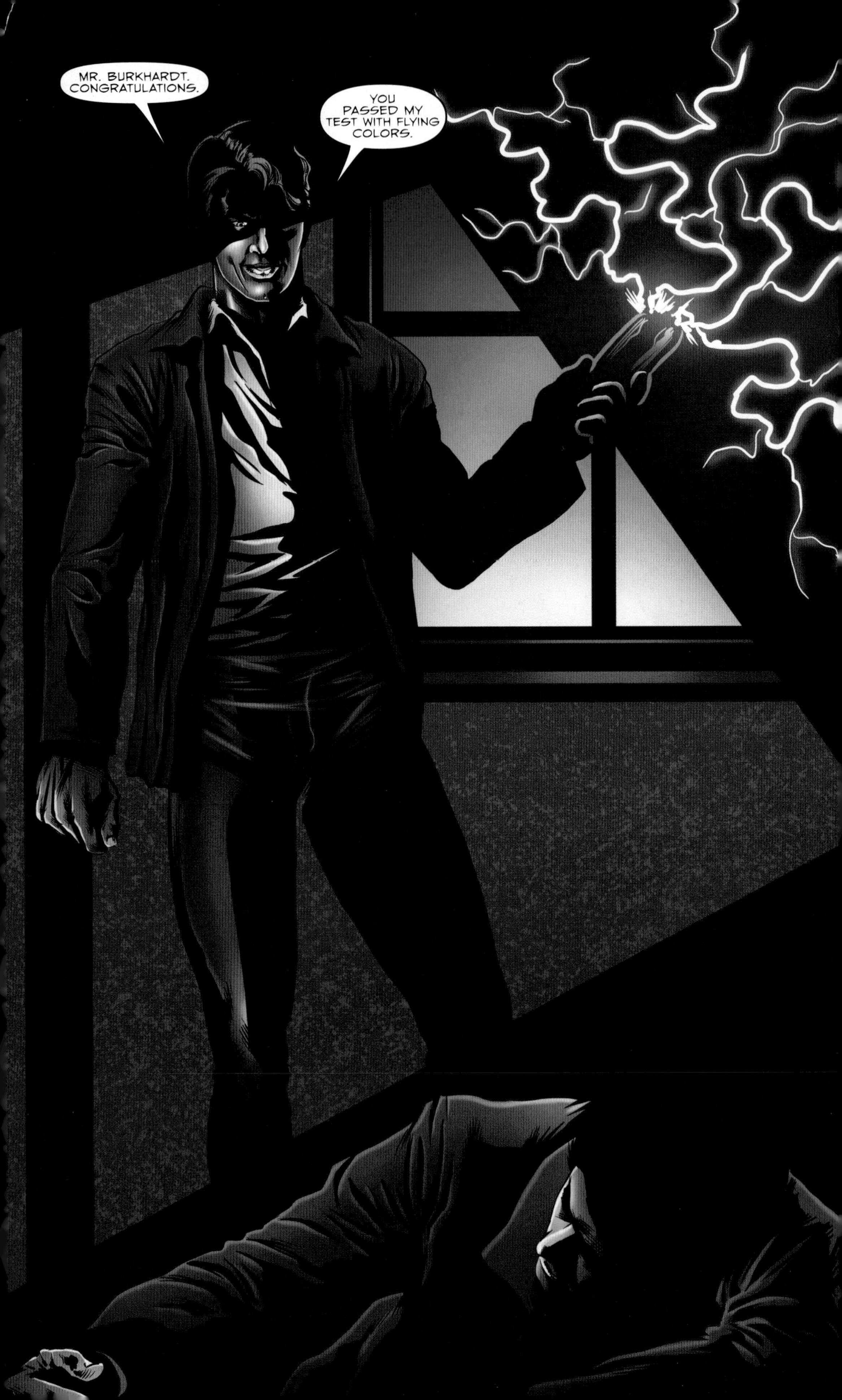
MR. BURKHARDT. CONGRATULATIONS.
YOU PASSED MY TEST WITH FLYING COLORS.

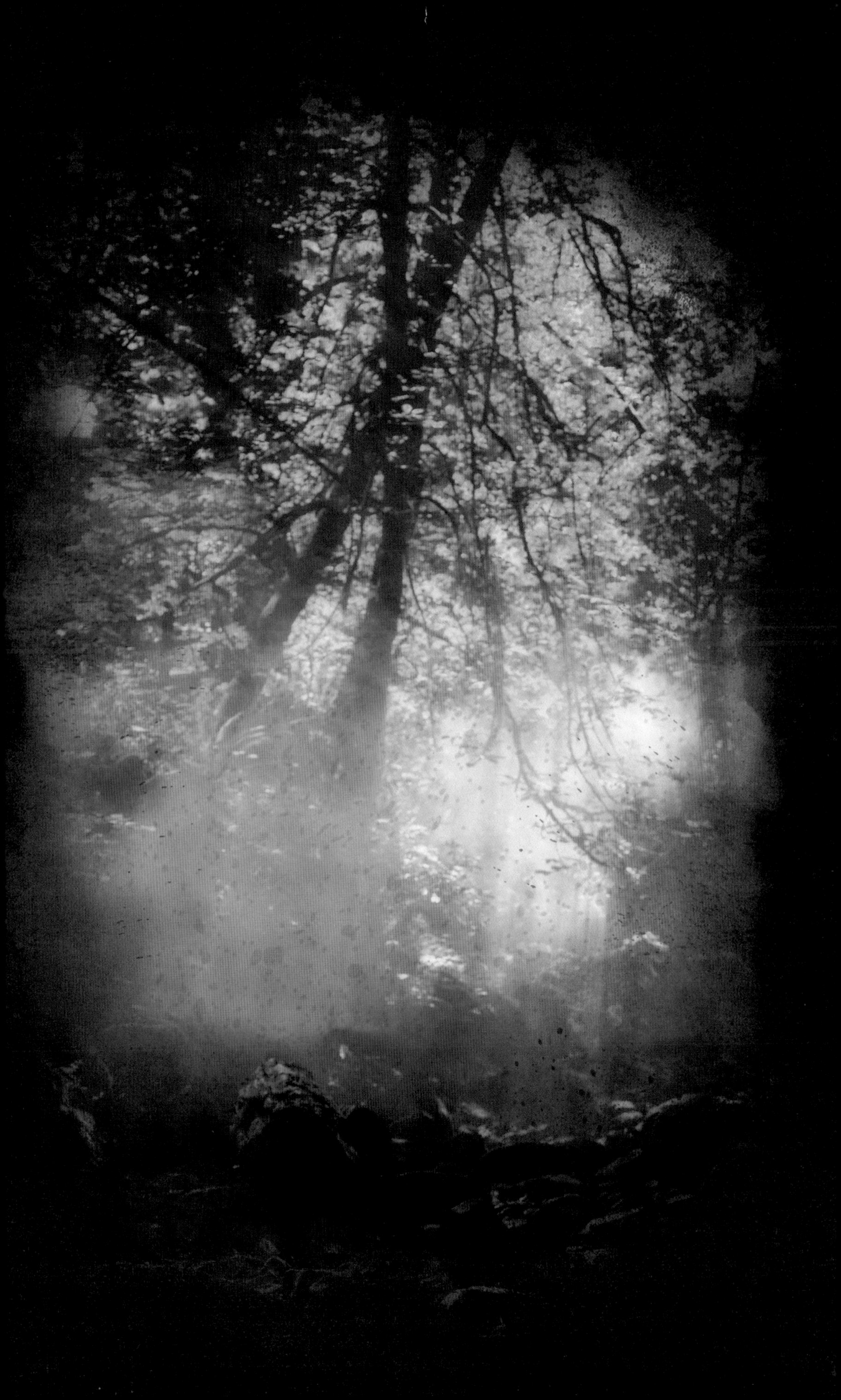

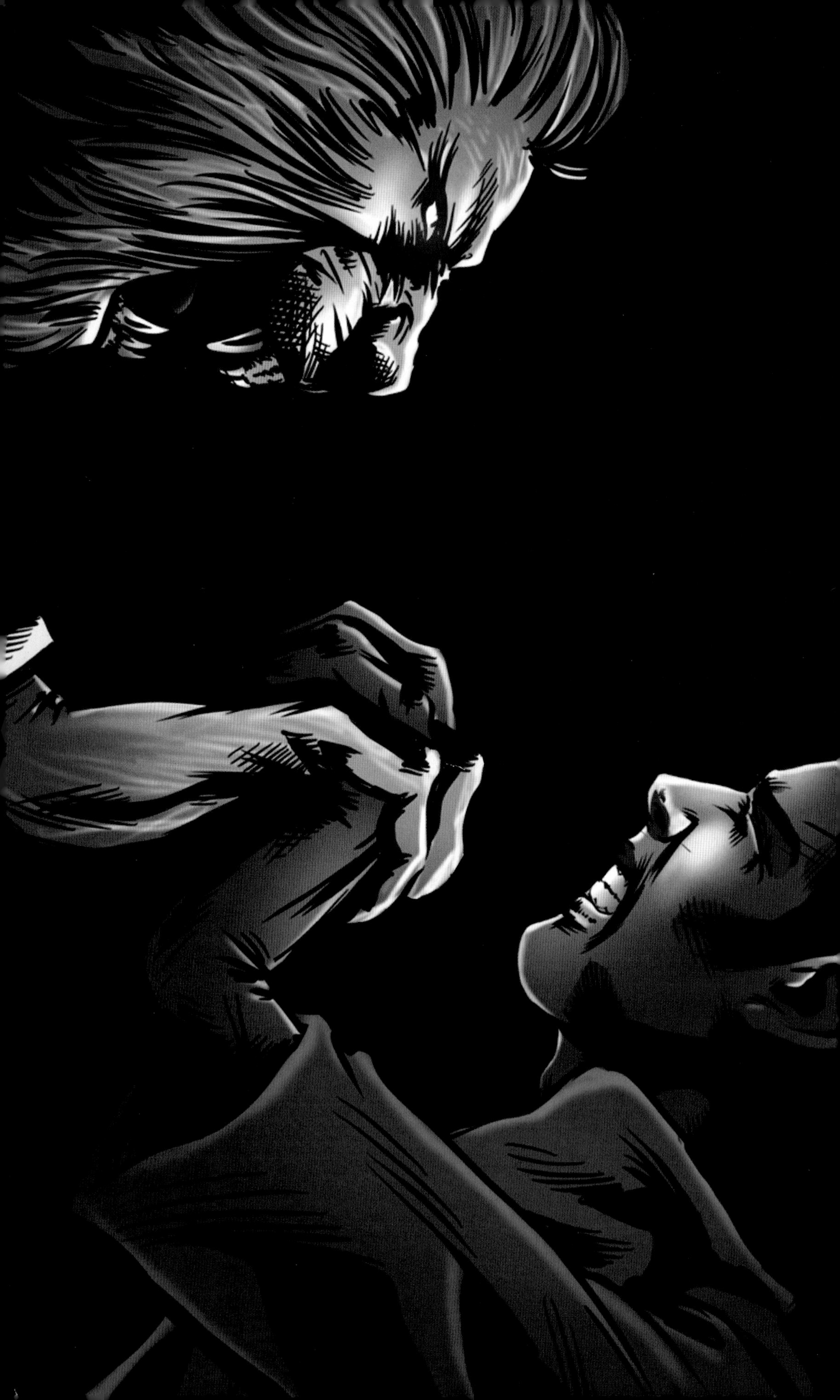

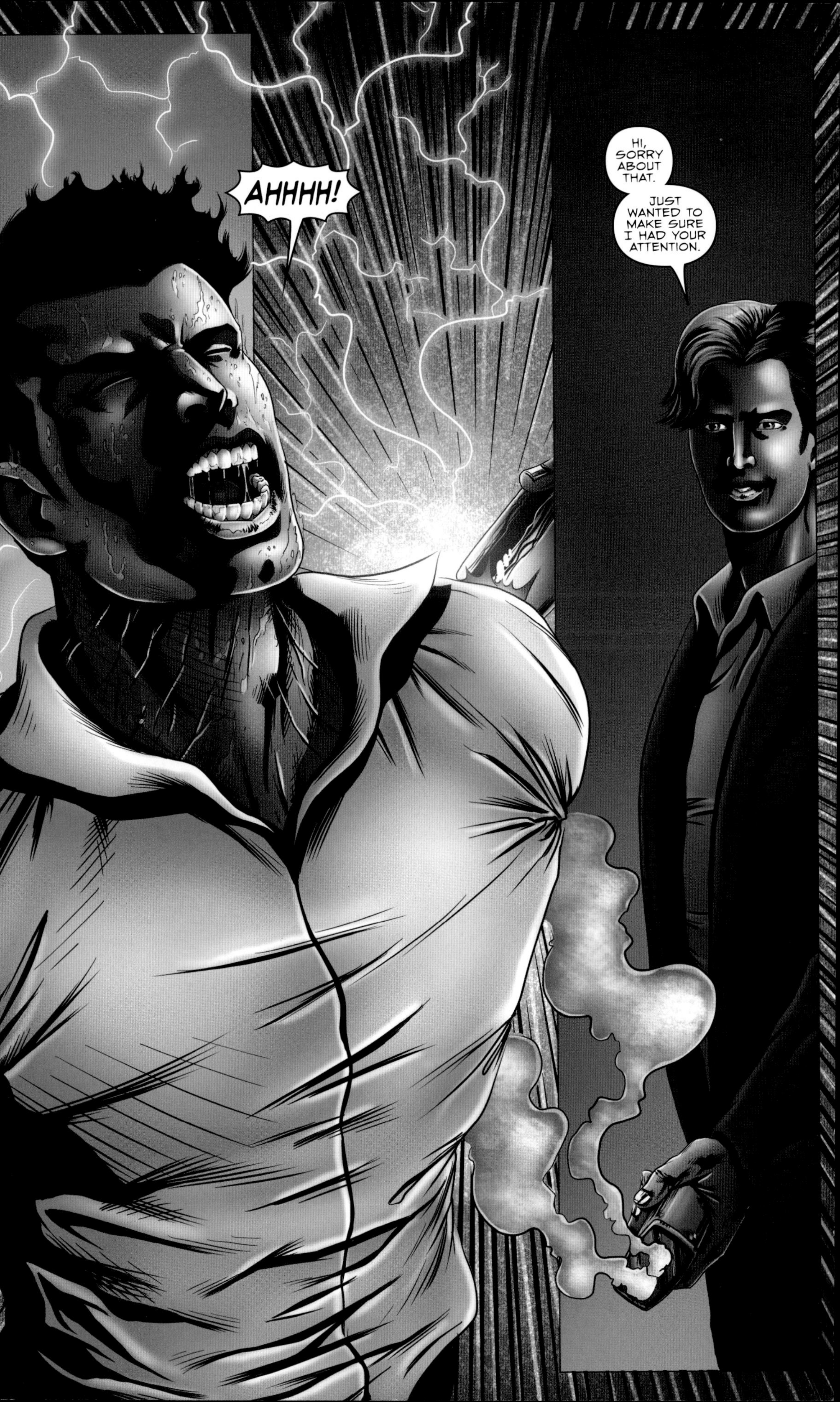
AHHHH!
HI, SORRY ABOUT THAT.
JUST WANTED TO MAKE SURE I HAD YOUR ATTENTION.

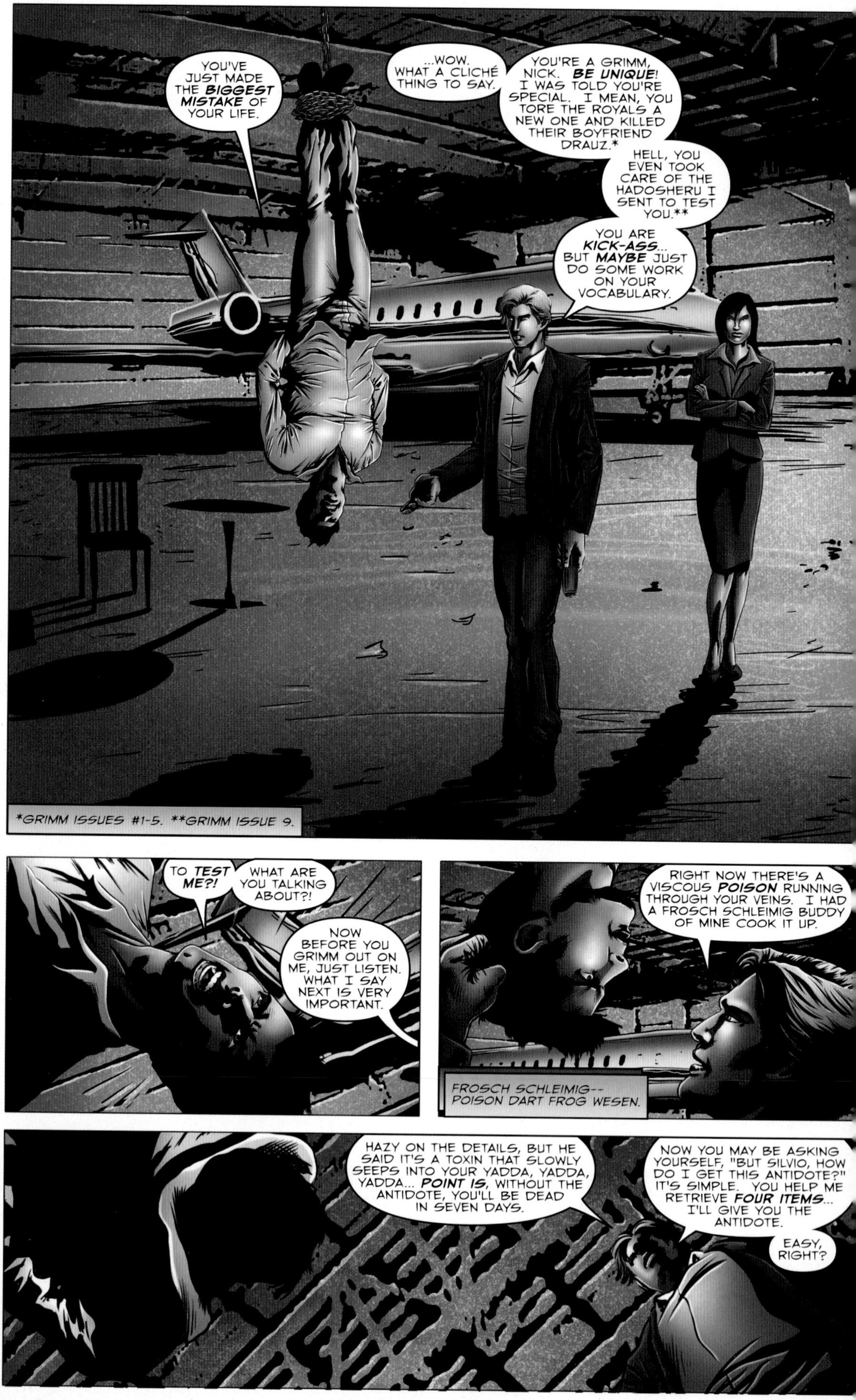

YOU'VE JUST MADE THE BIGGEST MISTAKE OF YOUR LIFE.
...WOW. WHAT A CLICHÉ THING TO SAY.
YOU'RE A GRIMM, NICK. BE UNIQUE! I WAS TOLD YOU'RE SPECIAL. I MEAN, YOU TORE THE ROYALS A NEW ONE AND KILLED THEIR BOYFRIEND DRAUZ.*
HELL, YOU EVEN TOOK CARE OF THE HADOSHERU I SENT TO TEST YOU.**
YOU ARE KICK-ASS... BUT MAYBE JUST DO SOME WORK ON YOUR VOCABULARY.
*GRIMM ISSUES #1-5. **GRIMM ISSUE 9.
TO TEST ME?!
WHAT ARE YOU TALKING ABOUT?!
NOW BEFORE YOU GRIMM OUT ON ME, JUST LISTEN. WHAT I SAY NEXT IS VERY IMPORTANT.
RIGHT NOW THERE'S A VISCOUS POISON RUNNING THROUGH YOUR VEINS. I HAD A FROSCH SCHLEIMIG BUDDY OF MINE COOK IT UP.
FROSCH SCHLEIMIG-- POISON DART FROG WESEN.
HAZY ON THE DETAILS, BUT HE SAID IT'S A TOXIN THAT SLOWLY SEEPS INTO YOUR YADDA, YADDA, YADDA... POINT IS, WITHOUT THE ANTIDOTE, YOU'LL BE DEAD IN SEVEN DAYS.
NOW YOU MAY BE ASKING YOURSELF, "BUT SILVIO, HOW DO I GET THIS ANTIDOTE?" IT'S SIMPLE. YOU HELP ME RETRIEVE FOUR ITEMS... I'LL GIVE YOU THE ANTIDOTE.
EASY, RIGHT?

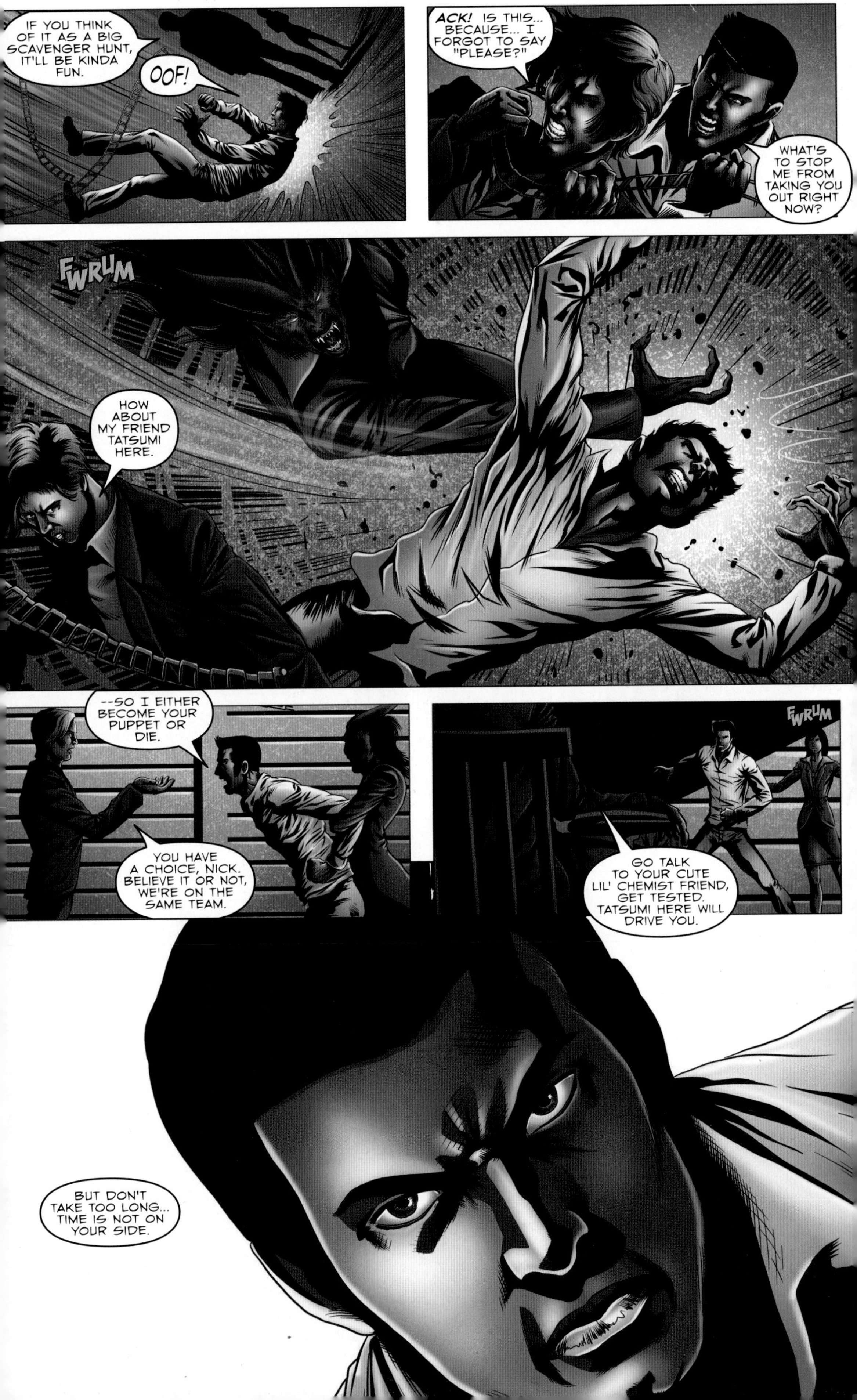
IF YOU THINK OF IT AS A BIG SCAVENGER HUNT, IT'LL BE KINDA FUN.
OOF!
ACK! IS THIS... BECAUSE... I FORGOT TO SAY "PLEASE?"
WHAT'S TO STOP ME FROM TAKING YOU OUT RIGHT NOW?
FWRUM
HOW ABOUT MY FRIEND TATSUMI HERE.
--SO I EITHER BECOME YOUR PUPPET OR DIE.
YOU HAVE A CHOICE, NICK. BELIEVE IT OR NOT, WE'RE ON THE SAME TEAM.
FWRUM
GO TALK TO YOUR CUTE LIL' CHEMIST FRIEND, GET TESTED. TATSUMI HERE WILL DRIVE YOU.
BUT DON'T TAKE TOO LONG... TIME IS NOT ON YOUR SIDE.

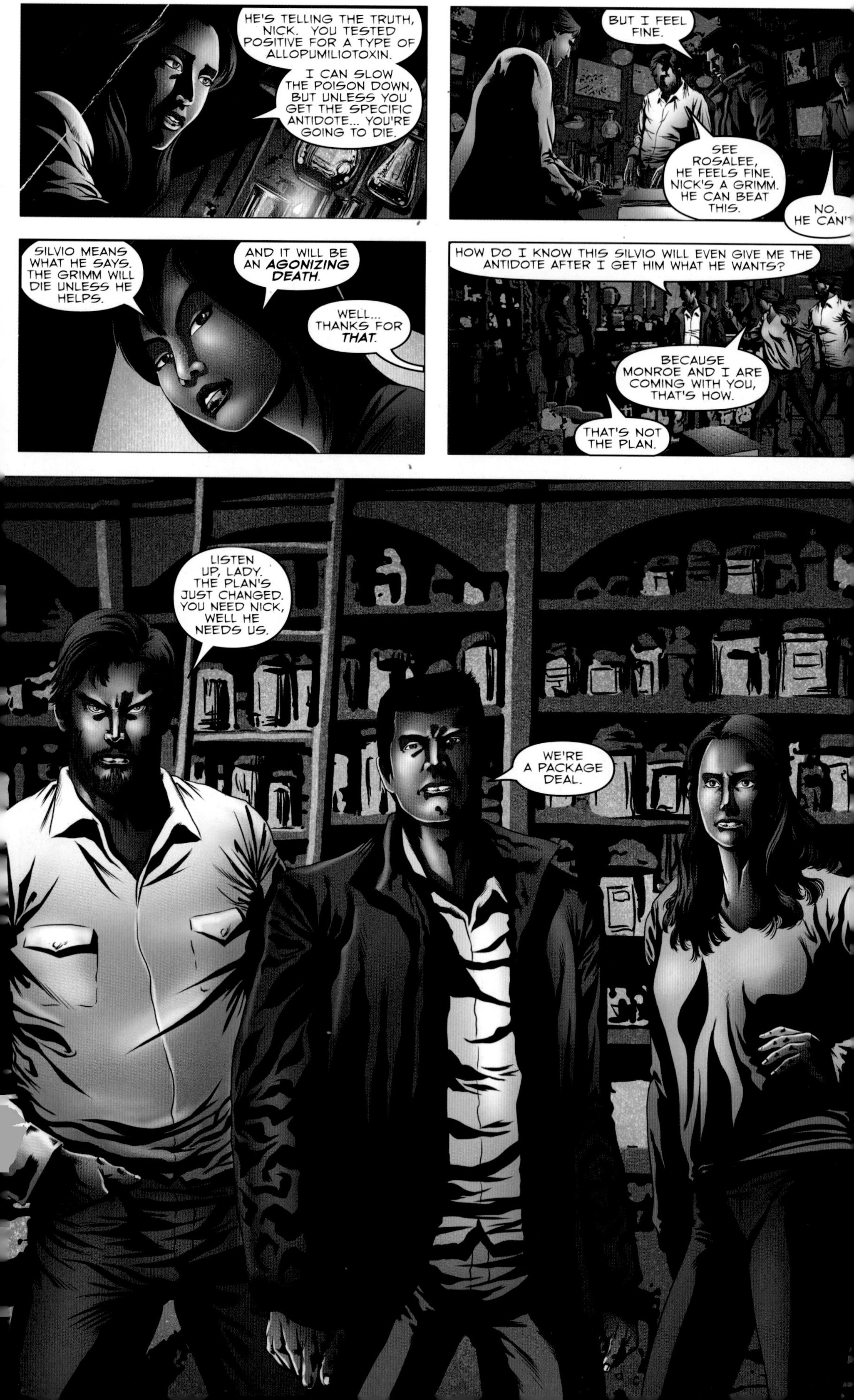
HE'S TELLING THE TRUTH, NICK. YOU TESTED POSITIVE FOR A TYPE OF ALLOPUMILIOTOXIN.
I CAN SLOW THE POISON DOWN, BUT UNLESS YOU GET THE SPECIFIC ANTIDOTE... YOU'RE GOING TO DIE.
BUT I FEEL FINE.
SEE ROSALEE, HE FEELS FINE. NICK'S A GRIMM. HE CAN BEAT THIS.
NO. HE CAN'T
SILVIO MEANS WHAT HE SAYS. THE GRIMM WILL DIE UNLESS HE HELPS.
AND IT WILL BE AN **AGONIZING DEATH**.
WELL... THANKS FOR ***THAT***.
HOW DO I KNOW THIS SILVIO WILL EVEN GIVE ME THE ANTIDOTE AFTER I GET HIM WHAT HE WANTS?
BECAUSE MONROE AND I ARE COMING WITH YOU, THAT'S HOW.
THAT'S NOT THE PLAN.
LISTEN UP, LADY. THE PLAN'S JUST CHANGED. YOU NEED NICK, WELL HE NEEDS US.
WE'RE A PACKAGE DEAL.

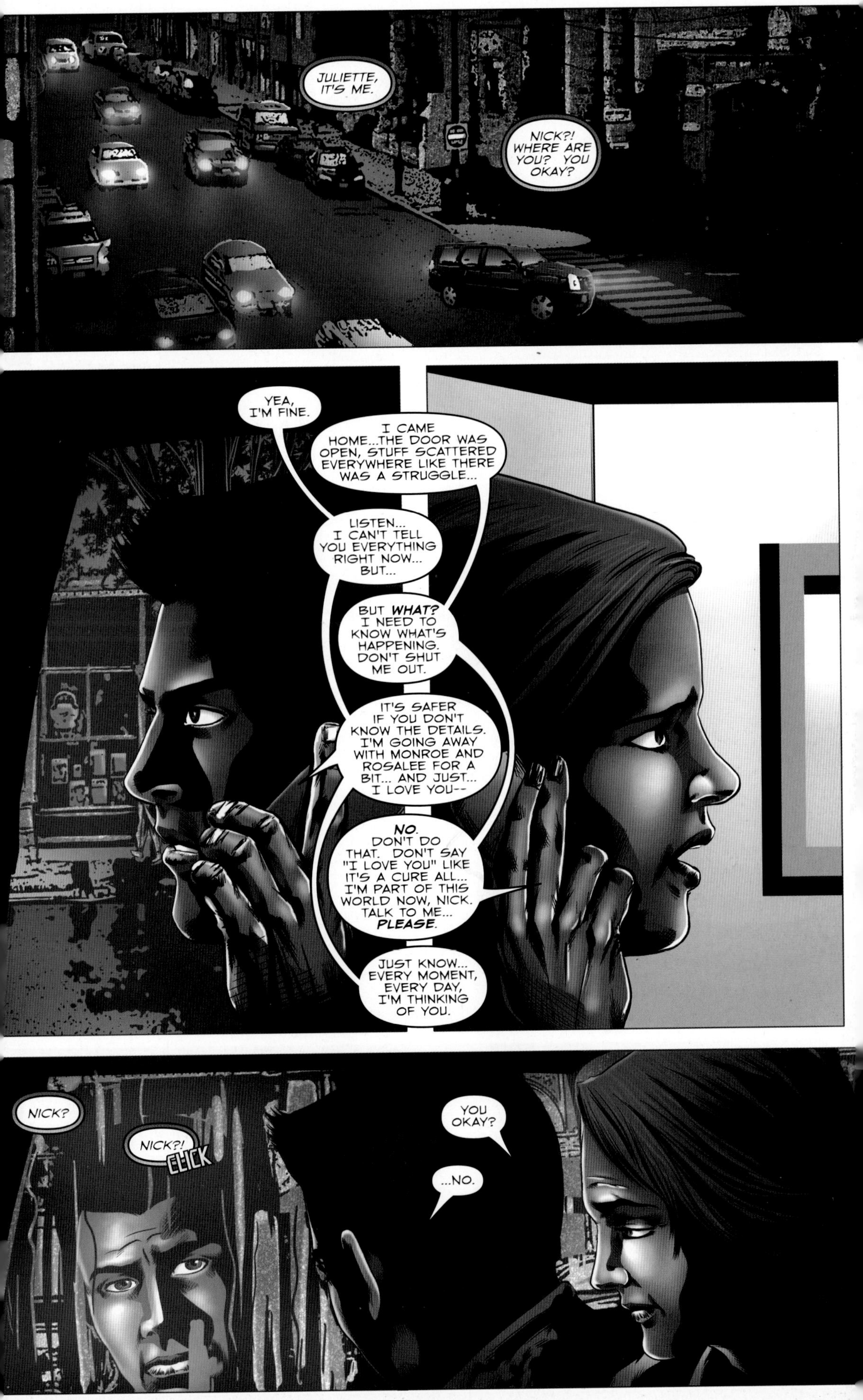

JULIETTE, IT'S ME.
NICK?! WHERE ARE YOU? YOU OKAY?
YEA, I'M FINE.
I CAME HOME...THE DOOR WAS OPEN, STUFF SCATTERED EVERYWHERE LIKE THERE WAS A STRUGGLE...
LISTEN... I CAN'T TELL YOU EVERYTHING RIGHT NOW... BUT...
BUT WHAT? I NEED TO KNOW WHAT'S HAPPENING. DON'T SHUT ME OUT.
IT'S SAFER IF YOU DON'T KNOW THE DETAILS. I'M GOING AWAY WITH MONROE AND ROSALEE FOR A BIT... AND JUST... I LOVE YOU--
NO. DON'T DO THAT. DON'T SAY "I LOVE YOU" LIKE IT'S A CURE ALL... I'M PART OF THIS WORLD NOW, NICK. TALK TO ME... PLEASE.
JUST KNOW... EVERY MOMENT, EVERY DAY, I'M THINKING OF YOU.
NICK?
NICK?!
CLICK
YOU OKAY?
...NO.

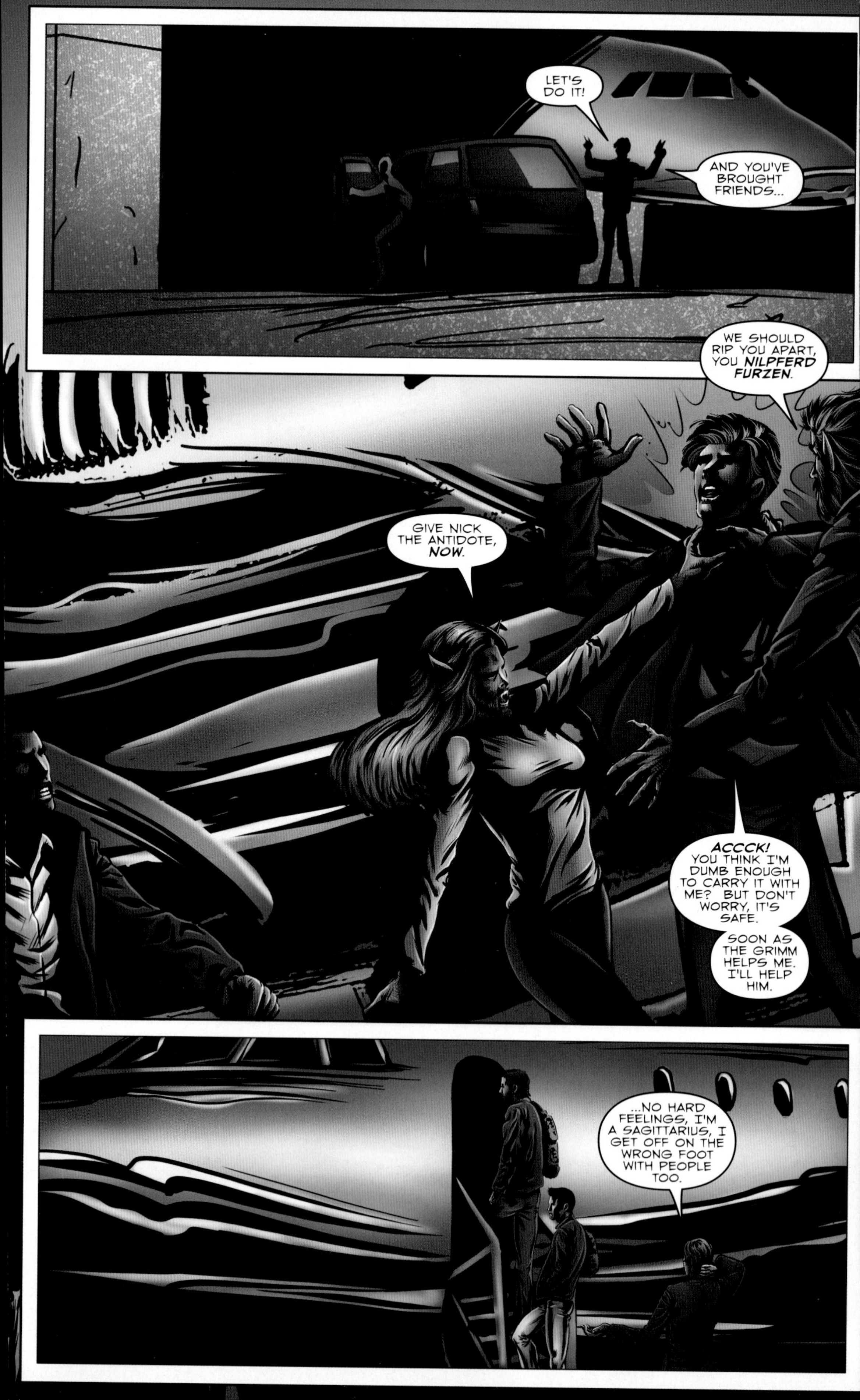
LET'S DO IT!
AND YOU'VE BROUGHT FRIENDS...
WE SHOULD RIP YOU APART, YOU *NILPFERD FURZEN*.
GIVE NICK THE ANTIDOTE, *NOW*.
ACCCK! YOU THINK I'M DUMB ENOUGH TO CARRY IT WITH ME? BUT DON'T WORRY, IT'S SAFE.
SOON AS THE GRIMM HELPS ME. I'LL HELP HIM.
...NO HARD FEELINGS, I'M A SAGITTARIUS, I GET OFF ON THE WRONG FOOT WITH PEOPLE TOO.

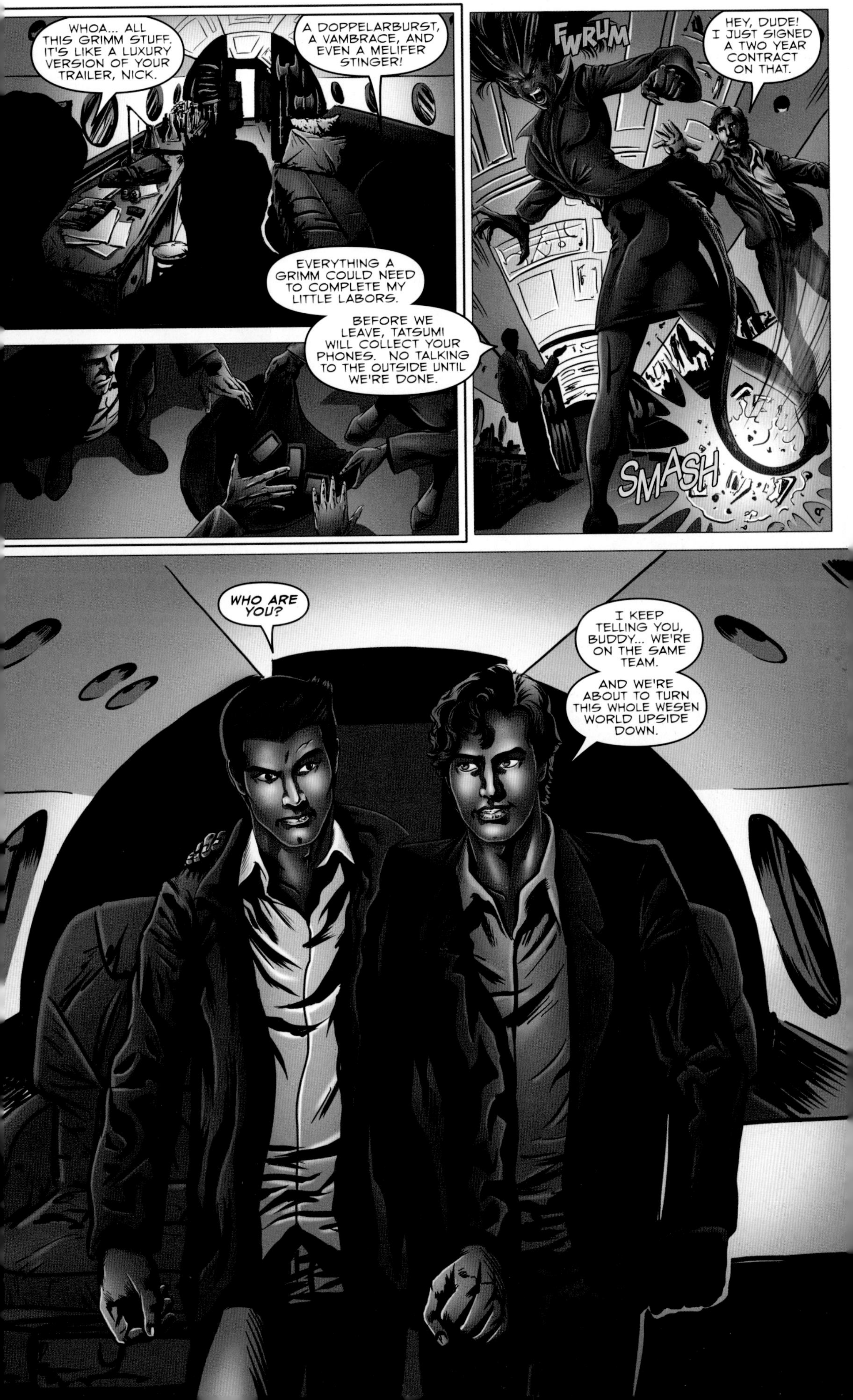
WHOA... ALL THIS GRIMM STUFF. IT'S LIKE A LUXURY VERSION OF YOUR TRAILER, NICK.
A DOPPELARBURST, A VAMBRACE, AND EVEN A MELIFER STINGER!
EVERYTHING A GRIMM COULD NEED TO COMPLETE MY LITTLE LABORS.
BEFORE WE LEAVE, TATSUMI WILL COLLECT YOUR PHONES. NO TALKING TO THE OUTSIDE UNTIL WE'RE DONE.
FWRUM
HEY, DUDE! I JUST SIGNED A TWO YEAR CONTRACT ON THAT.
SMASH
WHO ARE YOU?
I KEEP TELLING YOU, BUDDY... WE'RE ON THE SAME TEAM.
AND WE'RE ABOUT TO TURN THIS WHOLE WESEN WORLD UPSIDE DOWN.

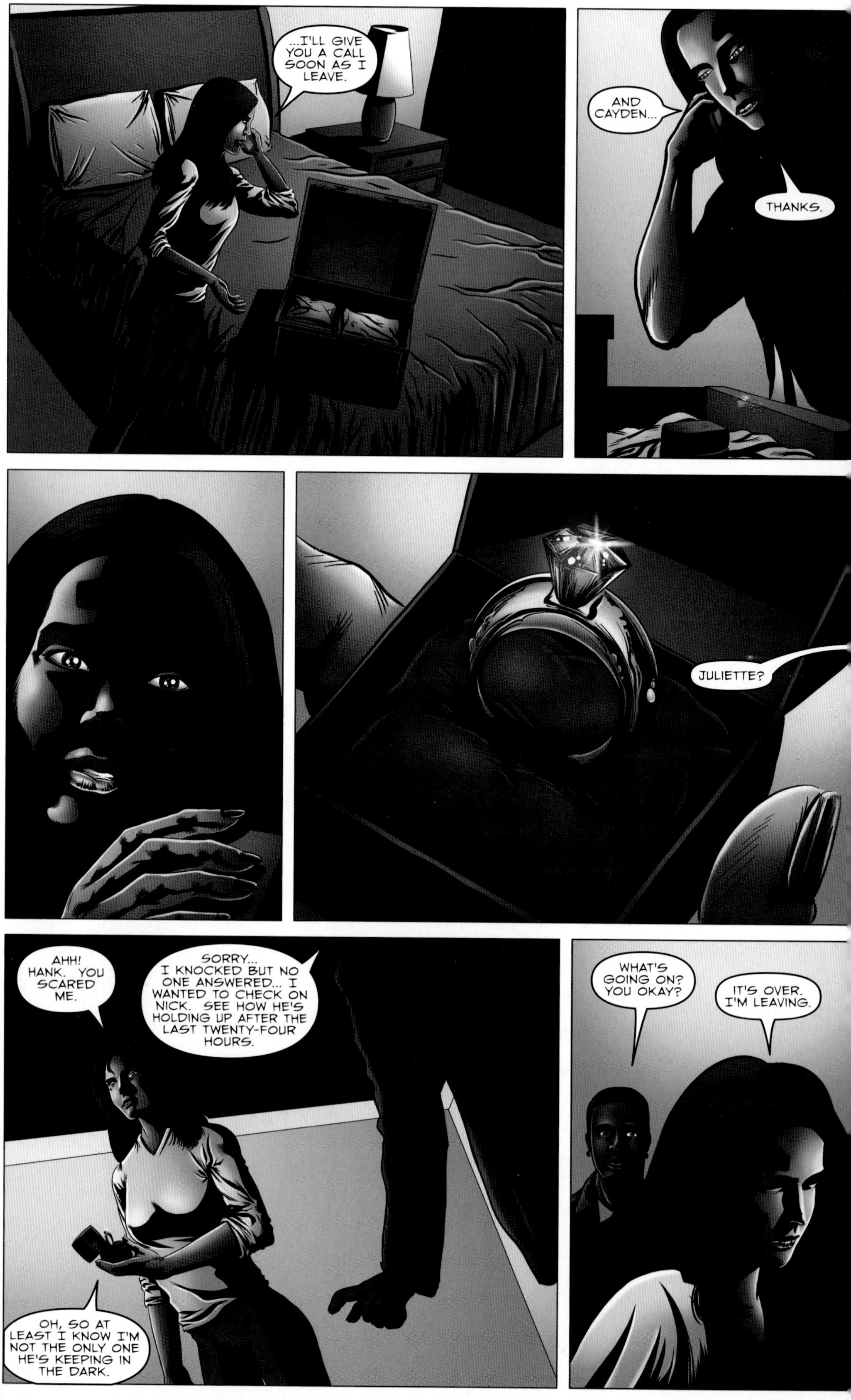
...I'LL GIVE YOU A CALL SOON AS I LEAVE.
AND CAYDEN...
THANKS.
JULIETTE?
AHH! HANK. YOU SCARED ME.
SORRY... I KNOCKED BUT NO ONE ANSWERED... I WANTED TO CHECK ON NICK. SEE HOW HE'S HOLDING UP AFTER THE LAST TWENTY-FOUR HOURS.
OH, SO AT LEAST I KNOW I'M NOT THE ONLY ONE HE'S KEEPING IN THE DARK.
WHAT'S GOING ON? YOU OKAY?
IT'S OVER. I'M LEAVING.

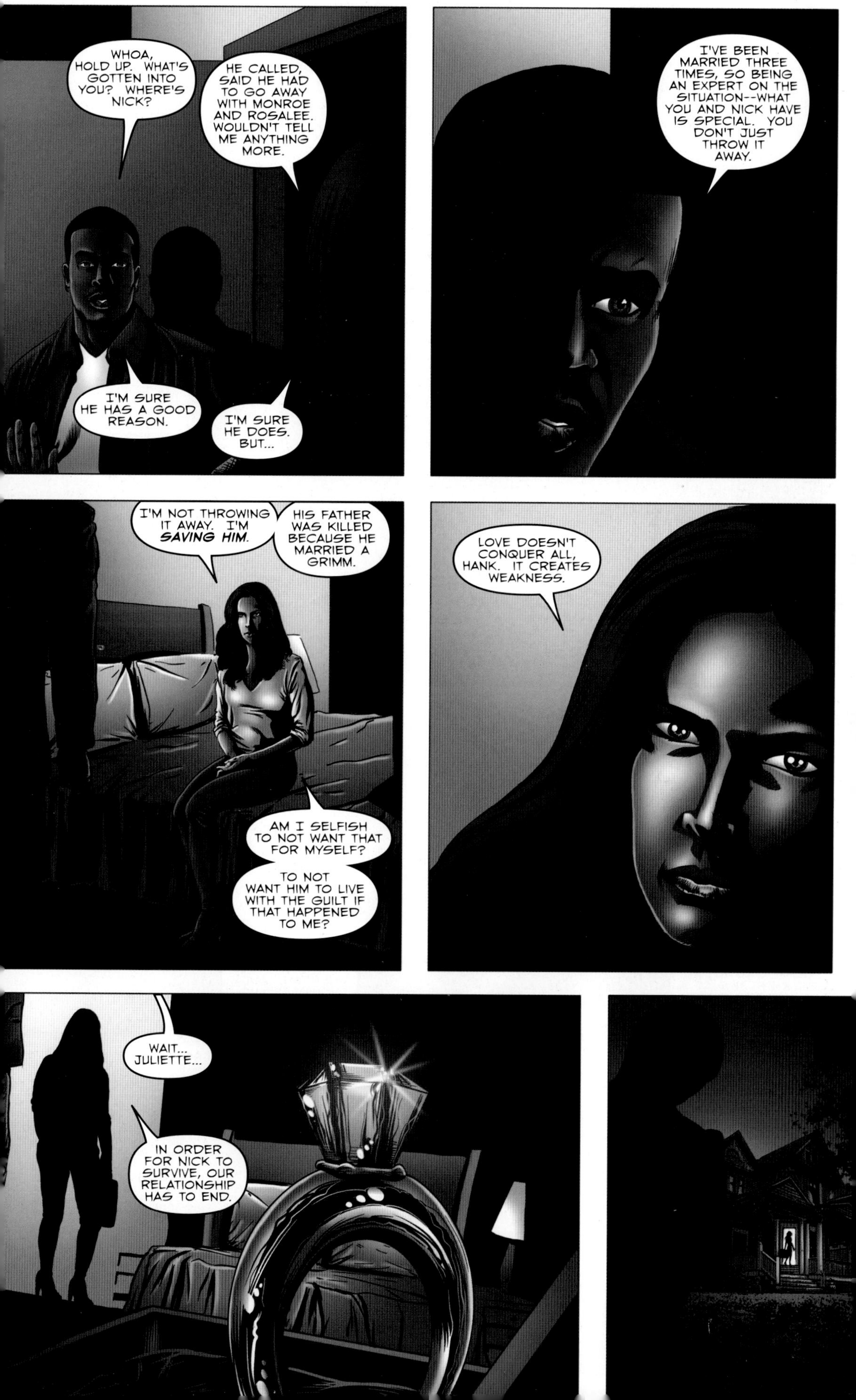
WHOA, HOLD UP. WHAT'S GOTTEN INTO YOU? WHERE'S NICK?
HE CALLED, SAID HE HAD TO GO AWAY WITH MONROE AND ROSALEE. WOULDN'T TELL ME ANYTHING MORE.
I'M SURE HE HAS A GOOD REASON.
I'M SURE HE DOES. BUT...
I'VE BEEN MARRIED THREE TIMES, SO BEING AN EXPERT ON THE SITUATION--WHAT YOU AND NICK HAVE IS SPECIAL. YOU DON'T JUST THROW IT AWAY.
I'M NOT THROWING IT AWAY. I'M *SAVING HIM*.
HIS FATHER WAS KILLED BECAUSE HE MARRIED A GRIMM.
AM I SELFISH TO NOT WANT THAT FOR MYSELF?
TO NOT WANT HIM TO LIVE WITH THE GUILT IF THAT HAPPENED TO ME?
LOVE DOESN'T CONQUER ALL, HANK. IT CREATES WEAKNESS.
WAIT... JULIETTE...
IN ORDER FOR NICK TO SURVIVE, OUR RELATIONSHIP HAS TO END.

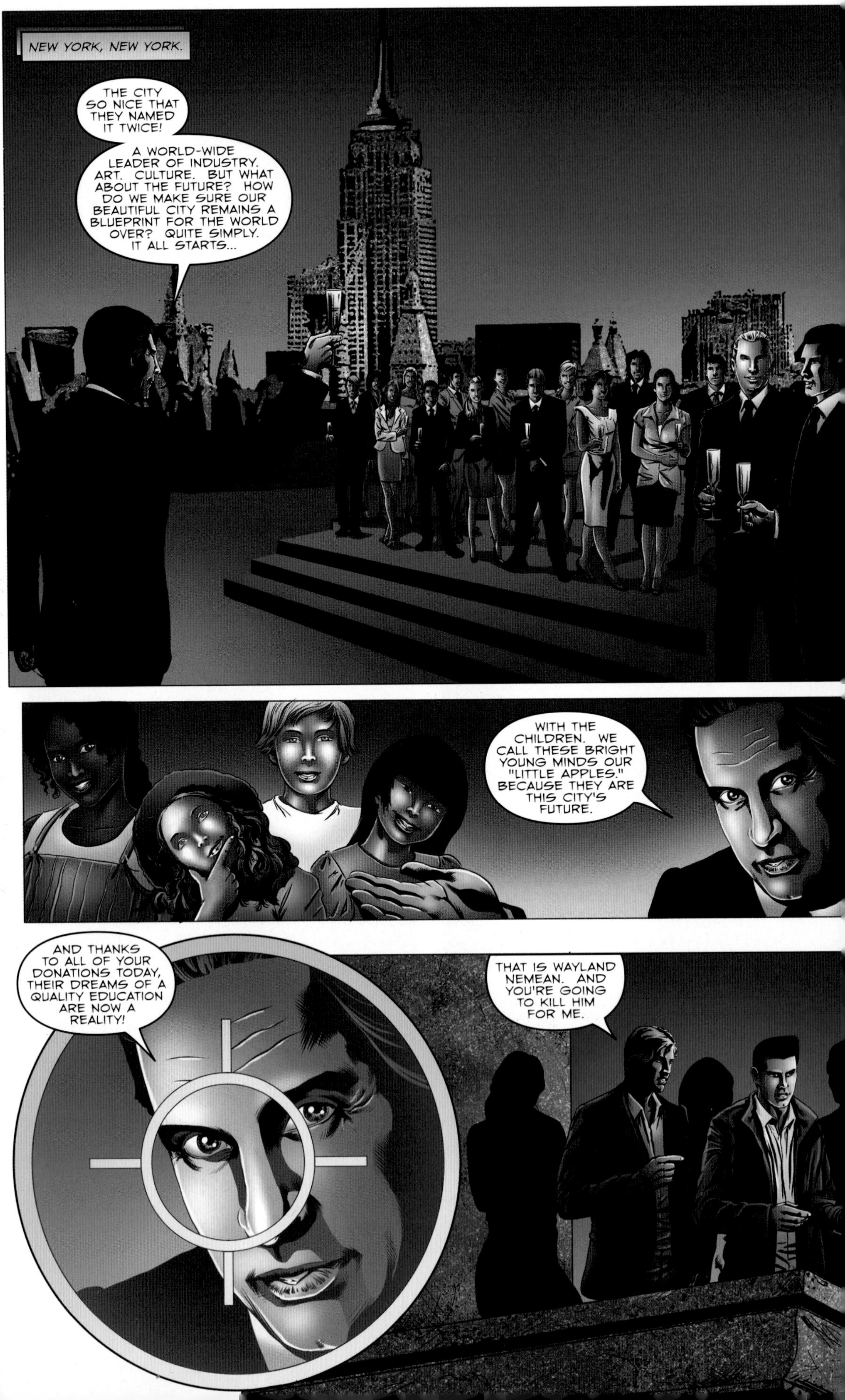
NEW YORK, NEW YORK.
THE CITY SO NICE THAT THEY NAMED IT TWICE!
A WORLD-WIDE LEADER OF INDUSTRY. ART. CULTURE. BUT WHAT ABOUT THE FUTURE? HOW DO WE MAKE SURE OUR BEAUTIFUL CITY REMAINS A BLUEPRINT FOR THE WORLD OVER? QUITE SIMPLY. IT ALL STARTS...
WITH THE CHILDREN. WE CALL THESE BRIGHT YOUNG MINDS OUR "LITTLE APPLES." BECAUSE THEY ARE THIS CITY'S FUTURE.
AND THANKS TO ALL OF YOUR DONATIONS TODAY, THEIR DREAMS OF A QUALITY EDUCATION ARE NOW A REALITY!
THAT IS WAYLAND NEMEAN. AND YOU'RE GOING TO KILL HIM FOR ME.

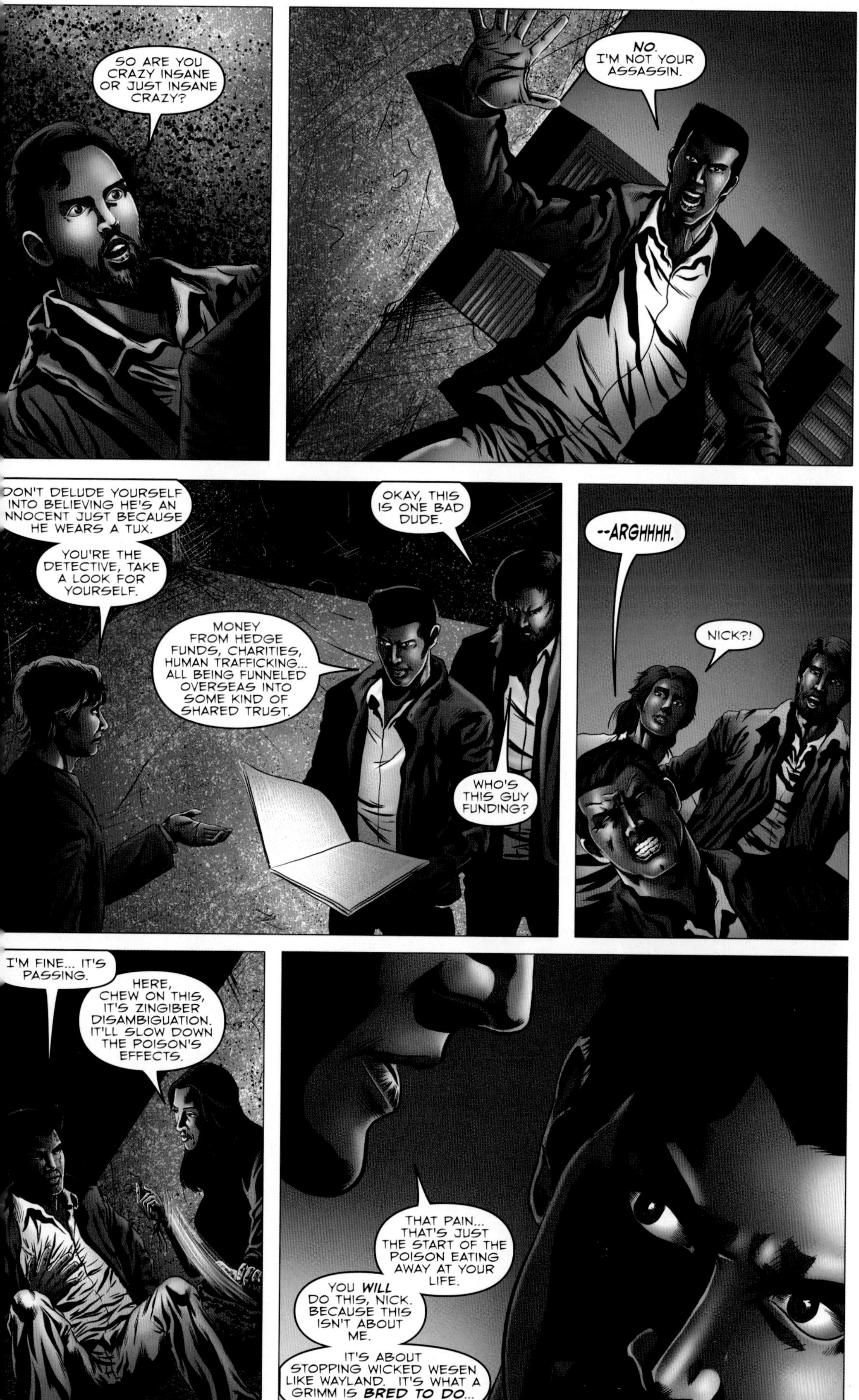

SO ARE YOU CRAZY INSANE OR JUST INSANE CRAZY?
NO. I'M NOT YOUR ASSASSIN.
DON'T DELUDE YOURSELF INTO BELIEVING HE'S AN INNOCENT JUST BECAUSE HE WEARS A TUX.
YOU'RE THE DETECTIVE, TAKE A LOOK FOR YOURSELF.
MONEY FROM HEDGE FUNDS, CHARITIES, HUMAN TRAFFICKING... ALL BEING FUNNELED OVERSEAS INTO SOME KIND OF SHARED TRUST.
OKAY, THIS IS ONE BAD DUDE.
WHO'S THIS GUY FUNDING?
--ARGHHHH.
NICK?!
I'M FINE... IT'S PASSING.
HERE, CHEW ON THIS, IT'S ZINGIBER DISAMBIGUATION. IT'LL SLOW DOWN THE POISON'S EFFECTS.
THAT PAIN... THAT'S JUST THE START OF THE POISON EATING AWAY AT YOUR LIFE.
YOU WILL DO THIS, NICK. BECAUSE THIS ISN'T ABOUT ME.
IT'S ABOUT STOPPING WICKED WESEN LIKE WAYLAND. IT'S WHAT A GRIMM IS BRED TO DO...

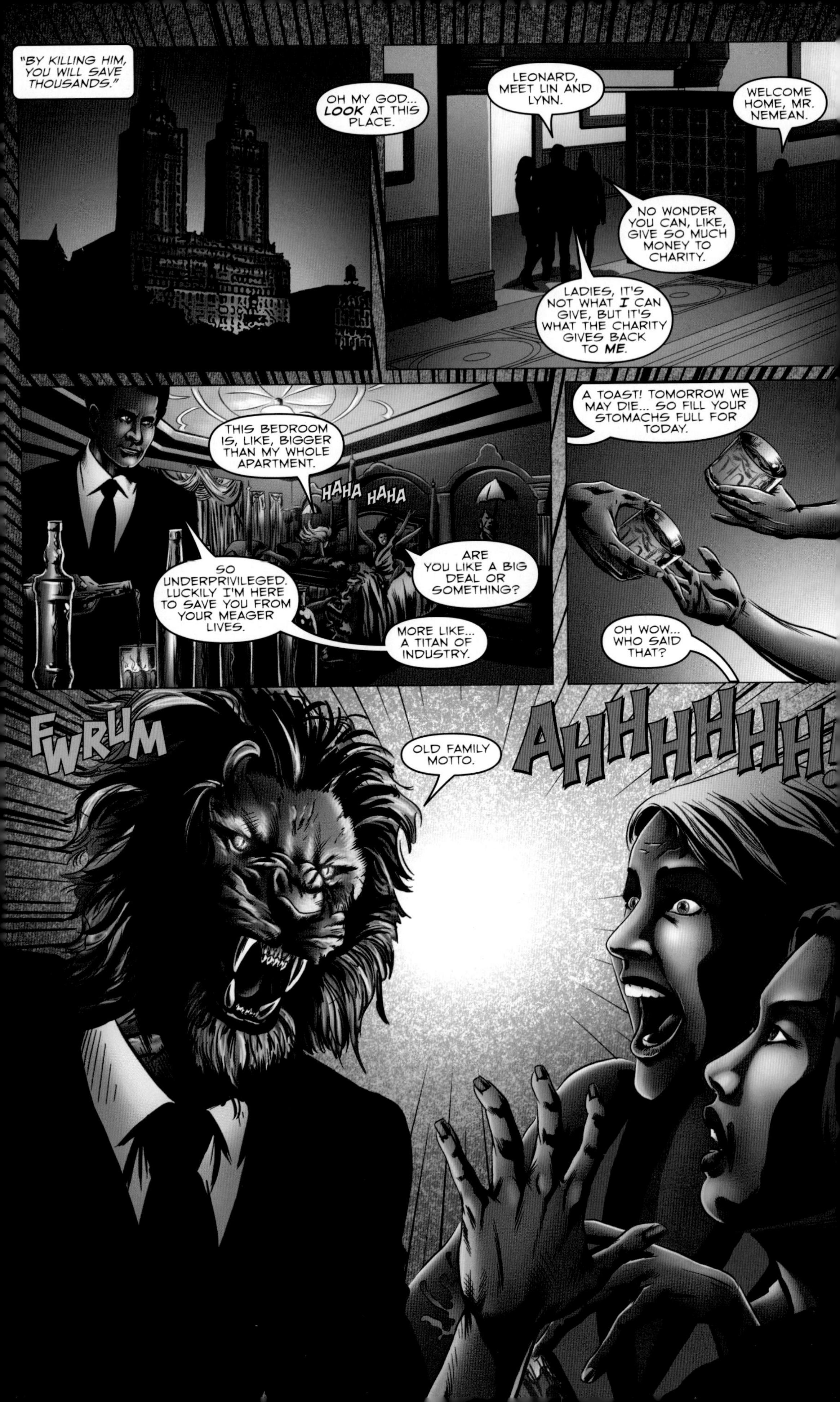
"BY KILLING HIM, YOU WILL SAVE THOUSANDS."
OH MY GOD... LOOK AT THIS PLACE.
LEONARD, MEET LIN AND LYNN.
WELCOME HOME, MR. NEMEAN.
NO WONDER YOU CAN, LIKE, GIVE SO MUCH MONEY TO CHARITY.
LADIES, IT'S NOT WHAT I CAN GIVE, BUT IT'S WHAT THE CHARITY GIVES BACK TO ME.
THIS BEDROOM IS, LIKE, BIGGER THAN MY WHOLE APARTMENT.
HAHA HAHA
SO UNDERPRIVILEGED. LUCKILY I'M HERE TO SAVE YOU FROM YOUR MEAGER LIVES.
ARE YOU LIKE A BIG DEAL OR SOMETHING?
MORE LIKE... A TITAN OF INDUSTRY.
A TOAST! TOMORROW WE MAY DIE... SO FILL YOUR STOMACHS FULL FOR TODAY.
OH WOW... WHO SAID THAT?
FWRUM
OLD FAMILY MOTTO.
AHHHHHH!

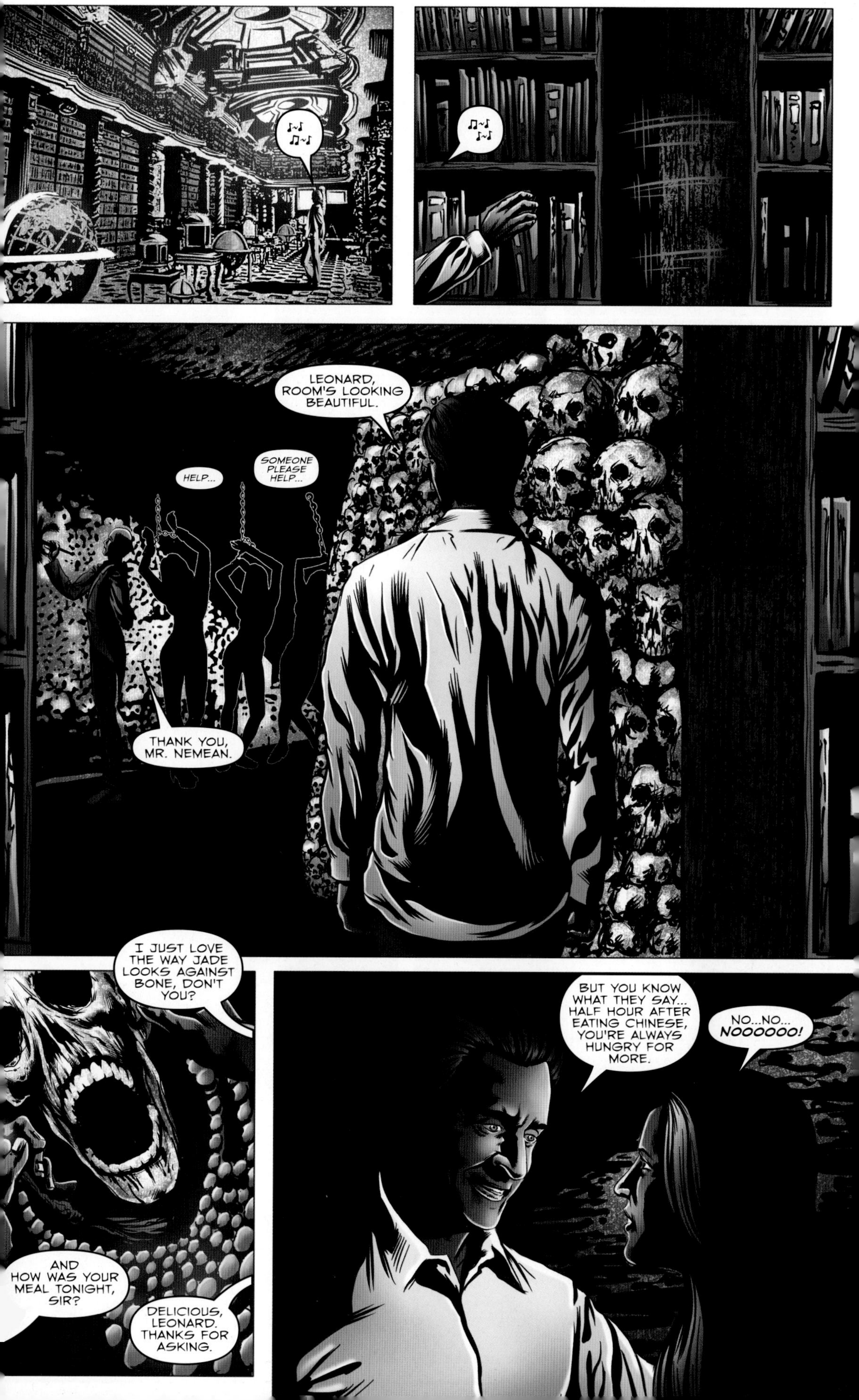
LEONARD, ROOM'S LOOKING BEAUTIFUL.
HELP...
SOMEONE PLEASE HELP...
THANK YOU, MR. NEMEAN.
I JUST LOVE THE WAY JADE LOOKS AGAINST BONE, DON'T YOU?
AND HOW WAS YOUR MEAL TONIGHT, SIR?
DELICIOUS, LEONARD. THANKS FOR ASKING.
BUT YOU KNOW WHAT THEY SAY... HALF HOUR AFTER EATING CHINESE, YOU'RE ALWAYS HUNGRY FOR MORE.
NO...NO... NOOOOOO!

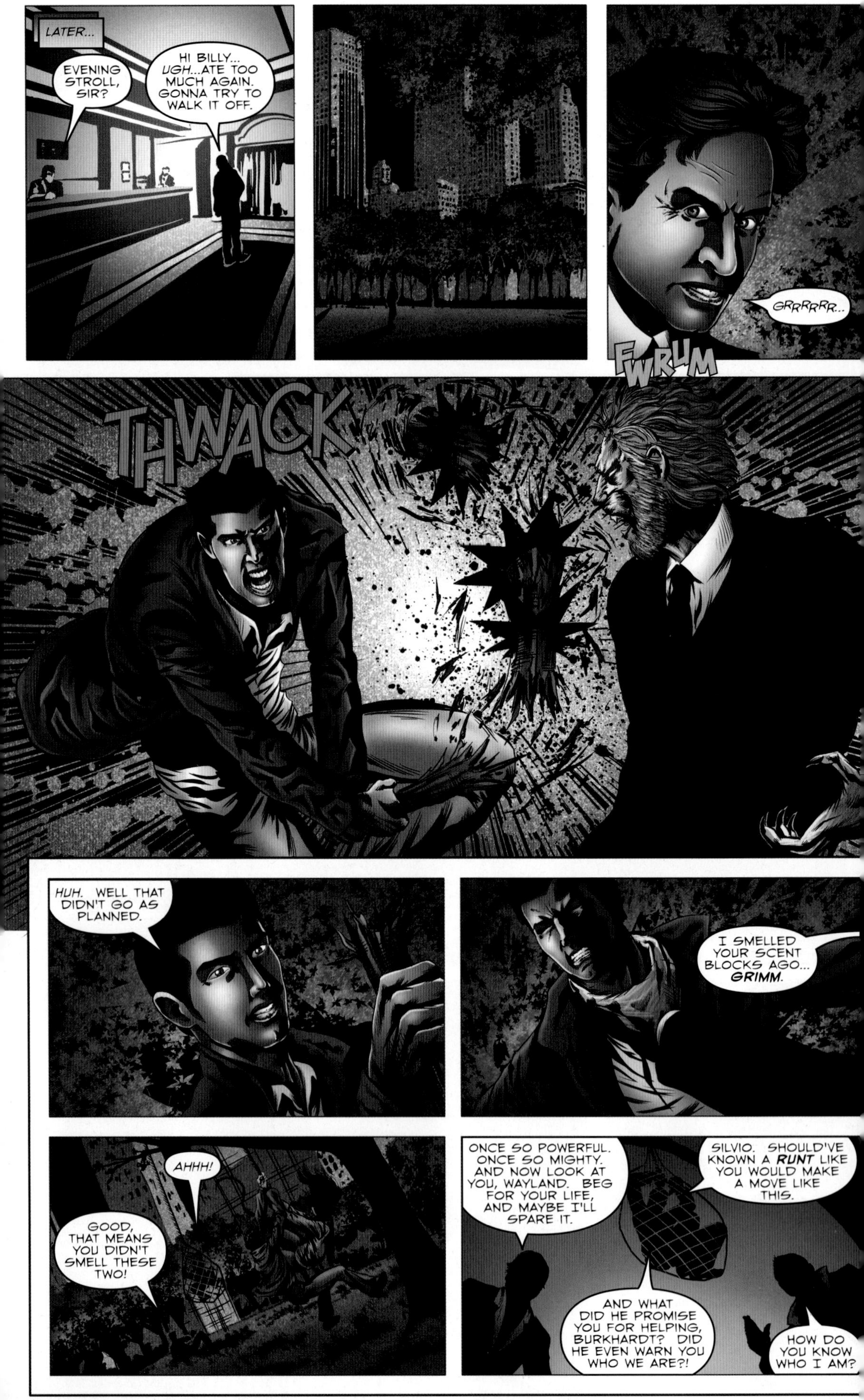
LATER...
EVENING STROLL, SIR?
HI BILLY... UGH...ATE TOO MUCH AGAIN. GONNA TRY TO WALK IT OFF.
GRRRRRR...
FWRUM
THWACK
HUH. WELL THAT DIDN'T GO AS PLANNED.
I SMELLED YOUR SCENT BLOCKS AGO... GRIMM.
AHHH!
GOOD, THAT MEANS YOU DIDN'T SMELL THESE TWO!
ONCE SO POWERFUL. ONCE SO MIGHTY. AND NOW LOOK AT YOU, WAYLAND. BEG FOR YOUR LIFE, AND MAYBE I'LL SPARE IT.
SILVIO. SHOULD'VE KNOWN A RUNT LIKE YOU WOULD MAKE A MOVE LIKE THIS.
AND WHAT DID HE PROMISE YOU FOR HELPING, BURKHARDT? DID HE EVEN WARN YOU WHO WE ARE?!
HOW DO YOU KNOW WHO I AM?

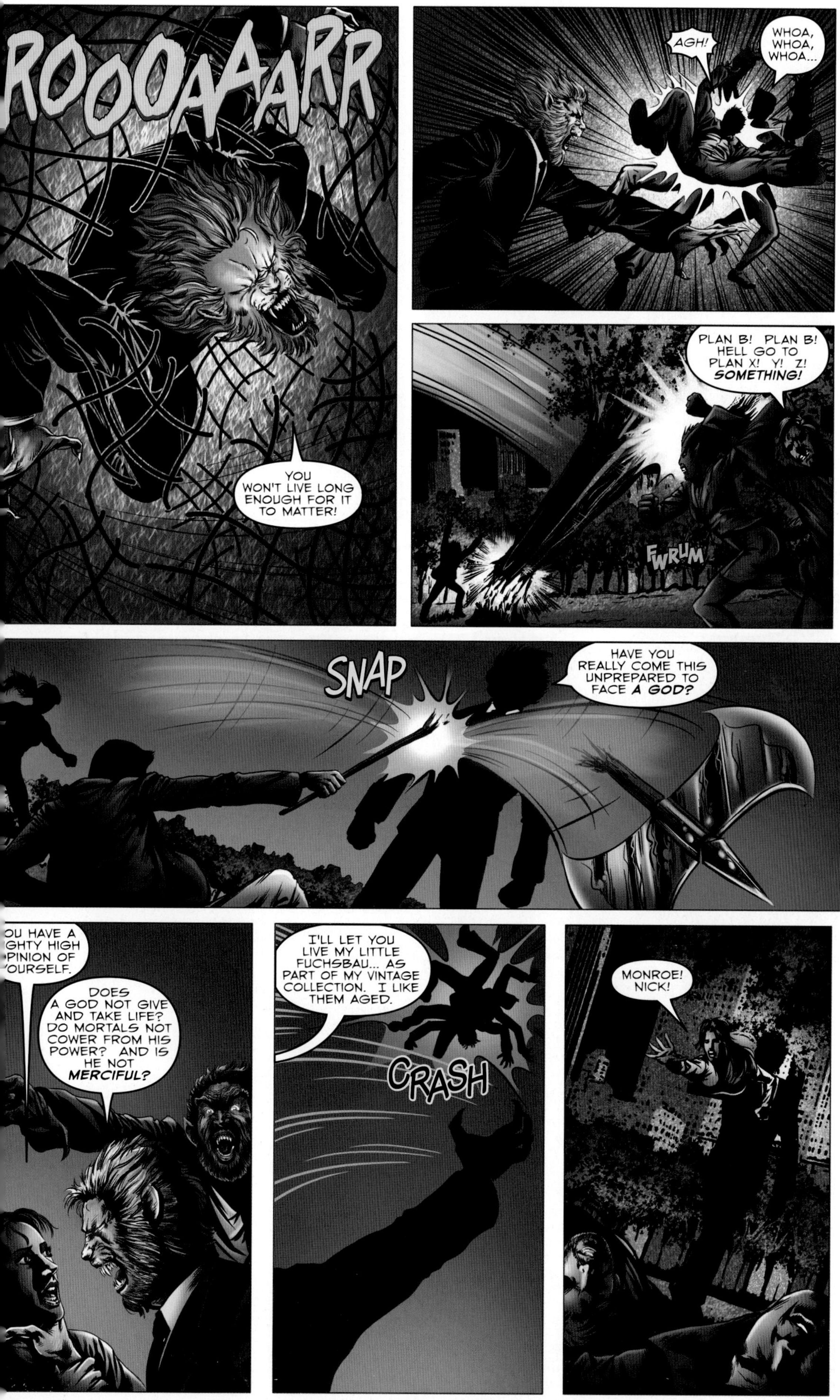
ROOOAAARR
YOU WON'T LIVE LONG ENOUGH FOR IT TO MATTER!
AGH!
WHOA, WHOA, WHOA...
PLAN B! PLAN B! HELL GO TO PLAN X! Y! Z! SOMETHING!
FWRUM
SNAP
HAVE YOU REALLY COME THIS UNPREPARED TO FACE A GOD?
OU HAVE A IGHTY HIGH PINION OF OURSELF.
DOES A GOD NOT GIVE AND TAKE LIFE? DO MORTALS NOT COWER FROM HIS POWER? AND IS HE NOT MERCIFUL?
I'LL LET YOU LIVE MY LITTLE FUCHSBAU... AS PART OF MY VINTAGE COLLECTION. I LIKE THEM AGED.
CRASH
MONROE! NICK!

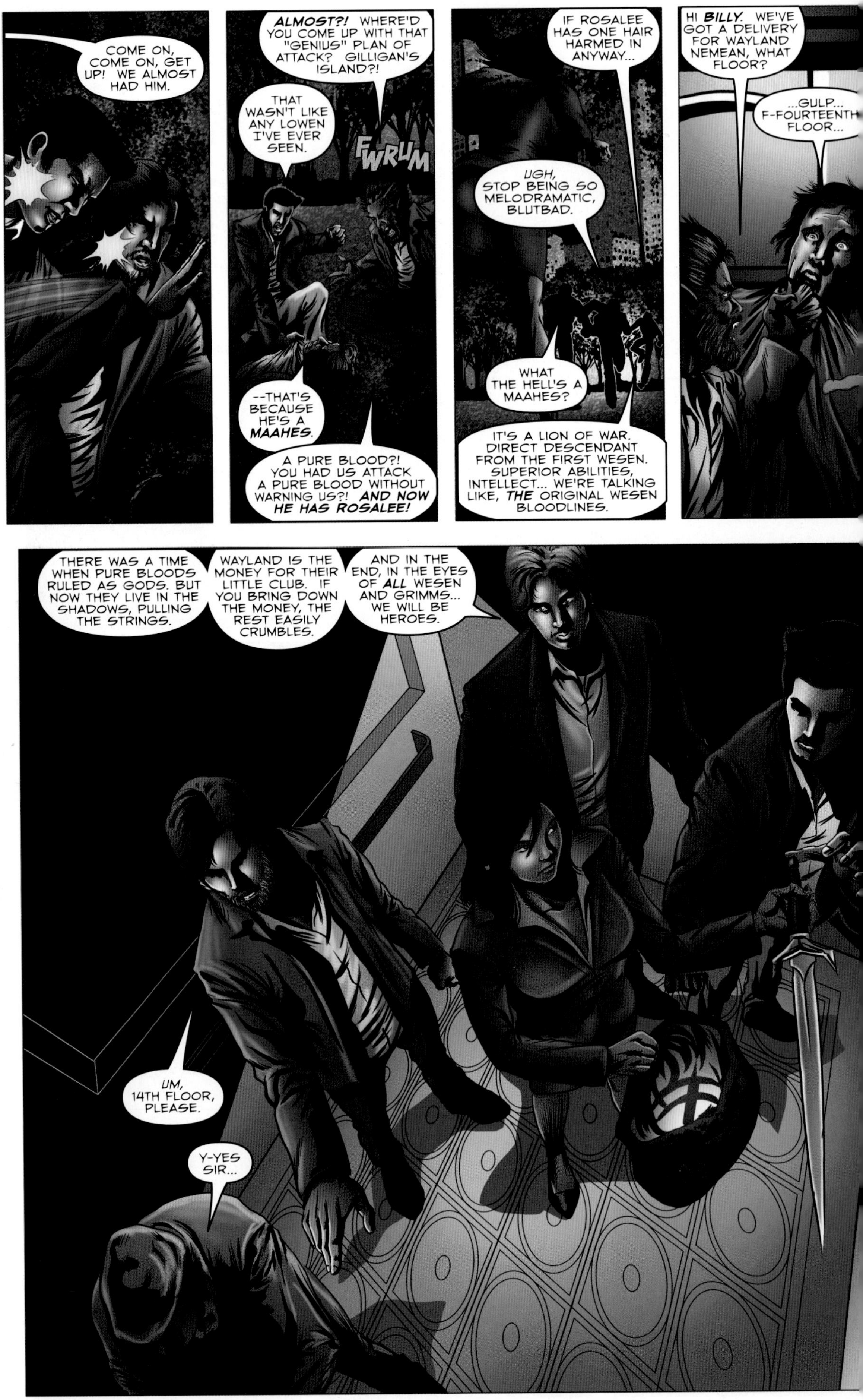
COME ON, COME ON, GET UP! WE ALMOST HAD HIM.
ALMOST?! WHERE'D YOU COME UP WITH THAT "GENIUS" PLAN OF ATTACK? GILLIGAN'S ISLAND?!
THAT WASN'T LIKE ANY LOWEN I'VE EVER SEEN.
FWRUM
--THAT'S BECAUSE HE'S A MAAHES.
A PURE BLOOD?! YOU HAD US ATTACK A PURE BLOOD WITHOUT WARNING US?! AND NOW HE HAS ROSALEE!
IF ROSALEE HAS ONE HAIR HARMED IN ANYWAY...
UGH, STOP BEING SO MELODRAMATIC, BLUTBAD.
WHAT THE HELL'S A MAAHES?
IT'S A LION OF WAR. DIRECT DESCENDANT FROM THE FIRST WESEN. SUPERIOR ABILITIES, INTELLECT... WE'RE TALKING LIKE, THE ORIGINAL WESEN BLOODLINES.
HI BILLY. WE'VE GOT A DELIVERY FOR WAYLAND NEMEAN, WHAT FLOOR?
...GULP... F-FOURTEENTH FLOOR...
THERE WAS A TIME WHEN PURE BLOODS RULED AS GODS. BUT NOW THEY LIVE IN THE SHADOWS, PULLING THE STRINGS.
WAYLAND IS THE MONEY FOR THEIR LITTLE CLUB. IF YOU BRING DOWN THE MONEY, THE REST EASILY CRUMBLES.
AND IN THE END, IN THE EYES OF ALL WESEN AND GRIMMS... WE WILL BE HEROES.
UM, 14TH FLOOR, PLEASE.
Y-YES SIR...

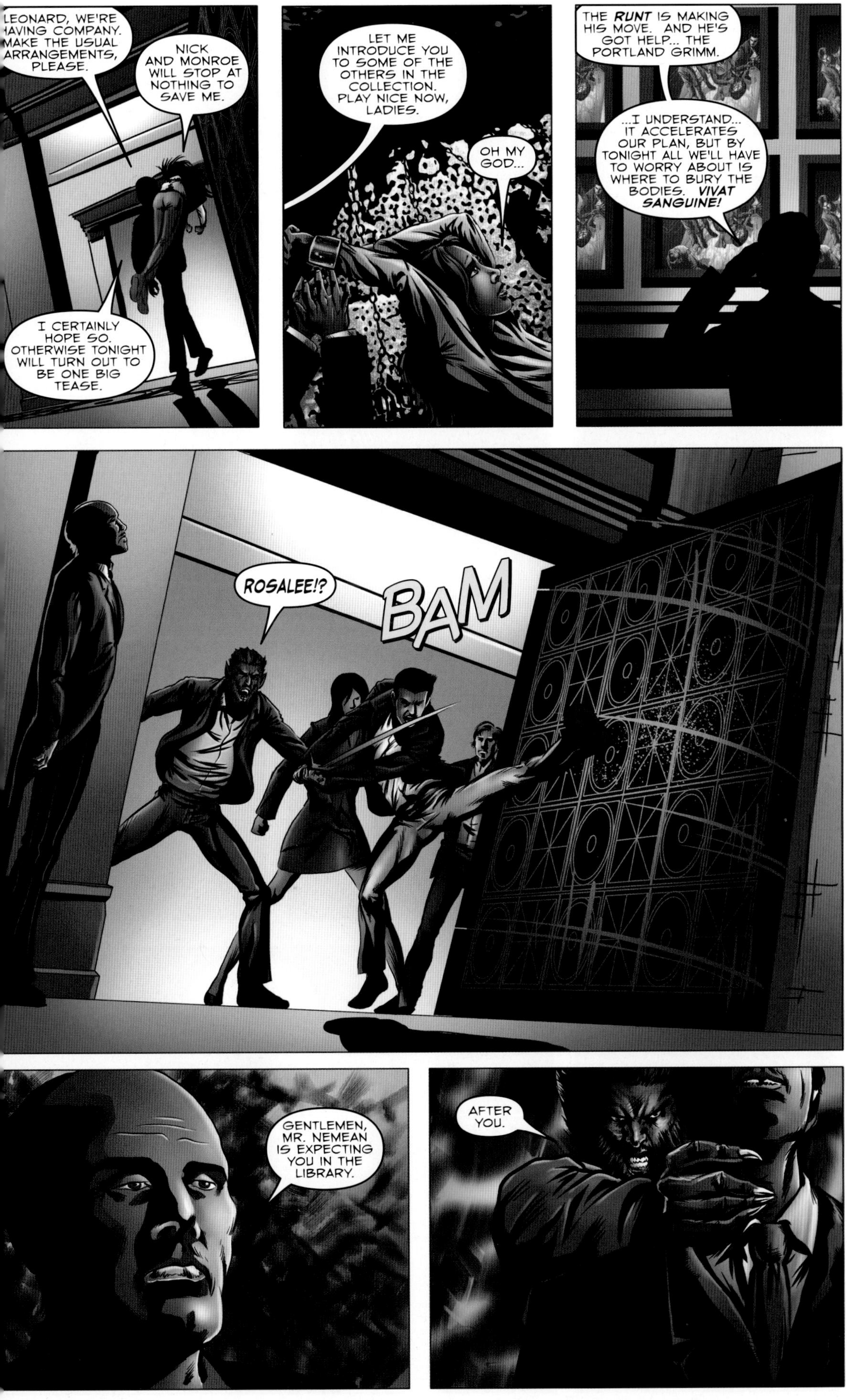
LEONARD, WE'RE HAVING COMPANY. MAKE THE USUAL ARRANGEMENTS, PLEASE.
NICK AND MONROE WILL STOP AT NOTHING TO SAVE ME.
I CERTAINLY HOPE SO. OTHERWISE TONIGHT WILL TURN OUT TO BE ONE BIG TEASE.
LET ME INTRODUCE YOU TO SOME OF THE OTHERS IN THE COLLECTION. PLAY NICE NOW, LADIES.
OH MY GOD...
THE RUNT IS MAKING HIS MOVE. AND HE'S GOT HELP... THE PORTLAND GRIMM.
...I UNDERSTAND... IT ACCELERATES OUR PLAN, BUT BY TONIGHT ALL WE'LL HAVE TO WORRY ABOUT IS WHERE TO BURY THE BODIES. VIVAT SANGUINE!
ROSALEE!?
BAM
GENTLEMEN, MR. NEMEAN IS EXPECTING YOU IN THE LIBRARY.
AFTER YOU.

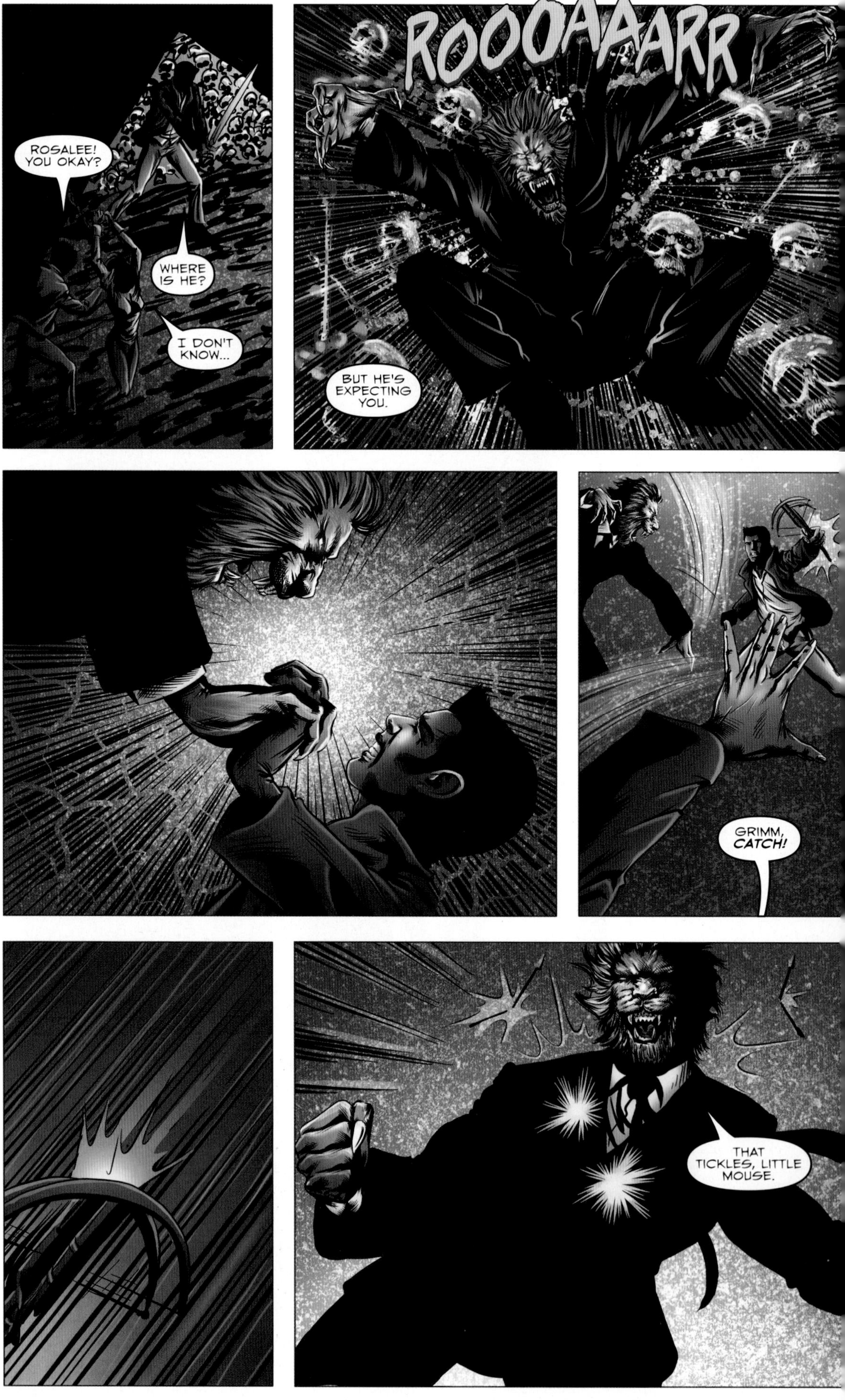
ROSALEE! YOU OKAY?
WHERE IS HE?
I DON'T KNOW...
ROOOAAARR
BUT HE'S EXPECTING YOU.
GRIMM, CATCH!
THAT TICKLES, LITTLE MOUSE.

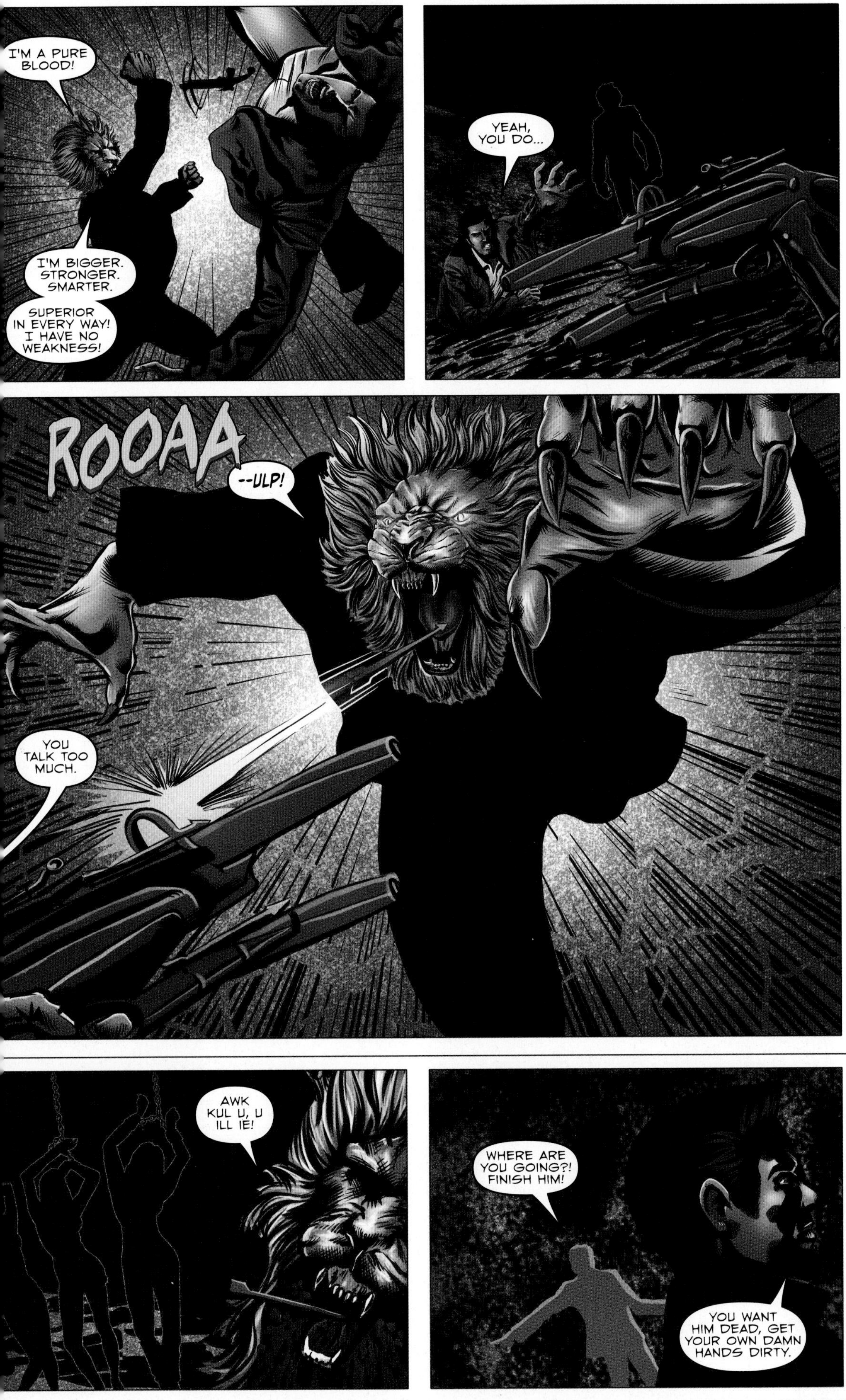
I'M A PURE BLOOD!
I'M BIGGER. STRONGER. SMARTER.
SUPERIOR IN EVERY WAY! I HAVE NO WEAKNESS!
YEAH, YOU DO...
ROOAA
--ULP!
YOU TALK TOO MUCH.
AWK KUL U, U ILL IE!
WHERE ARE YOU GOING?! FINISH HIM!
YOU WANT HIM DEAD, GET YOUR OWN DAMN HANDS DIRTY.

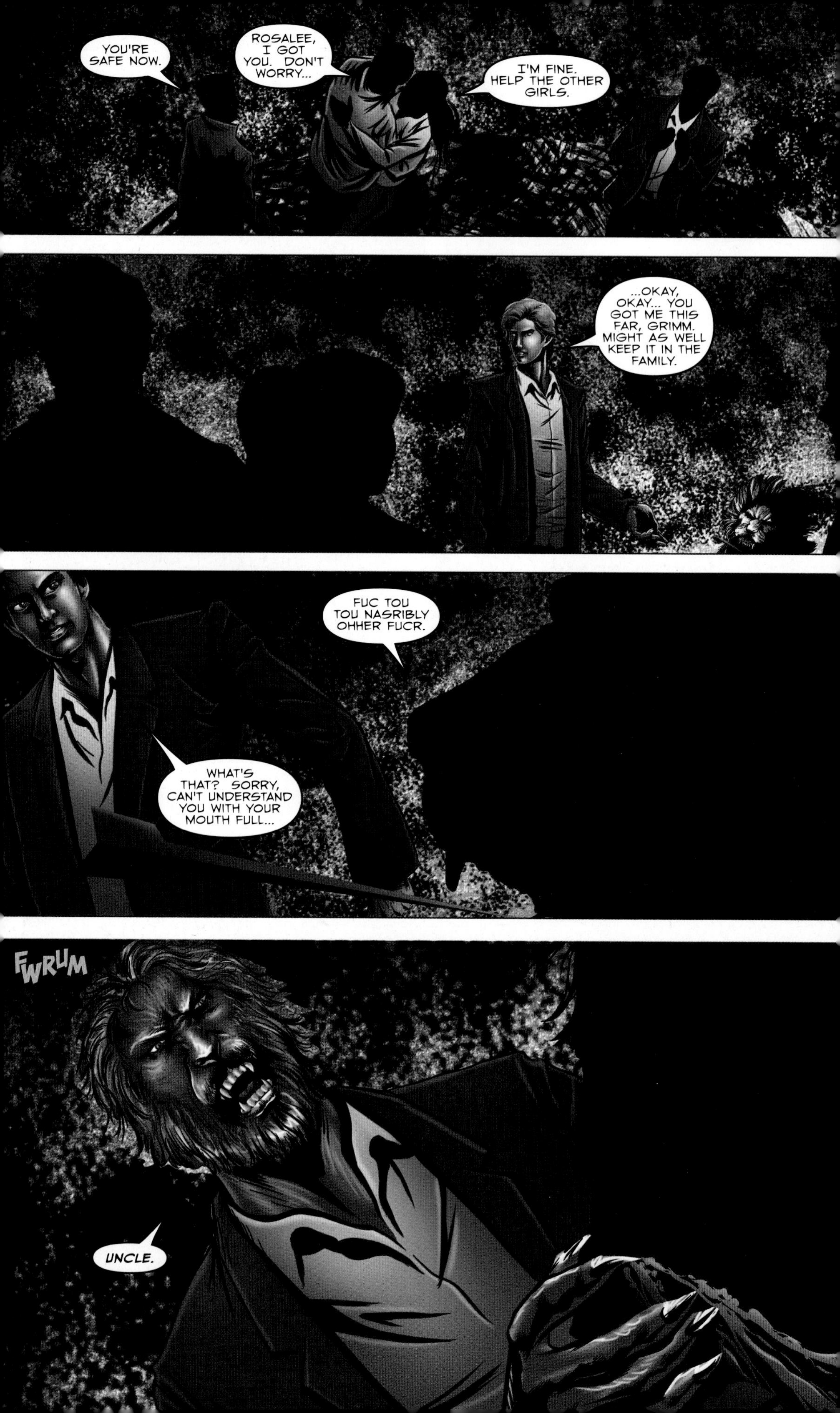
YOU'RE SAFE NOW.
ROSALEE, I GOT YOU. DON'T WORRY...
I'M FINE. HELP THE OTHER GIRLS.
...OKAY, OKAY... YOU GOT ME THIS FAR, GRIMM. MIGHT AS WELL KEEP IT IN THE FAMILY.
FUC TOU TOU NASRIBLY OHHER FUCR.
WHAT'S THAT? SORRY, CAN'T UNDERSTAND YOU WITH YOUR MOUTH FULL...
FWRUM
UNCLE.

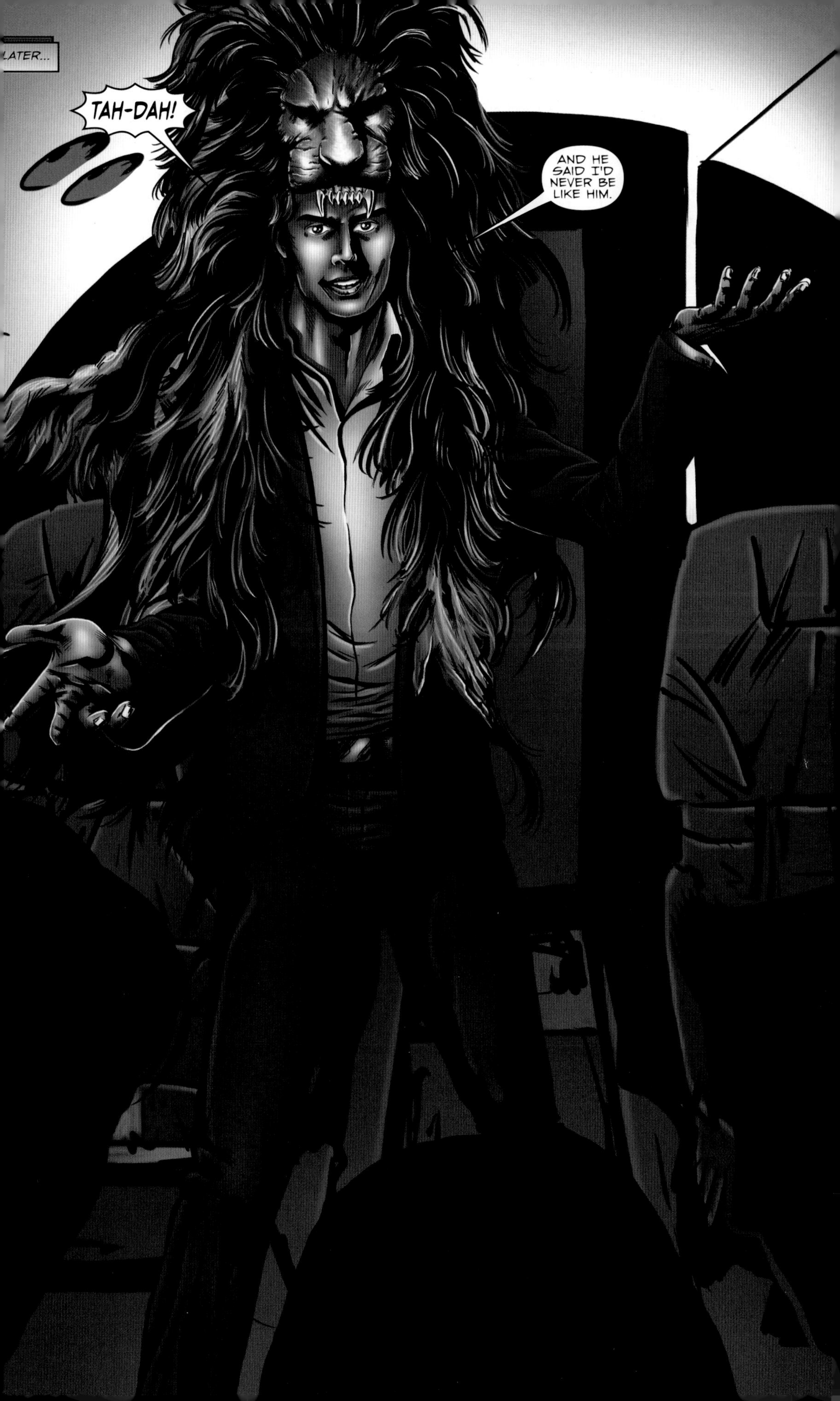
LATER...
TAH-DAH!
AND HE SAID I'D NEVER BE LIKE HIM.

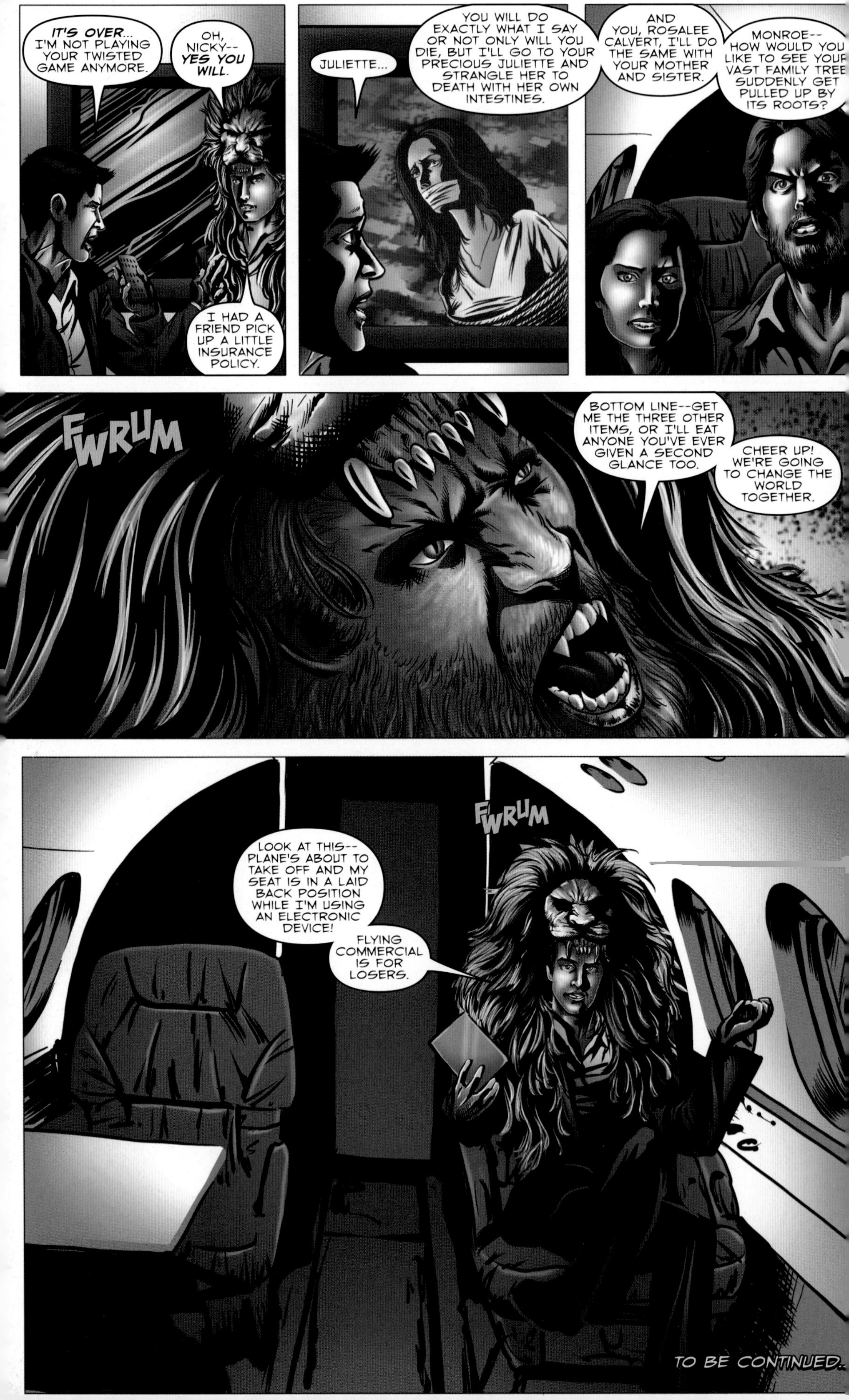
IT'S OVER... I'M NOT PLAYING YOUR TWISTED GAME ANYMORE.
OH, NICKY-- YES YOU WILL.
I HAD A FRIEND PICK UP A LITTLE INSURANCE POLICY.
JULIETTE...
YOU WILL DO EXACTLY WHAT I SAY OR NOT ONLY WILL YOU DIE, BUT I'LL GO TO YOUR PRECIOUS JULIETTE AND STRANGLE HER TO DEATH WITH HER OWN INTESTINES.
AND YOU, ROSALEE CALVERT, I'LL DO THE SAME WITH YOUR MOTHER AND SISTER.
MONROE-- HOW WOULD YOU LIKE TO SEE YOUR VAST FAMILY TREE SUDDENLY GET PULLED UP BY ITS ROOTS?
FWRUM
BOTTOM LINE--GET ME THE THREE OTHER ITEMS, OR I'LL EAT ANYONE YOU'VE EVER GIVEN A SECOND GLANCE TOO.
CHEER UP! WE'RE GOING TO CHANGE THE WORLD TOGETHER.
FWRUM
LOOK AT THIS-- PLANE'S ABOUT TO TAKE OFF AND MY SEAT IS IN A LAID BACK POSITION WHILE I'M USING AN ELECTRONIC DEVICE!
FLYING COMMERCIAL IS FOR LOSERS.
TO BE CONTINUED...

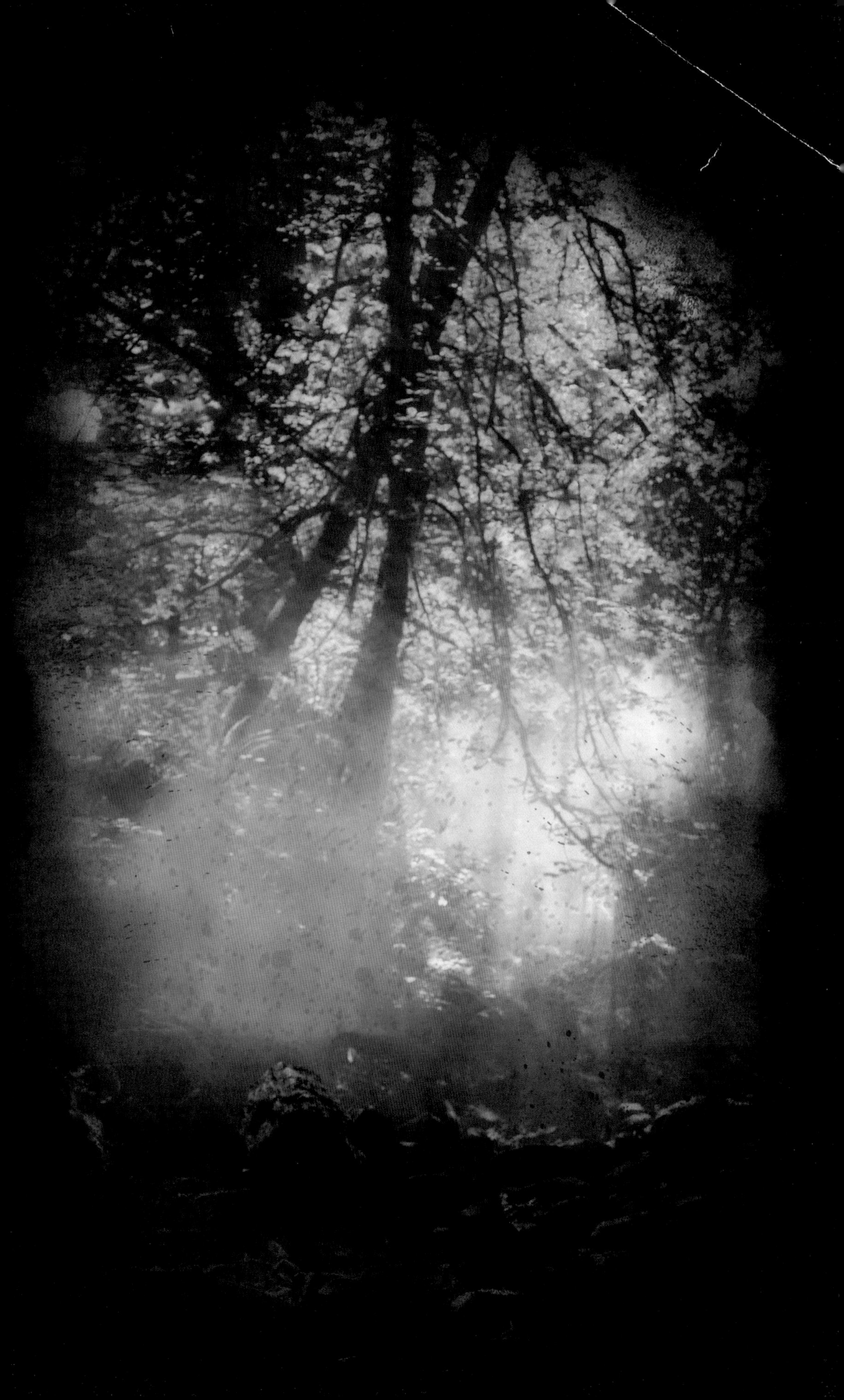

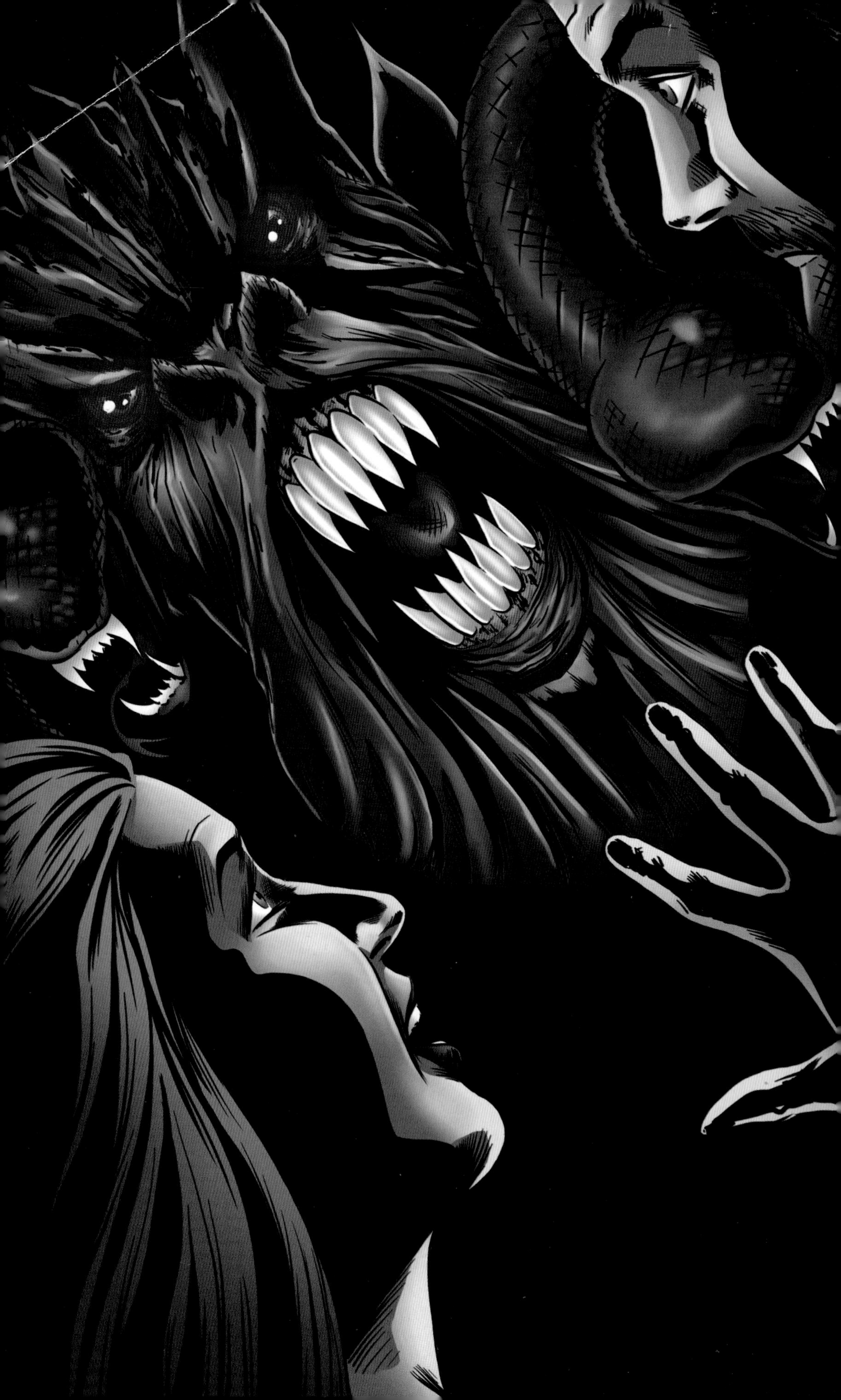

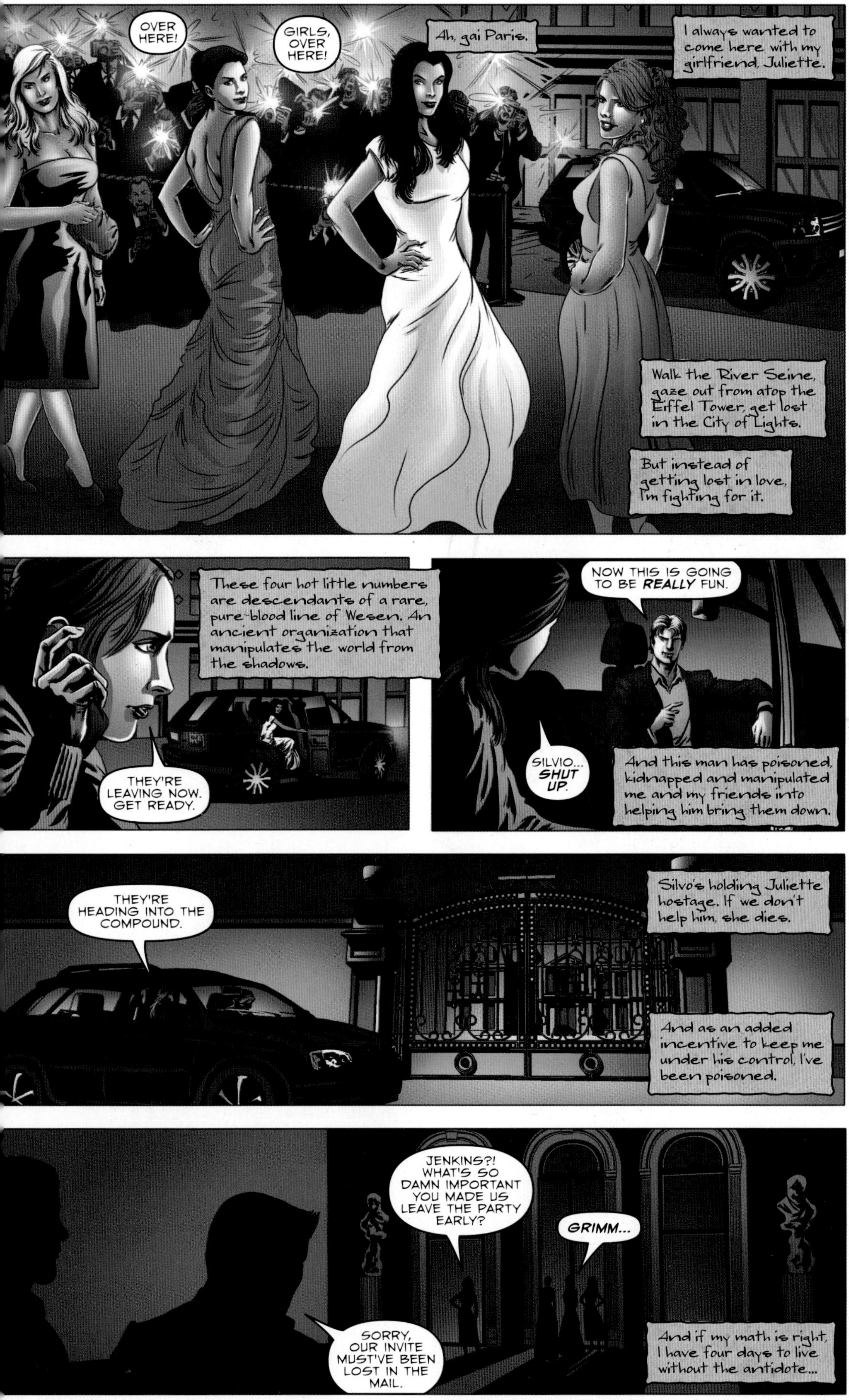
OVER HERE!
GIRLS, OVER HERE!
Ah, gai Paris.
I always wanted to come here with my girlfriend, Juliette.
Walk the River Seine, gaze out from atop the Eiffel Tower, get lost in the City of Lights.
But instead of getting lost in love, I'm fighting for it.
These four hot little numbers are descendants of a rare, pure-blood line of Wesen. An ancient organization that manipulates the world from the shadows.
THEY'RE LEAVING NOW. GET READY.
NOW THIS IS GOING TO BE REALLY FUN.
SILVIO... SHUT UP.
And this man has poisoned, kidnapped and manipulated me and my friends into helping him bring them down.
THEY'RE HEADING INTO THE COMPOUND.
Silvo's holding Juliette hostage. If we don't help him, she dies.
And as an added incentive to keep me under his control, I've been poisoned.
JENKINS?! WHAT'S SO DAMN IMPORTANT YOU MADE US LEAVE THE PARTY EARLY?
GRIMM...
SORRY, OUR INVITE MUST'VE BEEN LOST IN THE MAIL.
And if my math is right, I have four days to live without the antidote...

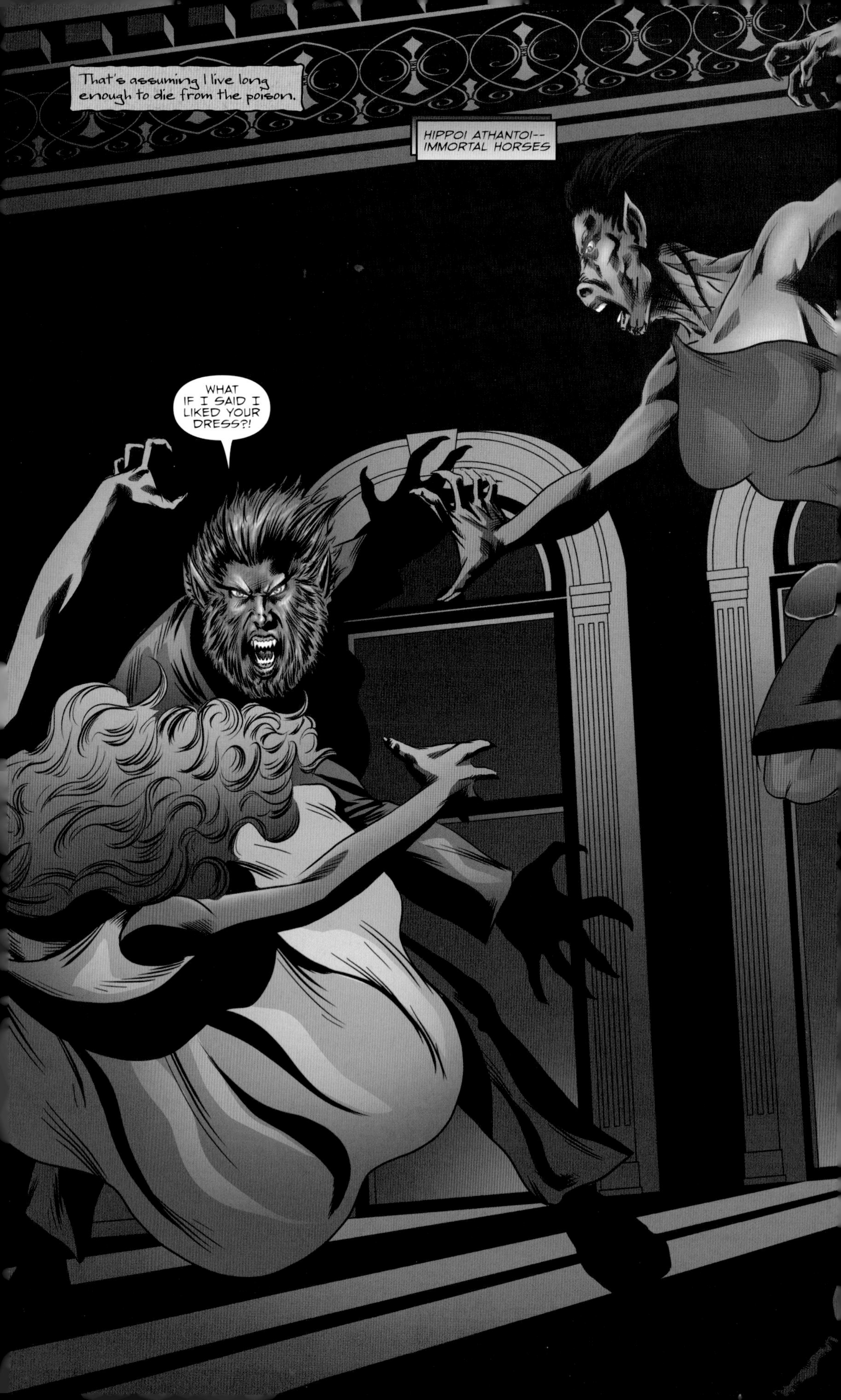
That's assuming I live long enough to die from the poison.
HIPPOI ATHANTOI-- IMMORTAL HORSES
WHAT IF I SAID I LIKED YOUR DRESS?!

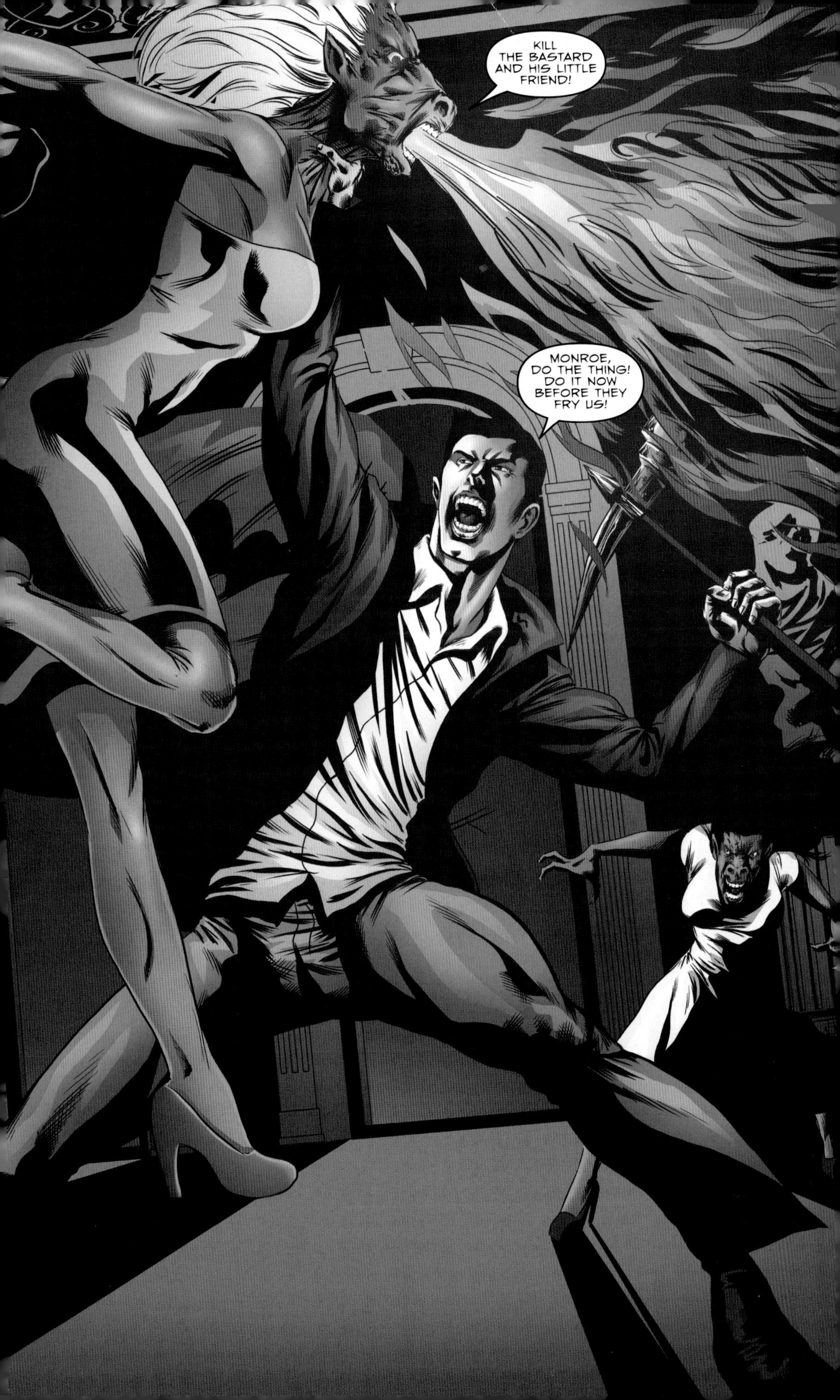
KILL THE BASTARD AND HIS LITTLE FRIEND!
MONROE, DO THE THING! DO IT NOW BEFORE THEY FRY US!

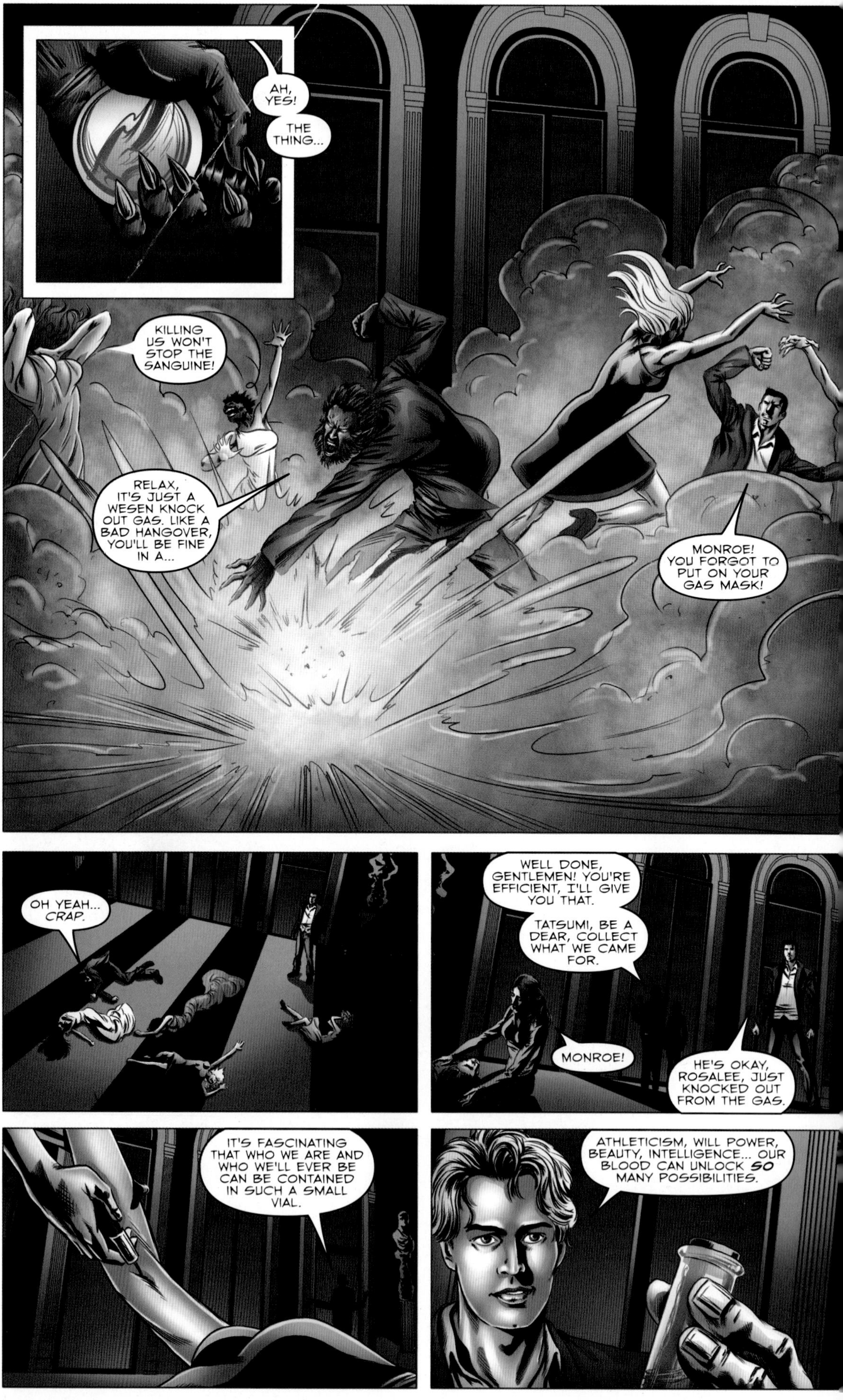

AH, YES!
THE THING...
KILLING US WON'T STOP THE SANGUINE!
RELAX, IT'S JUST A WESEN KNOCK OUT GAS. LIKE A BAD HANGOVER, YOU'LL BE FINE IN A...
MONROE! YOU FORGOT TO PUT ON YOUR GAS MASK!
OH YEAH... *CRAP.*
WELL DONE, GENTLEMEN! YOU'RE EFFICIENT, I'LL GIVE YOU THAT.
TATSUMI, BE A DEAR, COLLECT WHAT WE CAME FOR.
MONROE!
HE'S OKAY, ROSALEE, JUST KNOCKED OUT FROM THE GAS.
IT'S FASCINATING THAT WHO WE ARE AND WHO WE'LL EVER BE CAN BE CONTAINED IN SUCH A SMALL VIAL.
ATHLETICISM, WILL POWER, BEAUTY, INTELLIGENCE... OUR BLOOD CAN UNLOCK ***SO*** MANY POSSIBILITIES.

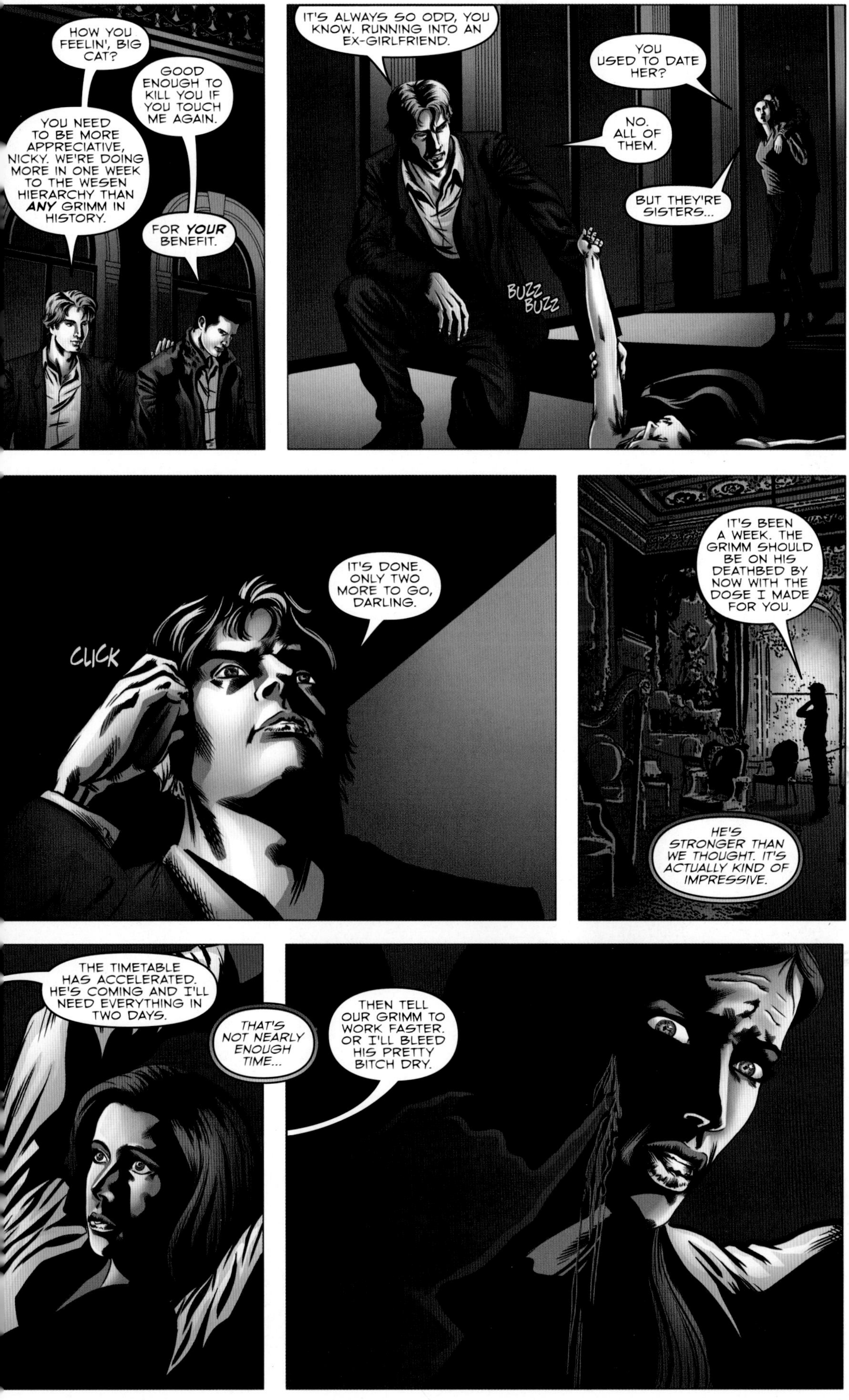
HOW YOU FEELIN', BIG CAT?
GOOD ENOUGH TO KILL YOU IF YOU TOUCH ME AGAIN.
YOU NEED TO BE MORE APPRECIATIVE, NICKY. WE'RE DOING MORE IN ONE WEEK TO THE WESEN HIERARCHY THAN ANY GRIMM IN HISTORY.
FOR YOUR BENEFIT.
IT'S ALWAYS SO ODD, YOU KNOW. RUNNING INTO AN EX-GIRLFRIEND.
YOU USED TO DATE HER?
NO. ALL OF THEM.
BUT THEY'RE SISTERS...
BUZZ BUZZ
CLICK
IT'S DONE. ONLY TWO MORE TO GO, DARLING.
IT'S BEEN A WEEK. THE GRIMM SHOULD BE ON HIS DEATHBED BY NOW WITH THE DOSE I MADE FOR YOU.
HE'S STRONGER THAN WE THOUGHT. IT'S ACTUALLY KIND OF IMPRESSIVE.
THE TIMETABLE HAS ACCELERATED. HE'S COMING AND I'LL NEED EVERYTHING IN TWO DAYS.
THAT'S NOT NEARLY ENOUGH TIME...
THEN TELL OUR GRIMM TO WORK FASTER. OR I'LL BLEED HIS PRETTY BITCH DRY.

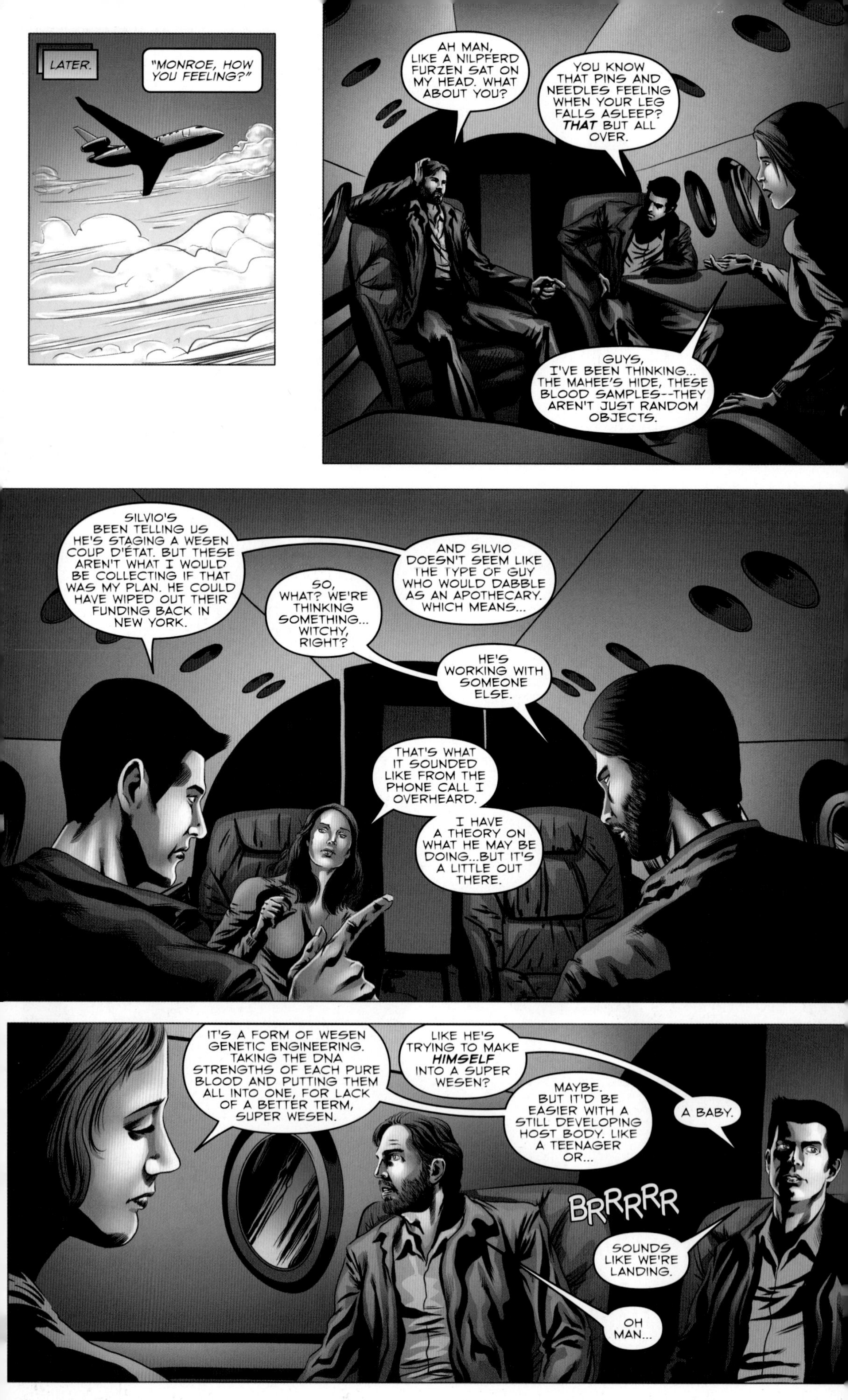
LATER.
"MONROE, HOW YOU FEELING?"
AH MAN, LIKE A NILPFERD FURZEN SAT ON MY HEAD. WHAT ABOUT YOU?
YOU KNOW THAT PINS AND NEEDLES FEELING WHEN YOUR LEG FALLS ASLEEP? THAT BUT ALL OVER.
GUYS, I'VE BEEN THINKING... THE MAHEE'S HIDE, THESE BLOOD SAMPLES--THEY AREN'T JUST RANDOM OBJECTS.
SILVIO'S BEEN TELLING US HE'S STAGING A WESEN COUP D'ÉTAT. BUT THESE AREN'T WHAT I WOULD BE COLLECTING IF THAT WAS MY PLAN. HE COULD HAVE WIPED OUT THEIR FUNDING BACK IN NEW YORK.
AND SILVIO DOESN'T SEEM LIKE THE TYPE OF GUY WHO WOULD DABBLE AS AN APOTHECARY. WHICH MEANS...
SO, WHAT? WE'RE THINKING SOMETHING... WITCHY, RIGHT?
HE'S WORKING WITH SOMEONE ELSE.
THAT'S WHAT IT SOUNDED LIKE FROM THE PHONE CALL I OVERHEARD.
I HAVE A THEORY ON WHAT HE MAY BE DOING...BUT IT'S A LITTLE OUT THERE.
IT'S A FORM OF WESEN GENETIC ENGINEERING. TAKING THE DNA STRENGTHS OF EACH PURE BLOOD AND PUTTING THEM ALL INTO ONE, FOR LACK OF A BETTER TERM, SUPER WESEN.
LIKE HE'S TRYING TO MAKE HIMSELF INTO A SUPER WESEN?
MAYBE. BUT IT'D BE EASIER WITH A STILL DEVELOPING HOST BODY. LIKE A TEENAGER OR...
A BABY.
BRRRRR
SOUNDS LIKE WE'RE LANDING.
OH MAN...

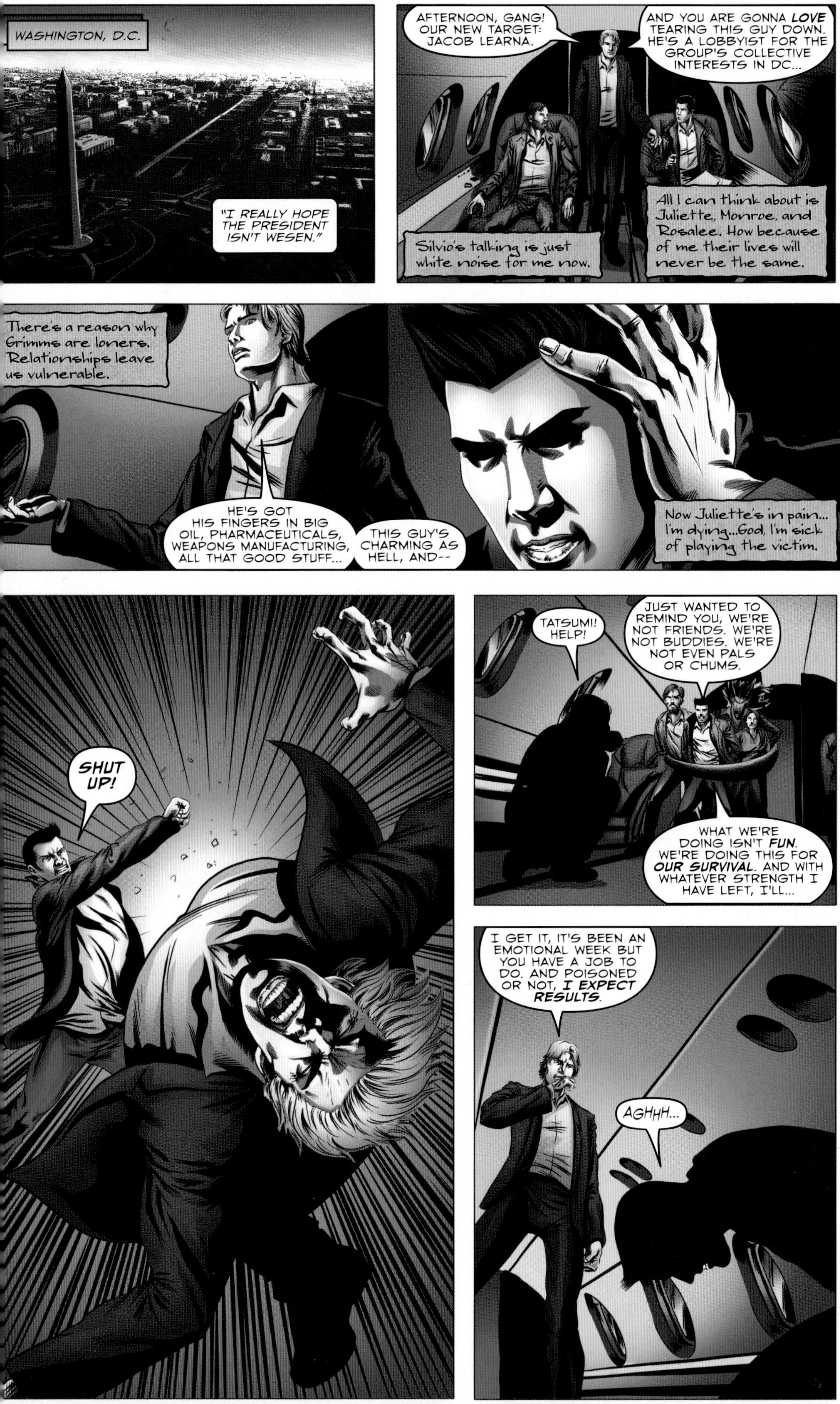
WASHINGTON, D.C.
"I REALLY HOPE THE PRESIDENT ISN'T WESEN."
AFTERNOON, GANG! OUR NEW TARGET: JACOB LEARNA.
AND YOU ARE GONNA LOVE TEARING THIS GUY DOWN. HE'S A LOBBYIST FOR THE GROUP'S COLLECTIVE INTERESTS IN DC...
Silvio's talking is just white noise for me now.
All I can think about is Juliette, Monroe, and Rosalee. How because of me their lives will never be the same.
There's a reason why Grimms are loners. Relationships leave us vulnerable.
HE'S GOT HIS FINGERS IN BIG OIL, PHARMACEUTICALS, WEAPONS MANUFACTURING, ALL THAT GOOD STUFF...
THIS GUY'S CHARMING AS HELL, AND--
Now Juliette's in pain... I'm dying...God, I'm sick of playing the victim.
SHUT UP!
TATSUMI! HELP!
JUST WANTED TO REMIND YOU, WE'RE NOT FRIENDS. WE'RE NOT BUDDIES. WE'RE NOT EVEN PALS OR CHUMS.
WHAT WE'RE DOING ISN'T FUN. WE'RE DOING THIS FOR OUR SURVIVAL. AND WITH WHATEVER STRENGTH I HAVE LEFT, I'LL...
I GET IT, IT'S BEEN AN EMOTIONAL WEEK BUT YOU HAVE A JOB TO DO. AND POISONED OR NOT, I EXPECT RESULTS.
AGHHH...

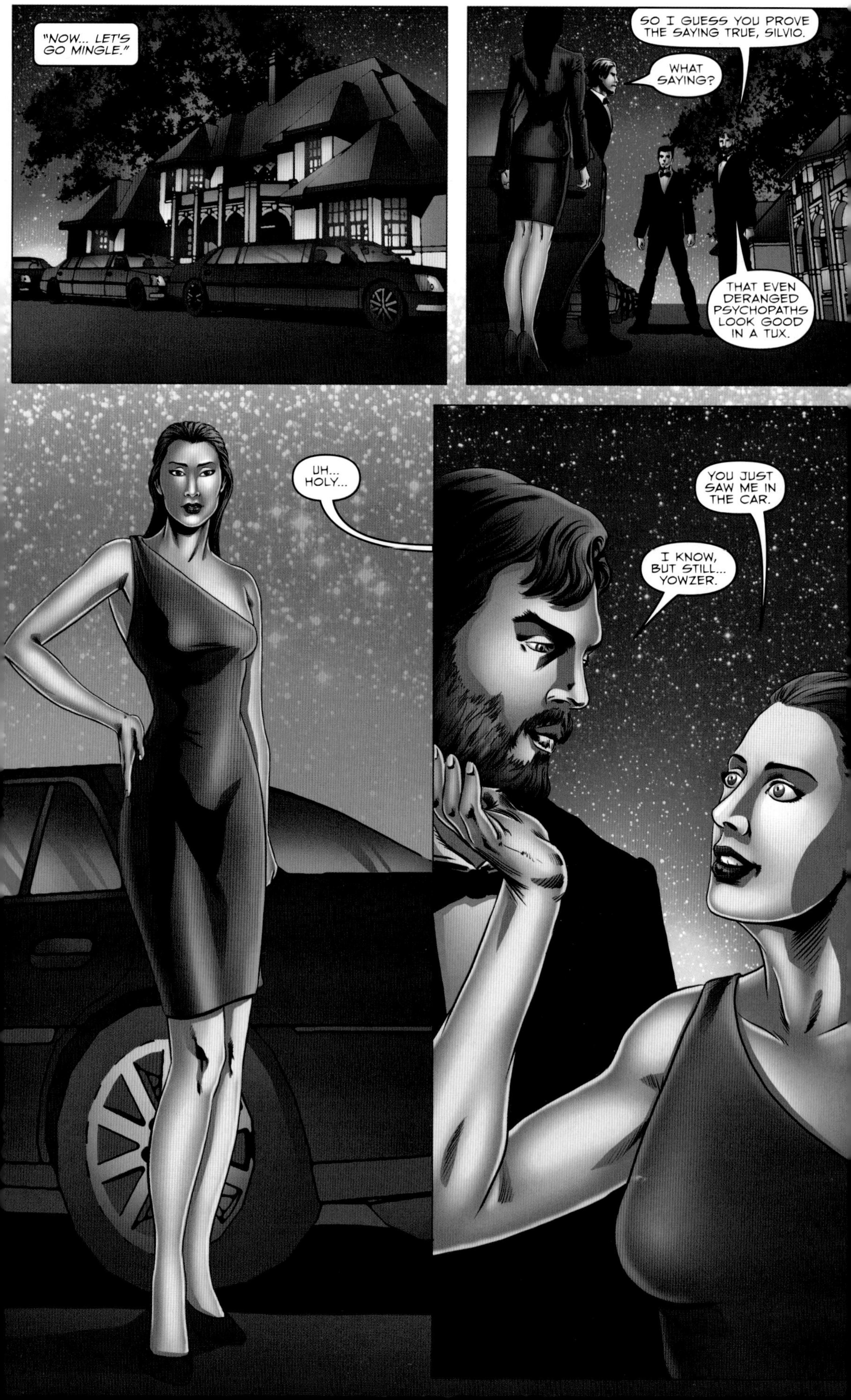
"NOW... LET'S GO MINGLE."
SO I GUESS YOU PROVE THE SAYING TRUE, SILVIO.
WHAT SAYING?
THAT EVEN DERANGED PSYCHOPATHS LOOK GOOD IN A TUX.
UH... HOLY...
YOU JUST SAW ME IN THE CAR.
I KNOW, BUT STILL... YOWZER.

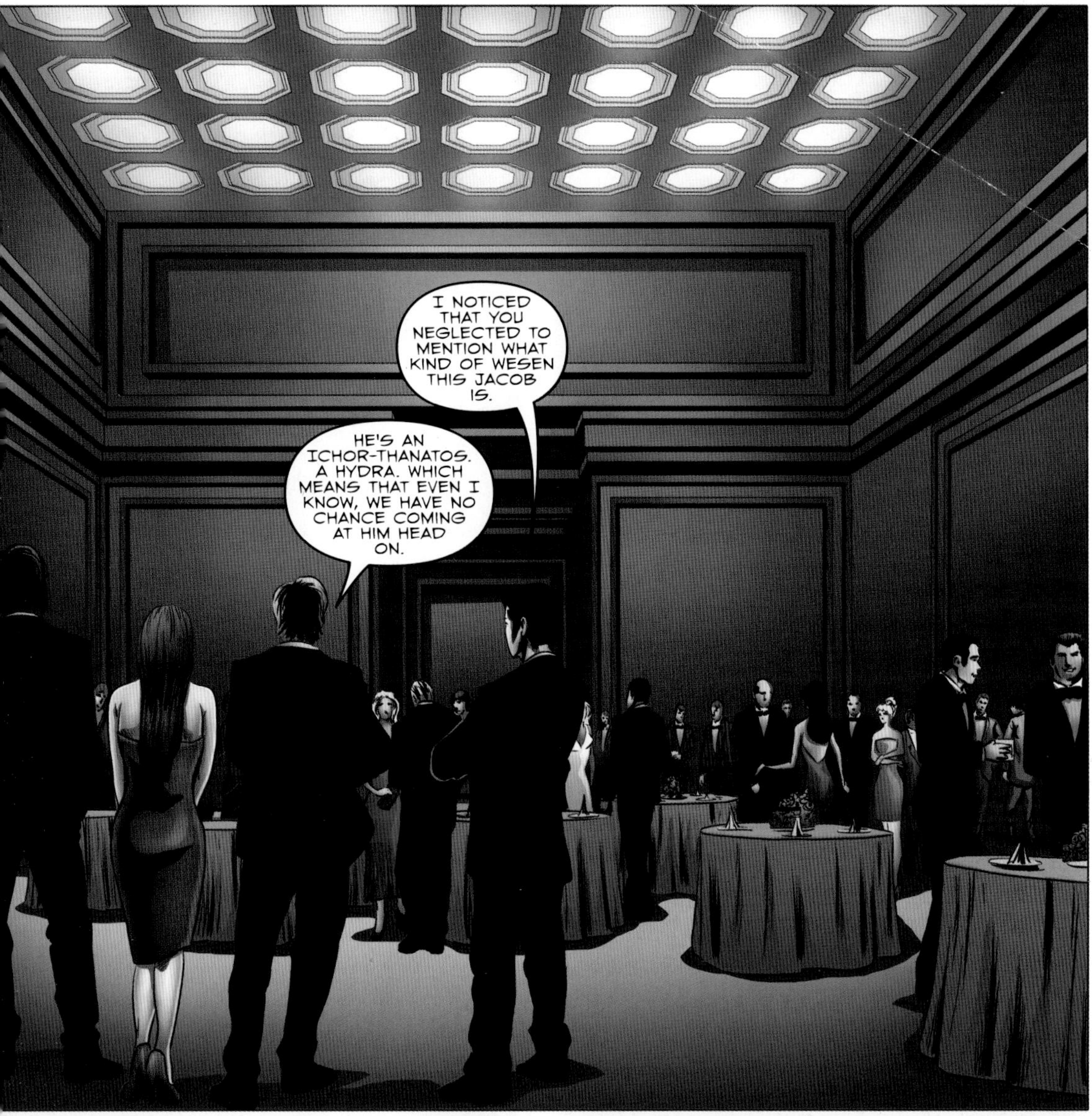

I NOTICED THAT YOU NEGLECTED TO MENTION WHAT KIND OF WESEN THIS JACOB IS.
HE'S AN ICHOR-THANATOS. A HYDRA. WHICH MEANS THAT EVEN I KNOW, WE HAVE NO CHANCE COMING AT HIM HEAD ON.

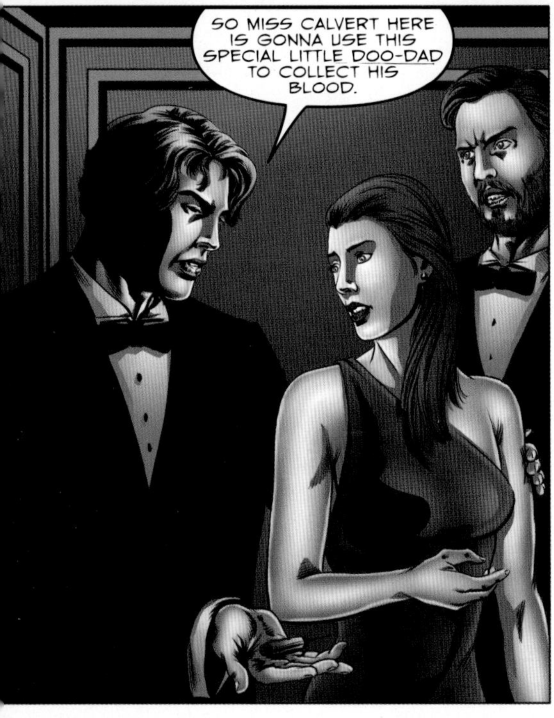

SO MISS CALVERT HERE IS GONNA USE THIS SPECIAL LITTLE DOO-DAD TO COLLECT HIS BLOOD.

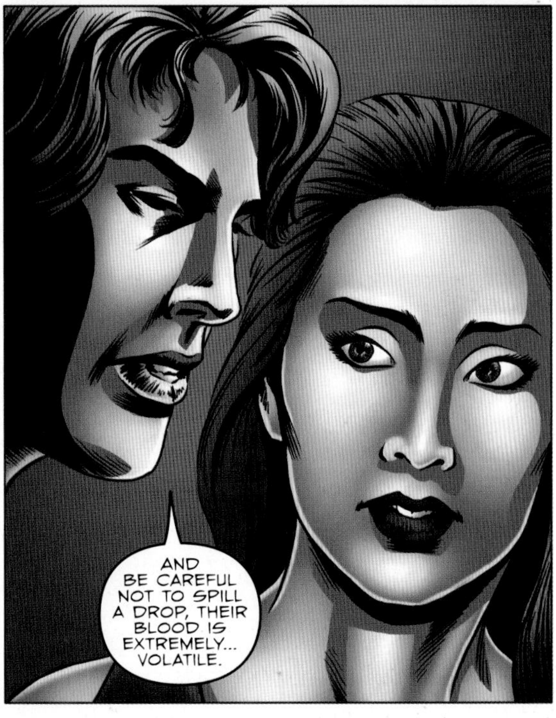

AND BE CAREFUL NOT TO SPILL A DROP, THEIR BLOOD IS EXTREMELY... VOLATILE.

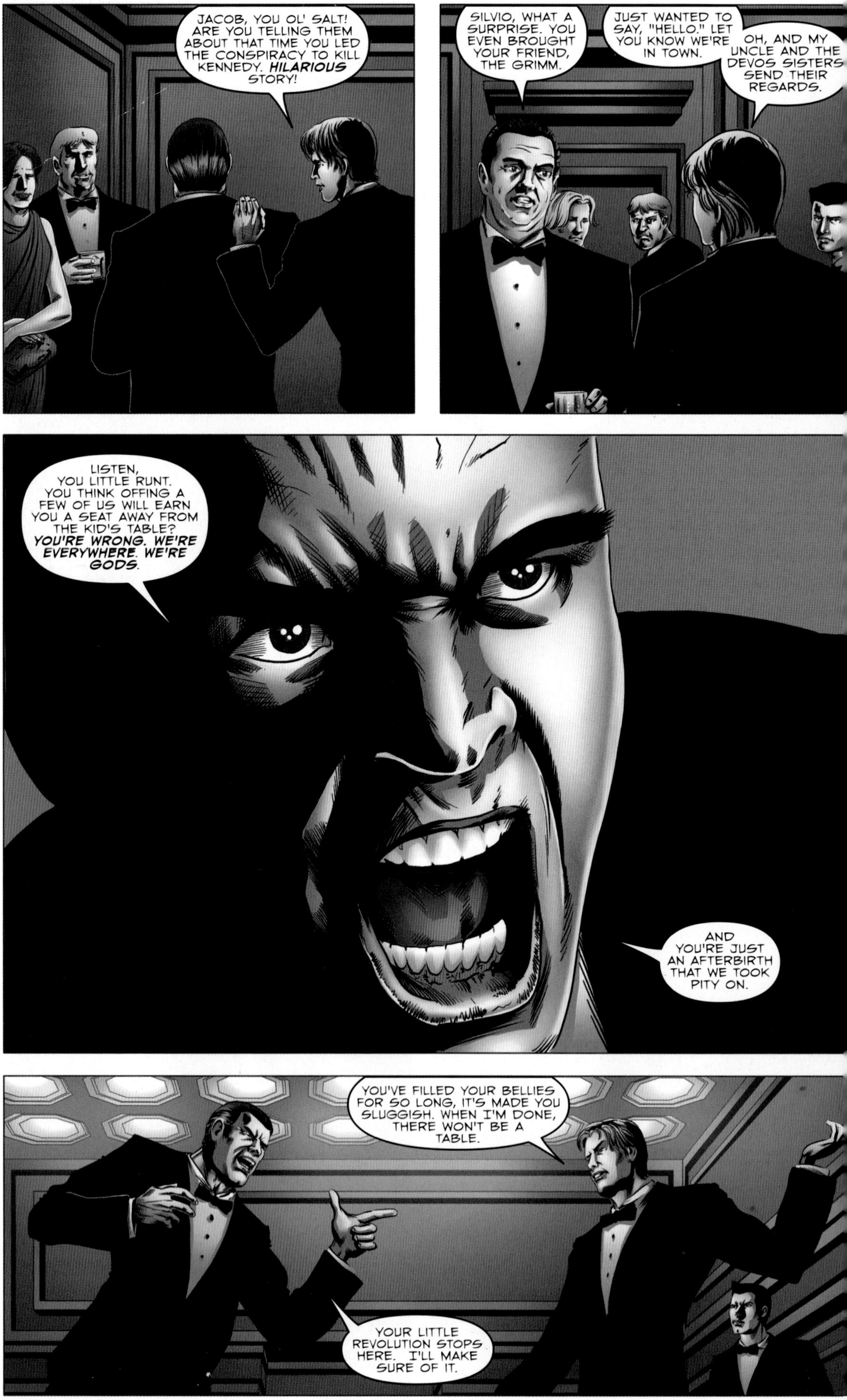
JACOB, YOU OL' SALT! ARE YOU TELLING THEM ABOUT THAT TIME YOU LED THE CONSPIRACY TO KILL KENNEDY. *HILARIOUS* STORY!
SILVIO, WHAT A SURPRISE. YOU EVEN BROUGHT YOUR FRIEND, THE GRIMM.
JUST WANTED TO SAY, "HELLO." LET YOU KNOW WE'RE IN TOWN.
OH, AND MY UNCLE AND THE DEVOS SISTERS SEND THEIR REGARDS.
LISTEN, YOU LITTLE RUNT. YOU THINK OFFING A FEW OF US WILL EARN YOU A SEAT AWAY FROM THE KID'S TABLE? *YOU'RE WRONG. WE'RE EVERYWHERE. WE'RE GODS.*
AND YOU'RE JUST AN AFTERBIRTH THAT WE TOOK PITY ON.
YOU'VE FILLED YOUR BELLIES FOR SO LONG, IT'S MADE YOU SLUGGISH. WHEN I'M DONE, THERE WON'T BE A TABLE.
YOUR LITTLE REVOLUTION STOPS HERE. I'LL MAKE SURE OF IT.

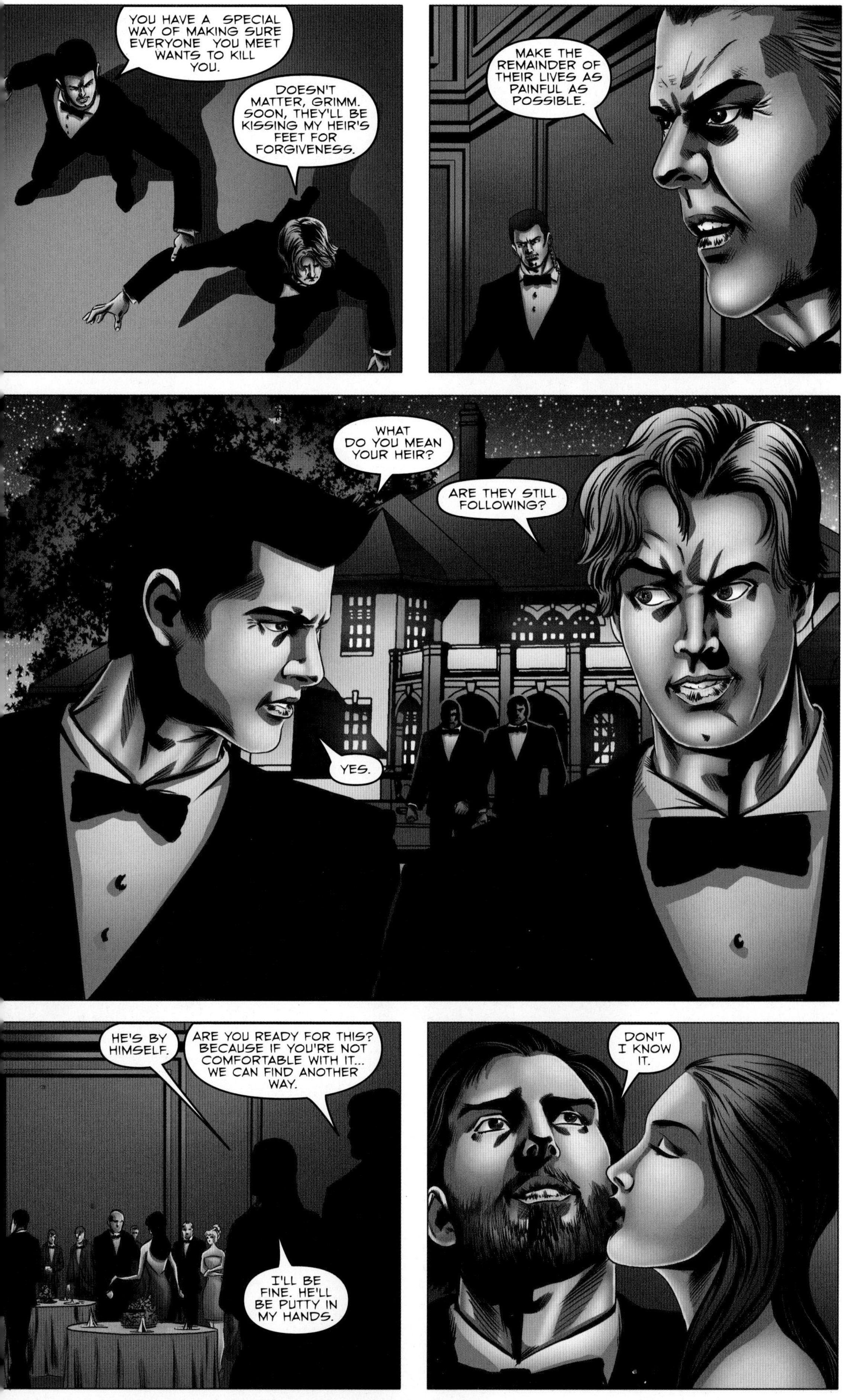
YOU HAVE A SPECIAL WAY OF MAKING SURE EVERYONE YOU MEET WANTS TO KILL YOU.
DOESN'T MATTER, GRIMM. SOON, THEY'LL BE KISSING MY HEIR'S FEET FOR FORGIVENESS.
MAKE THE REMAINDER OF THEIR LIVES AS PAINFUL AS POSSIBLE.
WHAT DO YOU MEAN YOUR HEIR?
ARE THEY STILL FOLLOWING?
YES.
HE'S BY HIMSELF.
ARE YOU READY FOR THIS? BECAUSE IF YOU'RE NOT COMFORTABLE WITH IT... WE CAN FIND ANOTHER WAY.
I'LL BE FINE. HE'LL BE PUTTY IN MY HANDS.
DON'T I KNOW IT.

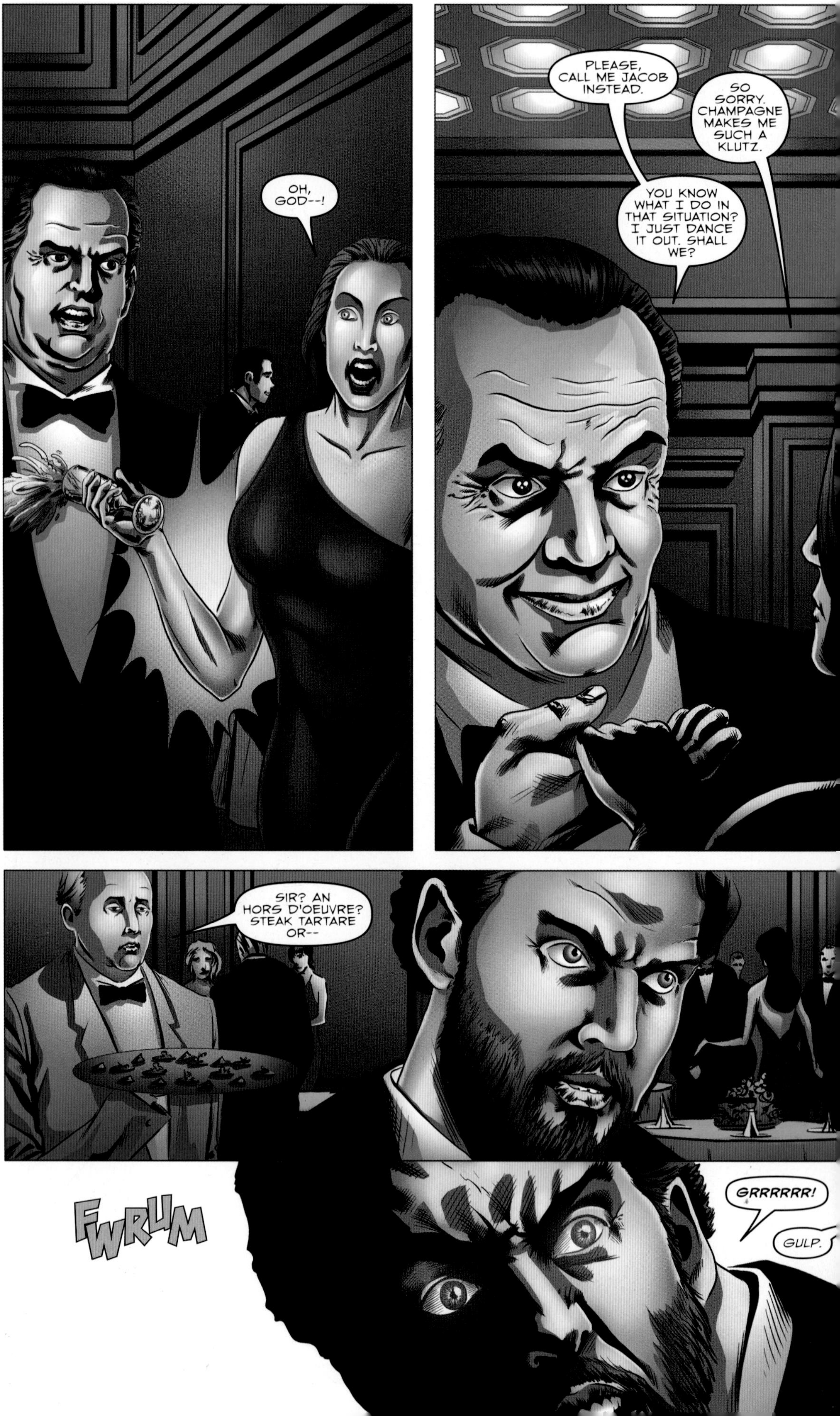
OH, GOD--!
PLEASE, CALL ME JACOB INSTEAD.
SO SORRY. CHAMPAGNE MAKES ME SUCH A KLUTZ.
YOU KNOW WHAT I DO IN THAT SITUATION? I JUST DANCE IT OUT. SHALL WE?
SIR? AN HORS D'OEUVRE? STEAK TARTARE OR--
FWRUM
GRRRRRR!
GULP.

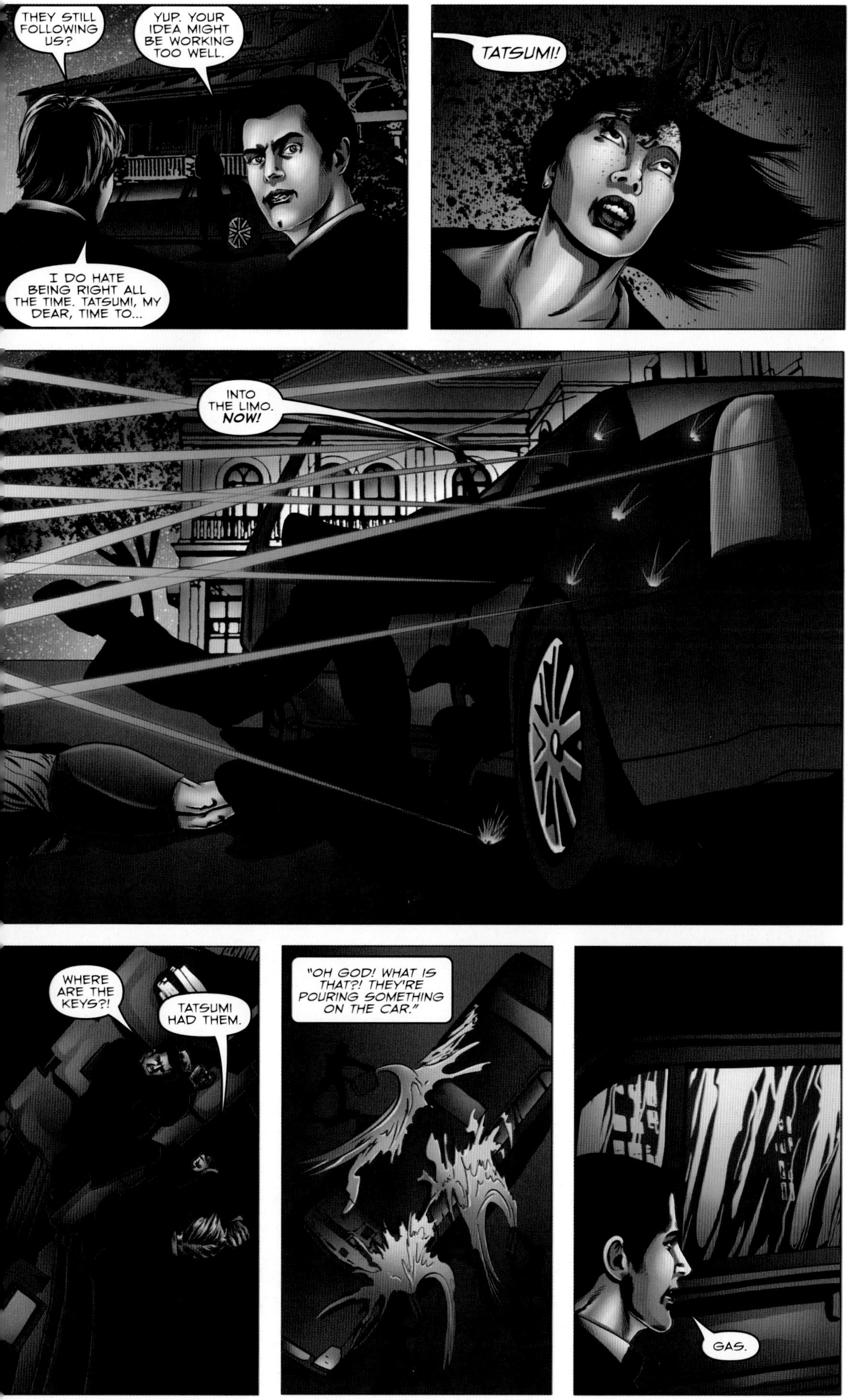
THEY STILL FOLLOWING US?
YUP. YOUR IDEA MIGHT BE WORKING TOO WELL.
I DO HATE BEING RIGHT ALL THE TIME. TATSUMI, MY DEAR, TIME TO...
BANG
TATSUMI!
INTO THE LIMO. NOW!
WHERE ARE THE KEYS?!
TATSUMI HAD THEM.
"OH GOD! WHAT IS THAT?! THEY'RE POURING SOMETHING ON THE CAR."
GAS.

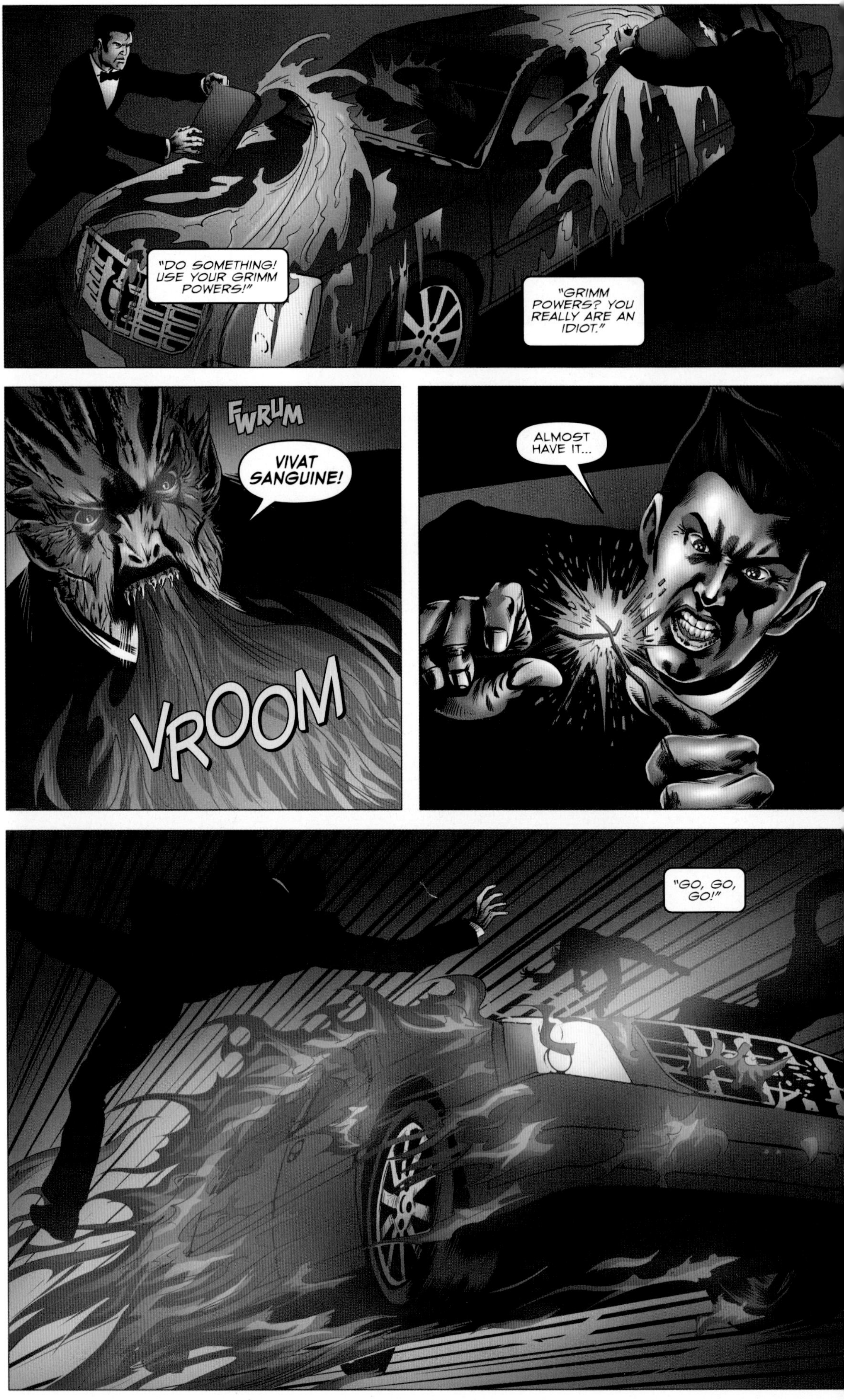
"DO SOMETHING! USE YOUR GRIMM POWERS!"
"GRIMM POWERS? YOU REALLY ARE AN IDIOT."
FWRUM
VIVAT SANGUINE!
VROOM
ALMOST HAVE IT...
"GO, GO, GO!"

YOU'RE A WONDERFUL DANCER FOR BEING SUCH A KLUTZ, MISS...

JONES. AND YOU'RE NOT SO BAD YOURSELF.

UGH. A DIP. GUY'S NOT EVEN IN TIME WITH THE DAMN MUSIC.

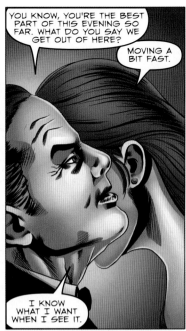

YOU KNOW, YOU'RE THE BEST PART OF THIS EVENING SO FAR. WHAT DO YOU SAY WE GET OUT OF HERE?

MOVING A BIT FAST.

I KNOW WHAT I WANT WHEN I SEE IT.

GOOD, BECAUSE SO DO I.

OW!

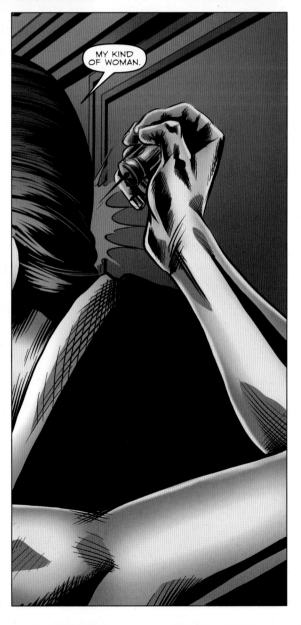

MY KIND OF WOMAN.

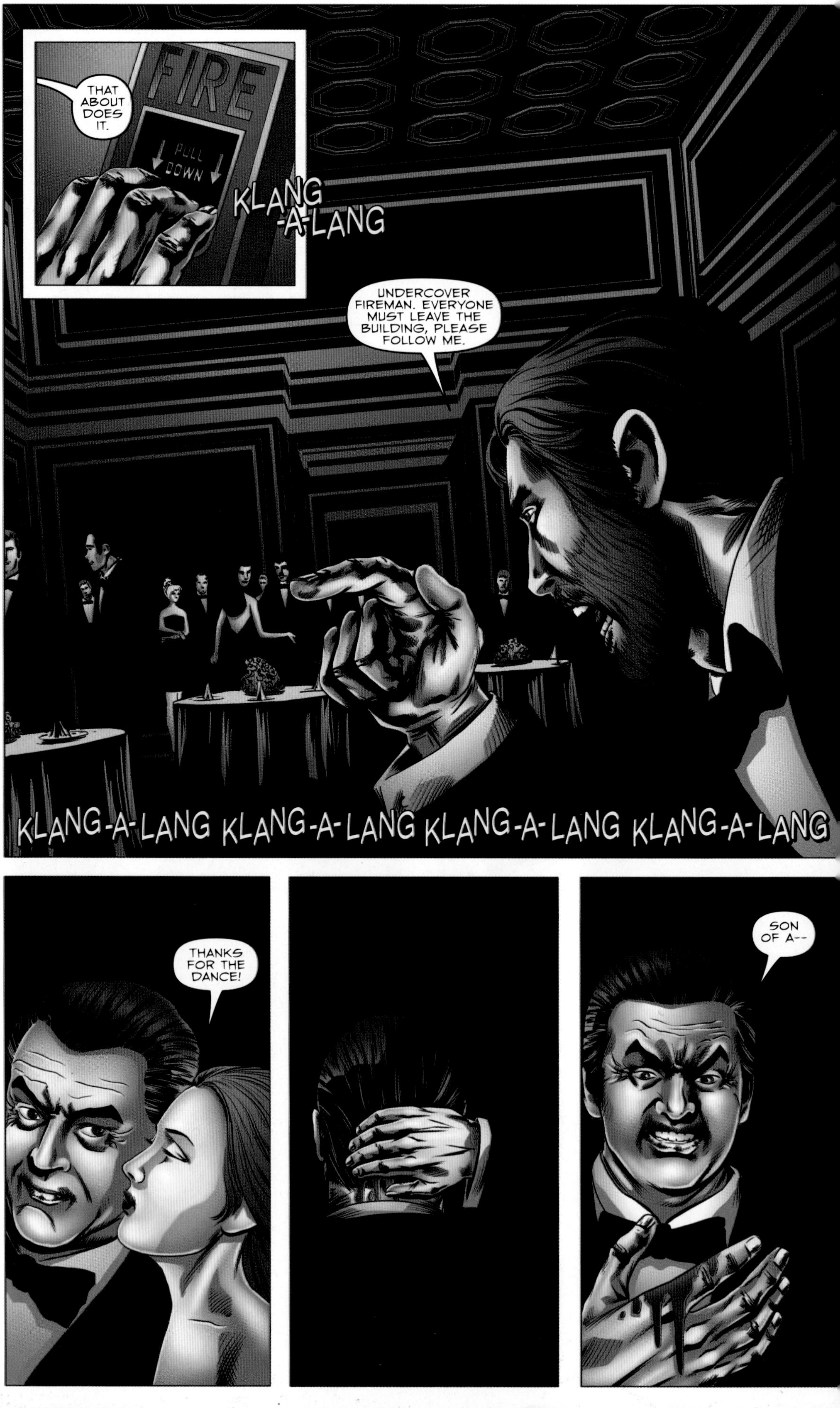

FIRE
PULL DOWN
THAT ABOUT DOES IT.
KLANG -A-LANG
UNDERCOVER FIREMAN. EVERYONE MUST LEAVE THE BUILDING, PLEASE FOLLOW ME.
KLANG-A-LANG KLANG-A-LANG KLANG-A-LANG KLANG-A-LANG
THANKS FOR THE DANCE!
SON OF A--

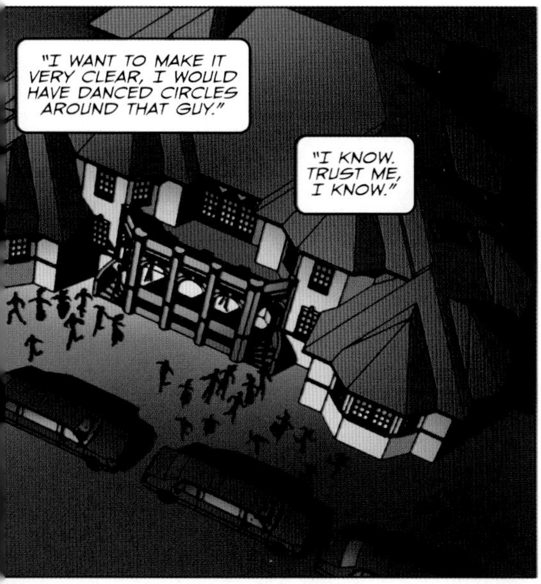
"I WANT TO MAKE IT VERY CLEAR, I WOULD HAVE DANCED CIRCLES AROUND THAT GUY."
"I KNOW. TRUST ME, I KNOW."

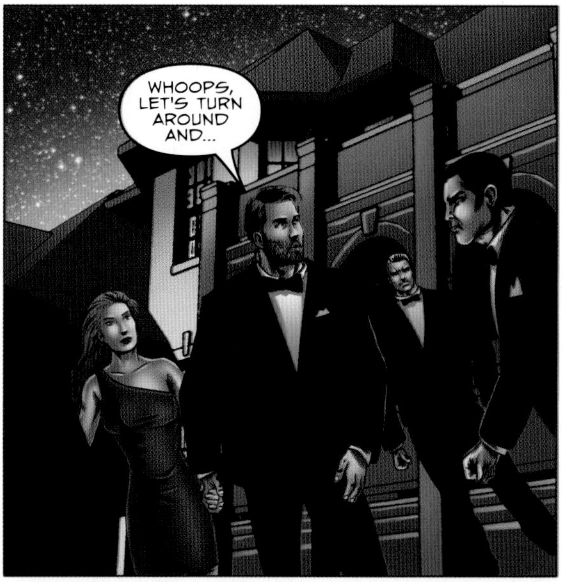
WHOOPS, LET'S TURN AROUND AND...

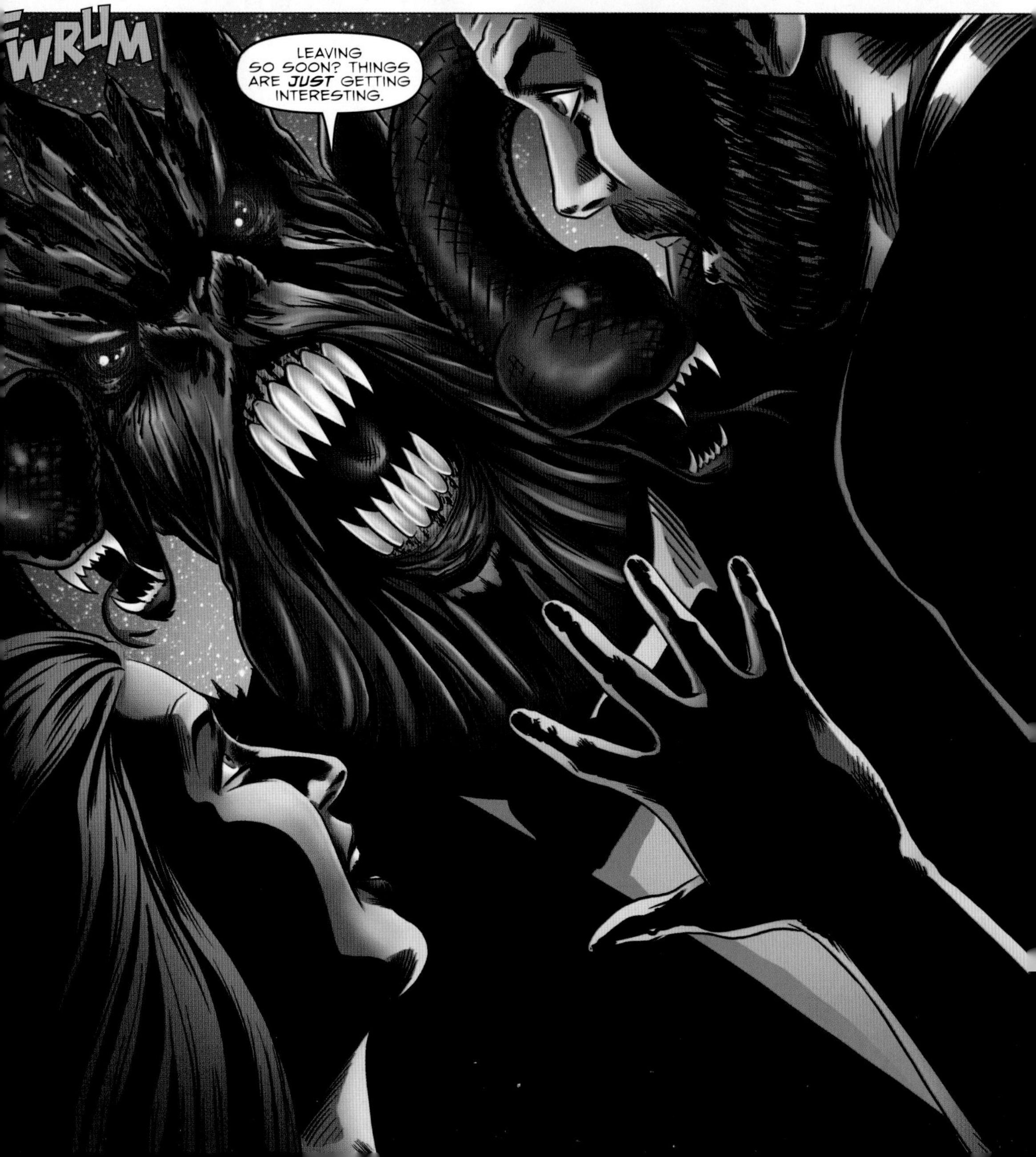
WRUM
LEAVING SO SOON? THINGS ARE **JUST** GETTING INTERESTING.

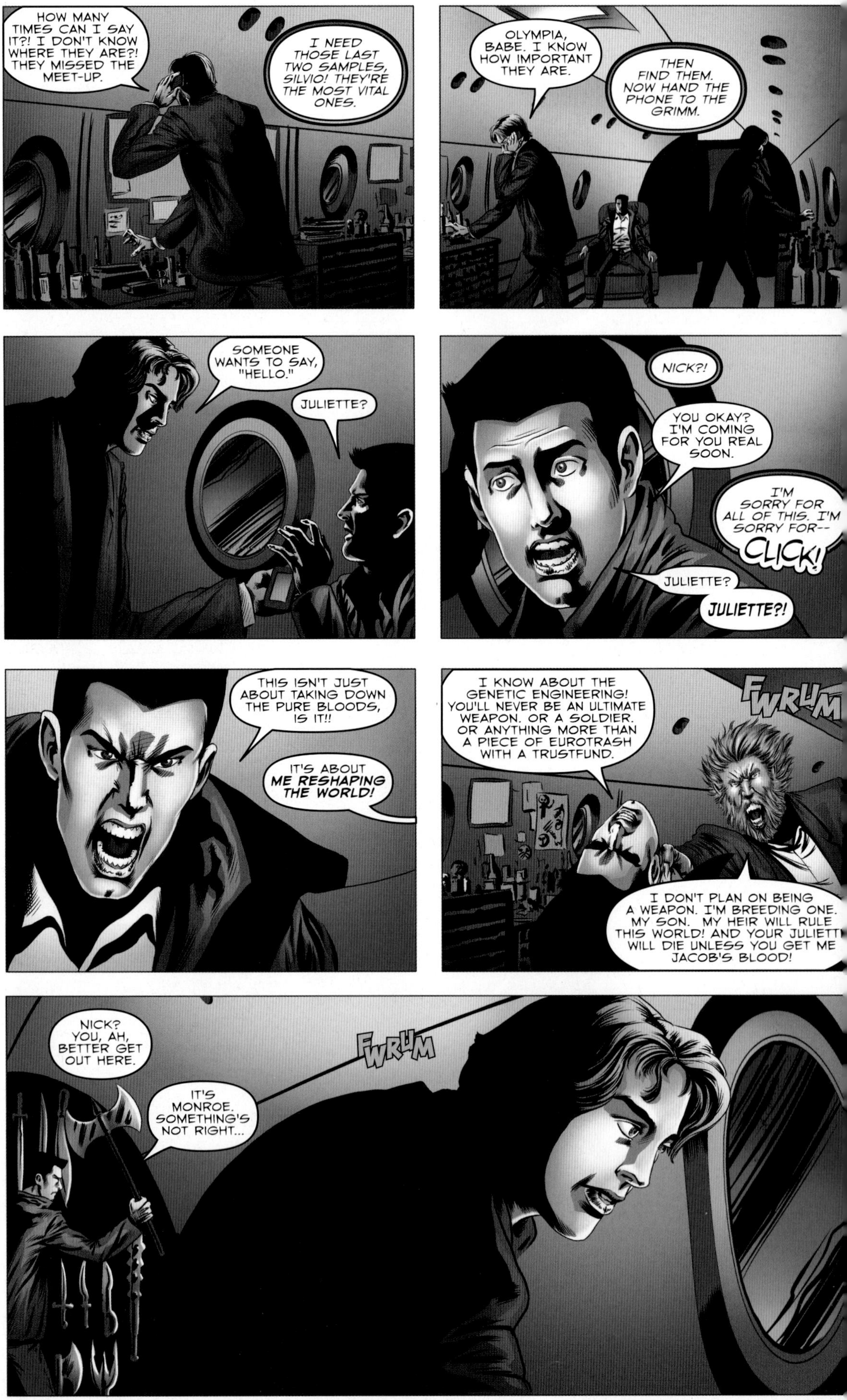

HOW MANY TIMES CAN I SAY IT?! I DON'T KNOW WHERE THEY ARE?! THEY MISSED THE MEET-UP.
I NEED THOSE LAST TWO SAMPLES, SILVIO! THEY'RE THE MOST VITAL ONES.
OLYMPIA, BABE. I KNOW HOW IMPORTANT THEY ARE.
THEN FIND THEM. NOW HAND THE PHONE TO THE GRIMM.
SOMEONE WANTS TO SAY, "HELLO."
JULIETTE?
NICK?!
YOU OKAY? I'M COMING FOR YOU REAL SOON.
I'M SORRY FOR ALL OF THIS. I'M SORRY FOR--
CLICK!
JULIETTE?
JULIETTE?!
THIS ISN'T JUST ABOUT TAKING DOWN THE PURE BLOODS, IS IT!!
IT'S ABOUT ME RESHAPING THE WORLD!
I KNOW ABOUT THE GENETIC ENGINEERING! YOU'LL NEVER BE AN ULTIMATE WEAPON. OR A SOLDIER. OR ANYTHING MORE THAN A PIECE OF EUROTRASH WITH A TRUSTFUND.
FWRUM
I DON'T PLAN ON BEING A WEAPON. I'M BREEDING ONE. MY SON. MY HEIR WILL RULE THIS WORLD! AND YOUR JULIETT WILL DIE UNLESS YOU GET ME JACOB'S BLOOD!
NICK? YOU, AH, BETTER GET OUT HERE.
FWRUM
IT'S MONROE. SOMETHING'S NOT RIGHT...

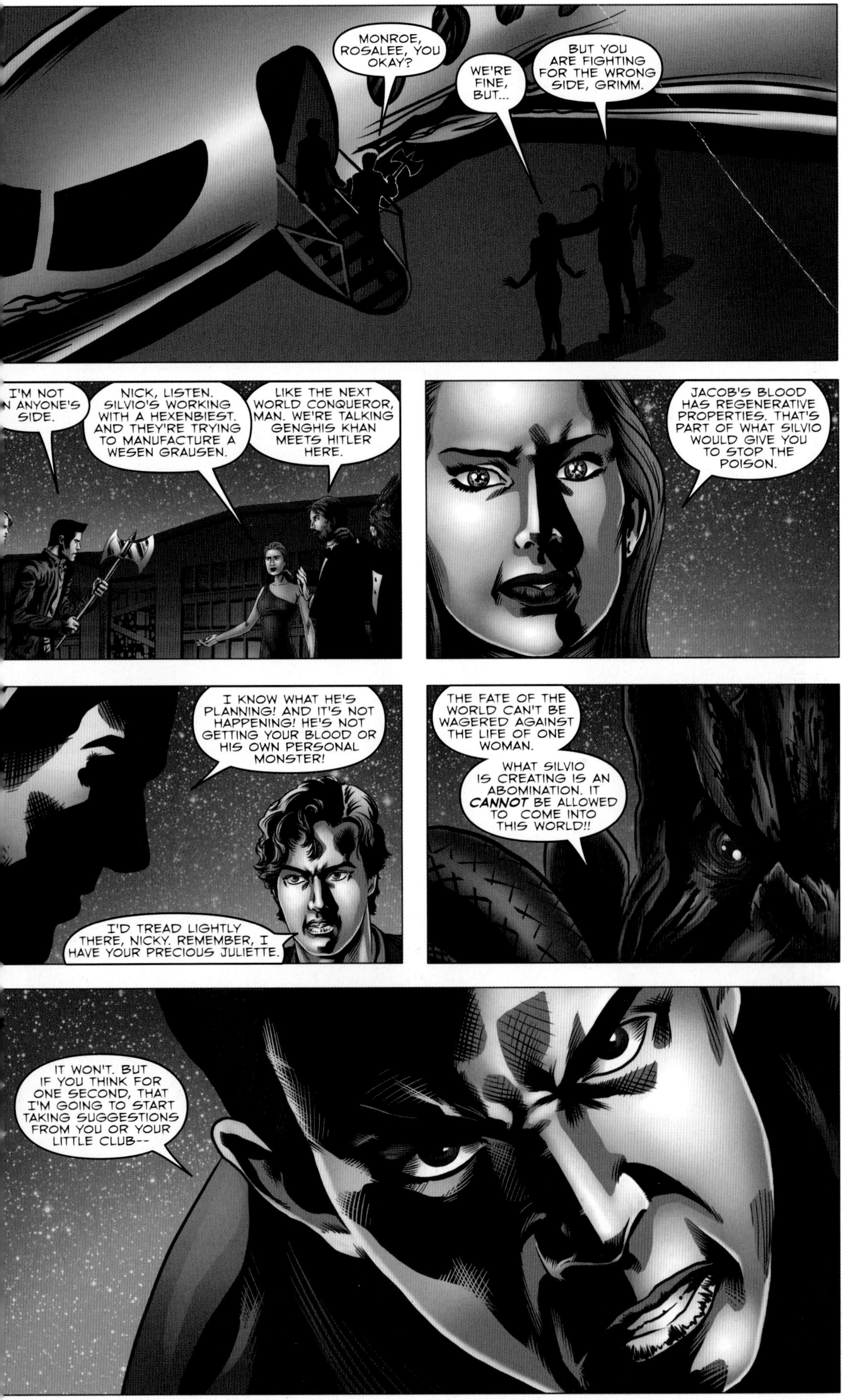
MONROE, ROSALEE, YOU OKAY?
WE'RE FINE, BUT...
BUT YOU ARE FIGHTING FOR THE WRONG SIDE, GRIMM.
I'M NOT ANYONE'S SIDE.
NICK, LISTEN. SILVIO'S WORKING WITH A HEXENBIEST. AND THEY'RE TRYING TO MANUFACTURE A WESEN GRAUSEN.
LIKE THE NEXT WORLD CONQUEROR, MAN. WE'RE TALKING GENGHIS KHAN MEETS HITLER HERE.
JACOB'S BLOOD HAS REGENERATIVE PROPERTIES. THAT'S PART OF WHAT SILVIO WOULD GIVE YOU TO STOP THE POISON.
I KNOW WHAT HE'S PLANNING! AND IT'S NOT HAPPENING! HE'S NOT GETTING YOUR BLOOD OR HIS OWN PERSONAL MONSTER!
I'D TREAD LIGHTLY THERE, NICKY. REMEMBER, I HAVE YOUR PRECIOUS JULIETTE.
THE FATE OF THE WORLD CAN'T BE WAGERED AGAINST THE LIFE OF ONE WOMAN.
WHAT SILVIO IS CREATING IS AN ABOMINATION. IT ***CANNOT*** BE ALLOWED TO COME INTO THIS WORLD!!
IT WON'T. BUT IF YOU THINK FOR ONE SECOND, THAT I'M GOING TO START TAKING SUGGESTIONS FROM YOU OR YOUR LITTLE CLUB--

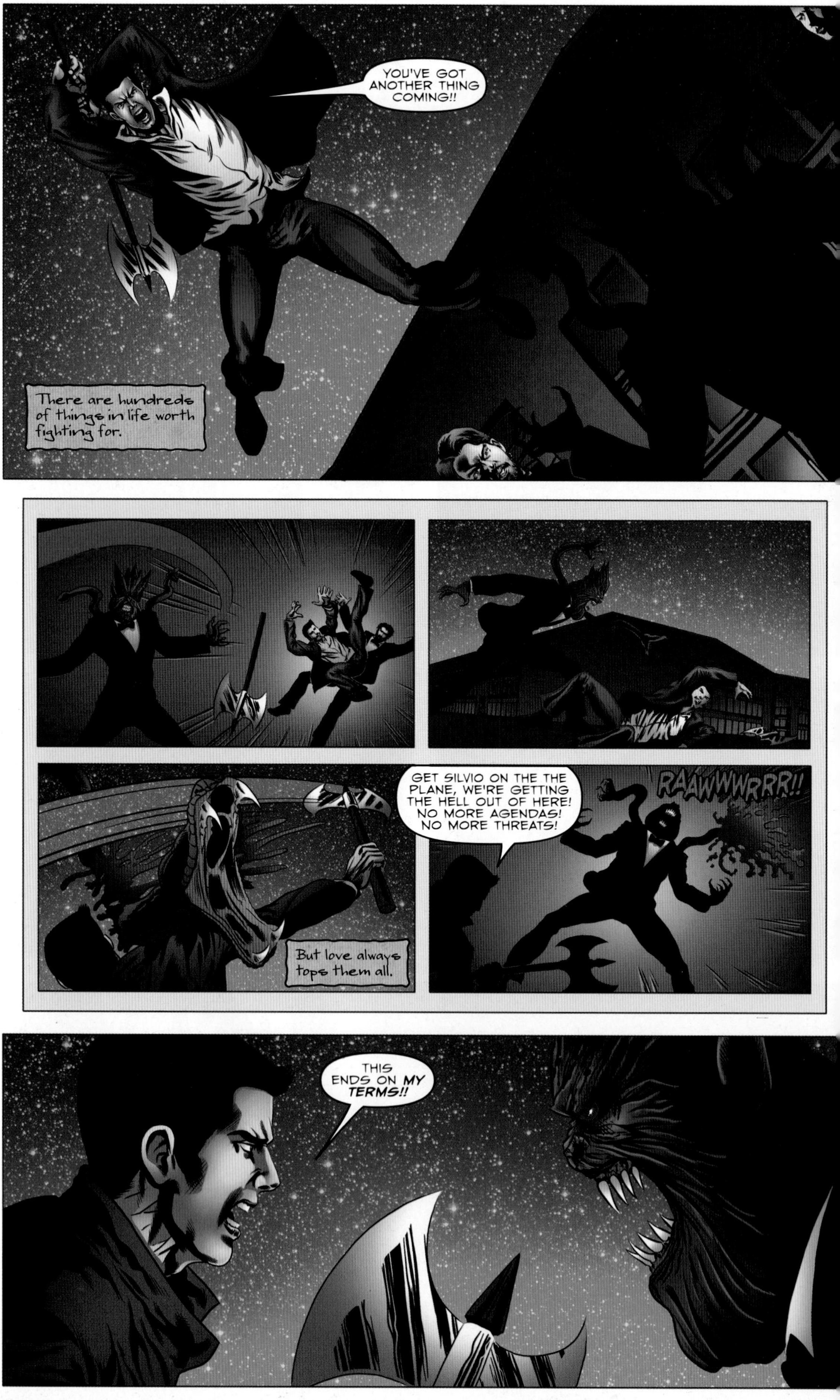
YOU'VE GOT ANOTHER THING COMING!!
There are hundreds of things in life worth fighting for.
But love always tops them all.
GET SILVIO ON THE THE PLANE, WE'RE GETTING THE HELL OUT OF HERE! NO MORE AGENDAS! NO MORE THREATS!
RAAWWWRRR!!
THIS ENDS ON MY TERMS!!

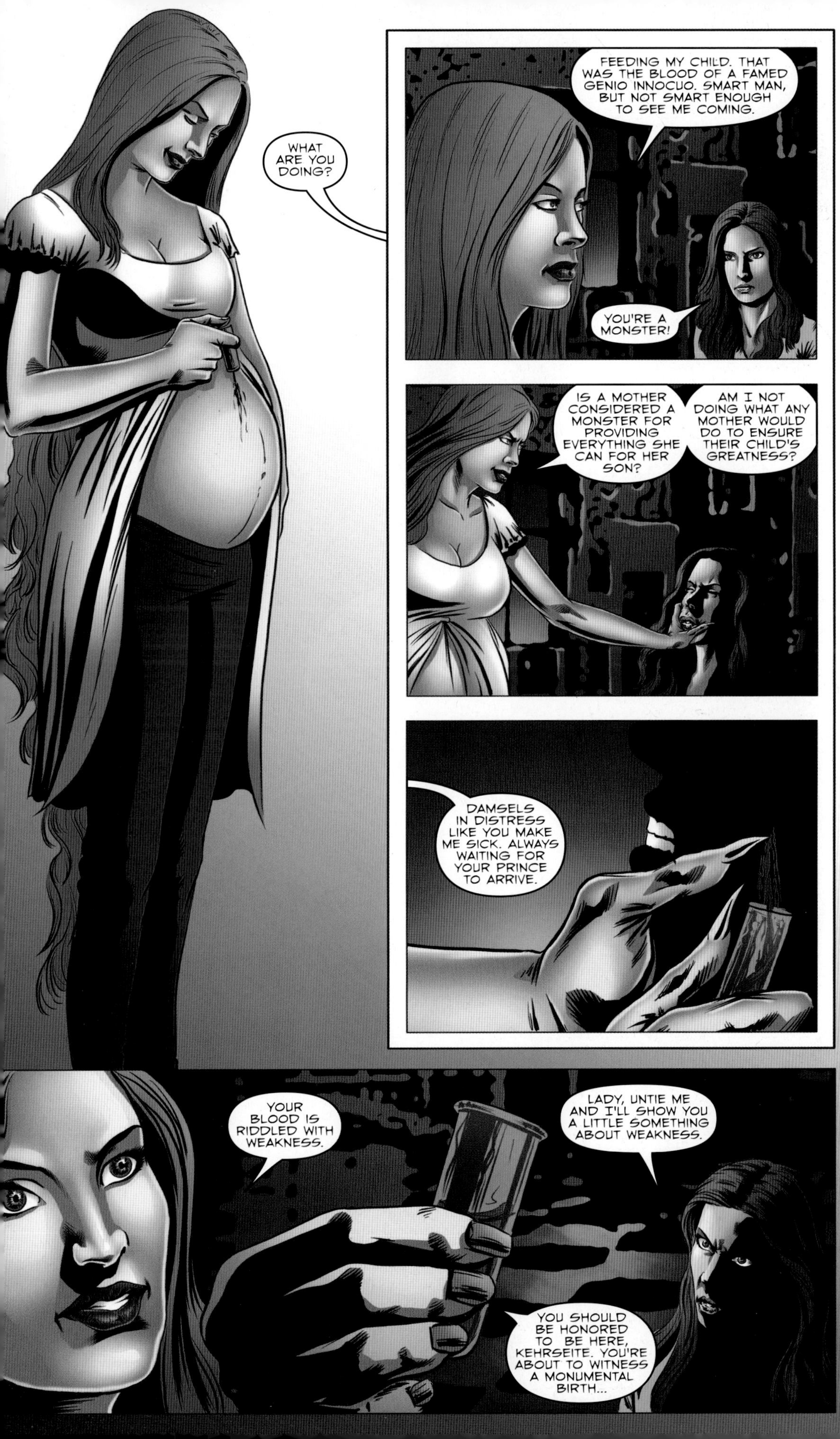
WHAT ARE YOU DOING?
FEEDING MY CHILD. THAT WAS THE BLOOD OF A FAMED GENIO INNOCUO. SMART MAN, BUT NOT SMART ENOUGH TO SEE ME COMING.
YOU'RE A MONSTER!
IS A MOTHER CONSIDERED A MONSTER FOR PROVIDING EVERYTHING SHE CAN FOR HER SON?
AM I NOT DOING WHAT ANY MOTHER WOULD DO TO ENSURE THEIR CHILD'S GREATNESS?
DAMSELS IN DISTRESS LIKE YOU MAKE ME SICK. ALWAYS WAITING FOR YOUR PRINCE TO ARRIVE.
YOUR BLOOD IS RIDDLED WITH WEAKNESS.
LADY, UNTIE ME AND I'LL SHOW YOU A LITTLE SOMETHING ABOUT WEAKNESS.
YOU SHOULD BE HONORED TO BE HERE, KEHRSEITE. YOU'RE ABOUT TO WITNESS A MONUMENTAL BIRTH...

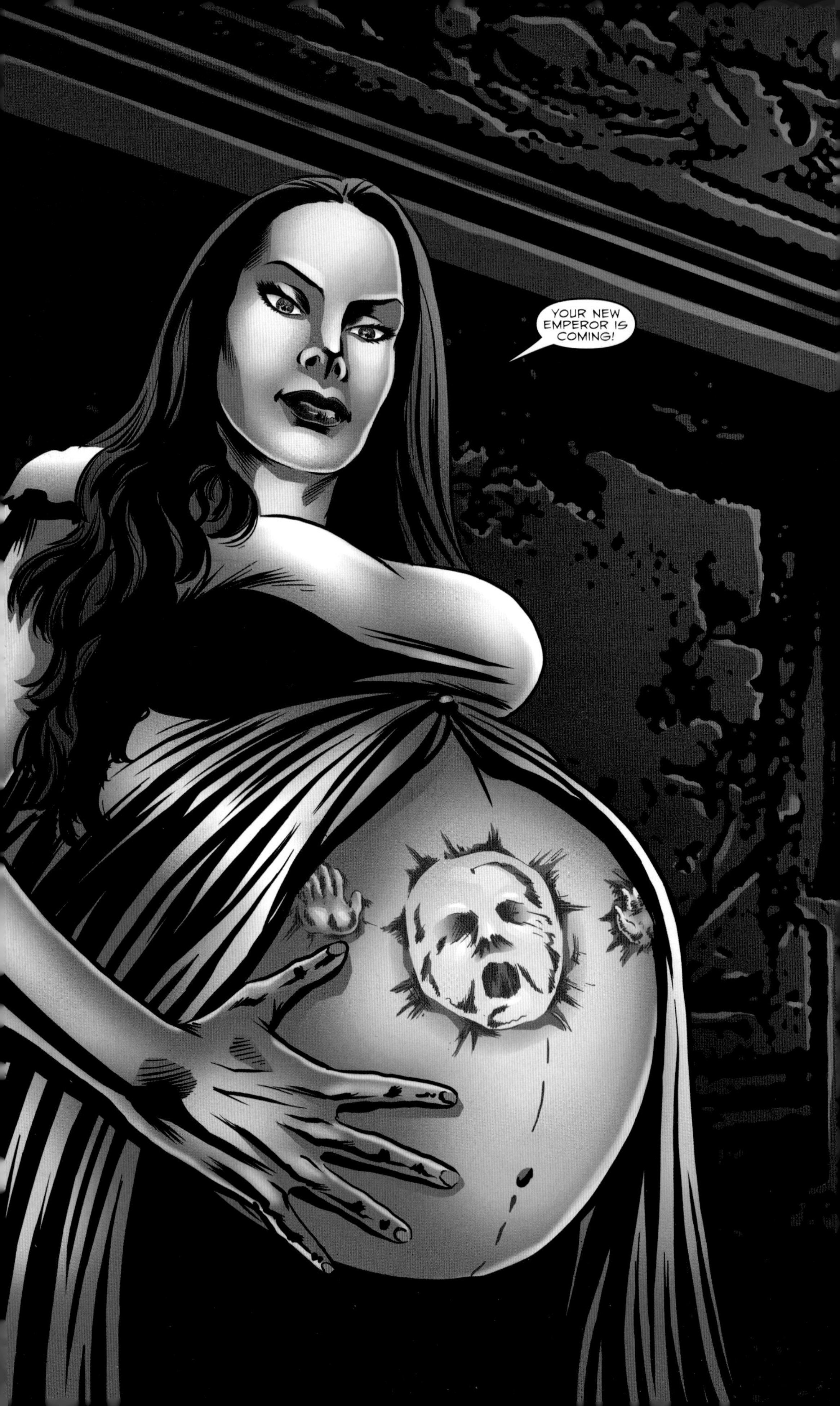
YOUR NEW EMPEROR IS COMING!

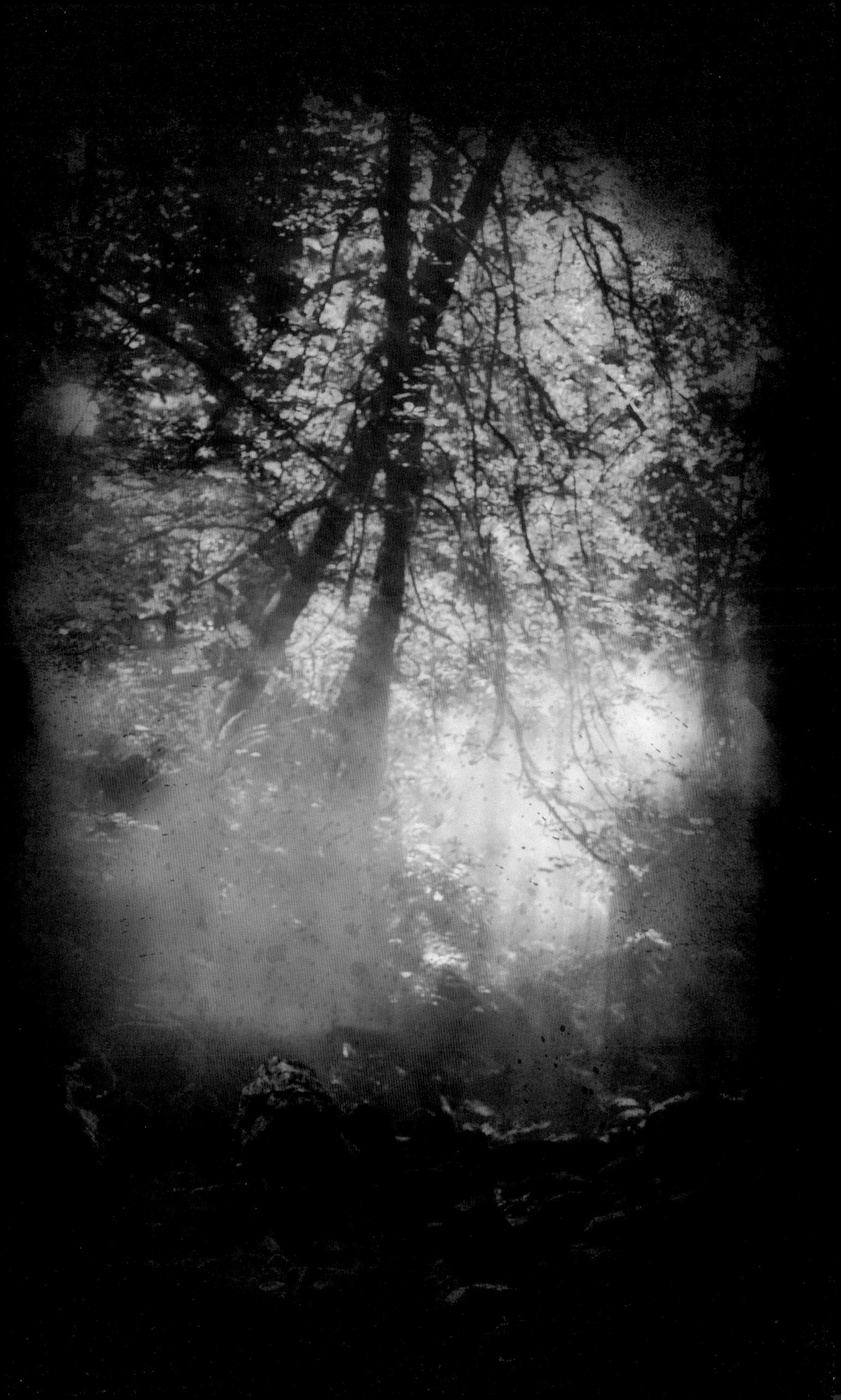

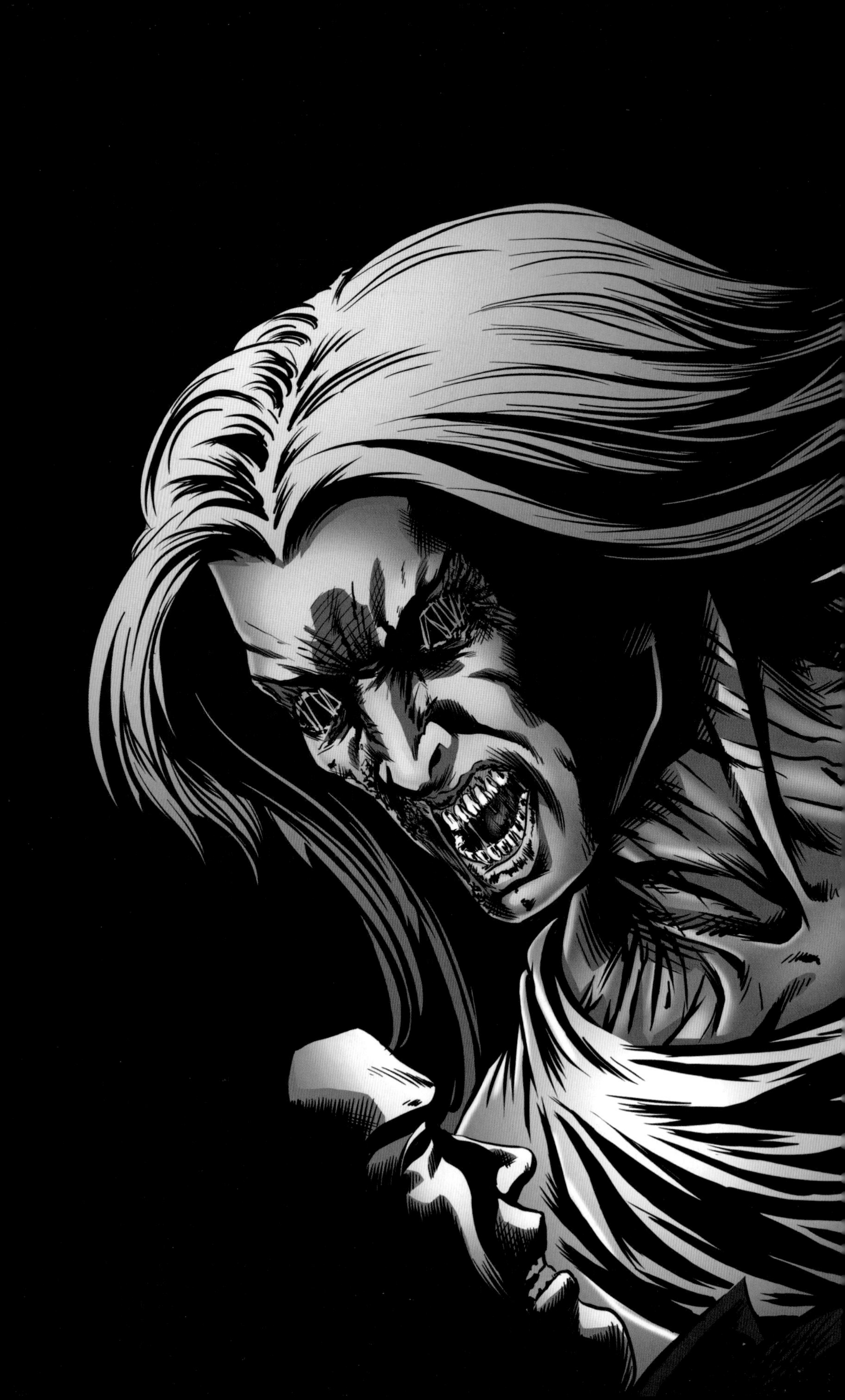

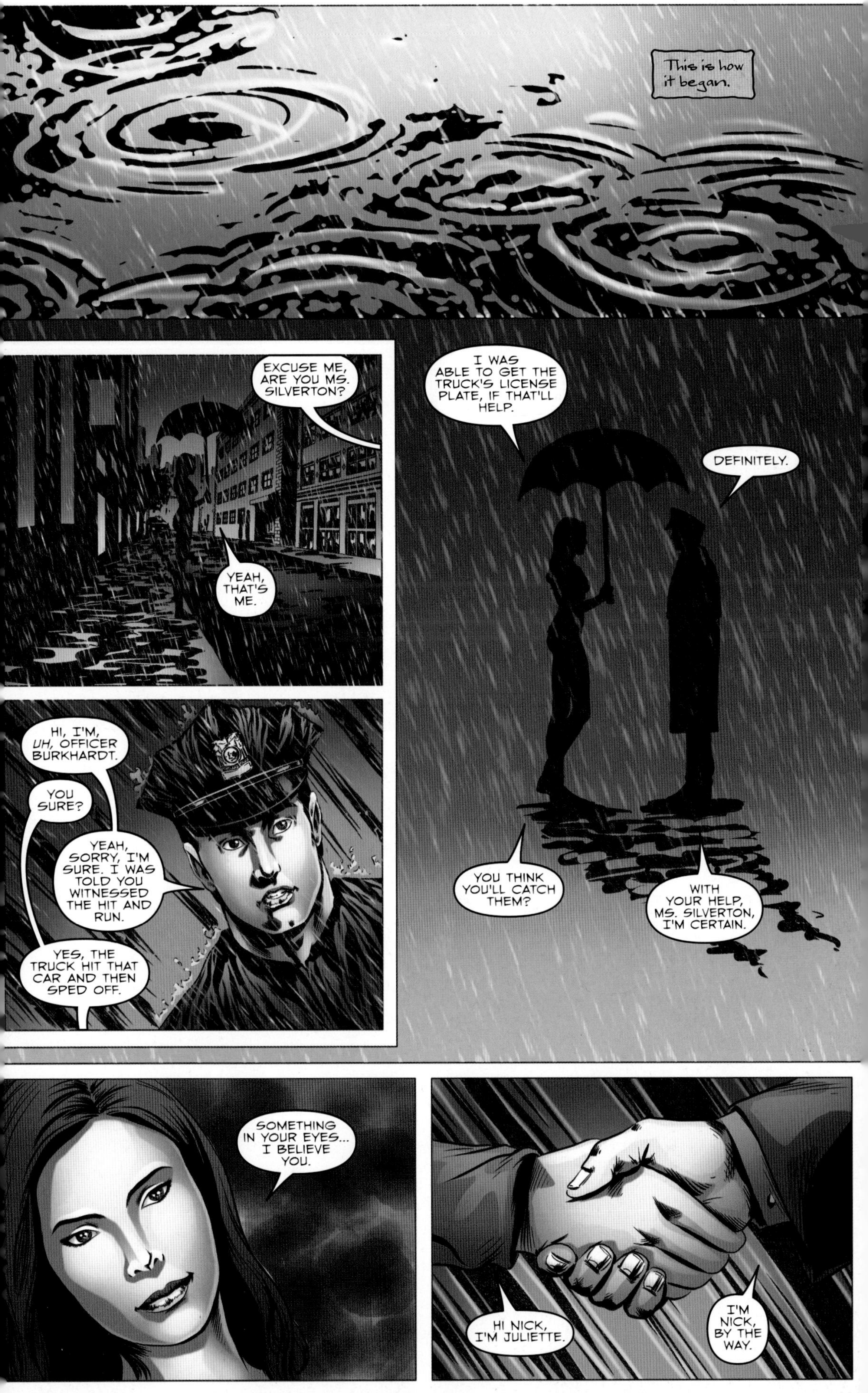
This is how it began.
EXCUSE ME, ARE YOU MS. SILVERTON?
YEAH, THAT'S ME.
HI, I'M, UH, OFFICER BURKHARDT.
YOU SURE?
YEAH, SORRY, I'M SURE. I WAS TOLD YOU WITNESSED THE HIT AND RUN.
YES, THE TRUCK HIT THAT CAR AND THEN SPED OFF.
I WAS ABLE TO GET THE TRUCK'S LICENSE PLATE, IF THAT'LL HELP.
DEFINITELY.
YOU THINK YOU'LL CATCH THEM?
WITH YOUR HELP, MS. SILVERTON, I'M CERTAIN.
SOMETHING IN YOUR EYES... I BELIEVE YOU.
I'M NICK, BY THE WAY.
HI NICK, I'M JULIETTE.

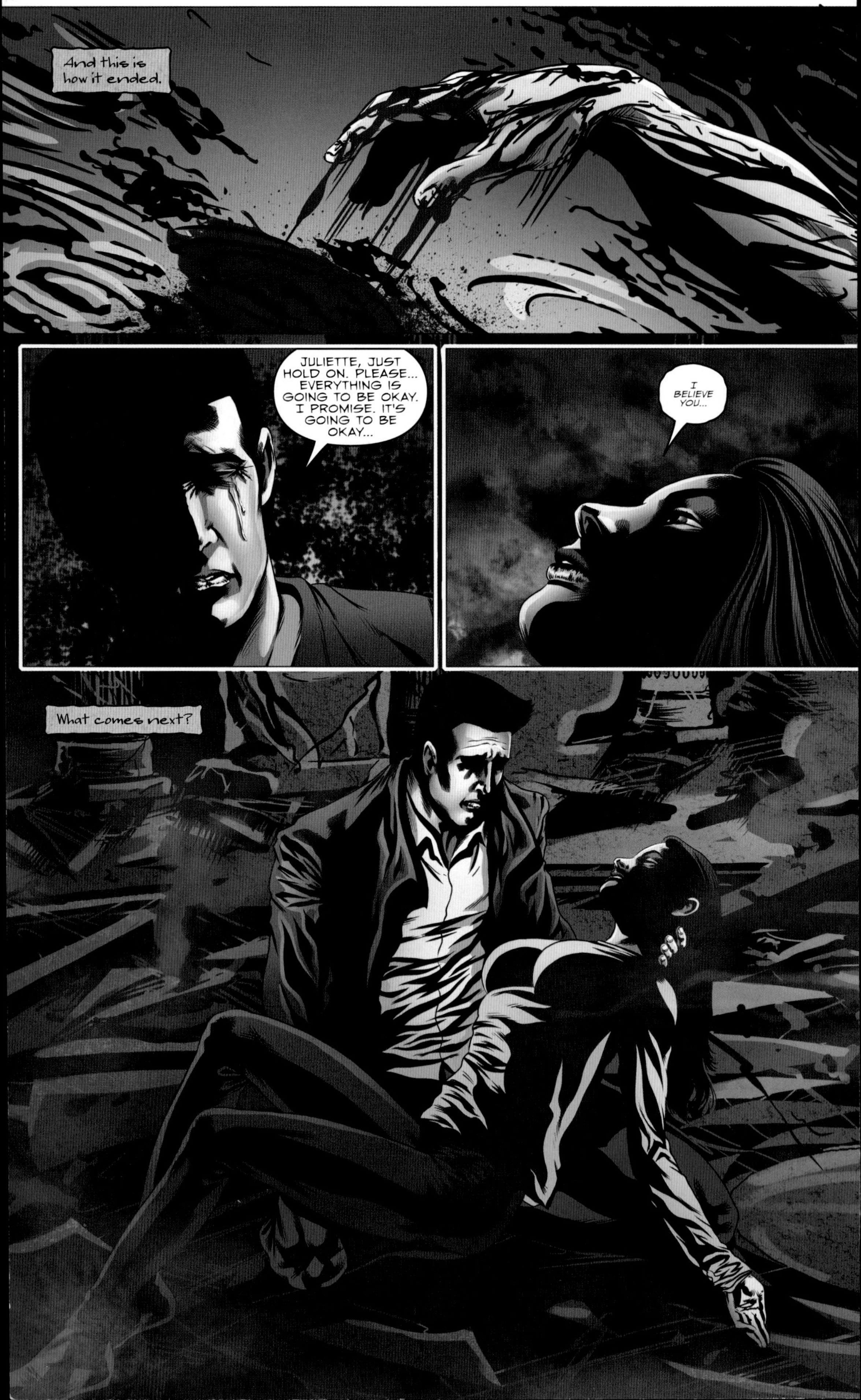
And this is how it ended.
JULIETTE, JUST HOLD ON. PLEASE... EVERYTHING IS GOING TO BE OKAY. I PROMISE. IT'S GOING TO BE OKAY...
I BELIEVE YOU...
What comes next?

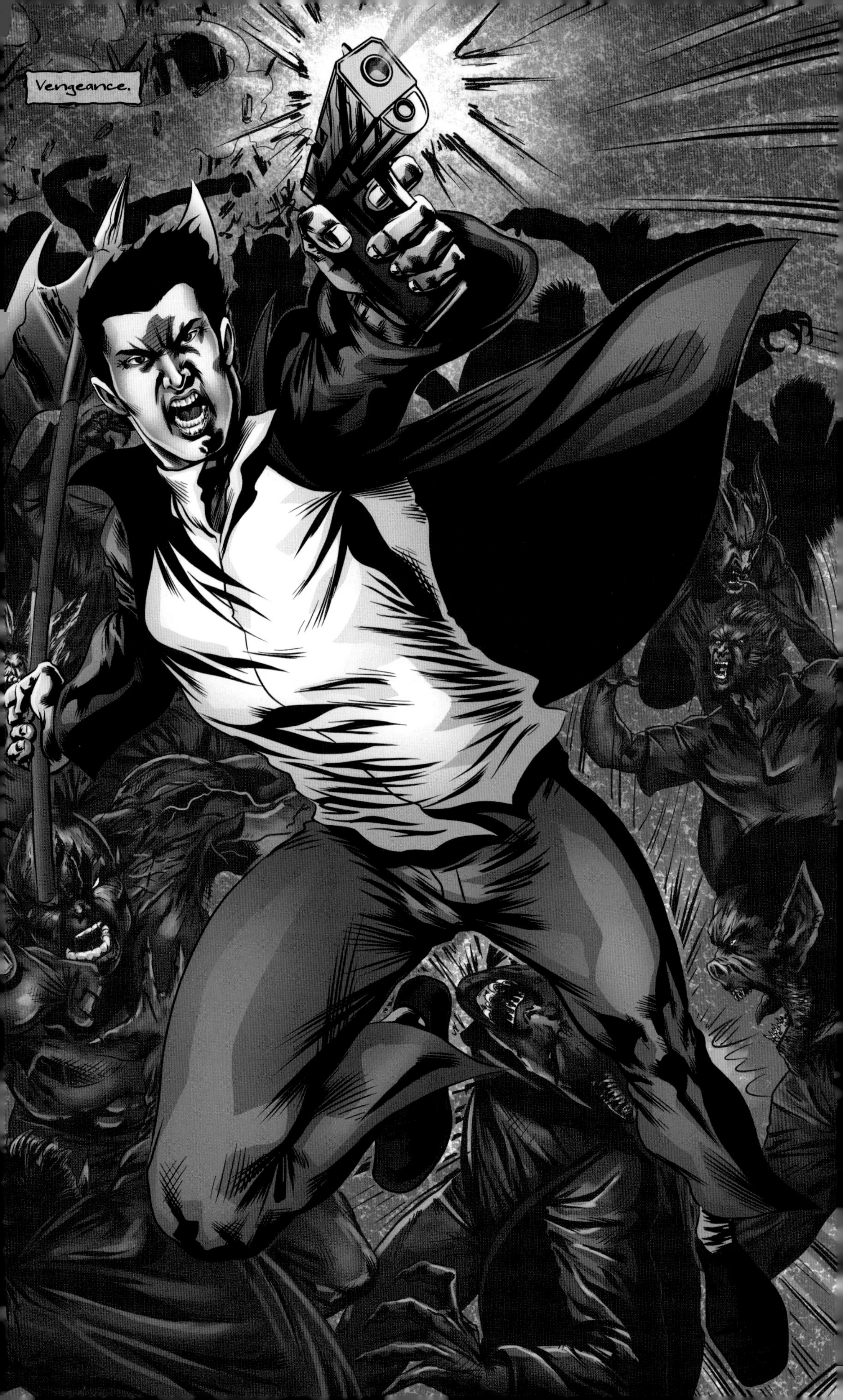
Vengeance.

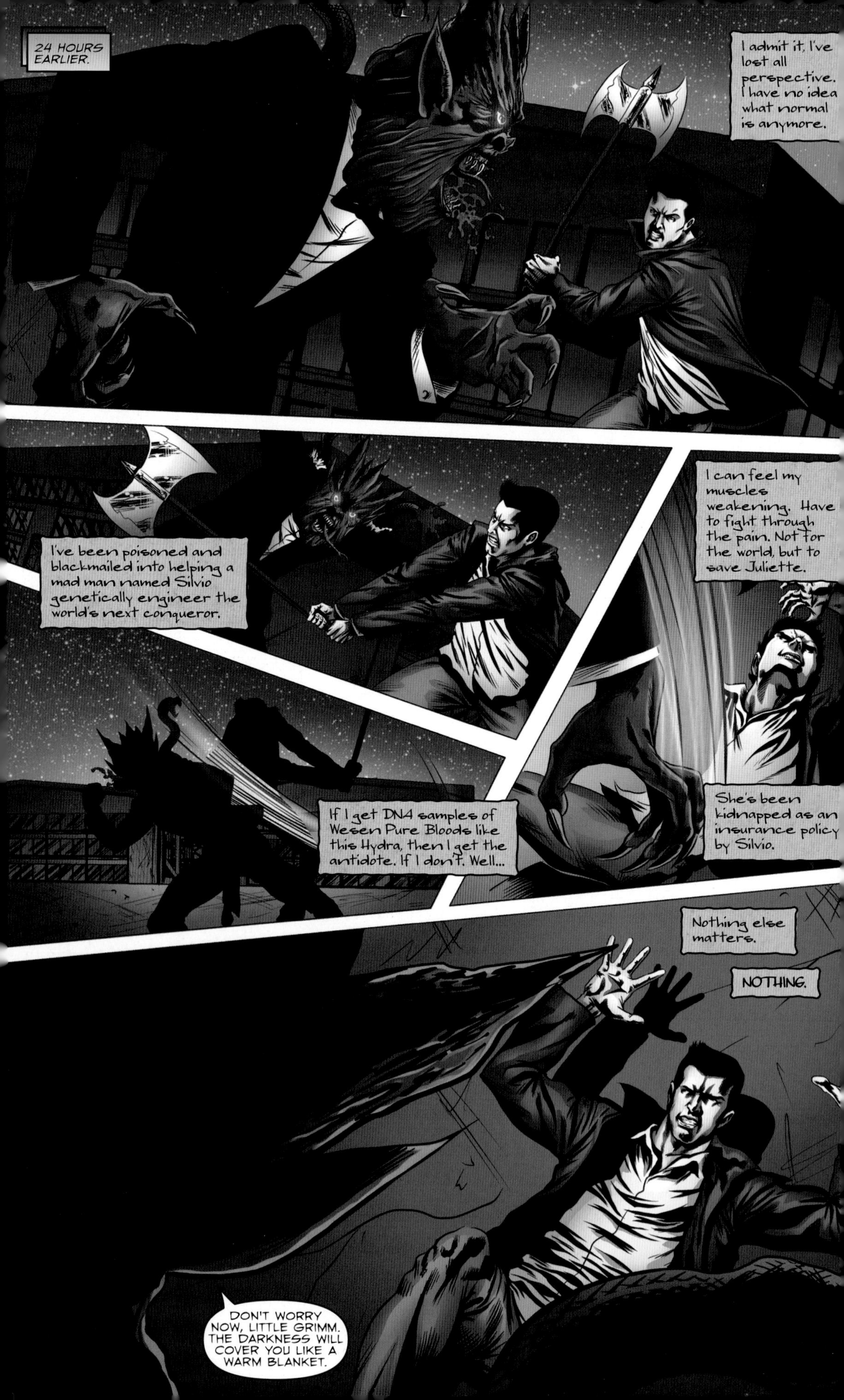
24 HOURS EARLIER.
I admit it, I've lost all perspective. I have no idea what normal is anymore.
I've been poisoned and blackmailed into helping a mad man named Silvio genetically engineer the world's next conqueror.
If I get DNA samples of Wesen Pure Bloods like this Hydra, then I get the antidote. If I don't. Well...
I can feel my muscles weakening. Have to fight through the pain. Not for the world, but to save Juliette.
She's been kidnapped as an insurance policy by Silvio.
Nothing else matters.
NOTHING.
DON'T WORRY NOW, LITTLE GRIMM. THE DARKNESS WILL COVER YOU LIKE A WARM BLANKET.

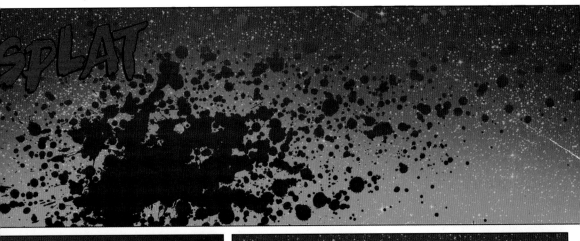

SPLAT

HIIISSSSS

THANKS FOR THE DISTRACTION, NICKY.

SILVIO, YOU'LL DOOM THE WORLD WITH YOUR ABOMINATION!

I REALLY WISH YOU COULD SEE THE POTENTIAL OF WHAT I'M CREATING HERE.

NICK! STAY WITH US. COME ON.

THE POISON'S IN THE FINAL STAGES.

AGHHH...

SILVIO, WE NEED THAT ANTIDOTE OR NICK WILL DIE. NOW!

UH...

NO PROBLEMO.

YOU CAN COOK IT UP ON THE WAY.

ON THE WAY, WHERE?

ON THE WAY TO HIS PRECIOUS JULIETTE. I TOLD YOU. I'M A MAN OF MY WORD.

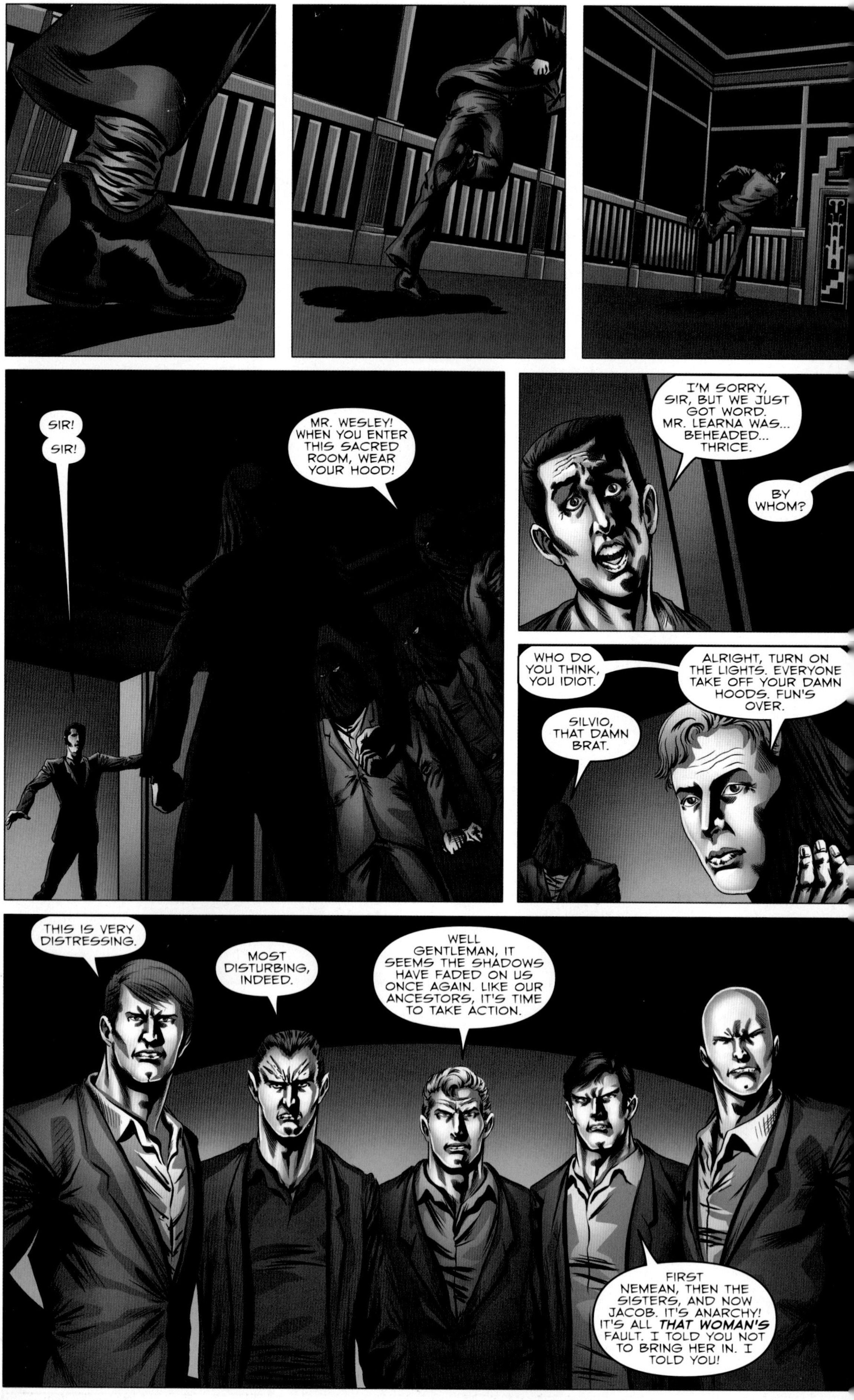
SIR!
SIR!
MR. WESLEY! WHEN YOU ENTER THIS SACRED ROOM, WEAR YOUR HOOD!
I'M SORRY, SIR, BUT WE JUST GOT WORD. MR. LEARNA WAS... BEHEADED... THRICE.
BY WHOM?
WHO DO YOU THINK, YOU IDIOT.
SILVIO, THAT DAMN BRAT.
ALRIGHT, TURN ON THE LIGHTS. EVERYONE TAKE OFF YOUR DAMN HOODS. FUN'S OVER.
THIS IS VERY DISTRESSING.
MOST DISTURBING, INDEED.
WELL GENTLEMAN, IT SEEMS THE SHADOWS HAVE FADED ON US ONCE AGAIN. LIKE OUR ANCESTORS, IT'S TIME TO TAKE ACTION.
FIRST NEMEAN, THEN THE SISTERS, AND NOW JACOB. IT'S ANARCHY! IT'S ALL ***THAT WOMAN'S*** FAULT. I TOLD YOU NOT TO BRING HER IN. I TOLD YOU!

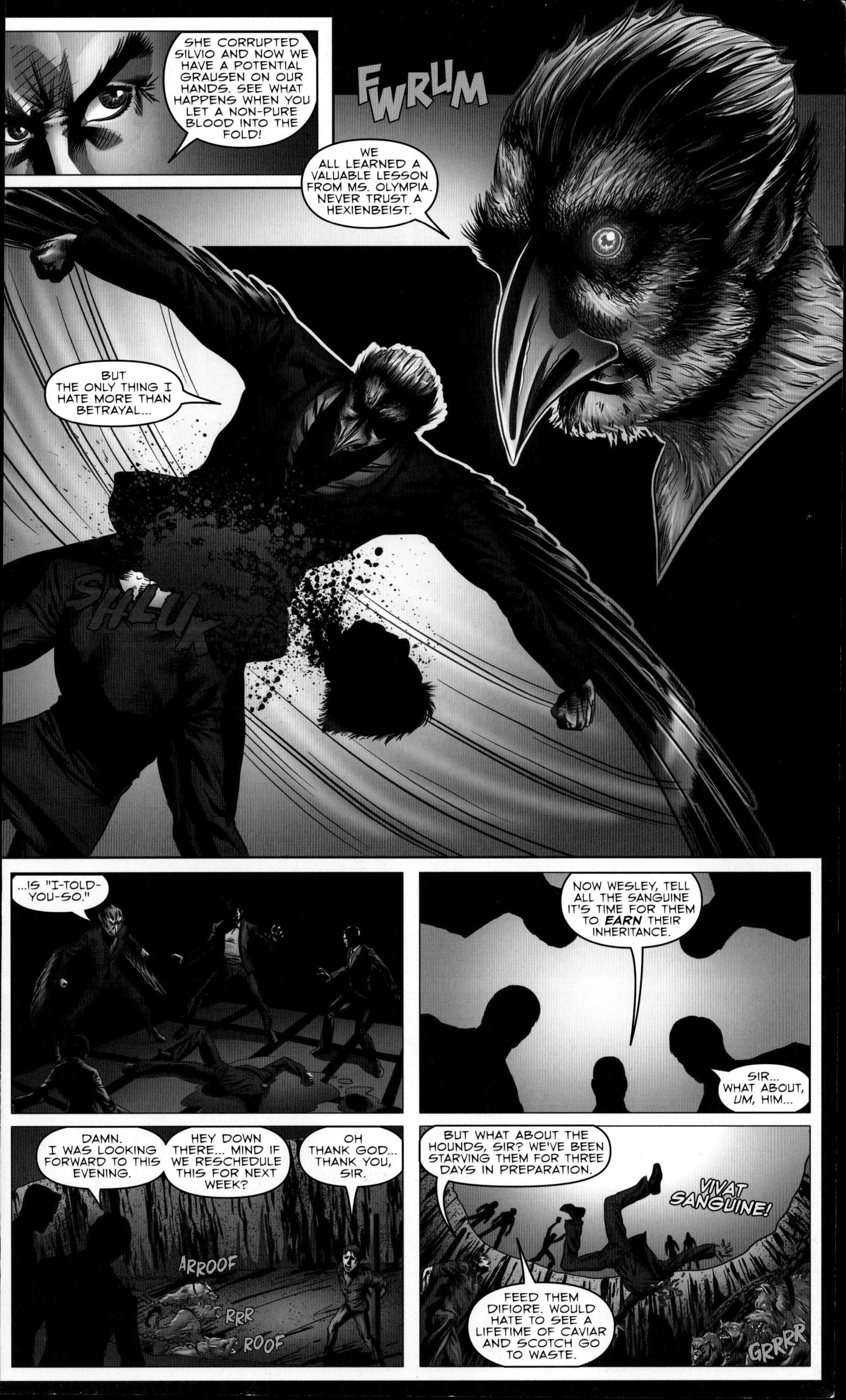
SHE CORRUPTED SILVIO AND NOW WE HAVE A POTENTIAL GRAUSEN ON OUR HANDS. SEE WHAT HAPPENS WHEN YOU LET A NON-PURE BLOOD INTO THE FOLD!
FWRUM
WE ALL LEARNED A VALUABLE LESSON FROM MS. OLYMPIA. NEVER TRUST A HEXIENBEIST.
BUT THE ONLY THING I HATE MORE THAN BETRAYAL...
SHLUK
...IS "I-TOLD-YOU-SO."
NOW WESLEY, TELL ALL THE SANGUINE IT'S TIME FOR THEM TO EARN THEIR INHERITANCE.
SIR... WHAT ABOUT, UM, HIM...
DAMN. I WAS LOOKING FORWARD TO THIS EVENING.
HEY DOWN THERE... MIND IF WE RESCHEDULE THIS FOR NEXT WEEK?
OH THANK GOD... THANK YOU, SIR.
ARROOF
RRR
ROOF
BUT WHAT ABOUT THE HOUNDS, SIR? WE'VE BEEN STARVING THEM FOR THREE DAYS IN PREPARATION.
VIVAT SANGUINE!
FEED THEM DIFIORE. WOULD HATE TO SEE A LIFETIME OF CAVIAR AND SCOTCH GO TO WASTE.
GRRRR

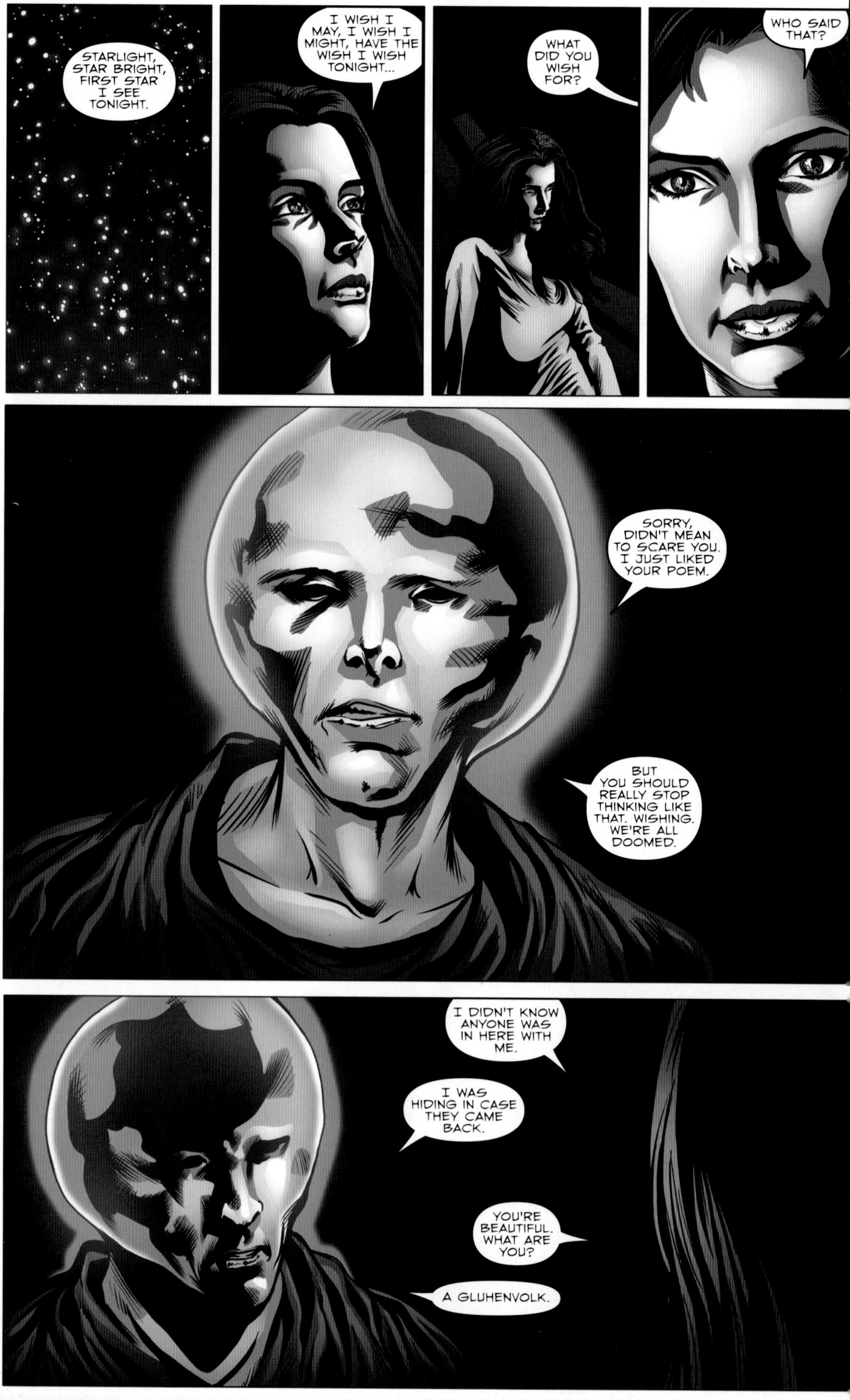
STARLIGHT, STAR BRIGHT, FIRST STAR I SEE TONIGHT.
I WISH I MAY, I WISH I MIGHT, HAVE THE WISH I WISH TONIGHT...
WHAT DID YOU WISH FOR?
WHO SAID THAT?
SORRY, DIDN'T MEAN TO SCARE YOU. I JUST LIKED YOUR POEM.
BUT YOU SHOULD REALLY STOP THINKING LIKE THAT. WISHING. WE'RE ALL DOOMED.
I DIDN'T KNOW ANYONE WAS IN HERE WITH ME.
I WAS HIDING IN CASE THEY CAME BACK.
YOU'RE BEAUTIFUL. WHAT ARE YOU?
A GLUHENVOLK.

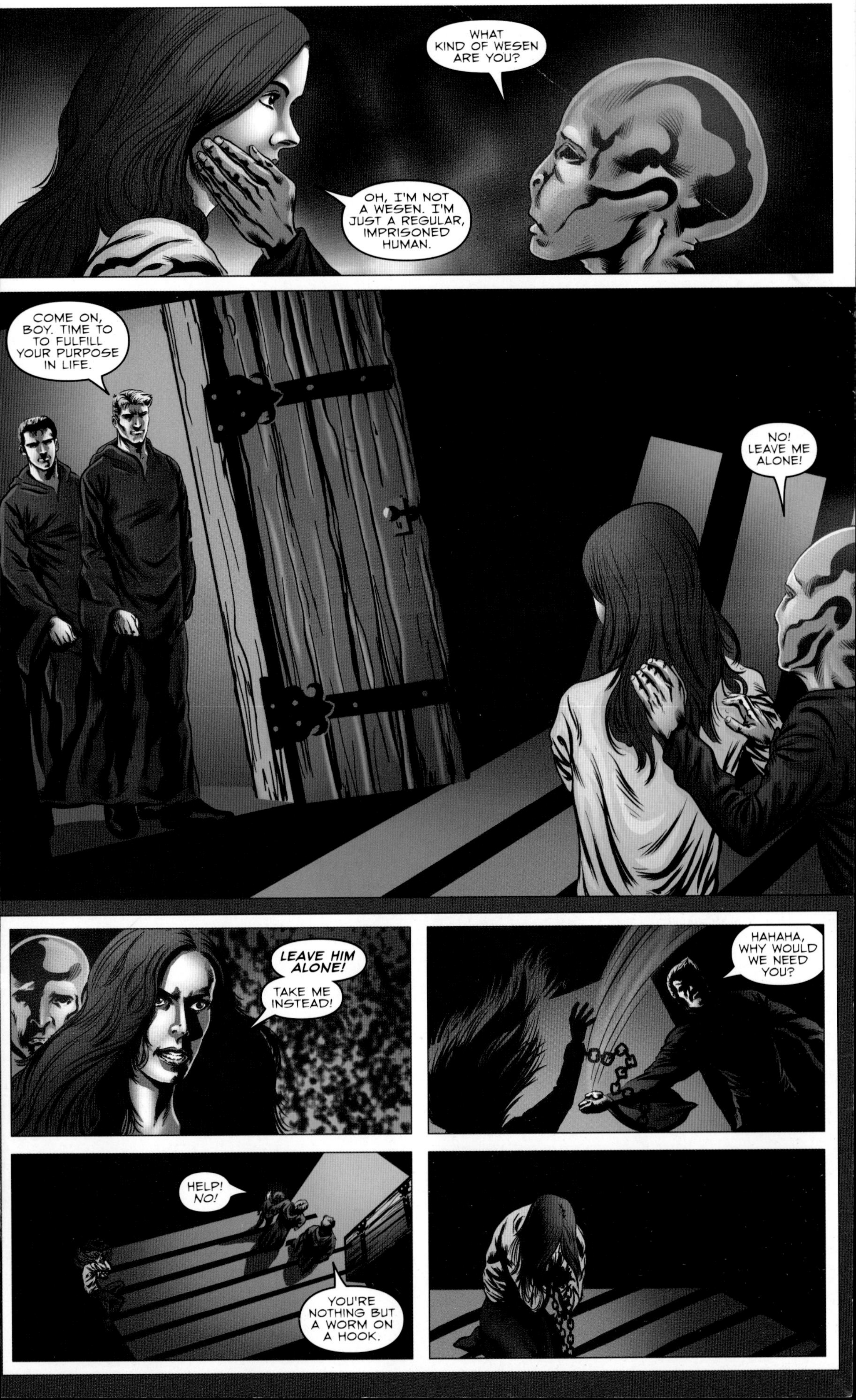
WHAT KIND OF WESEN ARE YOU?
OH, I'M NOT A WESEN. I'M JUST A REGULAR, IMPRISONED HUMAN.
COME ON, BOY. TIME TO TO FULFILL YOUR PURPOSE IN LIFE.
NO! LEAVE ME ALONE!
LEAVE HIM ALONE!
TAKE ME INSTEAD!
HAHAHA, WHY WOULD WE NEED YOU?
HELP! NO!
YOU'RE NOTHING BUT A WORM ON A HOOK.

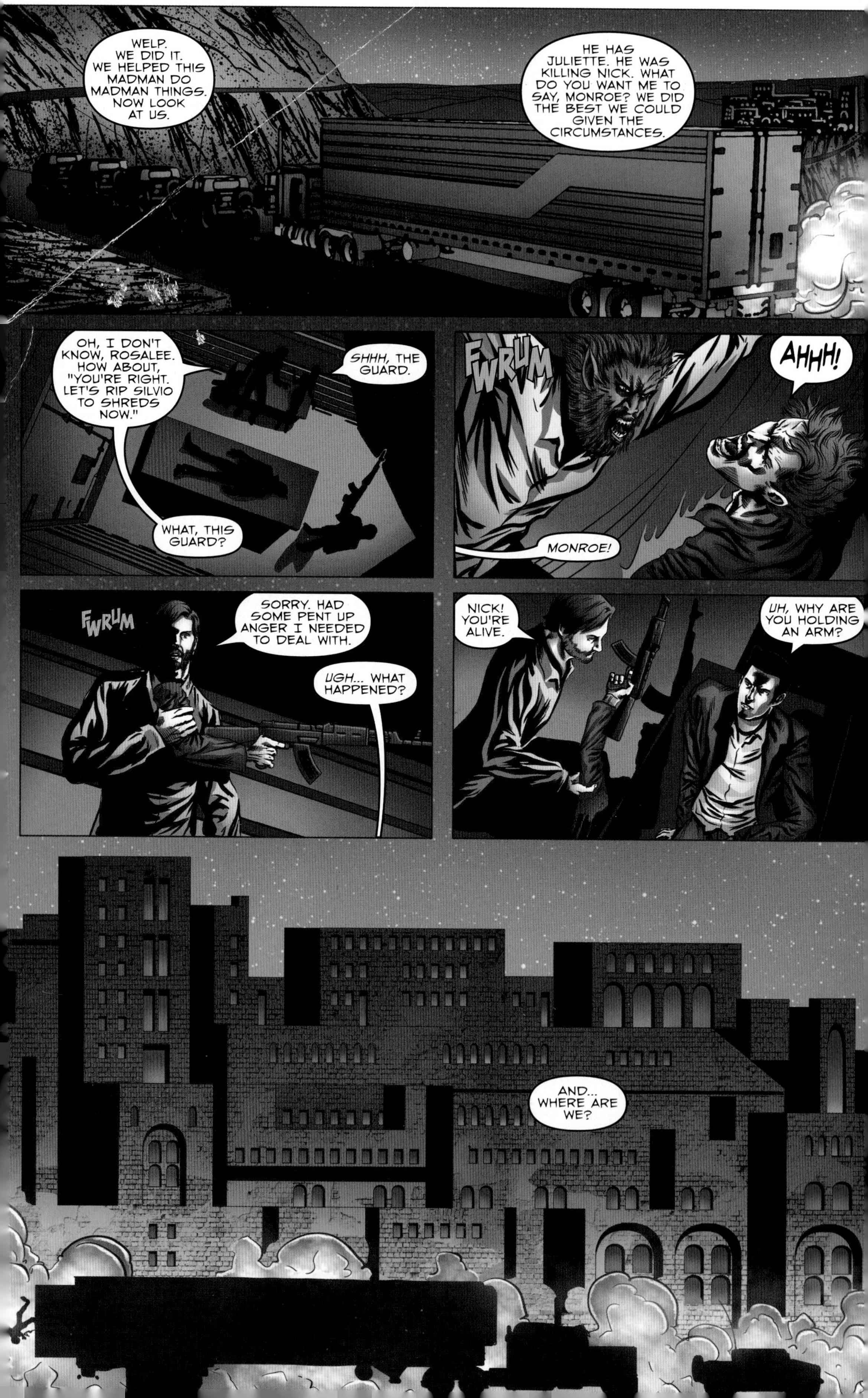
WELP. WE DID IT. WE HELPED THIS MADMAN DO MADMAN THINGS. NOW LOOK AT US.
HE HAS JULIETTE. HE WAS KILLING NICK. WHAT DO YOU WANT ME TO SAY, MONROE? WE DID THE BEST WE COULD GIVEN THE CIRCUMSTANCES.
OH, I DON'T KNOW, ROSALEE. HOW ABOUT, "YOU'RE RIGHT. LET'S RIP SILVIO TO SHREDS NOW."
SHHH, THE GUARD.
WHAT, THIS GUARD?
FWRUM
AHHH!
MONROE!
FWRUM
SORRY. HAD SOME PENT UP ANGER I NEEDED TO DEAL WITH.
UGH... WHAT HAPPENED?
NICK! YOU'RE ALIVE.
UH, WHY ARE YOU HOLDING AN ARM?
AND... WHERE ARE WE?

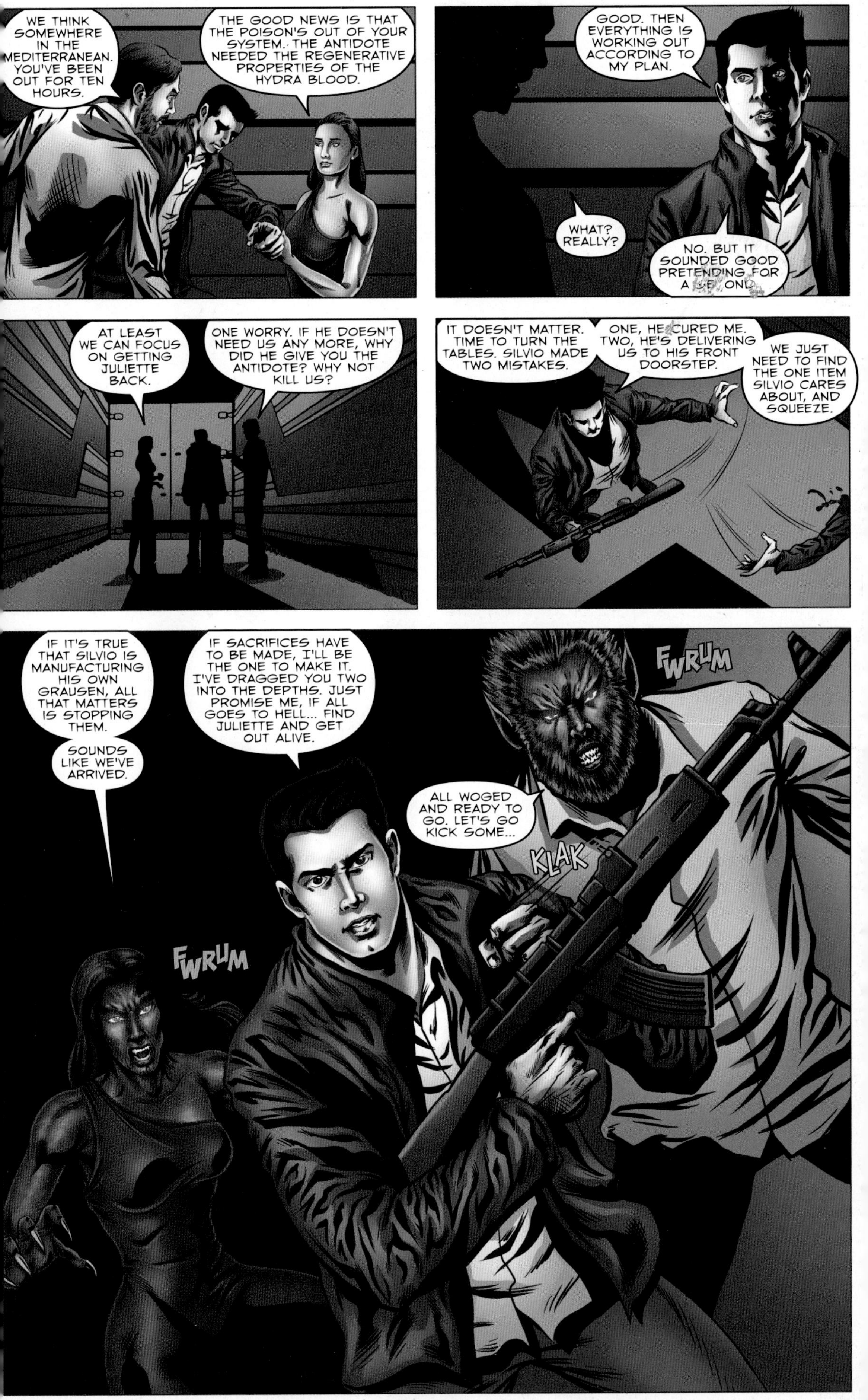

WE THINK SOMEWHERE IN THE MEDITERRANEAN. YOU'VE BEEN OUT FOR TEN HOURS.
THE GOOD NEWS IS THAT THE POISON'S OUT OF YOUR SYSTEM. THE ANTIDOTE NEEDED THE REGENERATIVE PROPERTIES OF THE HYDRA BLOOD.
GOOD. THEN EVERYTHING IS WORKING OUT ACCORDING TO MY PLAN.
WHAT? REALLY?
NO. BUT IT SOUNDED GOOD PRETENDING FOR A SE OND.
AT LEAST WE CAN FOCUS ON GETTING JULIETTE BACK.
ONE WORRY. IF HE DOESN'T NEED US ANY MORE, WHY DID HE GIVE YOU THE ANTIDOTE? WHY NOT KILL US?
IT DOESN'T MATTER. TIME TO TURN THE TABLES. SILVIO MADE TWO MISTAKES.
ONE, HE CURED ME. TWO, HE'S DELIVERING US TO HIS FRONT DOORSTEP.
WE JUST NEED TO FIND THE ONE ITEM SILVIO CARES ABOUT, AND SQUEEZE.
IF IT'S TRUE THAT SILVIO IS MANUFACTURING HIS OWN GRAUSEN, ALL THAT MATTERS IS STOPPING THEM.
SOUNDS LIKE WE'VE ARRIVED.
IF SACRIFICES HAVE TO BE MADE, I'LL BE THE ONE TO MAKE IT. I'VE DRAGGED YOU TWO INTO THE DEPTHS. JUST PROMISE ME, IF ALL GOES TO HELL... FIND JULIETTE AND GET OUT ALIVE.
FWRUM
ALL WOGED AND READY TO GO. LET'S GO KICK SOME...
KLAK
FWRUM

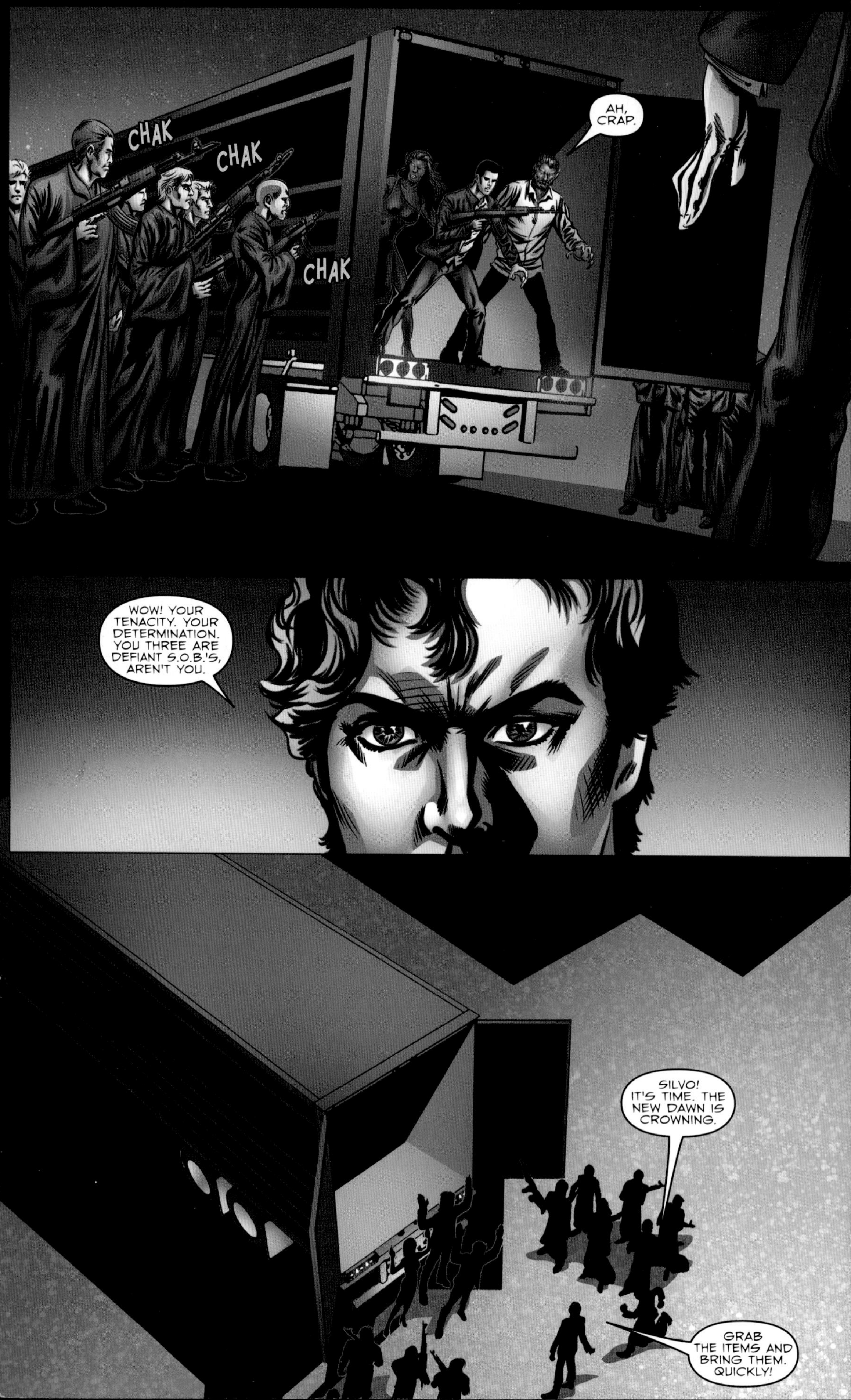
CHAK
CHAK
CHAK
AH, CRAP.
WOW! YOUR TENACITY. YOUR DETERMINATION. YOU THREE ARE DEFIANT S.O.B.'S, AREN'T YOU.
SILVO! IT'S TIME. THE NEW DAWN IS CROWNING.
GRAB THE ITEMS AND BRING THEM. QUICKLY!

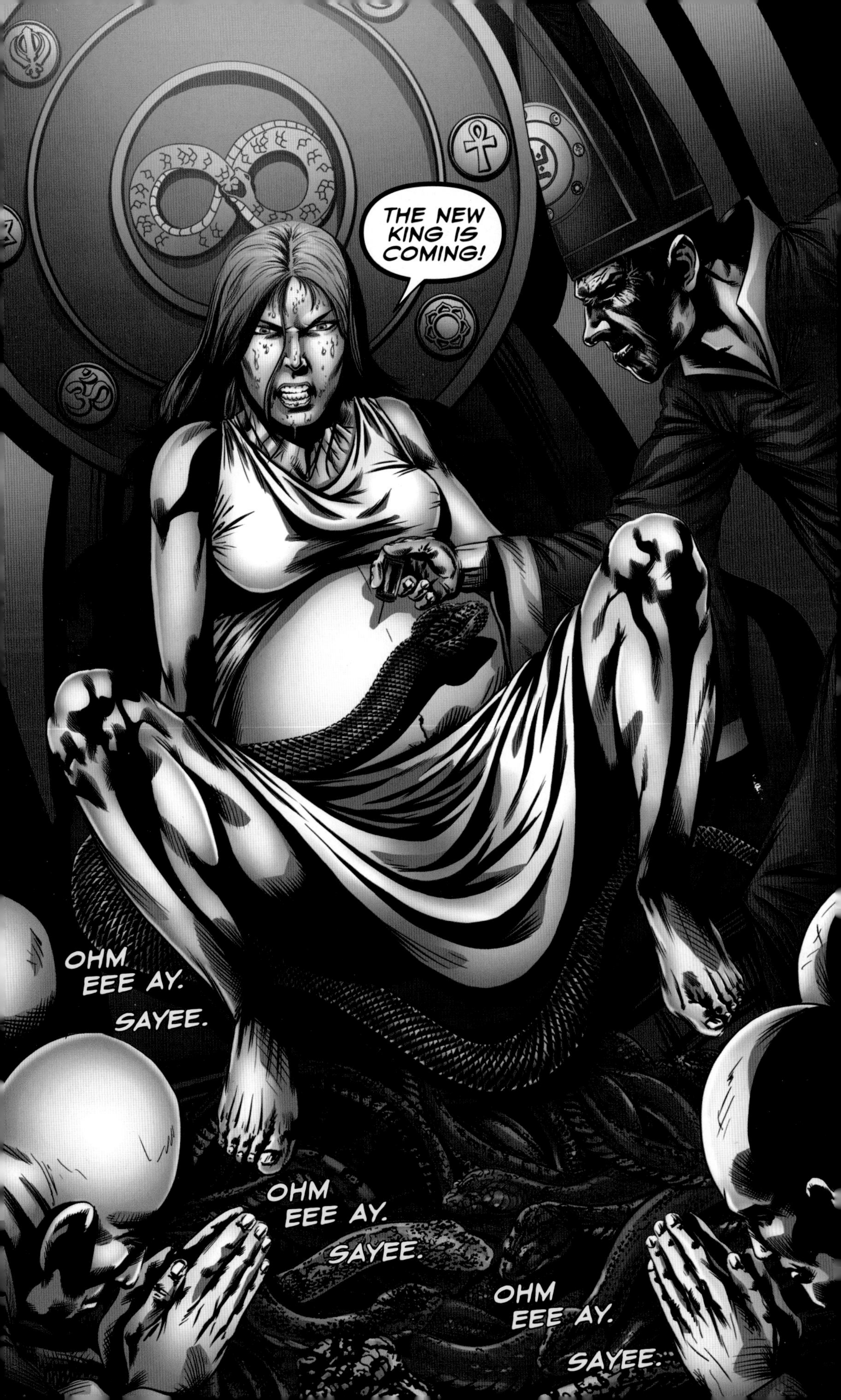
THE NEW KING IS COMING!
OHM EEE AY. SAYEE.
OHM EEE AY. SAYEE.
OHM EEE AY. SAYEE.

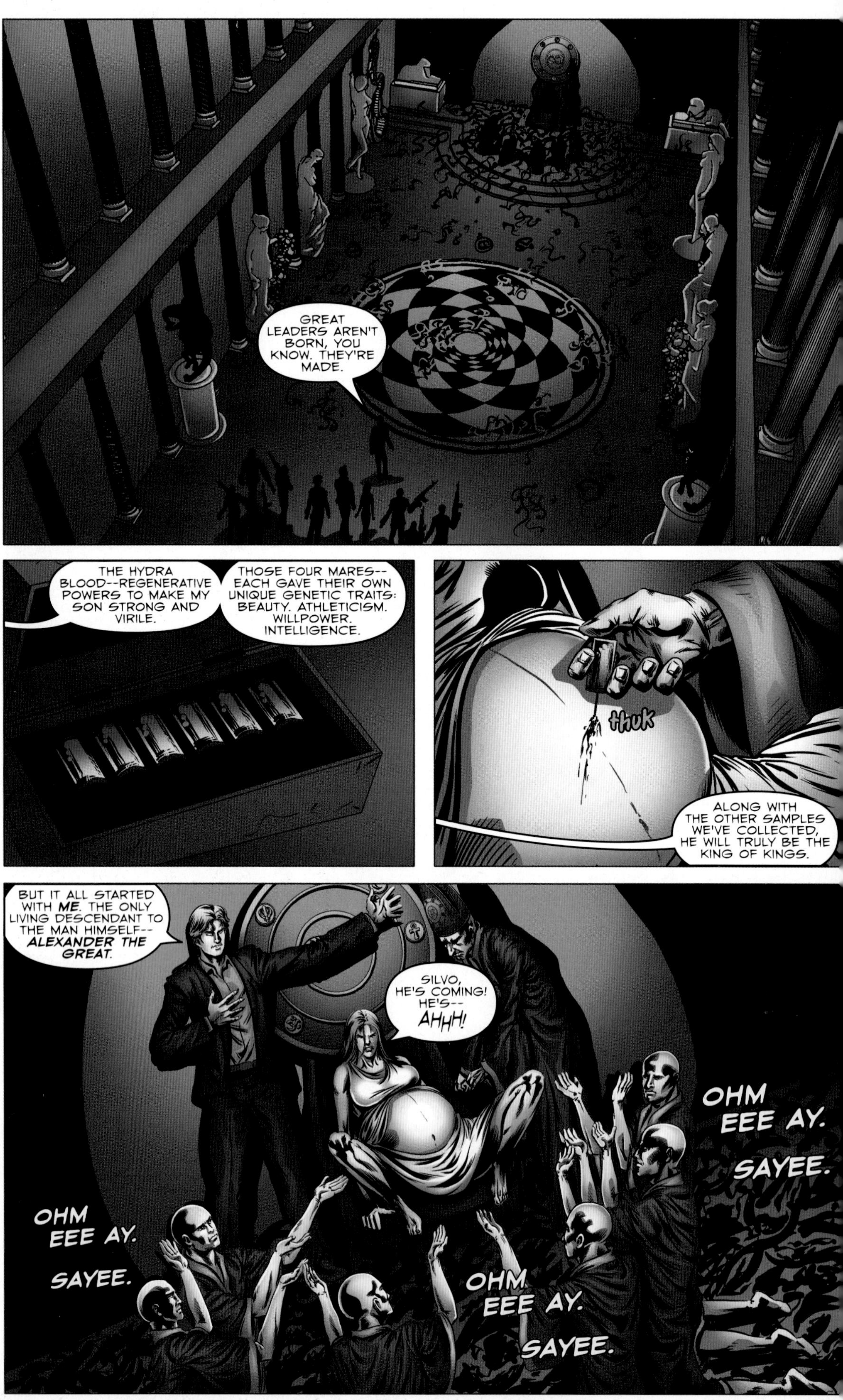
GREAT LEADERS AREN'T BORN, YOU KNOW. THEY'RE MADE.
THE HYDRA BLOOD--REGENERATIVE POWERS TO MAKE MY SON STRONG AND VIRILE.
THOSE FOUR MARES--EACH GAVE THEIR OWN UNIQUE GENETIC TRAITS: BEAUTY. ATHLETICISM. WILLPOWER. INTELLIGENCE.
thuk
ALONG WITH THE OTHER SAMPLES WE'VE COLLECTED, HE WILL TRULY BE THE KING OF KINGS.
BUT IT ALL STARTED WITH ME. THE ONLY LIVING DESCENDANT TO THE MAN HIMSELF--ALEXANDER THE GREAT.
SILVO, HE'S COMING! HE'S--AHHH!
OHM EEE AY. SAYEE.
OHM EEE AY. SAYEE.
OHM EEE AY. SAYEE.

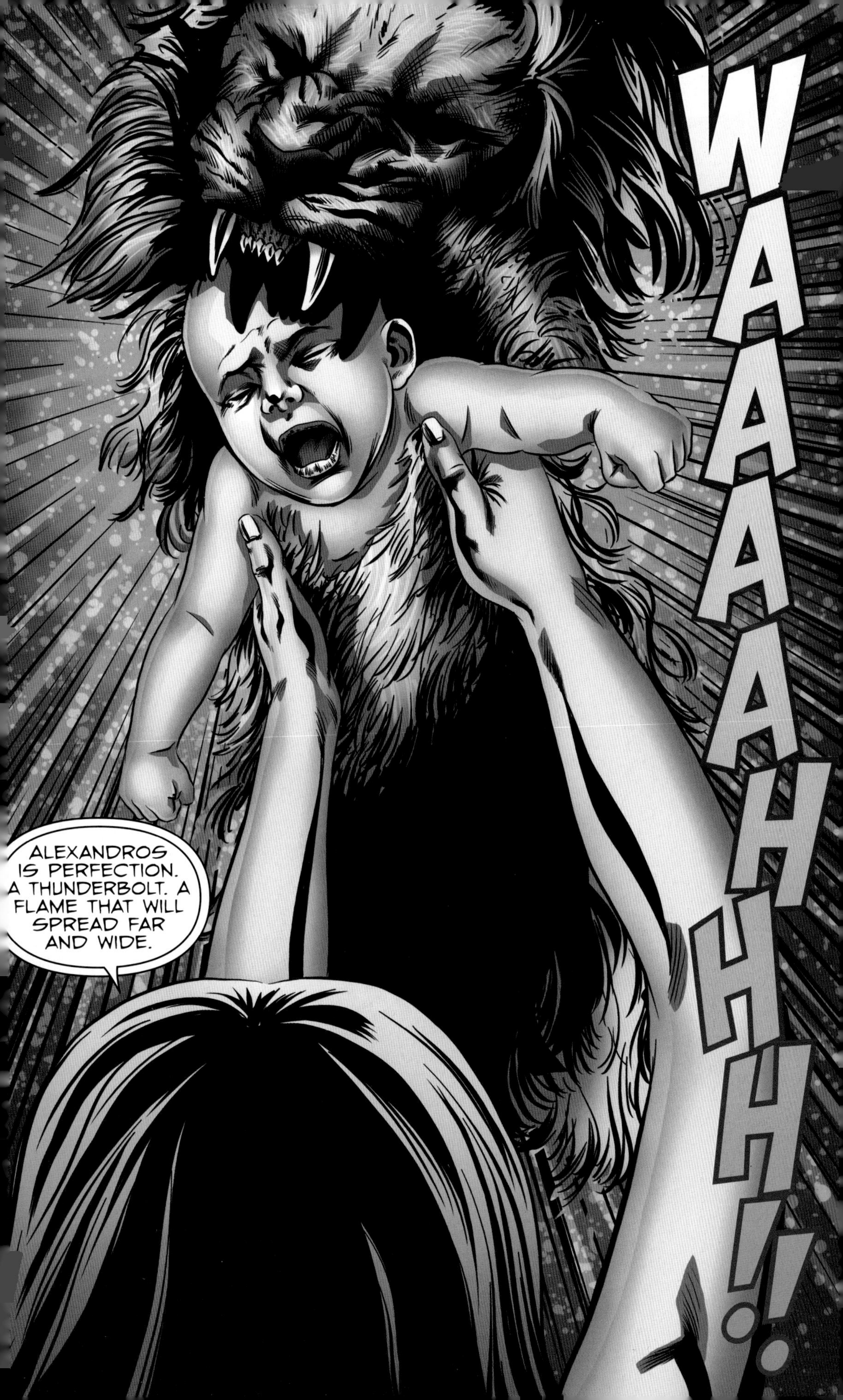
WAAAAAHHHH!!
ALEXANDROS IS PERFECTION. A THUNDERBOLT. A FLAME THAT WILL SPREAD FAR AND WIDE.

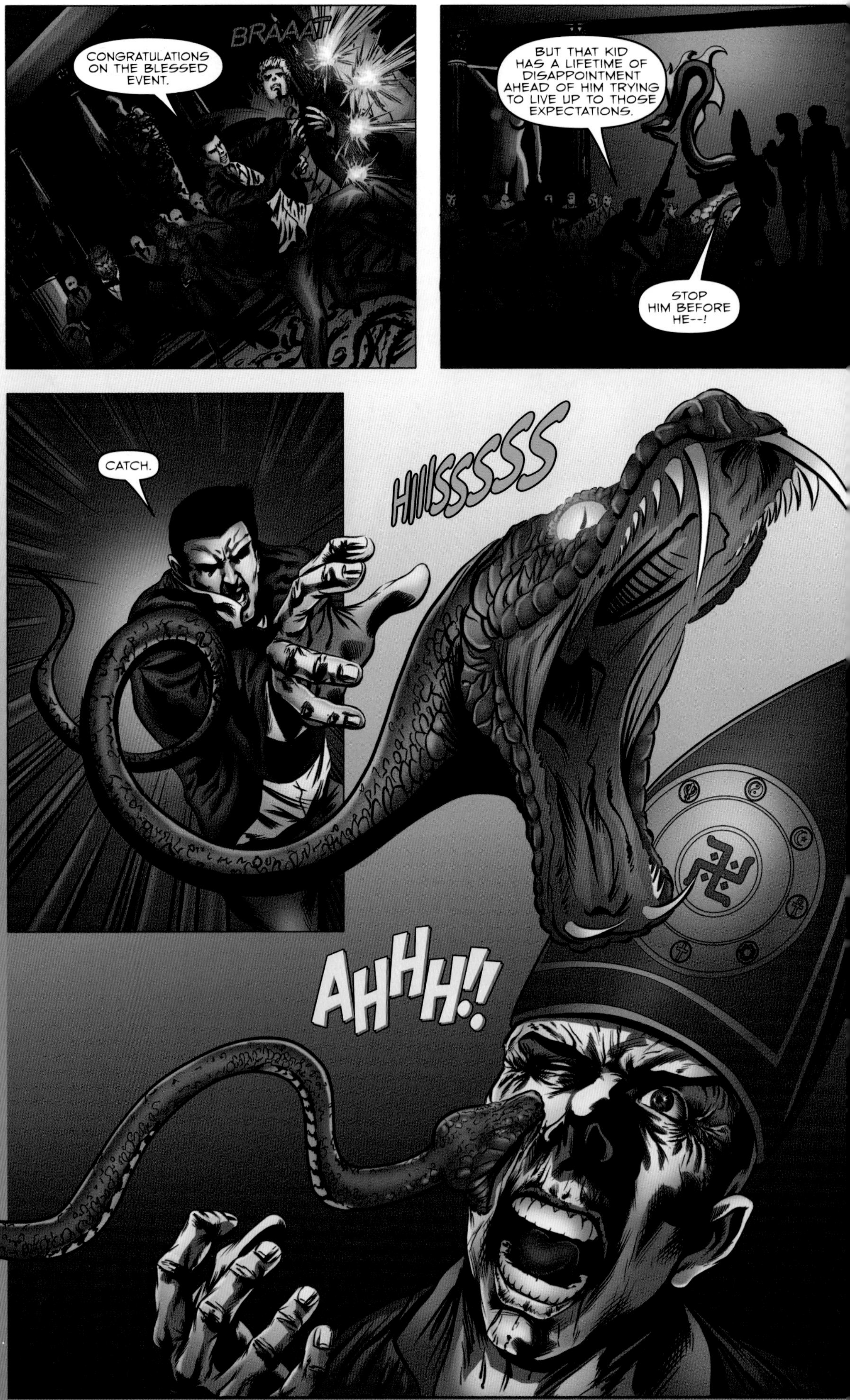
BRAAAT
CONGRATULATIONS ON THE BLESSED EVENT.
BUT THAT KID HAS A LIFETIME OF DISAPPOINTMENT AHEAD OF HIM TRYING TO LIVE UP TO THOSE EXPECTATIONS.
STOP HIM BEFORE HE--!
CATCH.
HIIISSSSS
AHHH!!

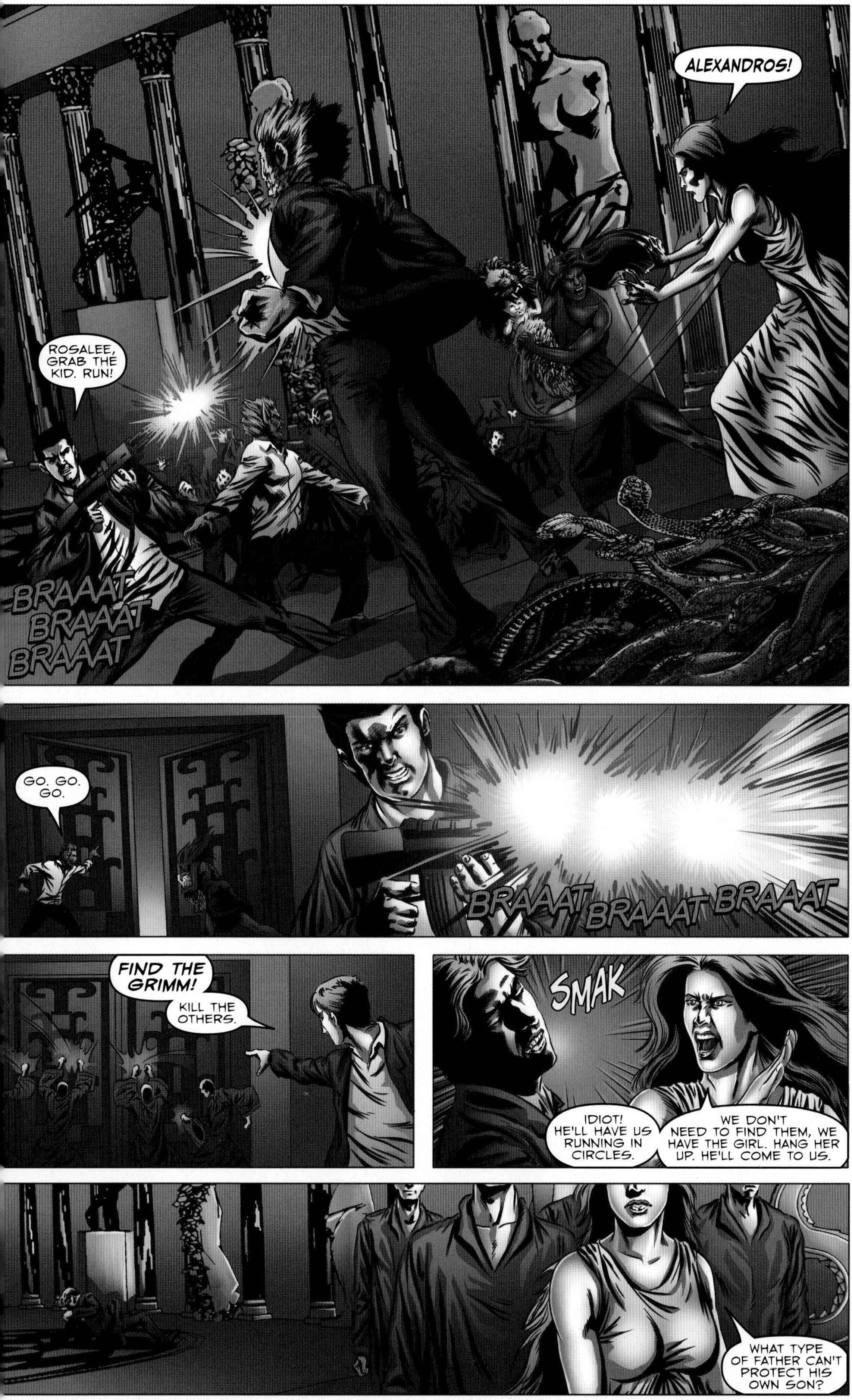
ALEXANDROS!
ROSALEE, GRAB THE KID. RUN!
BRAAAT BRAAAT BRAAAT
GO. GO. GO.
BRAAAT BRAAAT BRAAAT
FIND THE GRIMM!
KILL THE OTHERS.
SMAK
IDIOT! HE'LL HAVE US RUNNING IN CIRCLES.
WE DON'T NEED TO FIND THEM, WE HAVE THE GIRL. HANG HER UP. HE'LL COME TO US.
WHAT TYPE OF FATHER CAN'T PROTECT HIS OWN SON?

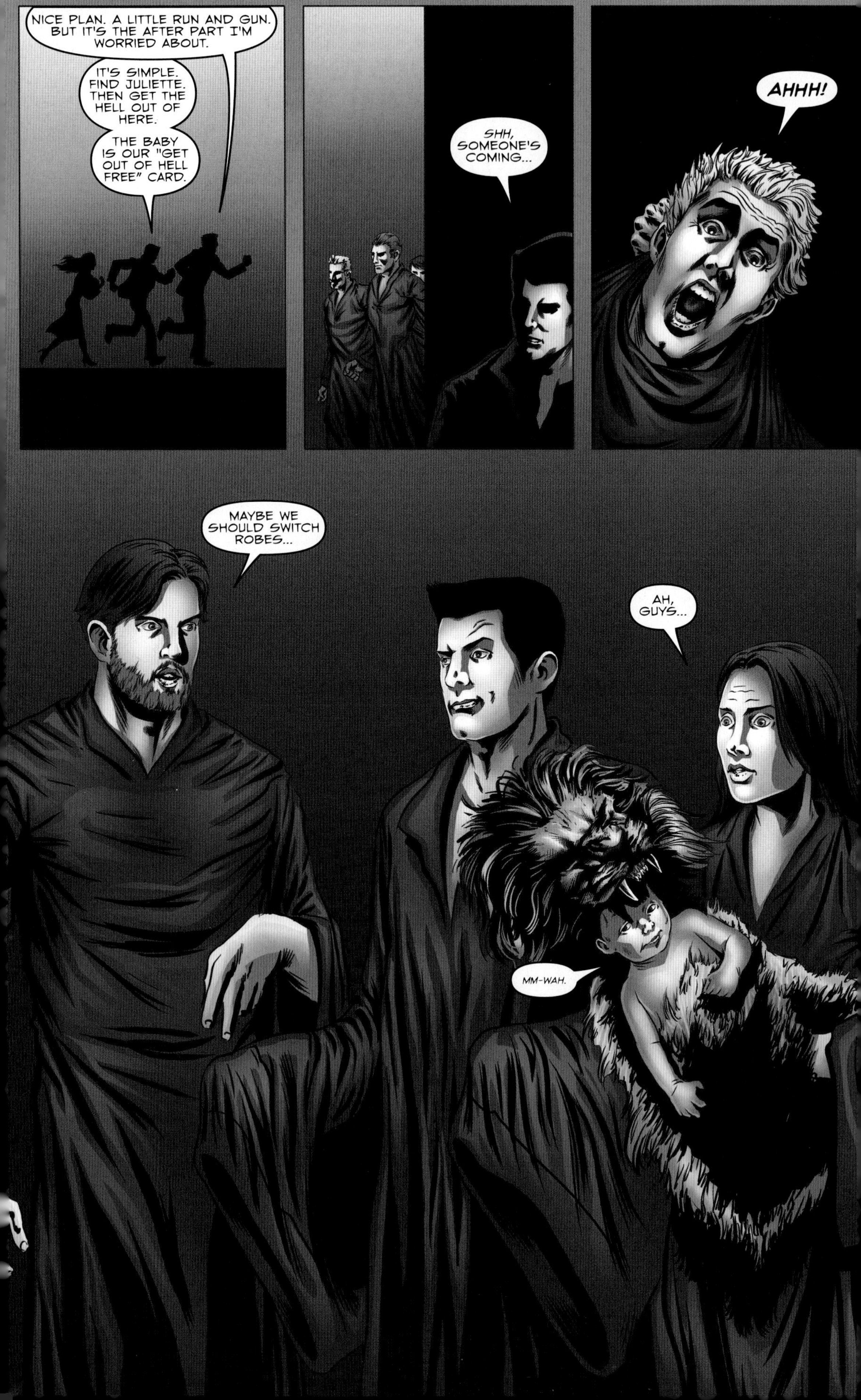
NICE PLAN. A LITTLE RUN AND GUN. BUT IT'S THE AFTER PART I'M WORRIED ABOUT.
IT'S SIMPLE. FIND JULIETTE. THEN GET THE HELL OUT OF HERE.
THE BABY IS OUR "GET OUT OF HELL FREE" CARD.
SHH, SOMEONE'S COMING...
AHHH!
MAYBE WE SHOULD SWITCH ROBES...
AH, GUYS...
MM-WAH.

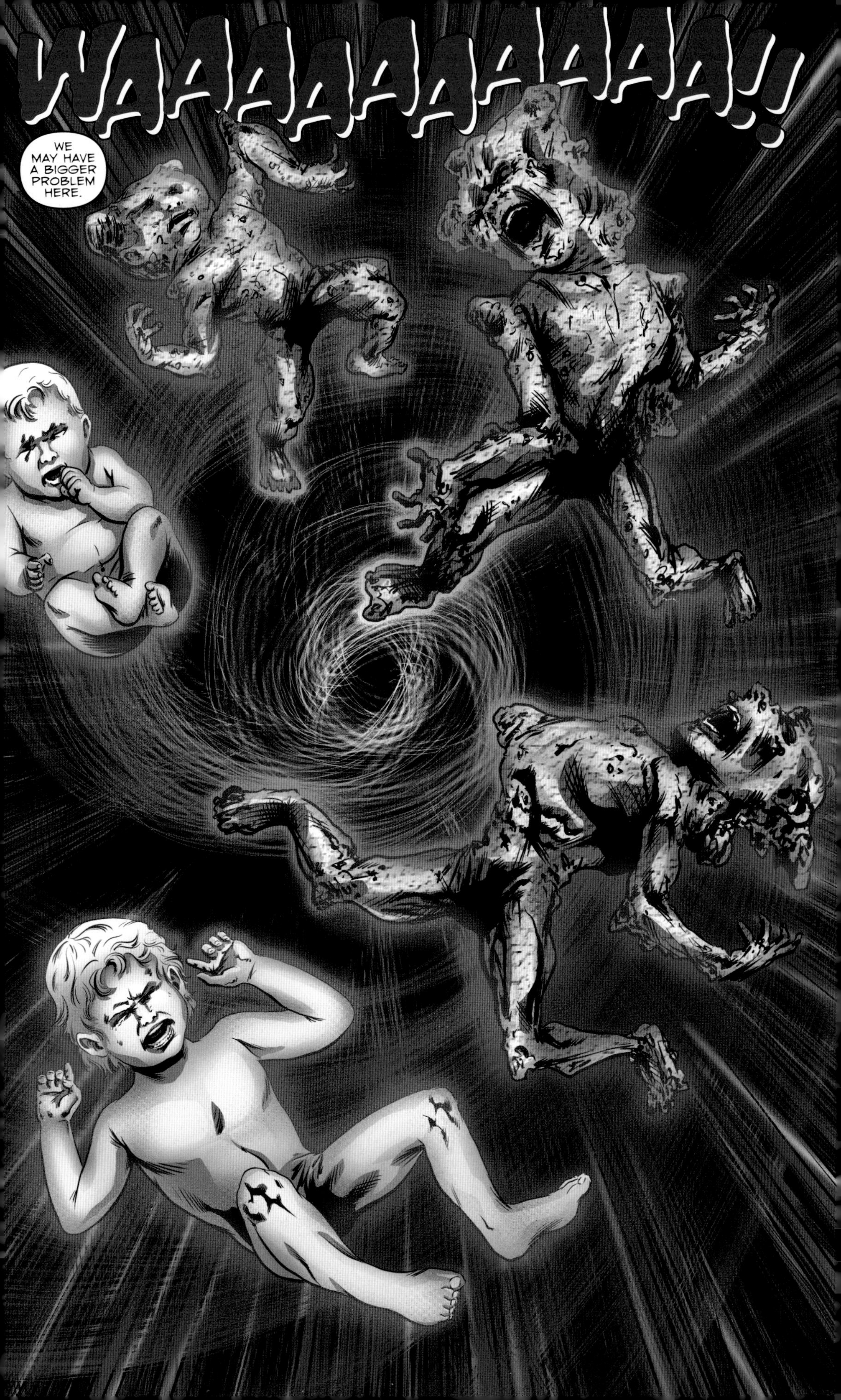
WAAAAAAAAAA!!
WE MAY HAVE A BIGGER PROBLEM HERE.

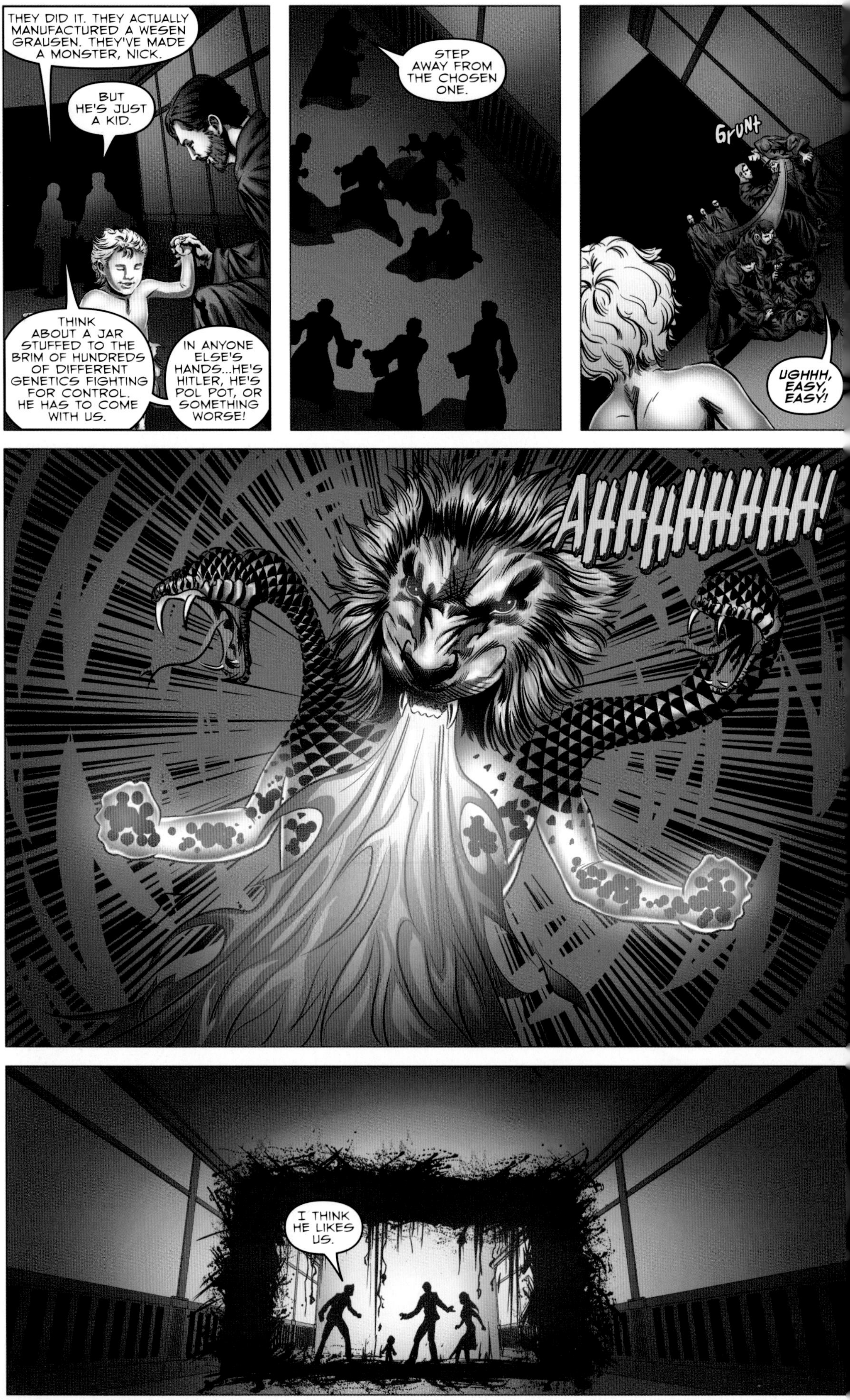
THEY DID IT. THEY ACTUALLY MANUFACTURED A WESEN GRAUSEN. THEY'VE MADE A MONSTER, NICK.
BUT HE'S JUST A KID.
THINK ABOUT A JAR STUFFED TO THE BRIM OF HUNDREDS OF DIFFERENT GENETICS FIGHTING FOR CONTROL. HE HAS TO COME WITH US.
IN ANYONE ELSE'S HANDS...HE'S HITLER, HE'S POL POT, OR SOMETHING WORSE!
STEP AWAY FROM THE CHOSEN ONE.
GRUNT
UGHHH, EASY, EASY!
AHHHHHHHH!
I THINK HE LIKES US.

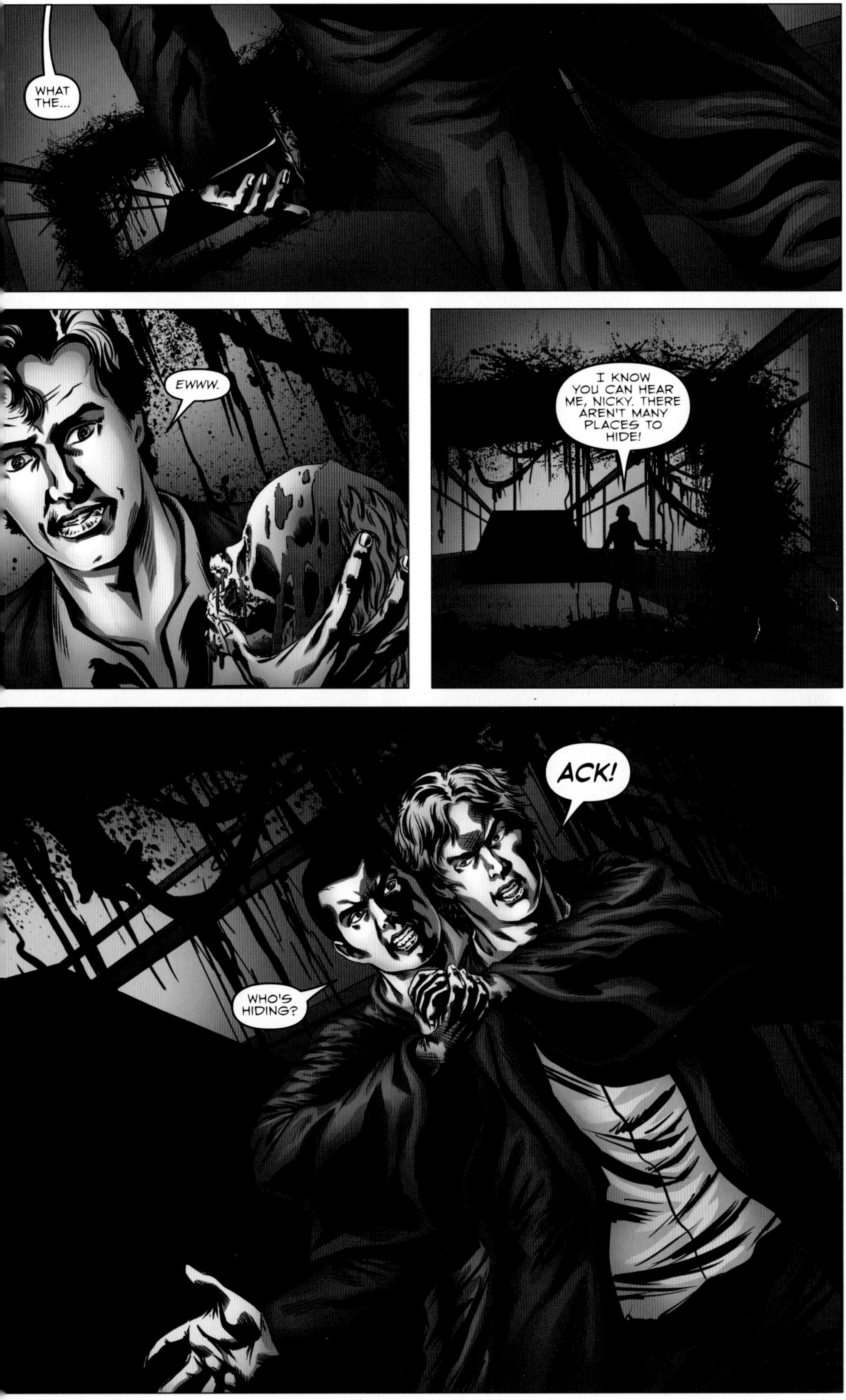
WHAT THE...
EWWW.
I KNOW YOU CAN HEAR ME, NICKY. THERE AREN'T MANY PLACES TO HIDE!
ACK!
WHO'S HIDING?

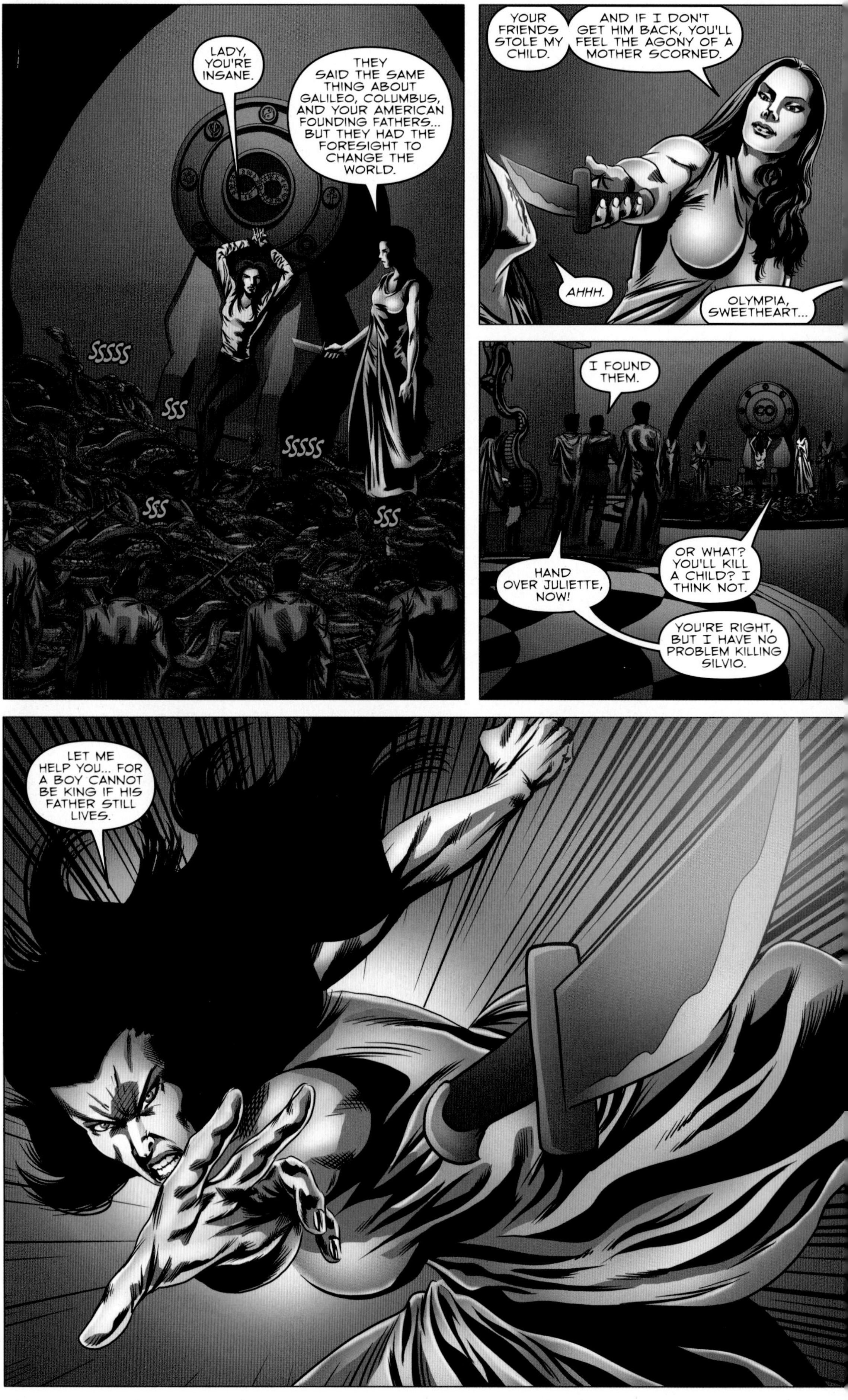
LADY, YOU'RE INSANE.
THEY SAID THE SAME THING ABOUT GALILEO, COLUMBUS, AND YOUR AMERICAN FOUNDING FATHERS... BUT THEY HAD THE FORESIGHT TO CHANGE THE WORLD.
SSSSS
SSS
SSSSS
SSS
SSS
YOUR FRIENDS STOLE MY CHILD.
AND IF I DON'T GET HIM BACK, YOU'LL FEEL THE AGONY OF A MOTHER SCORNED.
AHHH.
OLYMPIA, SWEETHEART...
I FOUND THEM.
HAND OVER JULIETTE, NOW!
OR WHAT? YOU'LL KILL A CHILD? I THINK NOT.
YOU'RE RIGHT, BUT I HAVE NO PROBLEM KILLING SILVIO.
LET ME HELP YOU... FOR A BOY CANNOT BE KING IF HIS FATHER STILL LIVES.

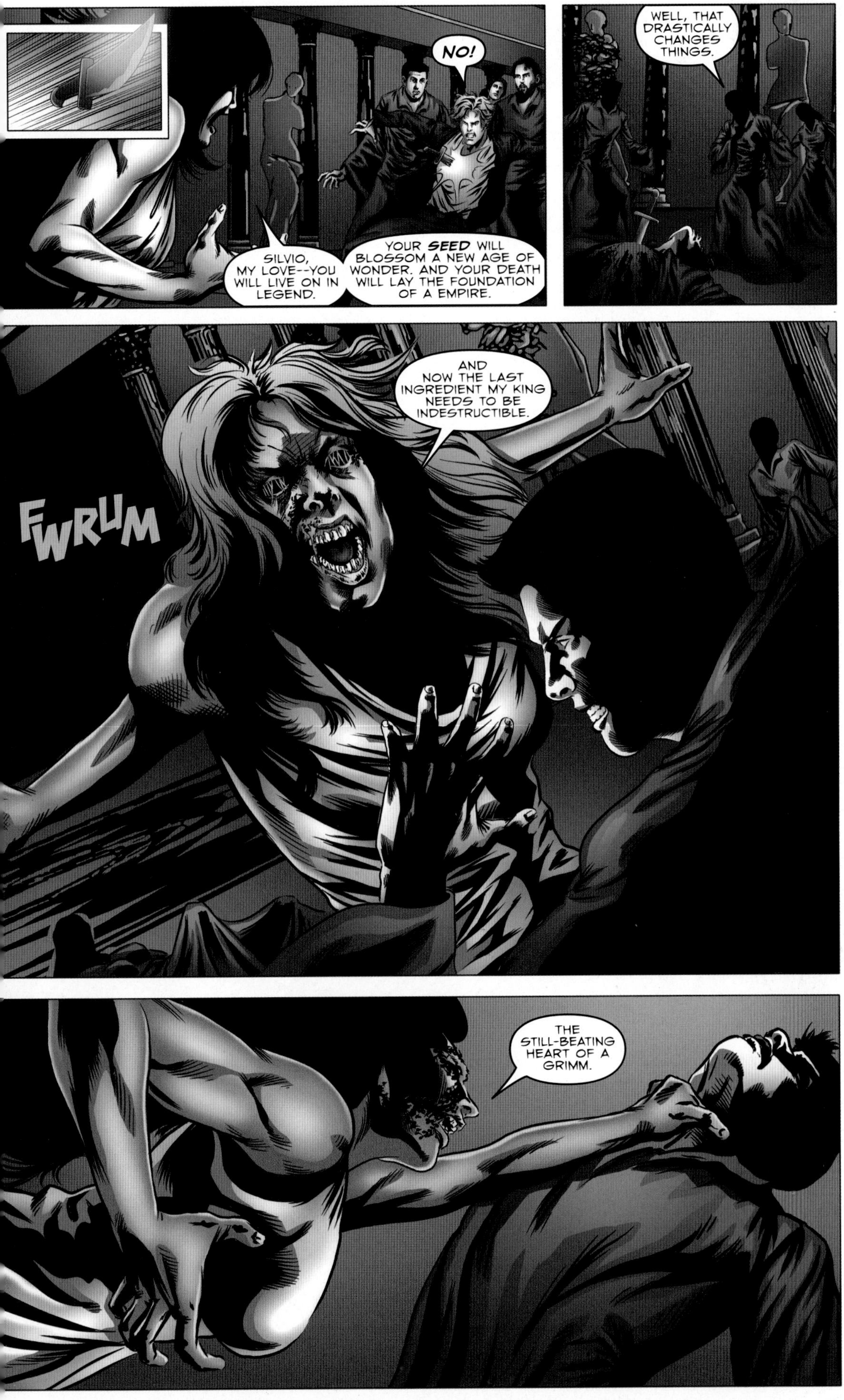
NO!
SILVIO, MY LOVE--YOU WILL LIVE ON IN LEGEND.
YOUR SEED WILL BLOSSOM A NEW AGE OF WONDER. AND YOUR DEATH WILL LAY THE FOUNDATION OF A EMPIRE.
WELL, THAT DRASTICALLY CHANGES THINGS.
AND NOW THE LAST INGREDIENT MY KING NEEDS TO BE INDESTRUCTIBLE.
FWRUM
THE STILL-BEATING HEART OF A GRIMM.

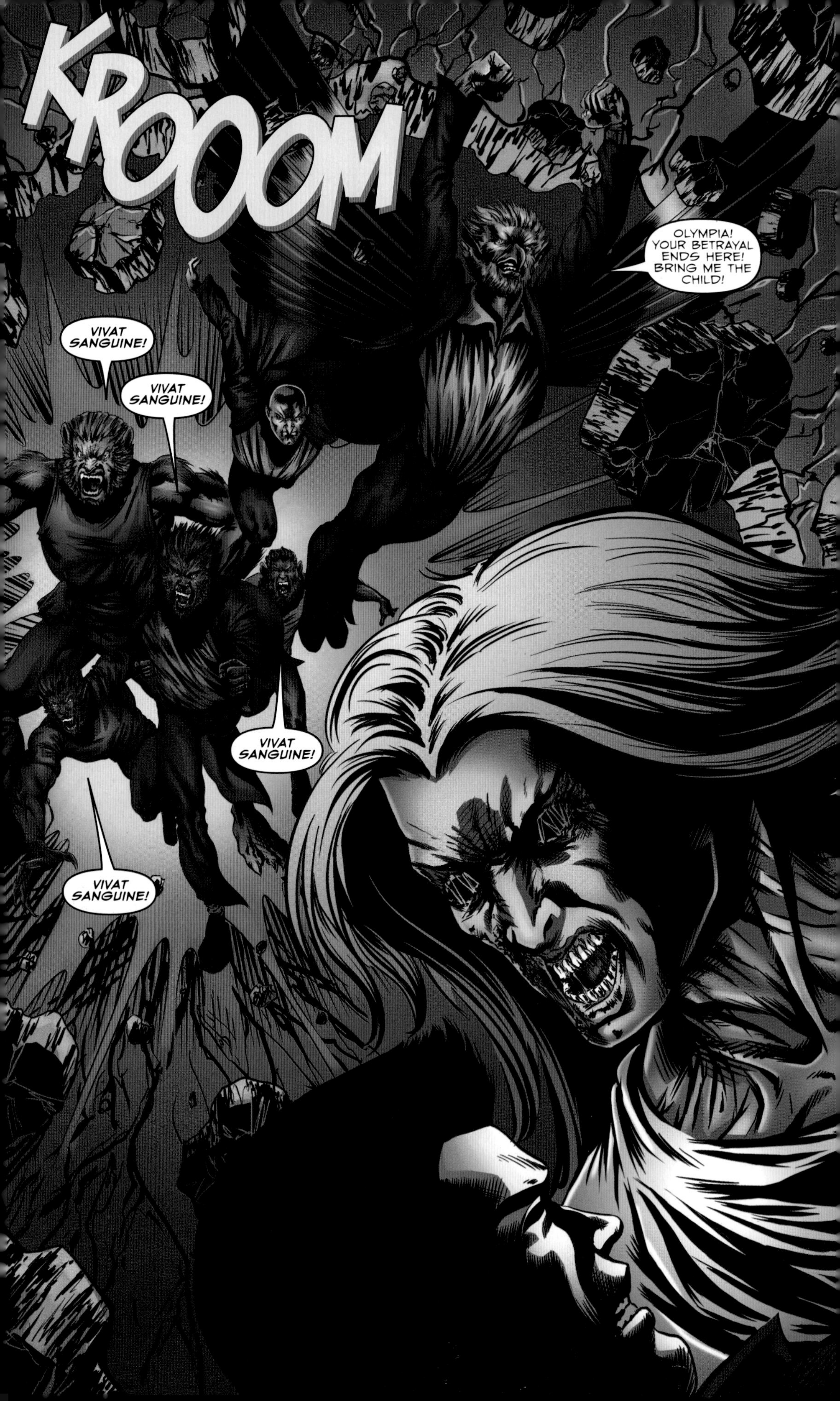
KROOOM
OLYMPIA! YOUR BETRAYAL ENDS HERE! BRING ME THE CHILD!
VIVAT SANGUINE!
VIVAT SANGUINE!
VIVAT SANGUINE!
VIVAT SANGUINE!

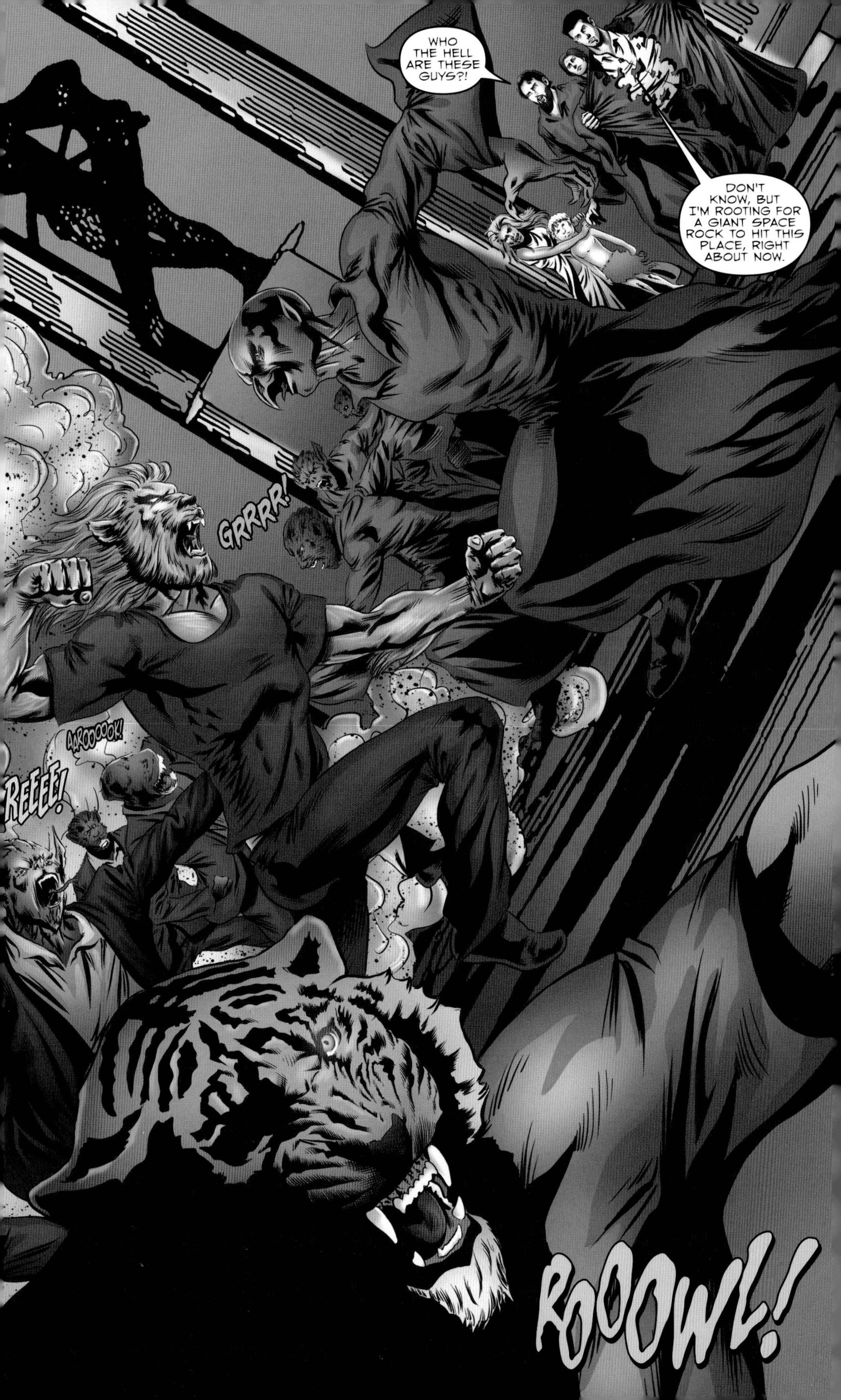

WHO THE HELL ARE THESE GUYS?!
DON'T KNOW, BUT I'M ROOTING FOR A GIANT SPACE ROCK TO HIT THIS PLACE, RIGHT ABOUT NOW.
GRRRR!
AAROOOOK!
REEEE!
ROOOWL!

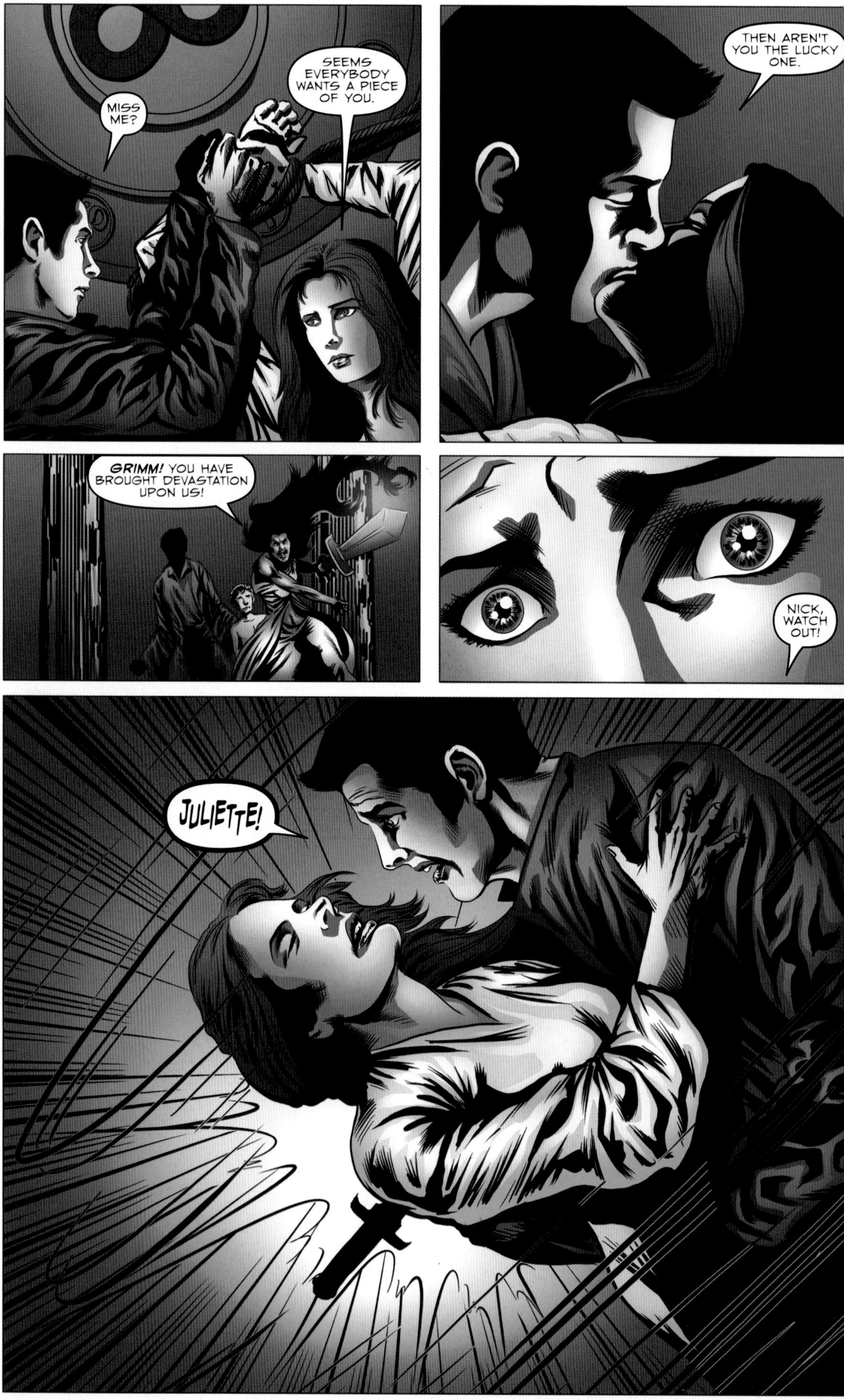
MISS ME?
SEEMS EVERYBODY WANTS A PIECE OF YOU.
THEN AREN'T YOU THE LUCKY ONE.
GRIMM! YOU HAVE BROUGHT DEVASTATION UPON US!
NICK, WATCH OUT!
JULIETTE!

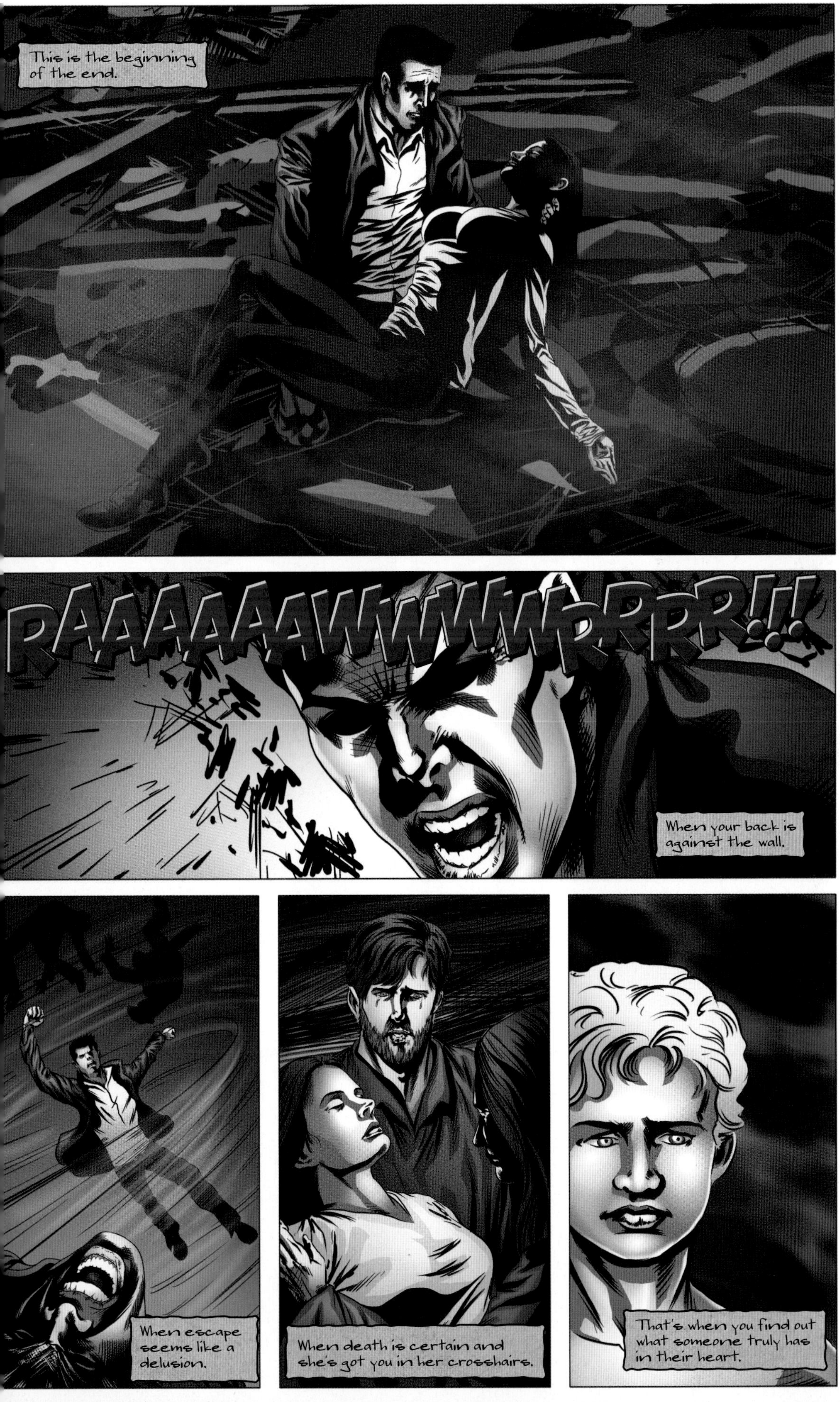

This is the beginning of the end.
RAAAAAAWWWWRRRR!!!
When your back is against the wall.
When escape seems like a delusion.
When death is certain and she's got you in her crosshairs.
That's when you find out what someone truly has in their heart.

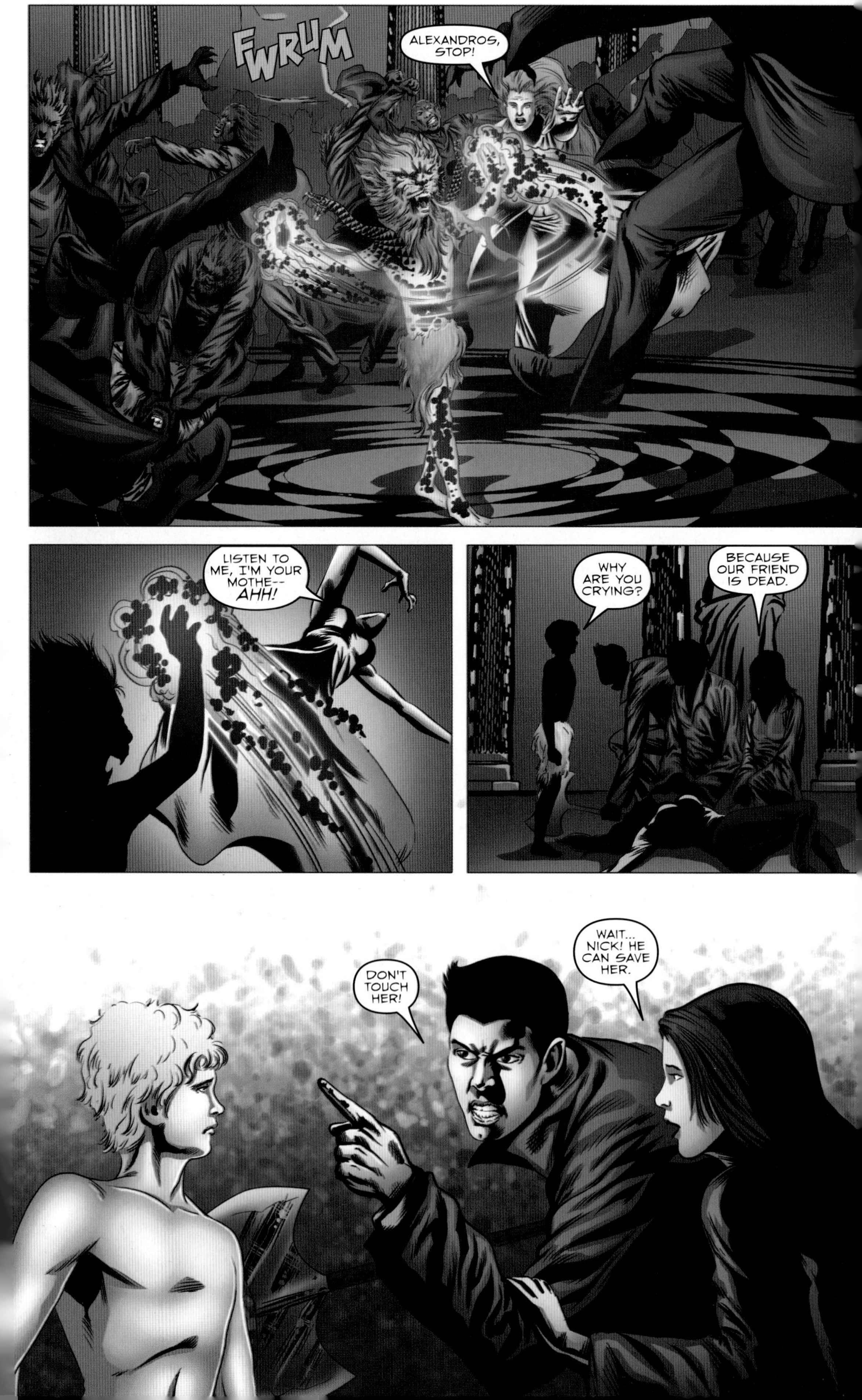
FWRUM
ALEXANDROS, STOP!
LISTEN TO ME, I'M YOUR MOTHE-- AHH!
WHY ARE YOU CRYING?
BECAUSE OUR FRIEND IS DEAD.
DON'T TOUCH HER!
WAIT... NICK! HE CAN SAVE HER.

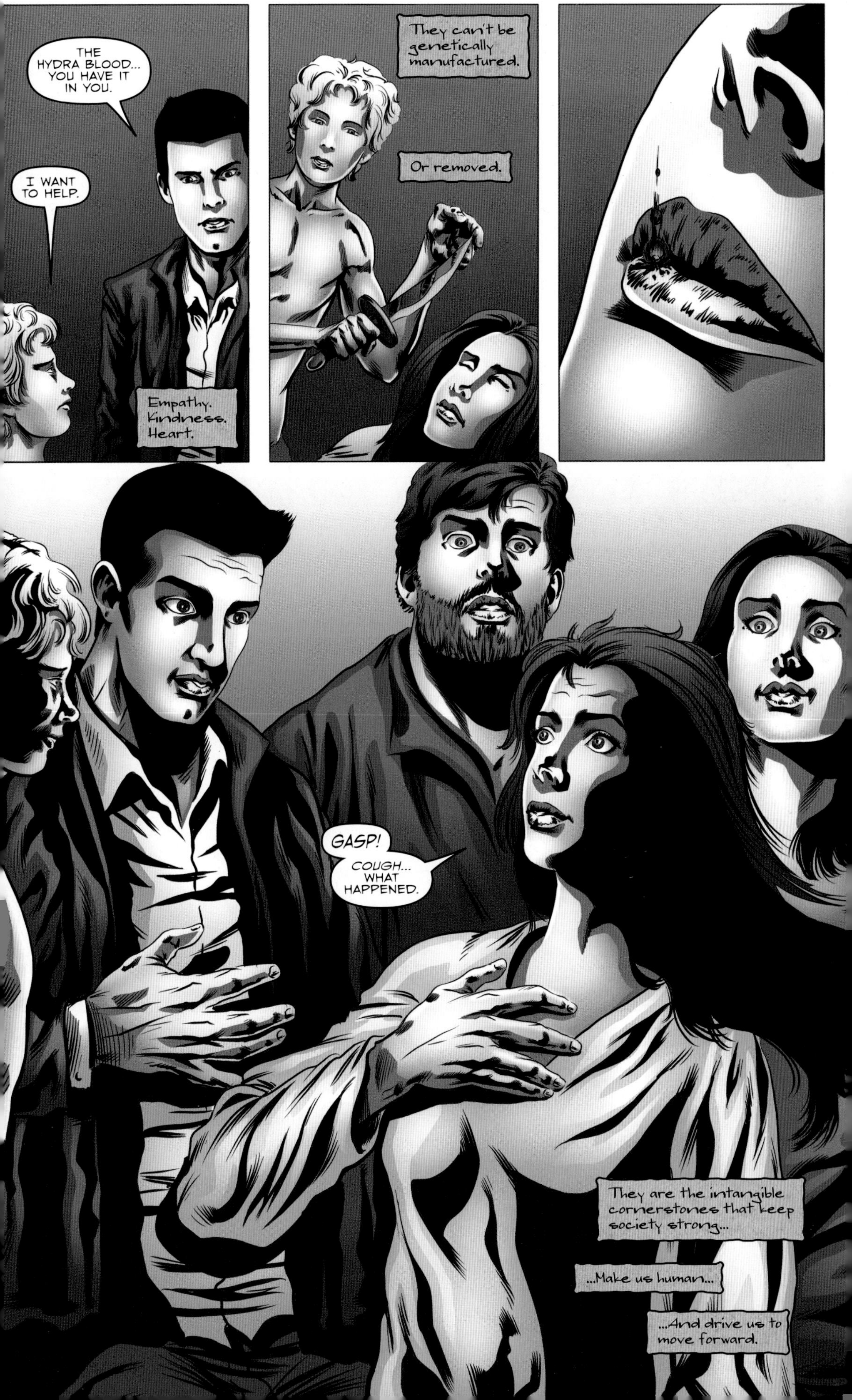
THE HYDRA BLOOD... YOU HAVE IT IN YOU.
I WANT TO HELP.
Empathy. Kindness. Heart.
They can't be genetically manufactured.
Or removed.
GASP!
COUGH... WHAT HAPPENED.
They are the intangible cornerstones that keep society strong...
...Make us human...
...And drive us to move forward.

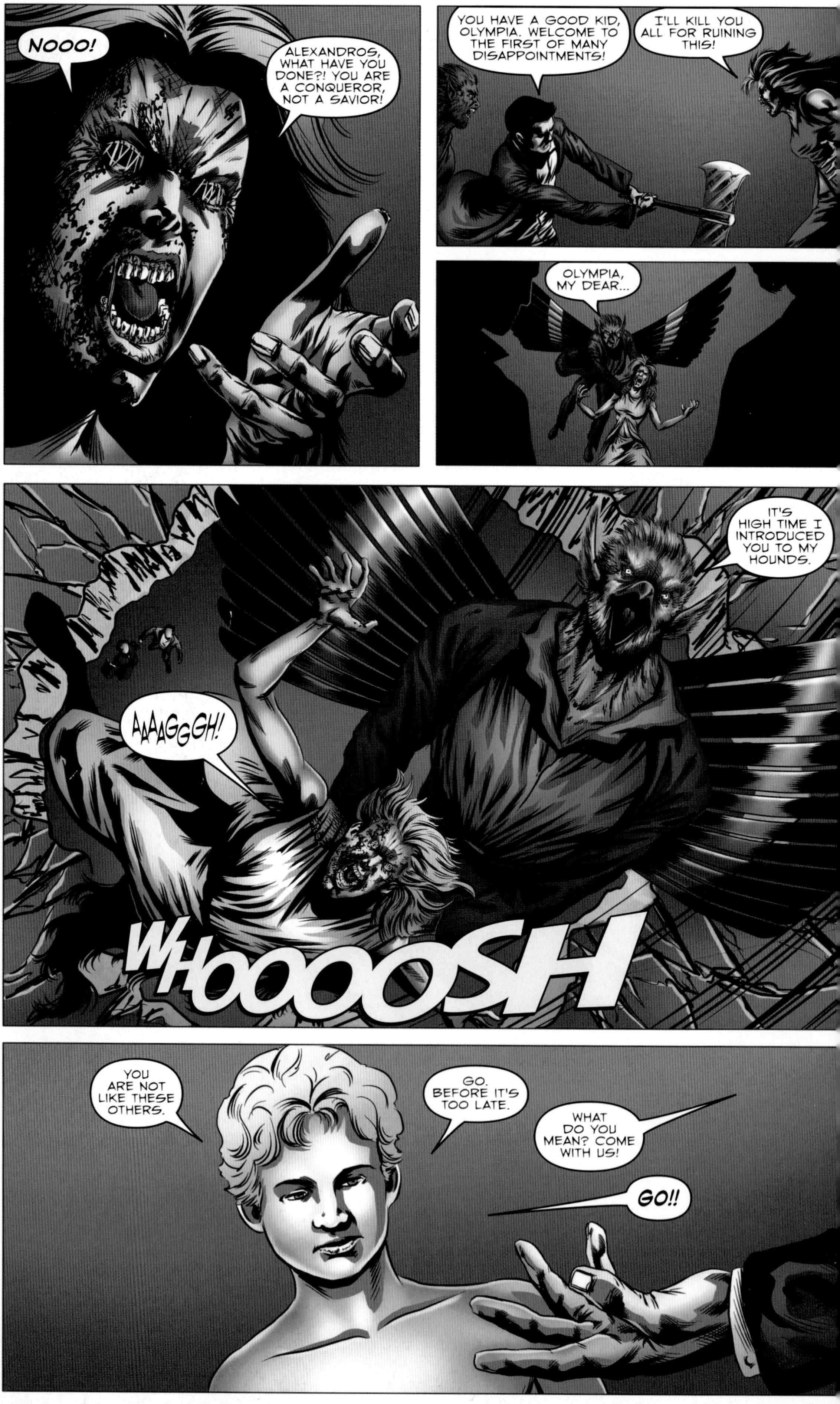
NOOO!
ALEXANDROS, WHAT HAVE YOU DONE?! YOU ARE A CONQUEROR, NOT A SAVIOR!
YOU HAVE A GOOD KID, OLYMPIA. WELCOME TO THE FIRST OF MANY DISAPPOINTMENTS!
I'LL KILL YOU ALL FOR RUINING THIS!
OLYMPIA, MY DEAR...
IT'S HIGH TIME I INTRODUCED YOU TO MY HOUNDS.
AAAAGGGH!
WHOOOOOSH
YOU ARE NOT LIKE THESE OTHERS.
GO. BEFORE IT'S TOO LATE.
WHAT DO YOU MEAN? COME WITH US!
GO!!

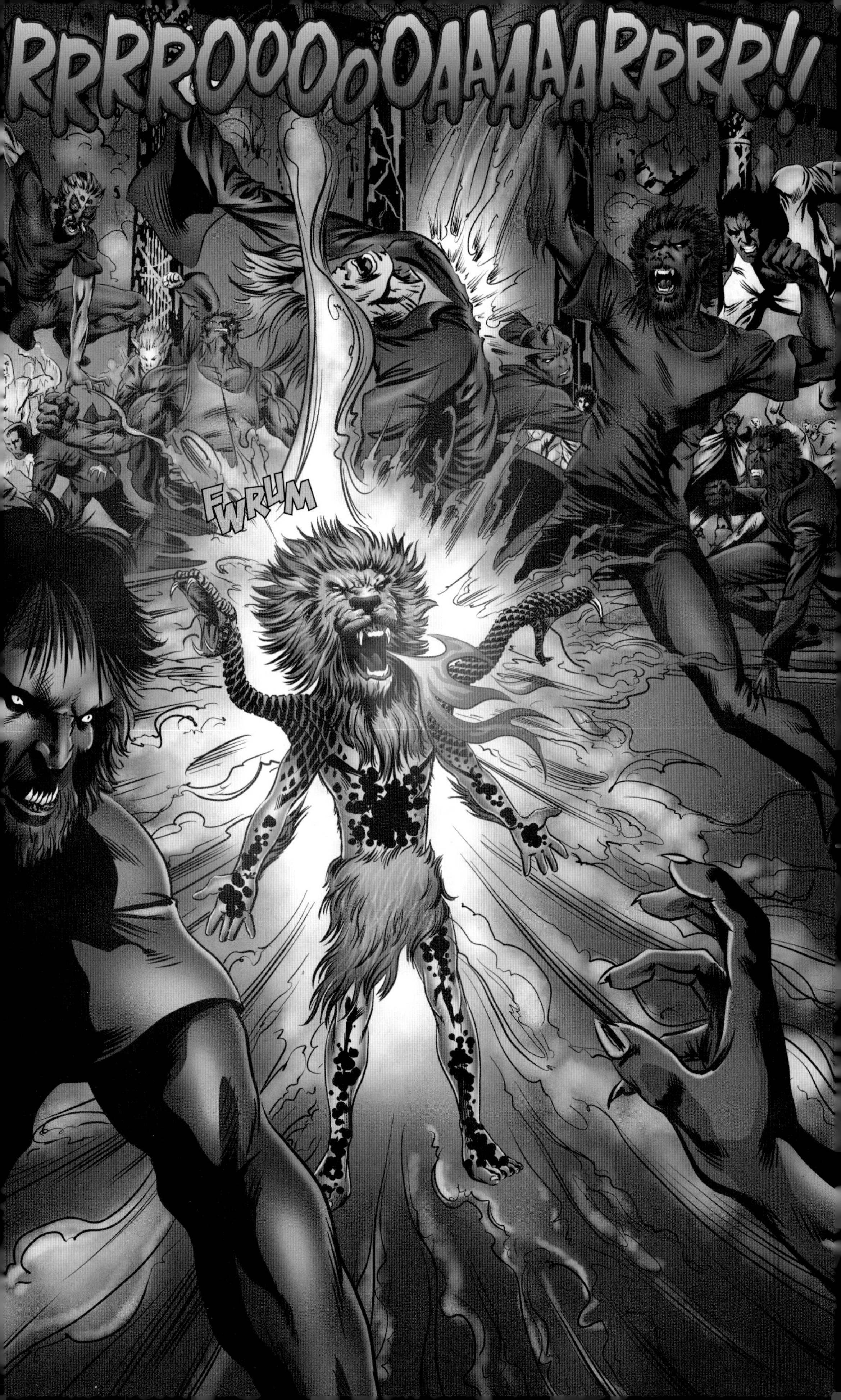
RRRROOOOOAAAAARRRR!!
FWRUM

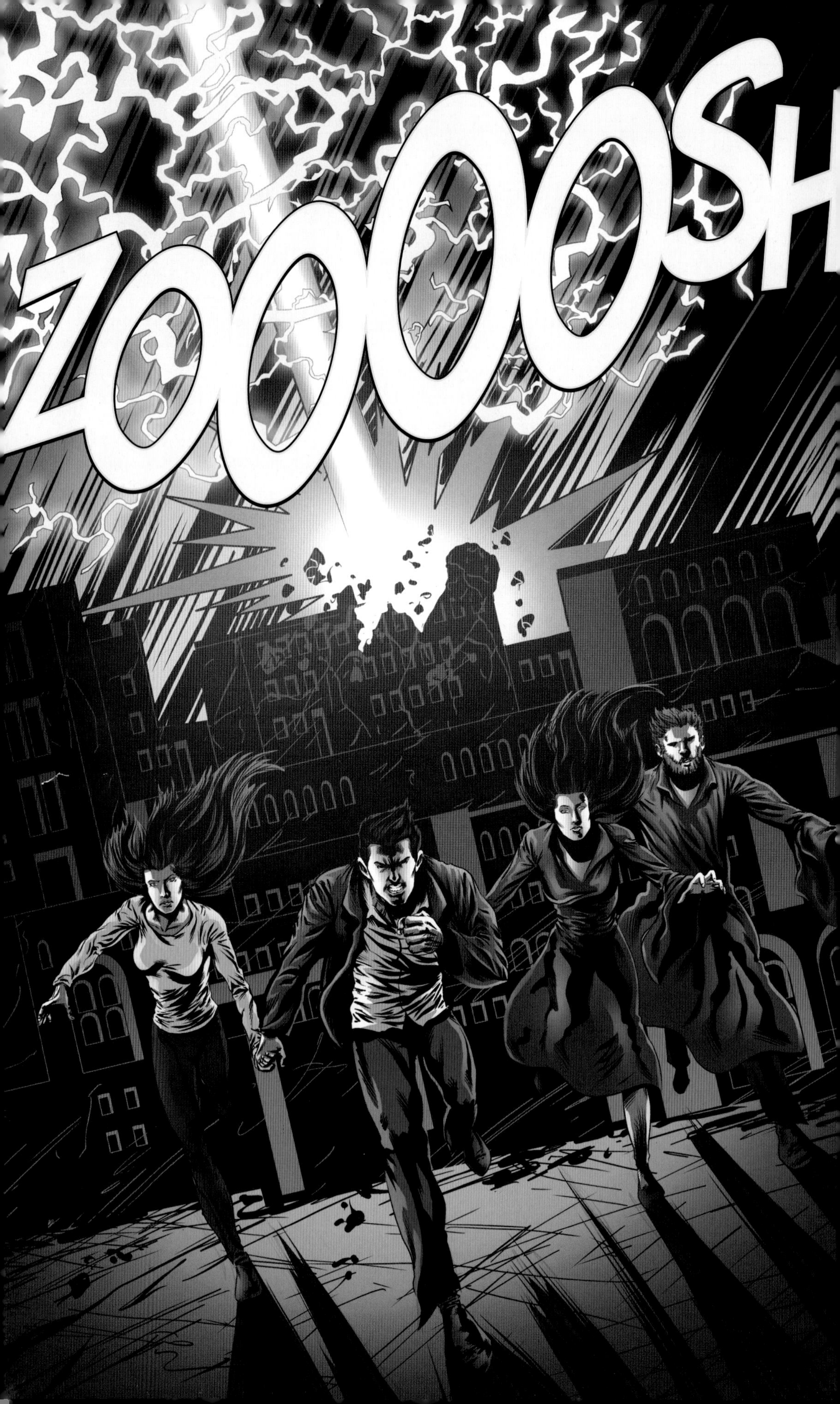
ZOOOOOSH

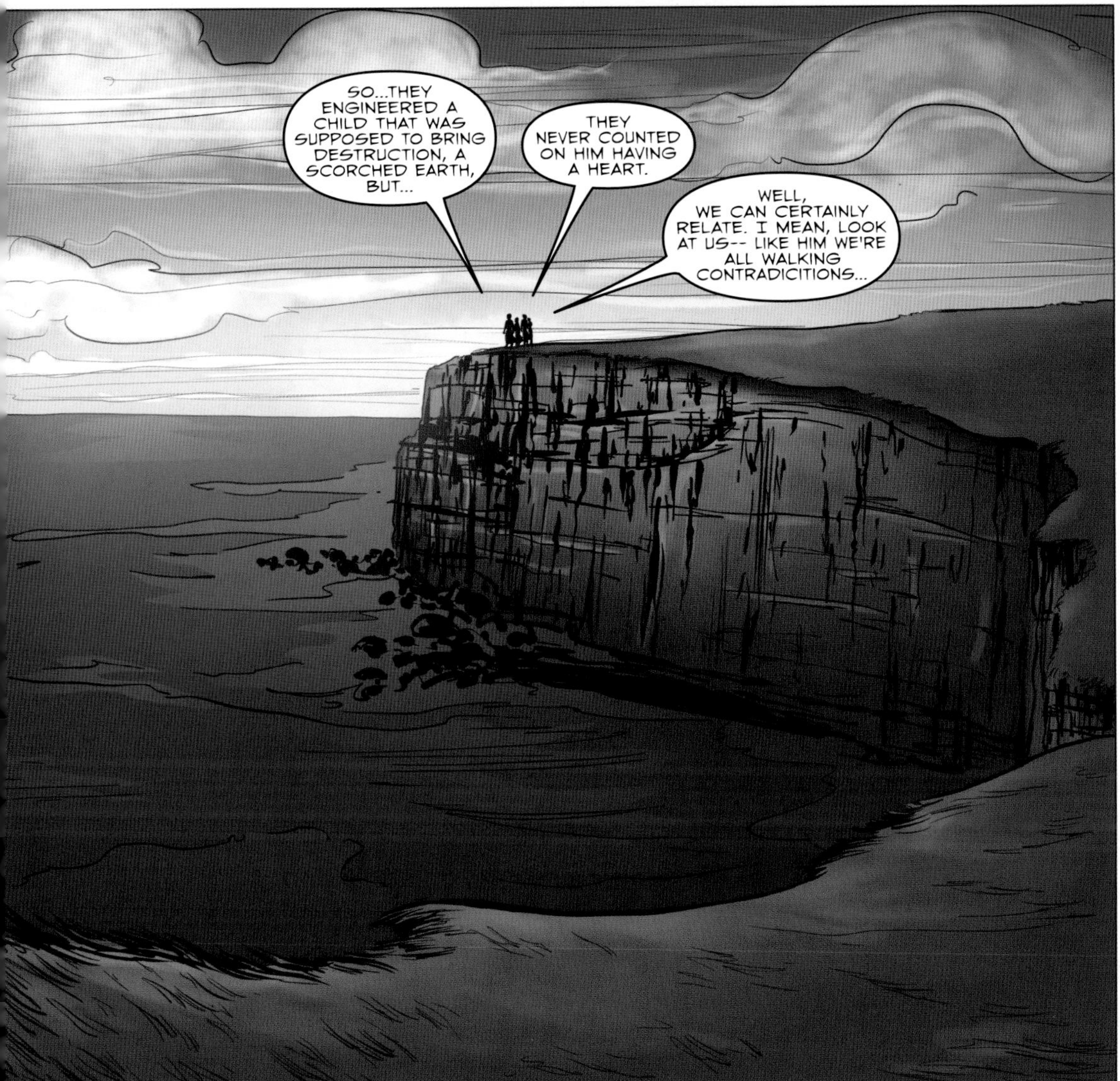
SO...THEY ENGINEERED A CHILD THAT WAS SUPPOSED TO BRING DESTRUCTION, A SCORCHED EARTH, BUT...
THEY NEVER COUNTED ON HIM HAVING A HEART.
WELL, WE CAN CERTAINLY RELATE. I MEAN, LOOK AT US-- LIKE HIM WE'RE ALL WALKING CONTRADICITIONS...

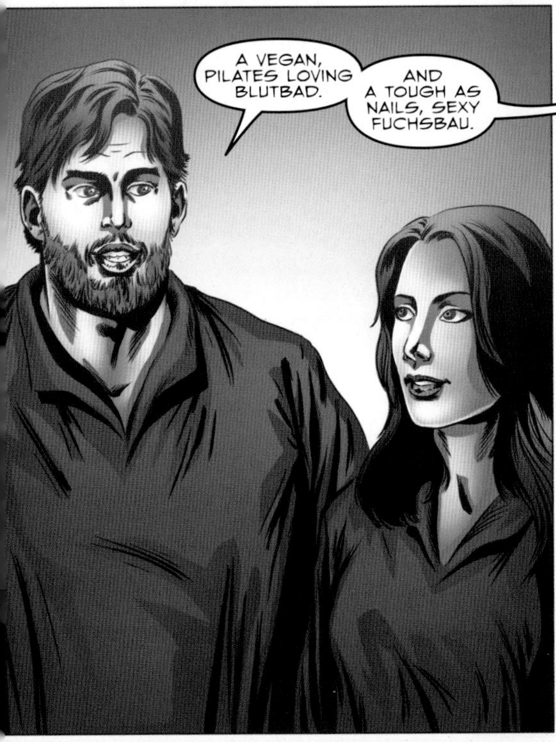
A VEGAN, PILATES LOVING BLUTBAD.
AND A TOUGH AS NAILS, SEXY FUCHSBAU.

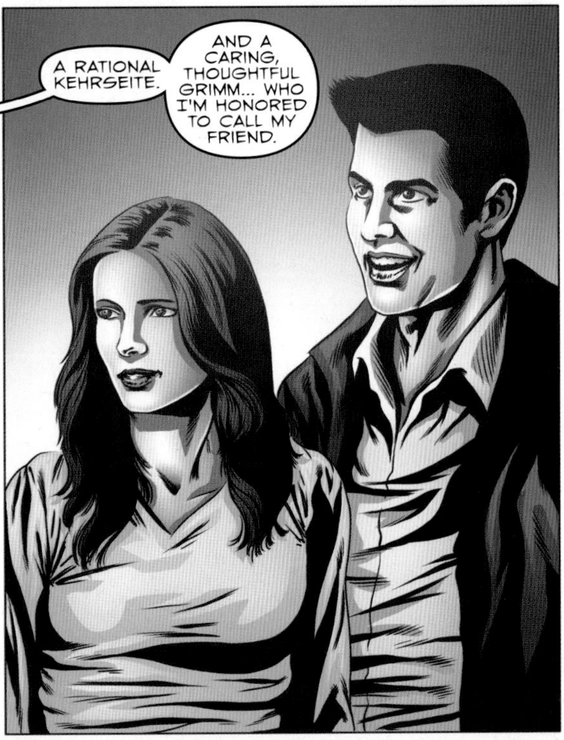
A RATIONAL KEHRSEITE.
AND A CARING, THOUGHTFUL GRIMM... WHO I'M HONORED TO CALL MY FRIEND.

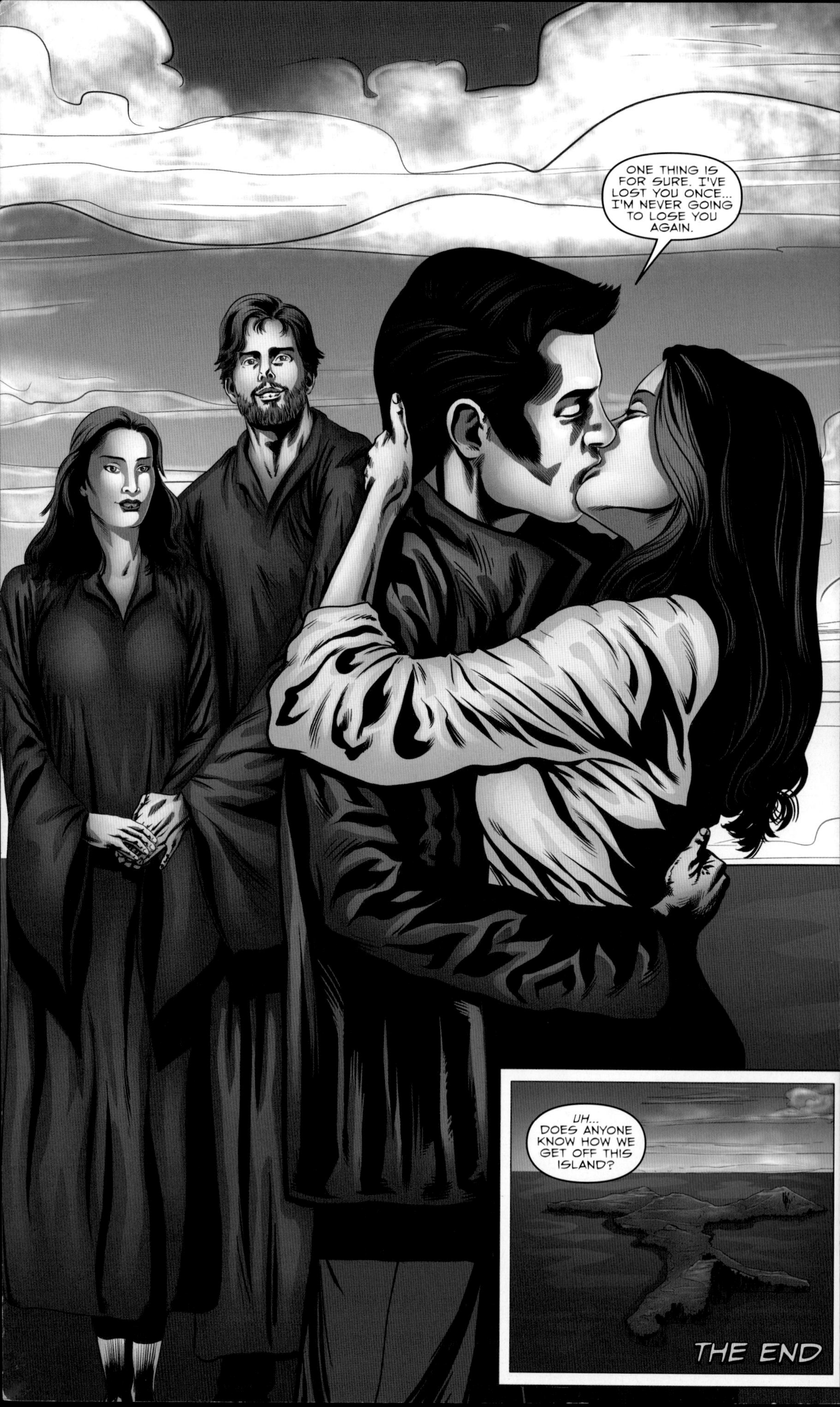
ONE THING IS FOR SURE. I'VE LOST YOU ONCE... I'M NEVER GOING TO LOSE YOU AGAIN.
UH... DOES ANYONE KNOW HOW WE GET OFF THIS ISLAND?
THE END

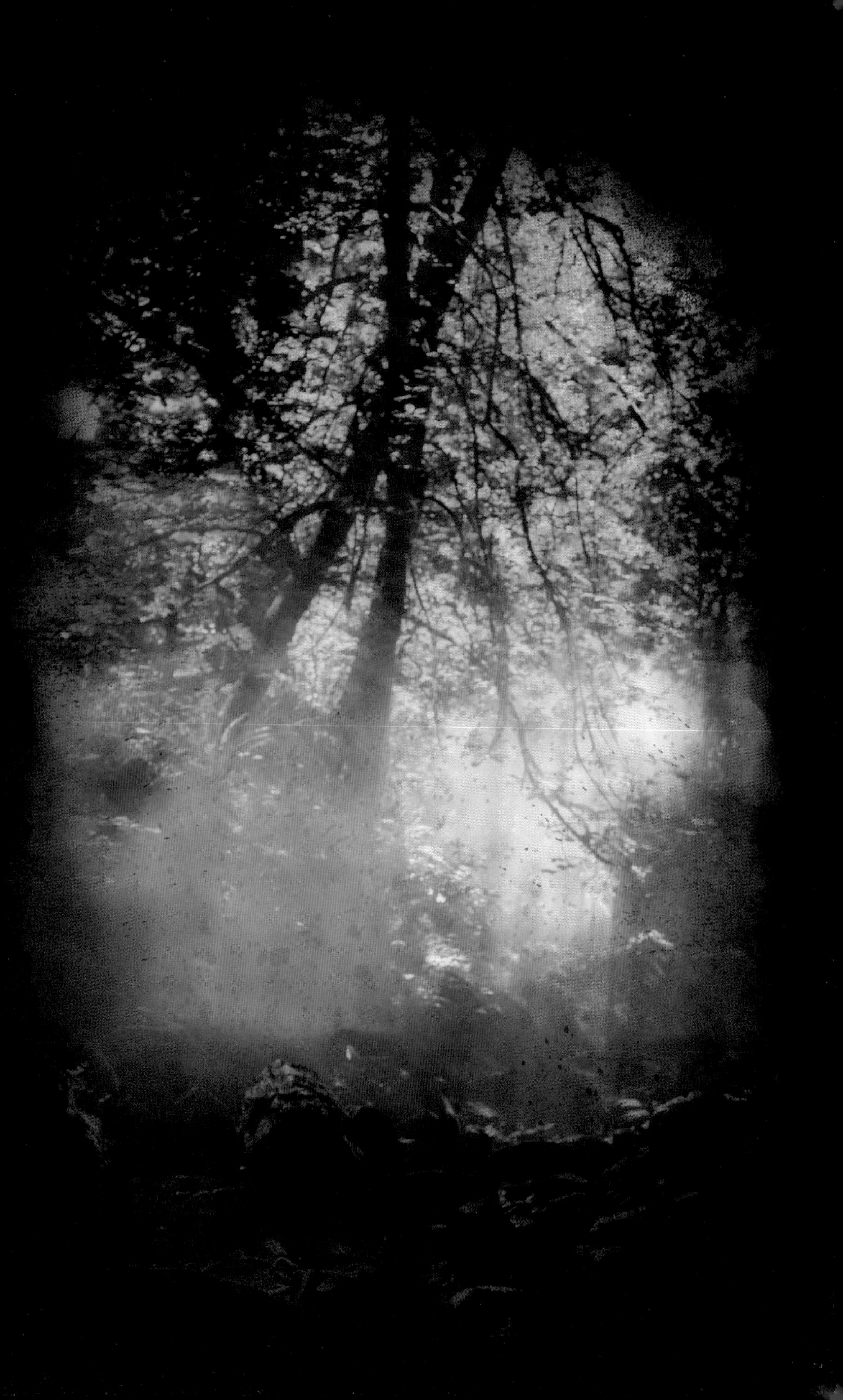

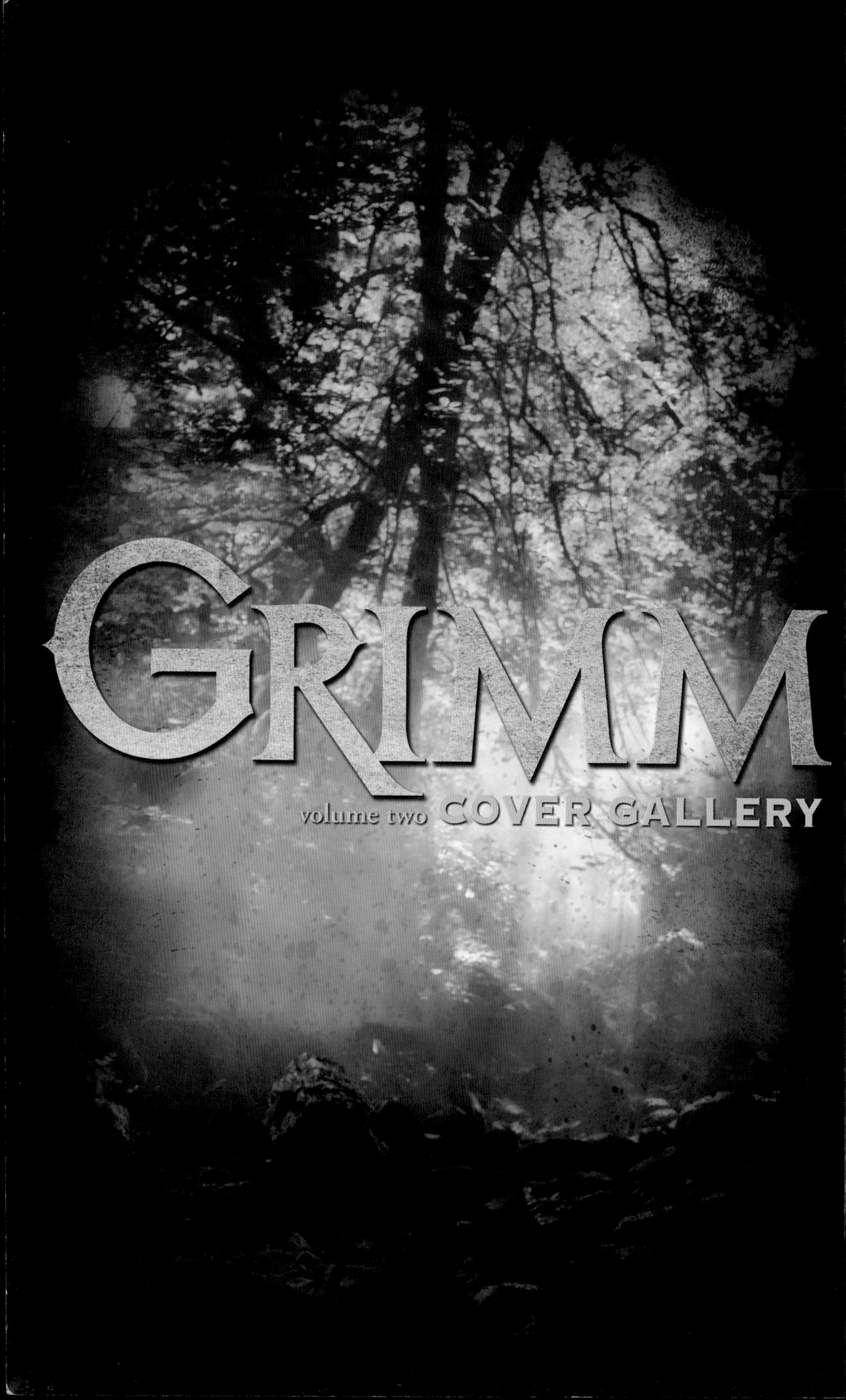
GRIMM
volume two COVER GALLERY

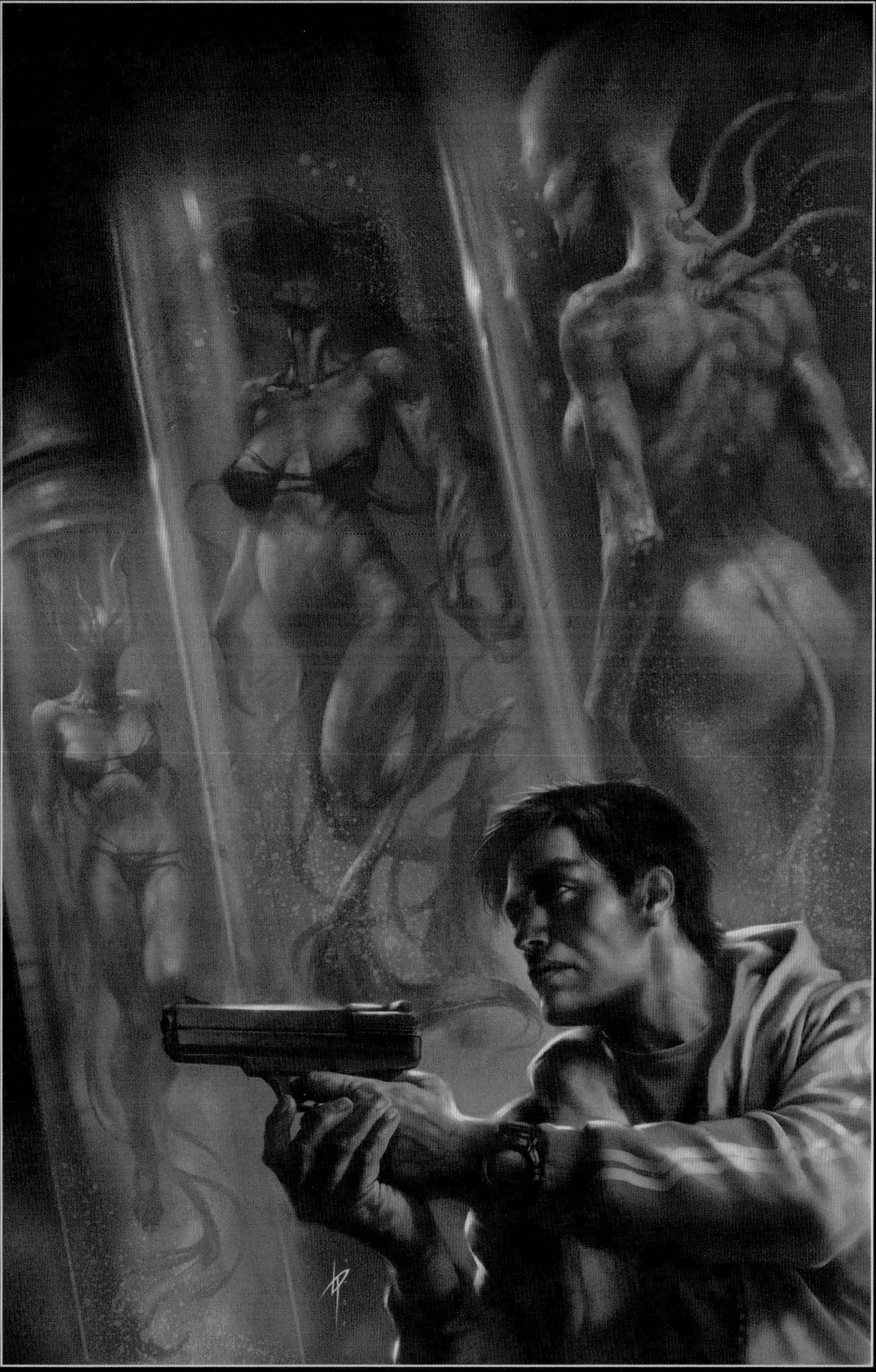

ISSUE #6 COVER BY LUCIO PARRILLO

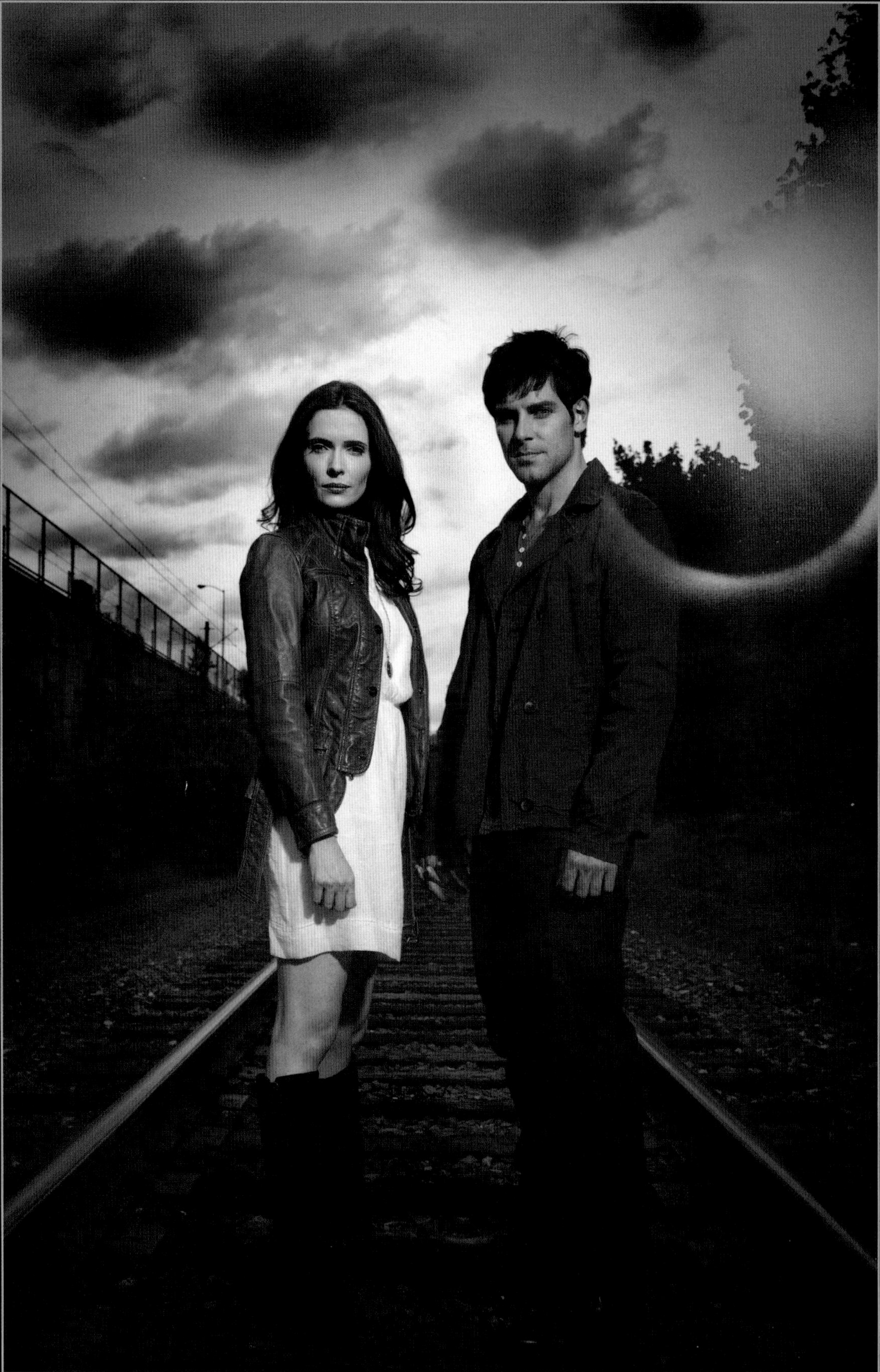

ISSUE #6 PHOTO EXCLUSIVE SUBSCRIPTION COVER

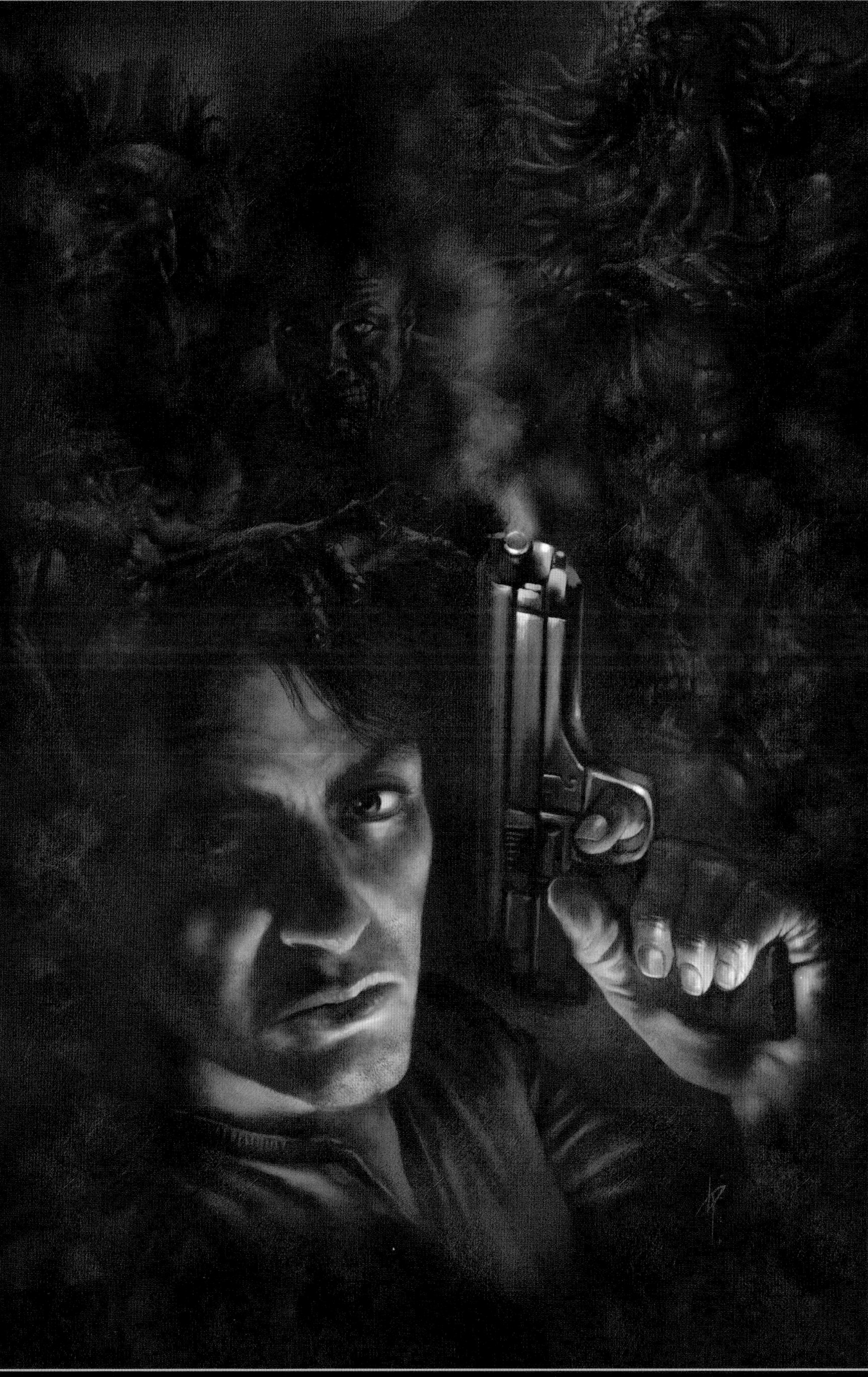

ISSUE #7 COVER BY LUCIO PARRILLO

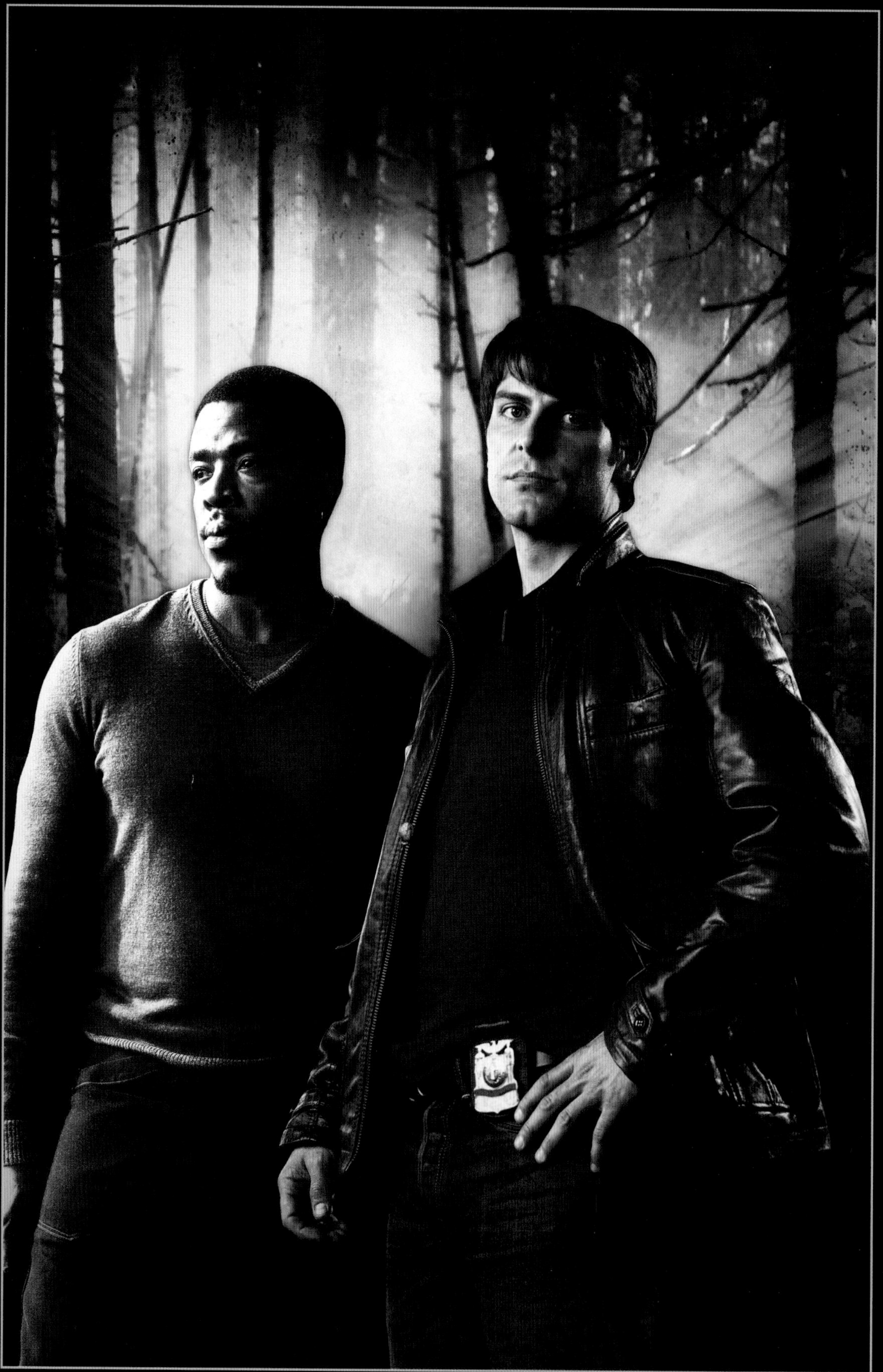

ISSUE #7 PHOTO EXCLUSIVE SUBSCRIPTION COVER

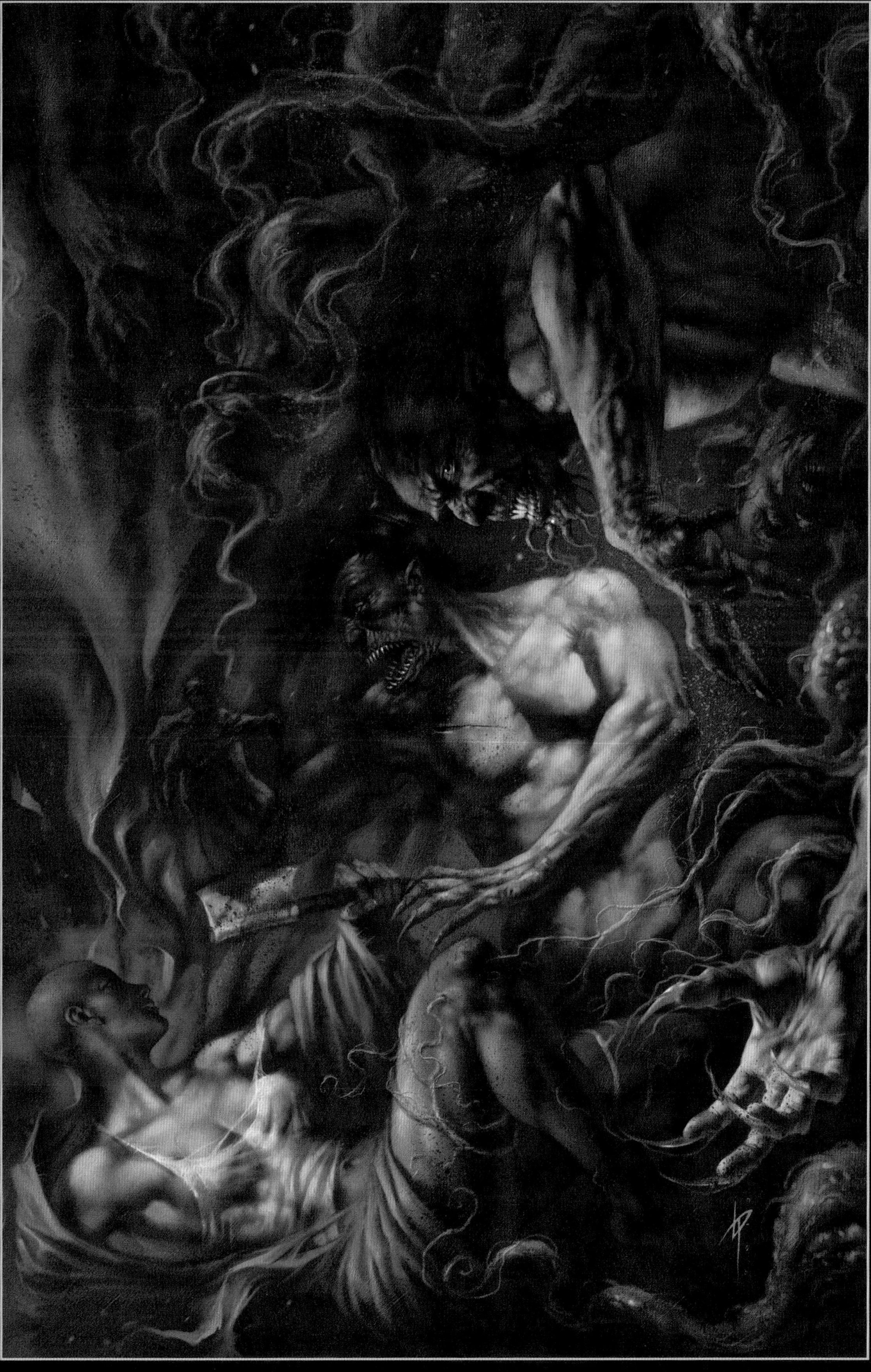

ISSUE #8 COVER BY LUCIO PARRILLO

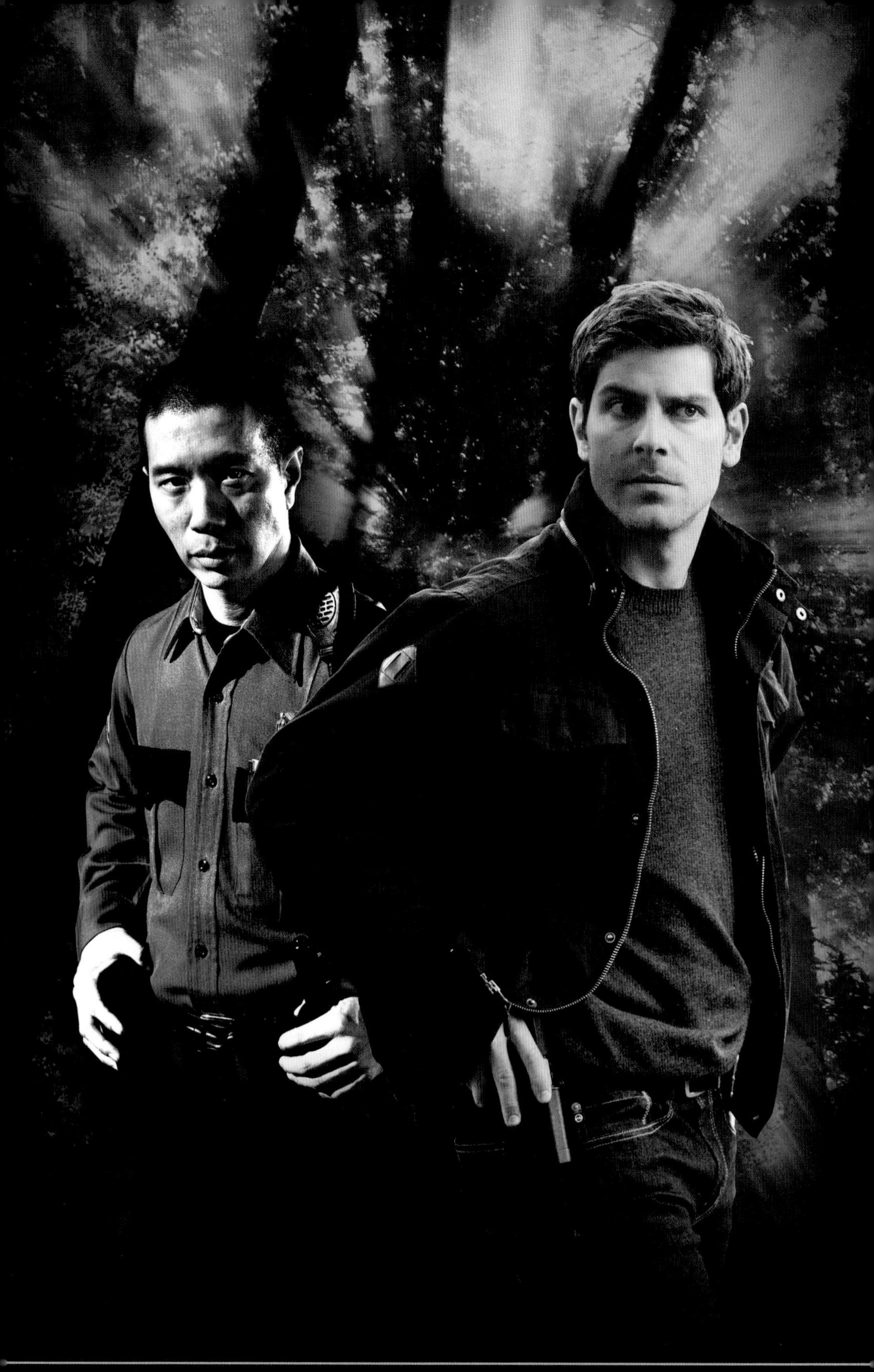

ISSUE #8 PHOTO EXCLUSIVE SUBSCRIPTION COVER

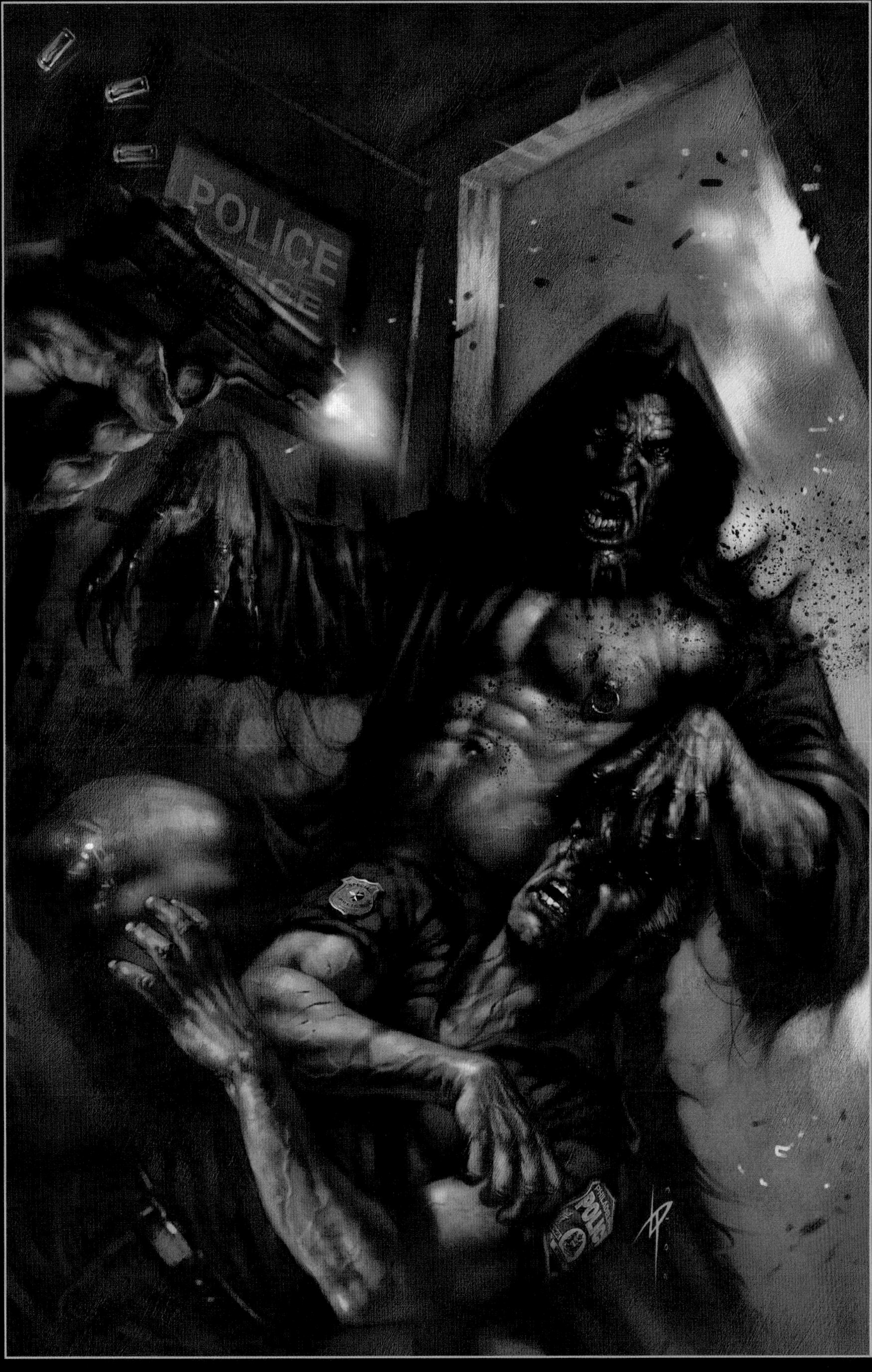
POLICE
POLICE

ISSUE #9 COVER BY LUCIO PARRILLO

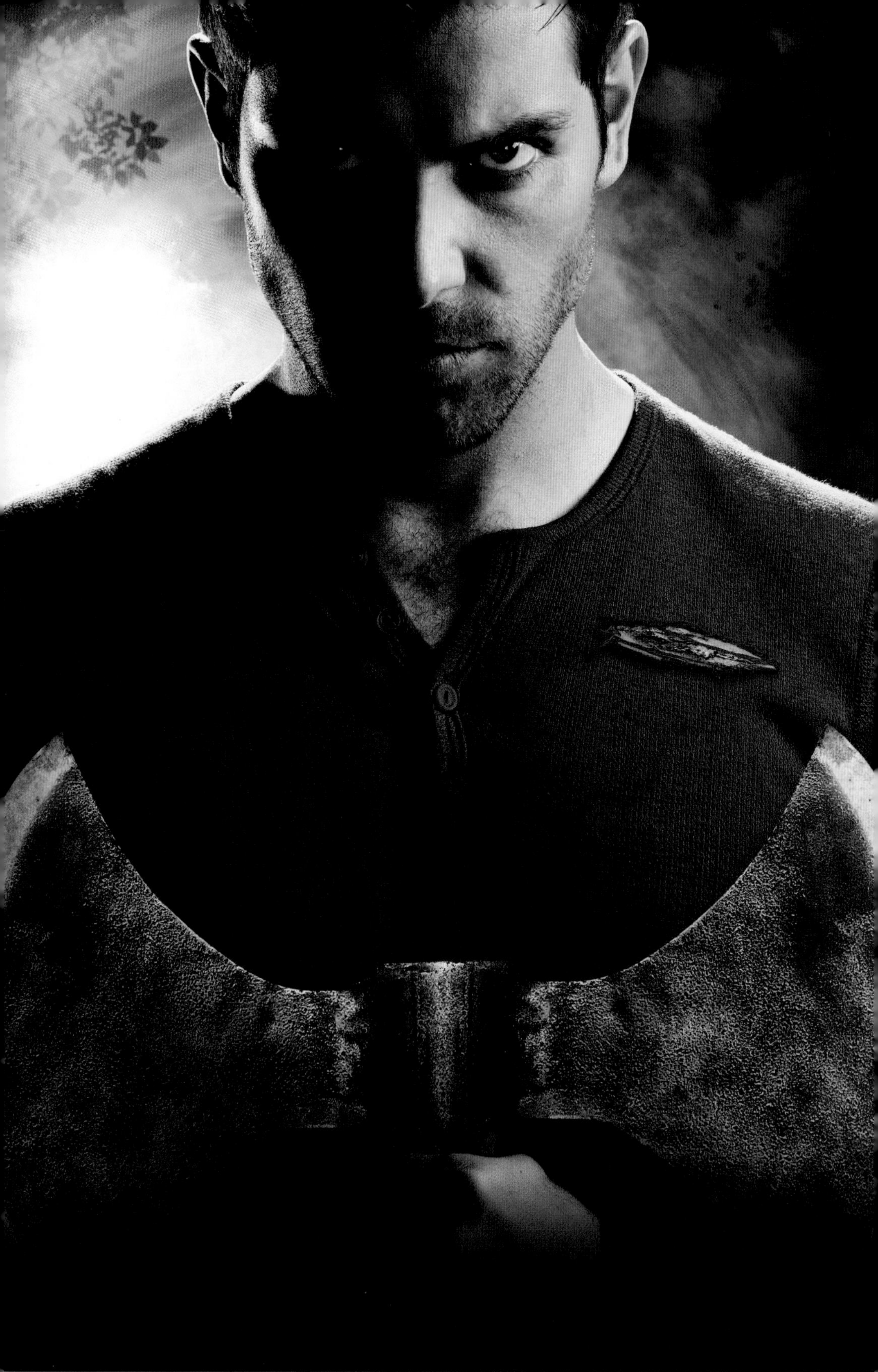

ISSUE #9 PHOTO EXCLUSIVE SUBSCRIPTION COVER

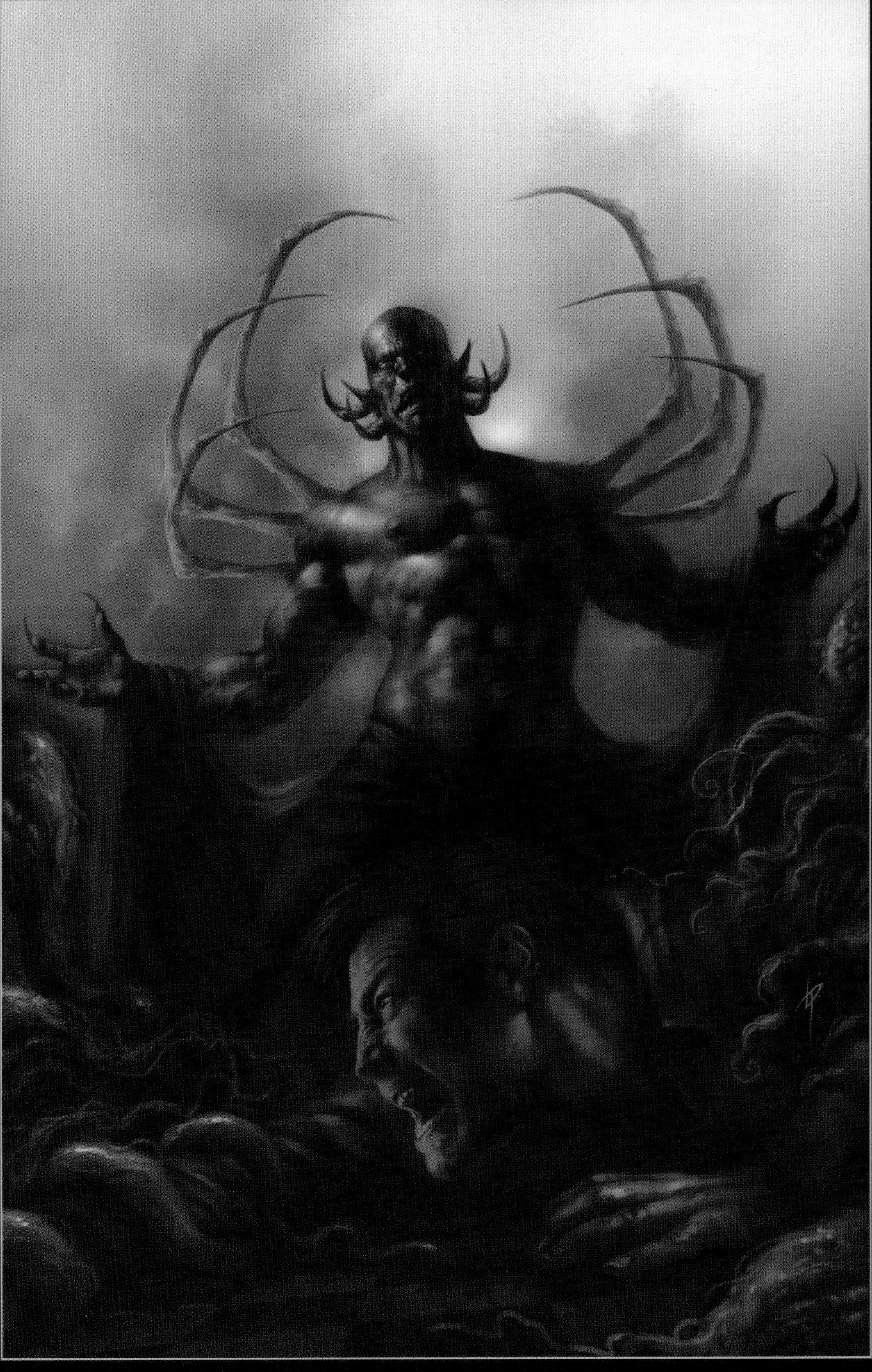

ISSUE #10 COVER BY LUCIO PARRILLO

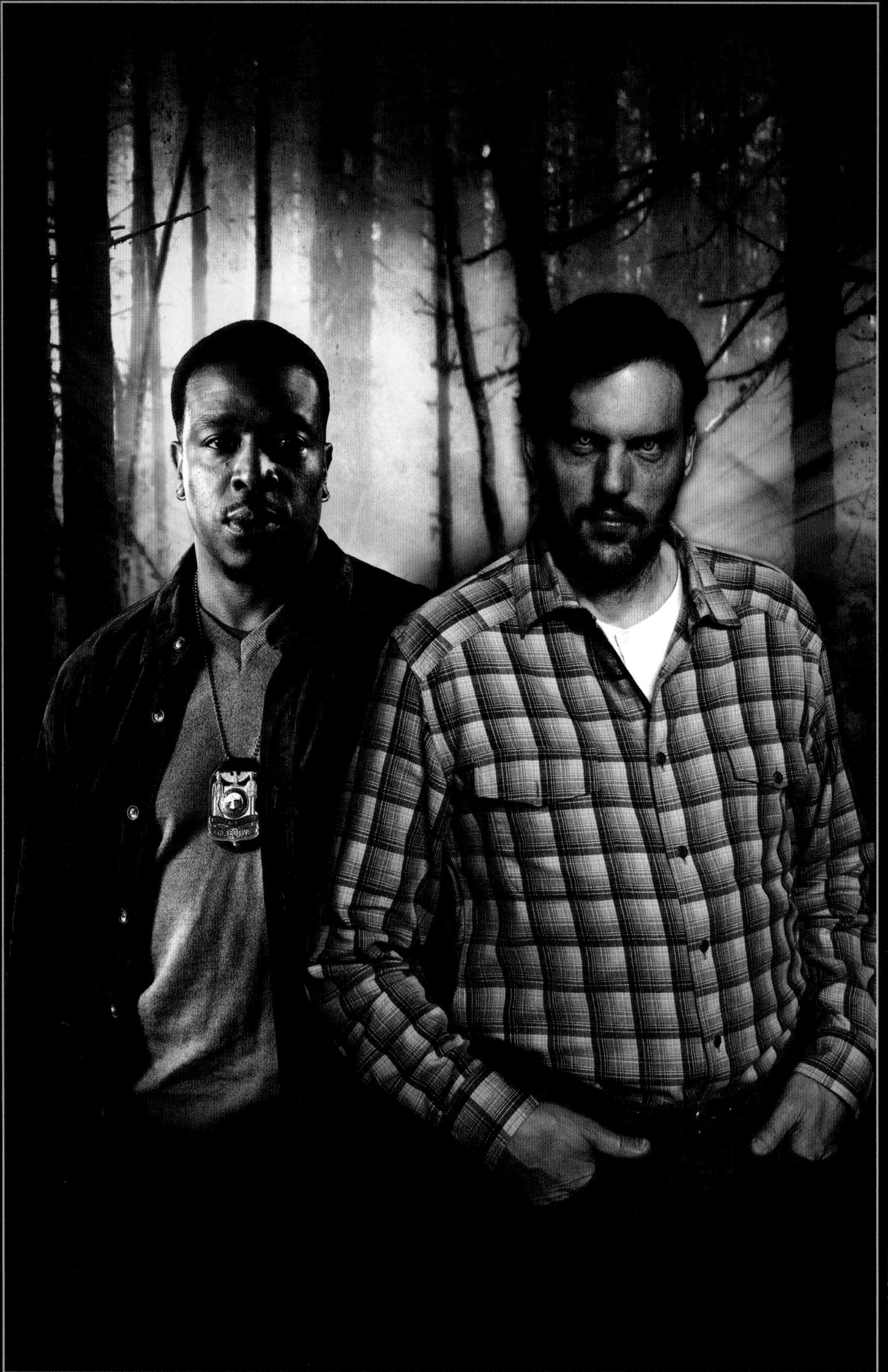

ISSUE #10 PHOTO EXCLUSIVE SUBSCRIPTION COVER

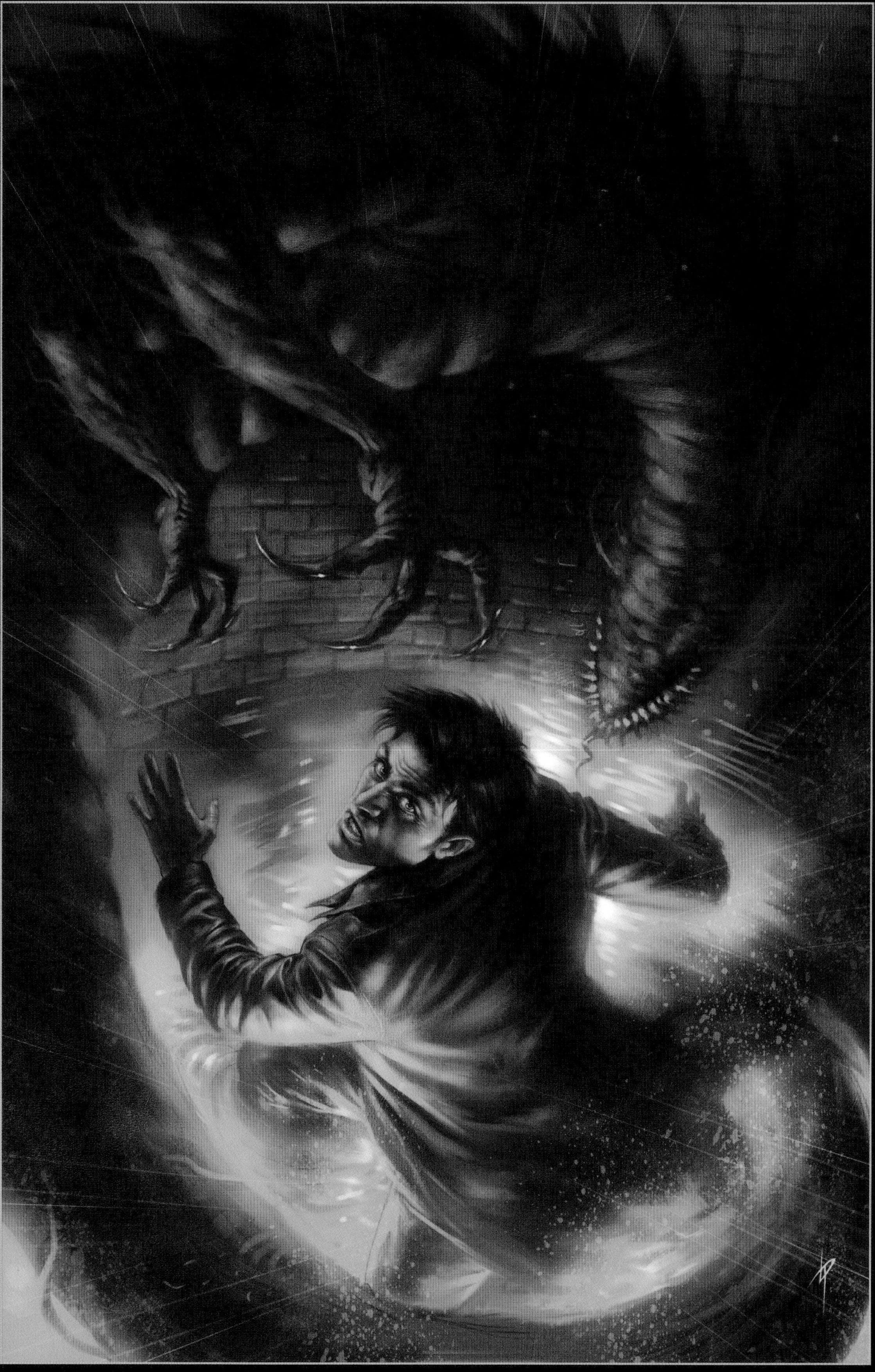

ISSUE #11 COVER BY LUCIO PARRILLO

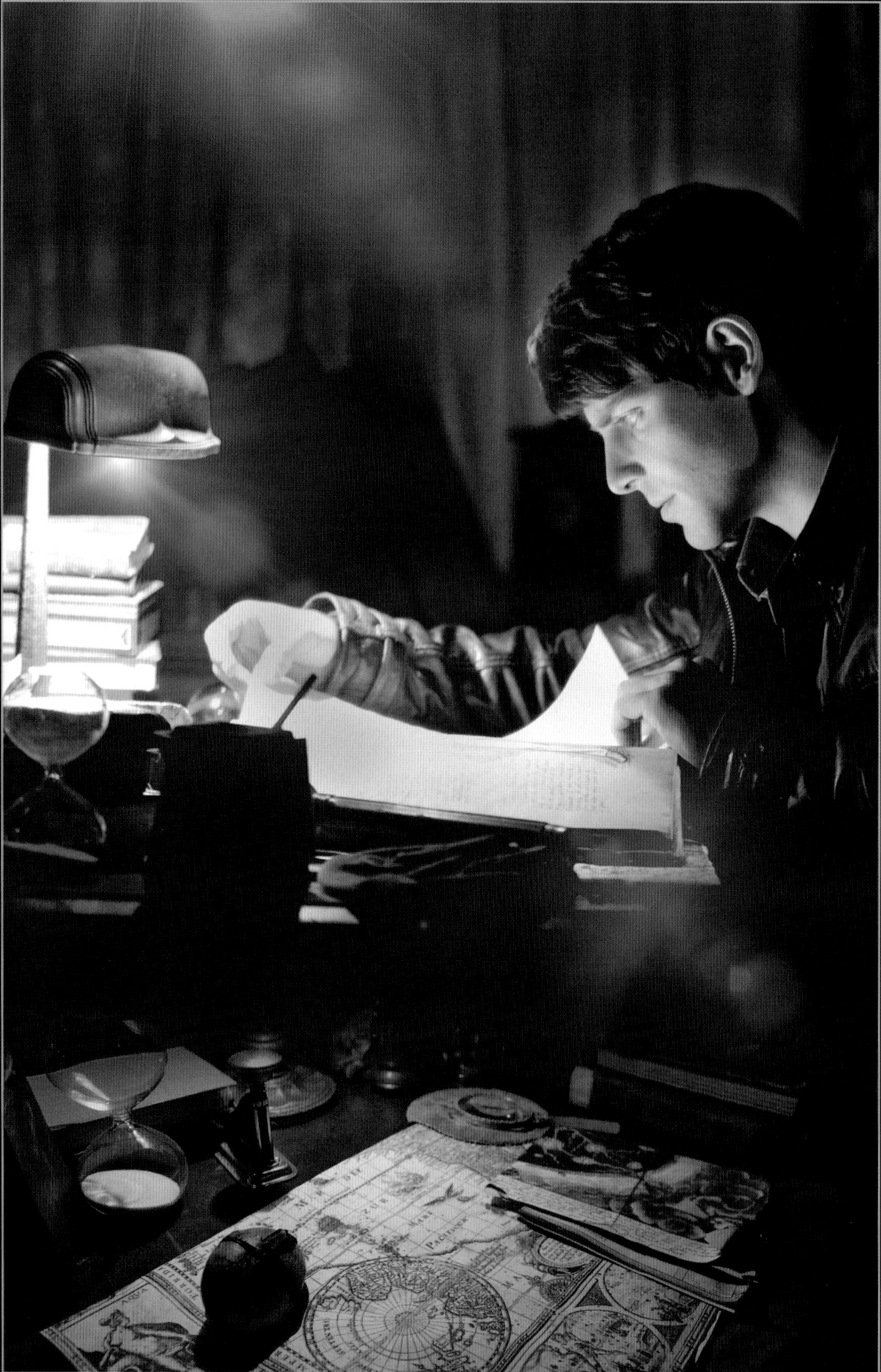

ISSUE #11 PHOTO EXCLUSIVE SUBSCRIPTION COVER

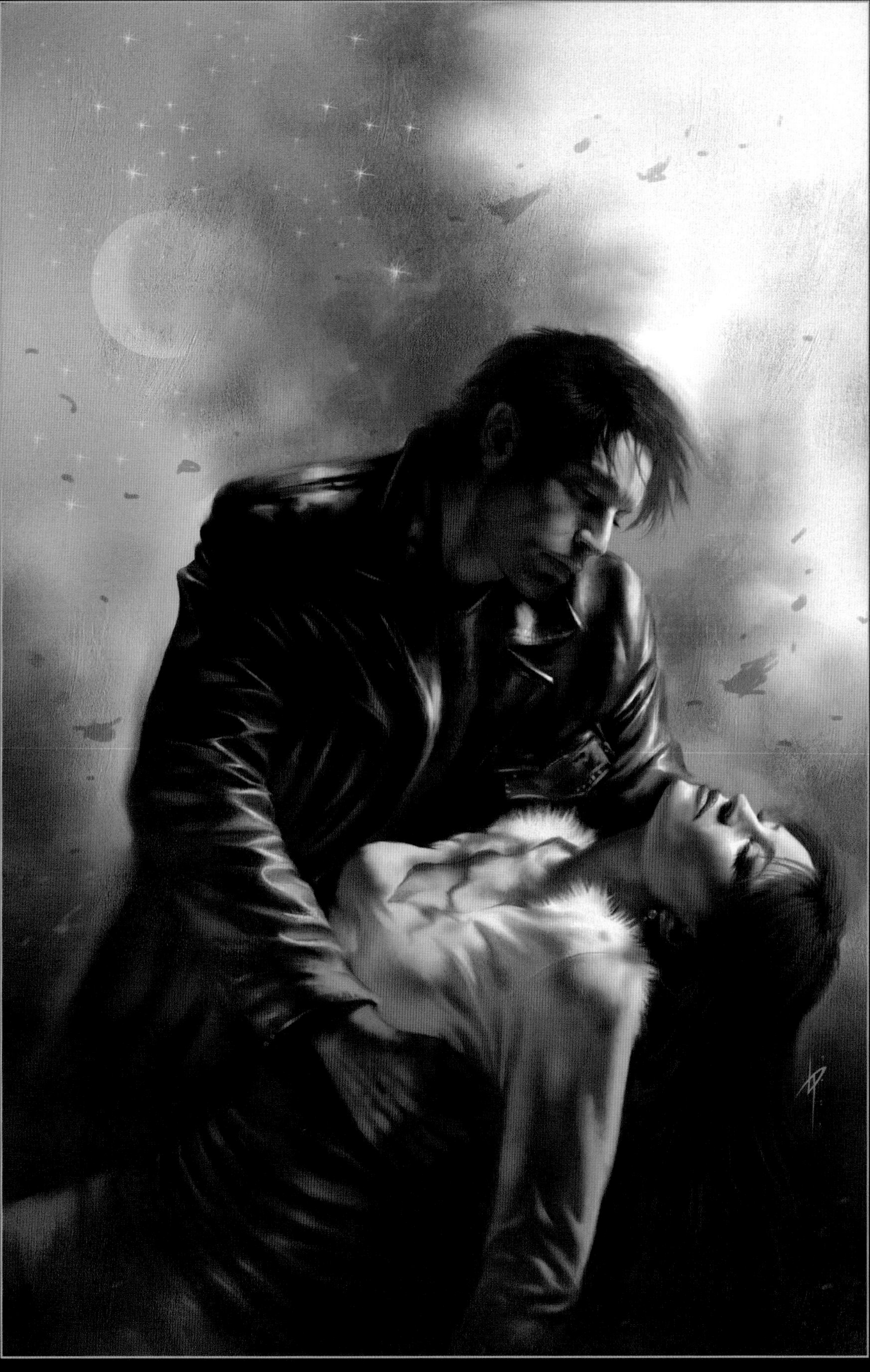

ISSUE #12 COVER BY LUCIO PARRILLO

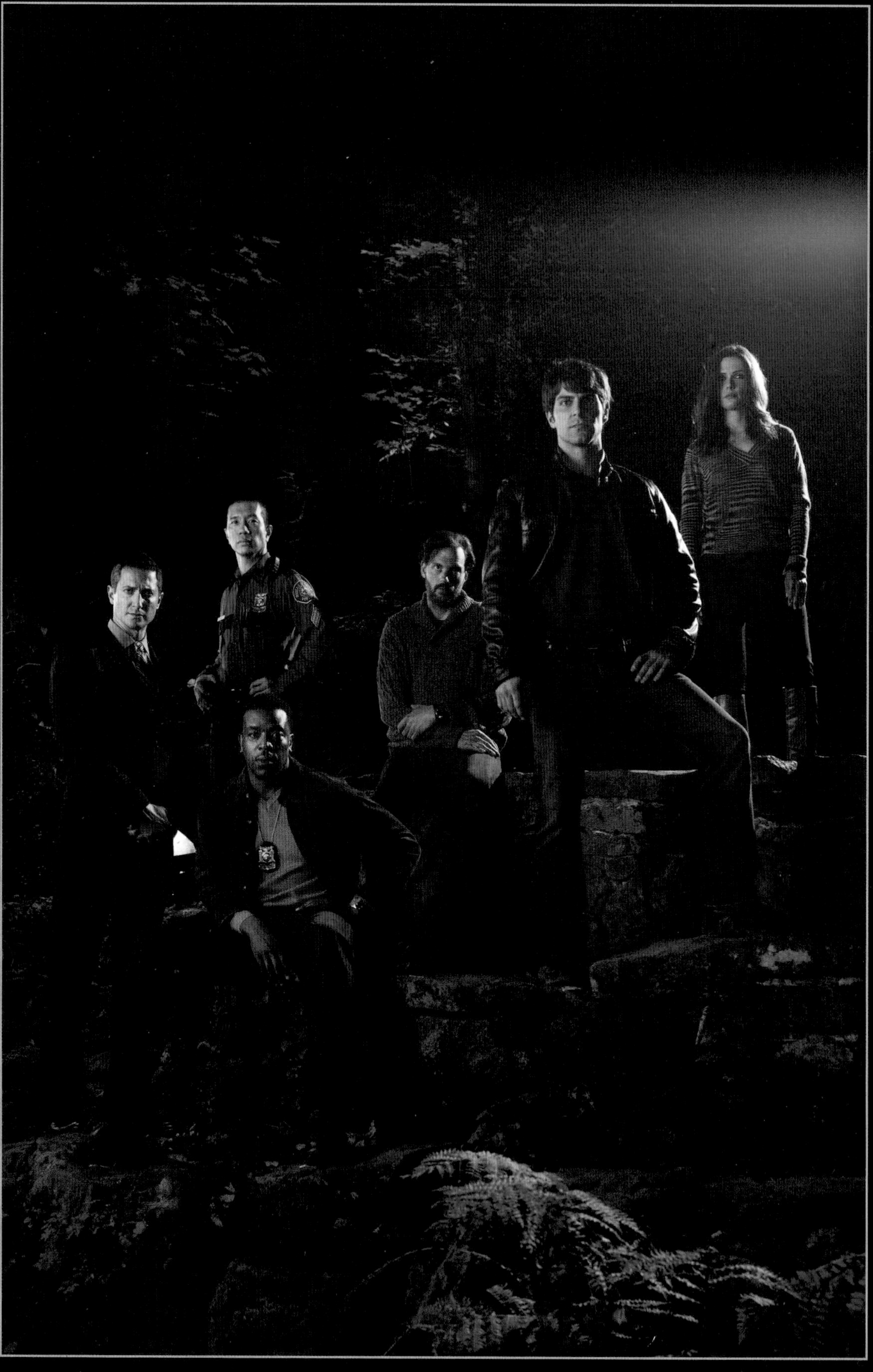

ISSUE #12 PHOTO EXCLUSIVE SUBSCRIPTION COVER

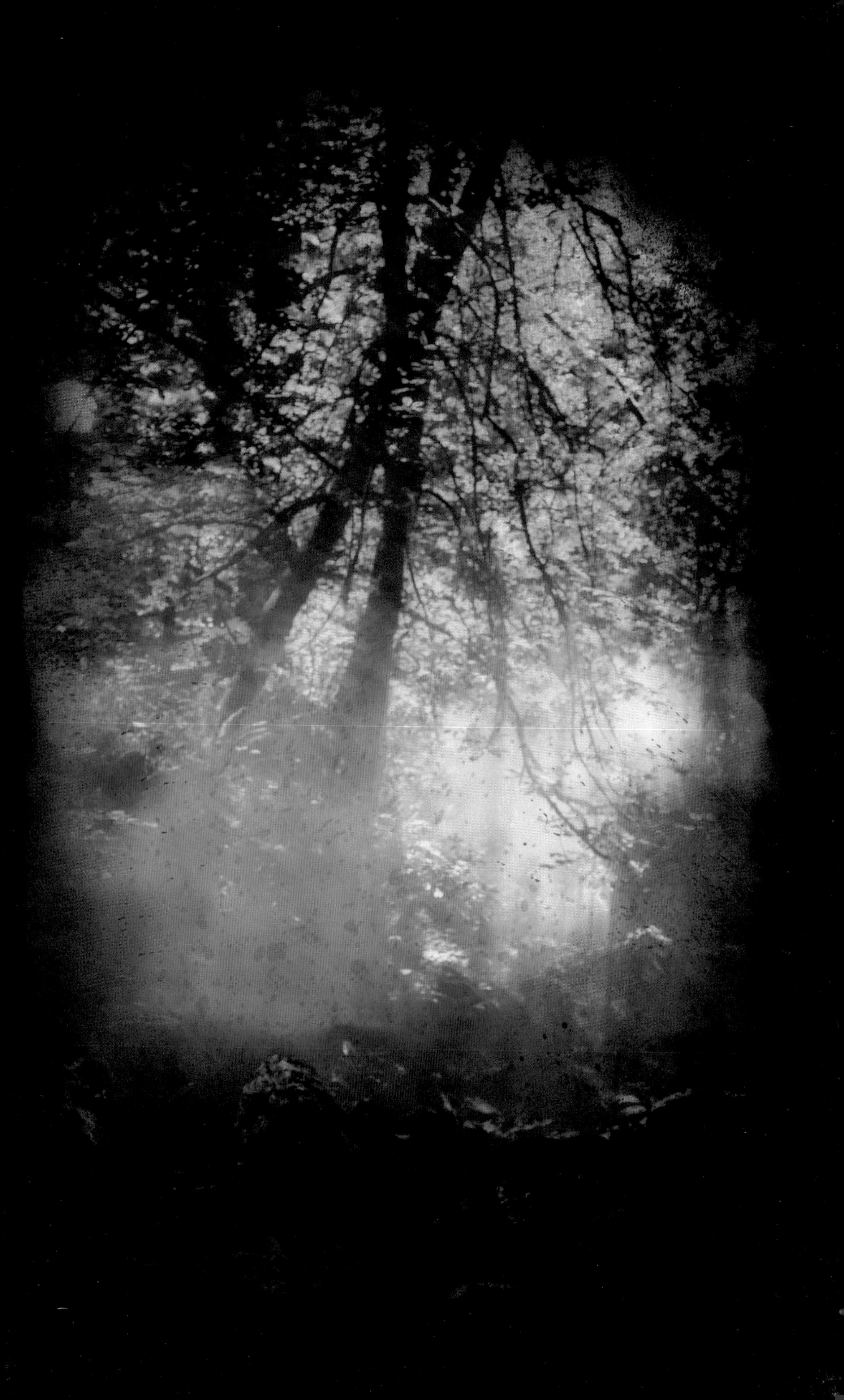

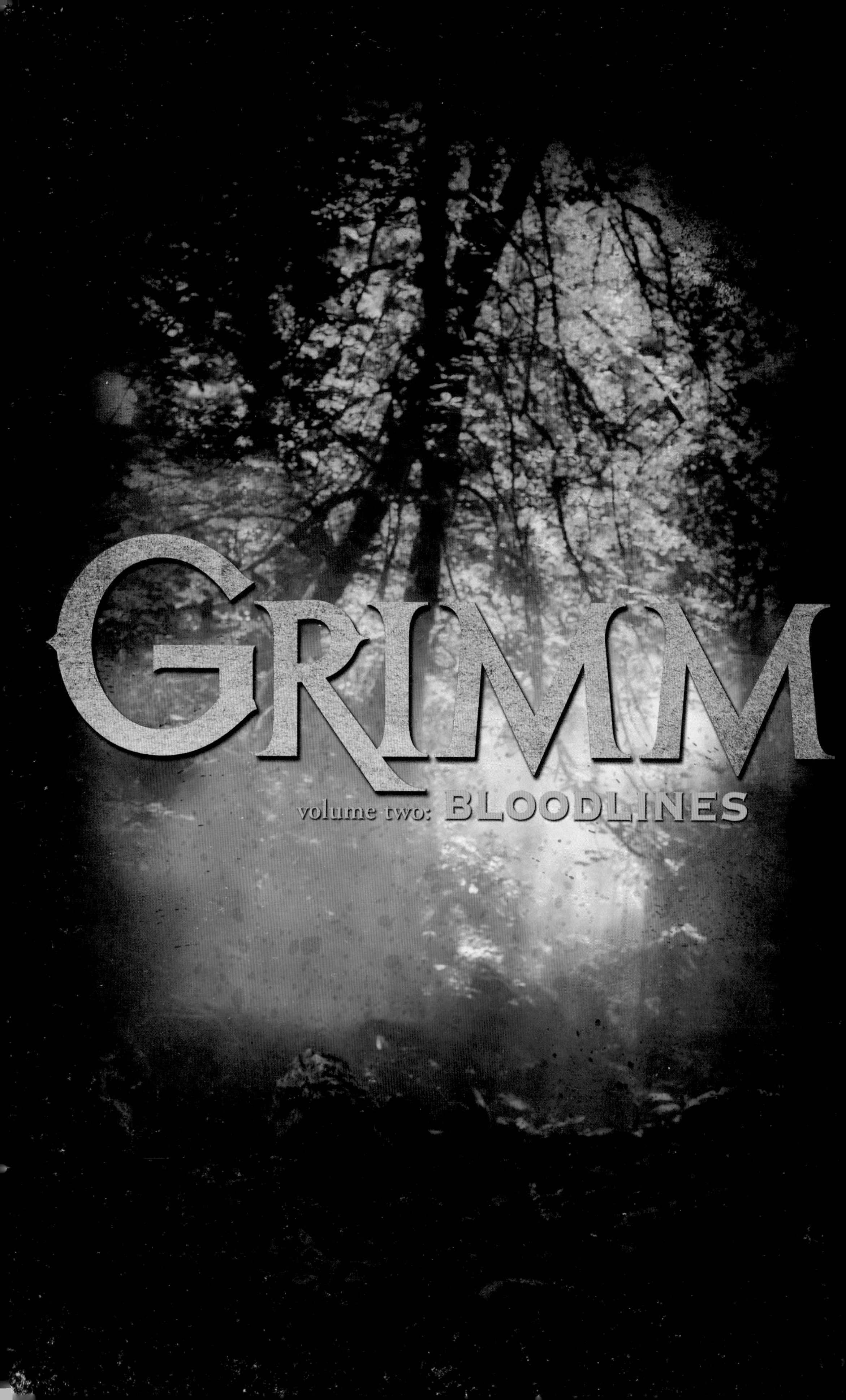
GRIMM
volume two: BLOODLINES